The Author

Arthur W. Pink was born in Notting-
ham, England. He died in Stornway,
Scotland, in 1952. His widespread ministry included pastorates in Australia and
the United States. He originated *Studies
in the Scriptures,* a monthly magazine
concerned solely with the exposition of
Scripture.

Mr. Pink's view of the Scriptures, of
doctrine, and of Christian practice was
not the view of the twentieth century, nor
even of many of his contemporary evan-
gelicals. Few men have traveled so widely
and yet remained so uninfluenced by prevailing opinions and accepted customs.
Independent Bible study convinced him
that much of modern evangelism was defective at its very foundations; when
Puritan and Reformed books were being
thrown out, he advanced the majority of
their principles with untiring zeal. He
was, in some ways, a Puritan born out
of time.

Events have justified his outlook. Two
world wars have substantiated his view
on human depravity; the progressive decline of his nation (Britain) was to him
the inevitable consequence of the prevalence of a gospel which is able neither
to wound nor heal.

Familiar with the whole range of revelation, Mr. Pink could divide the truth
with due weight, emphasis, and the proportion. He was rarely sidetracked from
the great themes of Scripture—grace,
justification, and sanctification. One looks
in vain for any quaint theories on prophecy and kindred subjects. The work of
God the Father and God the Holy Spirit
receive their proper emphasis as well as
the work of the Son.

GLEANINGS FROM PAUL

GLEANINGS FROM PAUL

STUDIES IN THE PRAYERS OF THE APOSTLE

By
ARTHUR W. PINK

MOODY PRESS
CHICAGO

FOREWORD

Men of the caliber of Arthur W. Pink appear on the religious horizon only rarely. His ability to apply the truths of Scripture to the lives of people, his vast and intimate knowledge of the Scriptures, and his clear-cut method of presenting the truths he experienced in his own life make his works not only vitally important for any serious Bible student—minister or layman—but also admirably adaptable for individual devotional reading.

The contents of this volume first appeared in the periodical *Studies in the Scriptures*. They appear now for the first time in book form to continue their service to an increasingly widening circle.

The author is now "for ever with the Lord," having departed to be with Christ on July 15, 1952, at the age of 66.

THE PUBLISHERS

CONTENTS

7

INTRODUCTION

MUCH HAS BEEN WRITTEN upon what is usually called "The Lord's Prayer" but which we prefer to term "The Family Prayer," and much upon the high priestly prayer of Christ in John 17, but very little upon the prayers of the apostles. Personally we know of no book devoted to the same, and except for a booklet on the two prayers of Ephesians 1 and 3 we have seen scarcely anything thereon. It is not easy to explain this omission, for one would think the apostolic prayers had such importance and value for us that they would attract the attention of those who wrote on devotional subjects. While we very much deprecate the efforts of those who would have us believe the prayers of the Old Testament are obsolete and unfitted for the saints of this dispensation, yet it seems evident that the prayers recorded in the epistles are peculiarly suited to Christians. Excepting only the prayers of the Redeemer, in the epistle prayers alone are the praises and petitions specifically addressed to "the Father," in them alone are they offered in the name of the Mediator, and in them alone do we find the full breathings of the Spirit of adoption.

How blessed it is to hear some aged saint, who has long walked with God and enjoyed intimate communion with Him, pouring out his heart before Him in adoration and supplication. But how much more blessed should we esteem it could we have listened to the utterances of those who companied with Christ in person during the days when He tabernacled in this scene. And if one of the apostles were still here upon earth what a high privilege we should deem it to hear him engage in prayer! Such a high privilege that most of us would be willing to go to considerable inconvenience and to travel a long distance in order to be thus favored. And if our desire were granted, how closely we would listen to his words, how diligently we would seek to treasure them up in our memories. Well, no such inconvenience, no such journey, is required: it has pleased the Holy Spirit to record quite a number of the apostolic prayers for our instruction and satisfaction. Do we evidence our appreciation of such a boon? Have we ever made a list of them and meditated upon their import?

No Prayers of the Apostles in Acts

In our preliminary task of surveying and tabulating the recorded prayers of the apostles, two things have impressed us, one at first quite surprising, the other to be expected. That which is apt to strike us as strange—to some of our readers it may be almost startling—is the book of Acts, which supplies us with most of the information we possess about the apostles, yet has not a single prayer of theirs in its twenty-eight chapters. Yet a little reflection should show us that this omission is in full accord with the special character of that book, for the book of Acts is much more historical than devotional, consisting far more of a chronicle of what the Spirit wrought through the apostles than of what He wrought in them. The public deeds of Christ's ambassadors are there made prominent, rather than their private exercises. True, they are shown to be men of prayer, as is seen by "We will give ourselves continually to prayer, and to the ministry of the word" (6:4). Again and again we behold them engaged in this holy exercise (9:40; 10:9; 20:36; 21:5; 28:8); yet we are not told what they *said,* the nearest approach being 8:15, for their words are not recorded. We regard the prayer of 1:24 as that of the hundred and twenty, and that of 4:24-30 as that of "their own company."

Paul Eminently a Man of Prayer

The second fact which impressed us while contemplating the field before us was that the great majority of the recorded prayers of the apostles issued from the heart of Paul; and this, as we have said, was really to be expected. You ask why? Several answers may be returned. Paul was preeminently the apostle to the Gentiles. Peter, James, and John ministered principally to Jewish believers (Gal. 2:9), and even in their unconverted days they had been accustomed to bow the knee before the Lord. But the Gentiles had come out of heathenism and it was fitting that their spiritual father should also be their devotional exemplar. Moreover, he wrote twice as many epistles as all the other apostles added together; nevertheless there are eight times as many prayers in his epistles as in all of theirs. But chiefly we call to mind the first thing said of Paul after his conversion: "Behold, he *prayeth*" (Acts 9:11). It is as though that struck the keynote of his subsequent life, that he would, to a special degree, be marked as a man of prayer.

The other apostles were not devoid of this spirit, for God does not employ prayerless ministers, as He has no dumb children. To "cry day and night unto him" is given as one of the distinguishing marks of His elect (Luke 18:7). Yet certain of His servants and some of his saints are permitted to enjoy closer and more constant fellowship with the Lord than others (excepting John), and such was obviously the case with the man who on one occasion was even caught up into Paradise. A special measure "of grace and of supplications" (Zech. 12:10) was vouchsafed him, so that he appears to have been favored above his fellows with a spirit of prayer which dwelt in him to a remarkable degree. Such was the fervor of his love for Christ and the members of His mystical body; such was his intense solicitude for their spiritual well-being and growth, that there continually gushed from his soul a flow of prayer to God for them, and thanksgiving on their behalf. Many illustrations of what has just been said will come before us, examples of where ebullitions of devotion broke forth in the midst of his doctrinal and practical instructions.

The Inclusiveness of Prayer

Before proceeding further it should be pointed out that in this series of studies we do not propose to confine ourselves to the petitionary prayers of the apostle, but rather take in a wider range. In Scripture "prayer" includes much more than making known our requests to God, and this is something which His people need reminding of, and some of them instructing in, in these days of superficiality and ignorance. The very verse that presents the privilege of spreading our needs before the Lord emphasizes this very thing: "In every thing by prayer and supplication *with thanksgiving* let your requests be made known unto God" (Phil. 4:6). Unless gratitude be expressed for mercies already received and thanks be given for granting us the continued favor of petitioning our Father, how can we expect to obtain His ear and receive answers of peace! Yet prayer, in its highest and fullest sense, rises above thanksgiving for gifts vouchsafed: the heart is drawn out in contemplating the Giver Himself so that the soul is prostrated before Him in worship and adoration.

Though we ought not to digress from our immediate theme and enter into the subject of prayer in general, it should be pointed out that there is yet another aspect which needs to take precedence over those referred to above, namely, self-abhorrence and confession of our unworthiness and sinfulness. The soul must solemnly remind itself of who it is that we are approaching, even the Most High, before whom the very seraphim veil their faces (Isa. 6). Though divine grace has made the Christian a "son," nevertheless he is still a creature, and as such at an infinite and inconceivable distance below the Creator; therefore it is fitting he should both deeply feel and acknowledge this by taking his place in the dust before Him. Moreover, we need to remember what we are, namely, not only creatures but (considered in ourselves) sinful creatures, and thus we need both a sense and an owning of this as we bow before the Holy One. Only thus can we, with any meaning and reality, plead the mediation and merits of Christ as the ground of our approach.

Thus, broadly speaking, prayer includes confession of sin, petitions for the supply of our needs, and the homage of our hearts unto the Giver Himself. Or, we may say prayer's principal branches are humiliation, supplication, and adoration. Hence we hope to embrace within the scope of this series not only passages such as Ephesians 1:16-19 and 3:14-21 but also such verses as II Corinthians 1:3 and Ephesians 1:3. Psalm 100:4 makes clear that "blessed be God" is itself a form of prayer: "Enter into his gates with thanksgiving, and into his courts with praise: be thankful unto him, and bless his name." Other references might be given, but let this suffice. The incense which was offered in the tabernacle and temple consisted of various spices compounded together (Exodus 30:34-35), and it was the blending of one with another that made the perfume so fragrant and refreshing. The incense was a type of the intercession of our great High Priest (Rev. 8:3-4) and the prayers of the saints (Mal. 1:11). Like the spices our humiliation, supplication, and adoration should be proportionately mingled in our approaches to the throne of grace—not one to the exclusion of the other but a blending together.

The Ministerial Duty of Prayer

The fact that so many prayers are found in the New Testament epistles calls attention to an important aspect of ministerial duty. The preacher's obligations are not fully discharged when he leaves the pulpit, for he needs to water the Seed which he has sown. We will enlarge a little upon this point for the benefit of young preachers. It has already been seen that the apostles devoted themselves "continually to prayer, and to the ministry of the word," and therein have they left an excellent example to be observed by all who follow them in the sacred vocation. Observe the order, and not only observe but heed and practice the same. The most laborious and carefully prepared sermon is likely to fall unctionless on the hearers unless it has been born out of travail of soul before God. Unless the sermon be the product of earnest prayer we must not expect it to awaken the spirit of prayer in those who hear it. As we have pointed out, Paul mingled supplications with his instructions. It is our privilege and duty to retire to the secret place after we leave the pulpit and beg God to write His Word on the hearts of those who have listened to us, to prevent the enemy from snatching away the Seed, to so bless our efforts that they may bear fruit to God's eternal praise.

Luther was wont to say, "There are three things which go to the making of a successful preacher: supplication, meditation, and tribulation." This was taken down by one of his students from his "Table Talks." We know not what elaboration the great Reformer made, but we suppose he meant that prayer is necessary to bring the preacher into a suitable frame to handle divine things and endue him with power; that meditation on the Word is essential in order to supply him with material for his message; and that tribulation is required as ballast for his vessel, for the minister of the gospel needs trials to keep him humble, as the apostle was given a thorn in the flesh that he might not be unduly exalted by the abundance of the revelations given him. Prayer is the appointed medium of receiving spiritual communications for the instruction of our people. We must be much with God before we are fitted to go forth and speak in His name. The Colossians were reminded that their minister was "always labouring fervently for you in prayers, that we may stand perfect and complete in all the will of God" (4:12). Could your church be truthfully told that of you?

The Duty of Believers to Pray

But let it not be thought this marked characteristic of the epistles points a lesson for preachers only. Far from it. These epistles are addressed to God's people at large, and everything in them is both needed by and suited to their Christian lives. Believers too should pray much, not only for themselves but also for all their brothers and sisters in Christ, and especially according to these apostolic models, petitioning for the particular blessing they specify. We have long been convinced there is no better way—no more practical, valuable, and effective way—of expressing solicitude and affection for our fellow saints than by bearing them up before God in the arms of our faith and love. By studying the prayers in these epistles and pondering them clause by clause we may learn more clearly what blessings we should desire for ourselves and others, what spiritual gifts and graces we most need to ask for. The very fact that these prayers, inspired by the Holy Spirit, have been placed on permanent record in the sacred Volume intimates the particular favors which are to be sought and obtained from God.

Believers to Address God as Father

We will conclude these preliminary and general observations by calling attention to a few of the more definite features of the apostolic prayers. Observe to whom these prayers are addressed. While there is not uniformity of expression but rather appropriate variety in this matter, yet the most frequent manner in which the Deity is addressed therein is as Father: "the Father of mercies" (II Cor. 1:3), "the God and Father of our Lord Jesus Christ" (Eph. 1:3; I Peter 1:3), "the Father of glory" (Eph. 1:17), "the Father of our Lord Jesus Christ" (Eph. 3:14). In this we may see how the apostles had heeded the injunction of their Master, for when they requested Him, "Lord, teach us to pray," He responded thus: "When ye pray, say, Our Father which art in heaven" (Luke 11:1-2), an example which He also set before them in John 17:1, 5, 11, 25. This has been recorded for our learning also. We are not unmindful of how many have unlawfully and lightly addressed God as "Father," yet their abuse does not warrant our disowning this blessed relationship. Nothing is more calculated to warm the heart and give liberty of utterance than a realization that we are approaching our "Father." If we have received "the Spirit of adoption" (Rom. 8:15), let us not quench the same.

The Brevity of the Apostles' Prayers

Next, we note the brevity of the prayers of the apostles. Not some, nor even most, but all of them are exceedingly brief, most of them comprised in but one or two verses, and the longest is only seven verses. How this rebukes the lengthy, lifeless, and wearisome prayers from many a pulpit. Wordy prayers are usually windy ones. To quote again from Martin Luther, this time from his comments on the Lord's Prayer to laymen: "When thou prayest let thy words be few, but thy thoughts and affections many, and above all let them be profound. The less thou speakest the better thou prayest . . . external and bodily prayer is that buzzing of the lips, that outside babble that is gone through without any attention, and which strikes the ears of men; but prayer in spirit and in truth is the inward desire, the motions, the sighs, which issue from the depths of the heart. The former is the prayer of hypocrites and of all who trust in themselves; the latter is the prayer of the children of God who walk in His fear."

Observe too the definiteness of the apostles' prayers. Though exceeding brief yet they are very explicit. They were not vague ramblings or mere generalizations, but specific requests for definite things. How much failure there is at this point. How many prayers have we heard that were so incoherent and aimless, so lacking in point and unity, that when the amen was reached we could scarcely remember one thing for which thanks had been given or request had been made, only a blurred impression remaining on the mind and a feeling that the supplicant had engaged more in a form of indirect preaching than in direct praying. But examine any of the prayers of the apostles, and it will be seen at a glance that theirs were like those of their Master's in Matthew 6:9-13 and John 17—made up of definite adorations and sharply defined petitions. There is no moralizing, no uttering of pious platitudes, but a spreading before God of certain needs and a simple asking for the supply of same.

Consider also the burden of these prayers. In the apostolic prayers there is no supplicating God for the supply of temporal needs and (with a single exception) no asking Him to interpose on their behalf in a providential way. Instead, the things asked for are wholly of a spiritual and gracious nature:

that the Father may give to us the spirit of understanding and revelation in the knowledge of Himself, the eyes of our understanding being enlightened so that we may know what is the hope of His calling, the riches of the glory of His inheritance in the saints, and the exceeding greatness of His power to usward (Eph. 1:17-19); that He would grant us according to the riches of His glory to be strengthened with might by His Spirit in the inner man, that Christ may dwell in our hearts by faith, that we might know the love of Christ which passeth knowledge, and be filled with all the knowledge of God (Eph. 3:16-19); that our love may abound more and more, that we might be sincere and without offense and be filled with the fruits of righteousness (Phil. 1:9-11); that we may walk worthy of the Lord unto all pleasing (Col. 1:10); that we might be sanctified wholly (I Thess. 5:23).

Note also the catholicity of the apostles' prayers. Not that it is either wrong or unspiritual to pray for ourselves individually any more than it is to supplicate for temporal and providential mercies; rather are we directing attention to where the apostles placed all their emphasis. In only one instance do we find Paul praying for himself, and rarely for particular individuals. His general custom was to pray for the whole household of faith. In this he adhered closely to the pattern prayer given us by Christ, which we like to think of as the Family Prayer. All its pronouns are in the plural: "give us" (not only me), "forgive us," and so on. Accordingly we find the apostle exhorting us to be making "supplication for *all* saints" (Eph. 6:18); and in his prayers he set us an example of this very thing. He asked that the Ephesian church might "be able to comprehend with all saints what is the breadth, and length, and depth, and height; And to know the love of Christ, which passeth knowledge" (3:18-19). What a corrective for self-centeredness! If I am praying for "all saints" I include myself.

A Striking Omission

Finally, let us point out a striking omission. If all the apostolic prayers be read attentively it will be found that in none of them is any place given to that which occupies such prominence in those of Arminians. Not once do we find God asked to save the world or pour out His Spirit on all flesh. The apostles did not so much as pray for the conversion of the city in which a particular Christian church was located. In this they conformed again to the example set them by Christ. "I pray not for the world," said He, "but for them which thou hast given me" (John 17:9). Should it be objected that the Lord Jesus was there praying only for His immediate apostles or disciples, the answer is that when He extended His prayer beyond them, it was not for the world, but only for His believing people unto the end of time (see vv. 20-21). True, the apostle exhorts that prayers "be made for all [classes of] men; For kings, and for all that are in authority" (I Tim. 2:1-2)—in which duty many are woefully remiss—yet it is not for their salvation but "that *we* may lead a quiet and peaceable life in all godliness and honesty" (2b). We may learn much from the prayers of the apostles.

Chapter 1

PRAYER AND PRAISE

ROMANS 1:8-12

As FOR PAUL'S PRAYERS we shall not take them up in their chronological order but according as they are found in his epistles in our present-day Bible. The Thessalonian epistles were written before the Roman letter, but as the book of Romans, because of its theme and importance, rightly comes first, we shall begin with Paul's prayers recorded therein. Opinion is divided as to whether the verses before us chronicle a particular prayer actually offered by Paul at that time, or whether he is here informing them how he was wont to remember them at the throne of grace. It appears to us the distinction is such a fine one that it makes little practical difference which view be adopted. Personally we incline to the former concept. This epistle was taken down by an amanuensis (16:22), and as the apostle dictated the words "to all that be in Rome, beloved of God" (1:7), his heart was immediately drawn out in thanksgiving that some of God's elect were to be found even in the capital of the Roman Empire, yea, in "Caesar's household" (Phil. 4:22).

Paul's Affection for the Saints at Rome

The position of Paul was somewhat delicate, as he was a stranger to the saints at Rome. No doubt they had often heard of him—at first as a dangerous person. When assured of his conversion, and learning that he was an apostle to the Gentiles, they probably wondered why he had not visited them, especially when he had been as near Rome as Corinth. So he made known his deep personal interest in them. They were continually upon his heart and in all his prayers. How his "I thank my God through Jesus Christ for you all" (1:8a) would draw out their affections to the writer of this epistle! How it would move them to read with warmer interest what he had sent to them! Nothing more endears one Christian to another than to know he is remembered by him before the throne of grace. As one of our readers recently wrote, "I prize the prayers of God's dear saints more than I would all the riches of the world. The latter would only prove a curse, while the former reaches to blessings in the highest heaven and lays me even lower before God's holy throne."

"First, I thank my God through Jesus Christ for you all, that your faith is spoken of throughout the whole world" (1:8). There are five things here which claim our attention. First, the manner, or method, of Paul's praying: the first note struck is one of praise. This is made very emphatic: "First, I thank my

15

God" takes precedence over the "making request" of verse 10. Thus we see how blessedly the apostle practiced what he preached: "In every thing by prayer and supplication with thanksgiving let your requests be made known unto God" (Phil. 4:6). Thanksgiving ought to have a prominent place in our prayers: to say the least, it is due to God. As one of the Puritans expressed it, "It is rent due Him for the mercies received." Thanksgiving is an effective means of strengthening faith, for it puts the heart into a more suitable frame to petition Him for further favors. It is conducive to joy in the Christian life: "I thank my God upon every remembrance of you, always in every prayer of mine for you all making request with joy" (Phil. 1:3-4). Nothing is more calculated to dispel a spirit of gloom from the soul than the cultivation of gratitude and praise. The same will cheer and encourage our fellow Christians. Piety is not commended by sadness and sourness.

Paul Blended Thanksgiving with Petitions

The above example is so far from being exceptional that it rather indicates the usual custom of the apostle. It is blessed to observe how frequently Paul blended thanksgiving with petitions. (Cf. I Cor. 1:4; Eph. 1:16; Col. 1:3; I Thess. 1:2; Philemon 4.) Remember that these examples have been recorded for our learning. Does not failure at this very point go far to explain why so many of our prayers remain unanswered? If we have not owned the goodness and grace of God for previous mercies, can we expect Him to continue bestowing them upon the ungrateful? Praise and petitions, thanksgiving and requests, should ever be conjoined (Col. 4:2). But we see here in the apostle much more than this—something nobler and more selfless. His heart was continually drawn out in gratitude to God for the wondrous things He had done for His people, and this emboldened him to seek further blessings for them.

Second, note the One whom Paul invoked, termed here "my God." It is indeed blessed to observe how the apostle regarded the Deity: not as an absolutely, infinitely removed, unrelated One. There was no formality, no sense of remoteness, no uncertainty: instead, God was a living and personal reality to him: "my God." This was an avowal of *covenant* relationship. The grand covenant promise is "I will be to them a God, and they shall be to me a people" (Heb. 8:10), which looks back to Jeremiah 24:7; 31:33; they in turn have their roots in Genesis 17:7 and Exodus 6:7. On that ground Moses and the children of Israel sang on the farther shores of the Red Sea, "The Lord is my strength and song, and he is become my salvation: he is *my God*" (Exodus 15:2). For that reason David exclaimed, "O God, thou art my God" (Ps. 63:1). In like manner we find that Caleb (Joshua 14:8), Ruth (1:16), Nehemiah (6:14), Daniel (9:4, 19) and Jonah (2:6) owned Him as "my God" in avowal of the covenant relationship.

"My God": expressive of a *personal* relationship. God was Paul's God by eternal election, having loved him with an everlasting love. He was Paul's God by redemption, having purchased him with precious blood. He was his God by regenerating power, having communicated spiritual life to him and having stamped the divine image upon his heart, making him manifestly His own dear child. He was Paul's God by personal choice, for when God was revealed to

Paul and in him, Paul had surrendered to His claims, saying, "What wilt thou have me do?" God, by bestowing upon Paul His own nature after the apostle's acceptance of His claims, had become Paul's everlasting portion, his all-satisfying inheritance. "My God": the One who had shown such sovereign and signal mercy to Paul. Their relationship was also *assured;* there was no doubting, hesitation, or uncertainty. Paul could say with Job, "I have heard of thee by the hearing of the ear: but now mine eye seeth thee" (42:5). And theirs was a *practical* relationship: "whom I serve" (Rom. 1:9).

Now put the two phrases together: "I thank . . . my God." What a fitting combination! Is not such a God worthy of infinite thanks? And if I know Him personally as *my* God, will not, must not, thanksgiving issue spontaneously from my heart and lips? The union of these phrases both opens the meaning of and gives due force to the opening word, "First, I thank my God"—not first in enumeration, but in emphasis, in spiritual order. If God Himself be mine, then everything that is pure, holy, lovely, satisfying, is mine. If that glorious fact, that infinitely grand truth, be the subject of constant meditation and adoration, then my heart will not be cold and dull, nor will my mouth be paralyzed when I draw near to the throne of grace. It is not an absolute and unrelated Deity whom I approach, but "my God." And that blessed and blissful relationship is to be duly acknowledged by the Christian when he bows the knee before Him. So far from being the language of presumption, it would be wicked presumption, insulting unbelief, to deny it.

Paul's Ground of Approach

Third, note *the ground of approach:* "through Jesus Christ." How thankful is the writer (and the reader too, if regenerate) for this clause. Though God be "my God" yet He ever remains the ineffably Holy One. How can I, conscious of pollution and utter unworthiness, think of approaching infinite purity? Ah, here is the blessed answer, the all-sufficient provision to meet my need: I may obtain access to the thrice holy God "through Jesus Christ." But suppose my assurance be dampened and through sad failure in my walk I no longer enjoy the conscious relationship of His being "my God." How can I then give thanks to Him? Again, the answer is "through Jesus Christ." As it is written, "By him [Jesus Christ] therefore [because of the merit and efficacy of His sanctifying blood; see previous verse] let us offer the sacrifice of praise to God continually, that is, the fruit of our lips giving *thanks* to his name" (Heb. 13:15). Whatever my case may be, however burdened with a sense of guilt and defilement, that should not keep me away from the throne of grace, neither should it deter me from giving thanks for Jesus Christ and God's provision of Him.

Grammatically the "through Jesus Christ" is connected with the giving of thanks, but theologically or doctrinally there is a double thought. God is "my God" through Jesus Christ. As He declared to His beloved disciples, "I ascend unto my Father, and your Father; and to my God, and your God" (John 20:17b)—"*your*" God because "*my*" God. And I give thanks unto my God "through Jesus Christ," for it is both the duty and the privilege of the regenerate, who are members of the holy priesthood, "to offer up spiritual sacrifices, acceptable to God by Jesus Christ" (I Peter 2:5*b*). There is no approach to God save "through Jesus Christ" the lone Mediator between God and men. Our worship is acceptable to God only through His merits (Col. 3:17). This fact must be the subject of the believer's constant meditation and adoration, for only thus will the blessed assurance of "my God" be maintained in the heart. Jesus Christ changes not: His mediation changes not. However deeply despondent I may be by my sense of unworthiness as I approach the throne, let me turn to and believingly ponder the infinite worthiness of Jesus Christ. Then I shall *"thank* my God."

"First, I thank my God through Jesus Christ." Upon these words the late Handley Moule most beautifully said, " 'My God' . . . it is the expression of an indescribable appropriation and reverent intimacy . . . it is the language of a personality wherein Christ has dethroned self in His own favor. . . . And this holy intimacy, with its action in thanks and petition, is all the while 'through Jesus Christ' the Mediator. The man knows God as 'my God' and deals with Him as such, never out of that beloved Son who is equally one with the believer and with the Father, no alien medium, but the living point of unity." In proportion to the soul's realization of this truth, in proportion to the faith mixed with the declarations of the Word thereon, there will be liberty and freedom, holy boldness, as we draw near the throne. Only thus will the Christian enjoy his birthright and live up to his blood-bought privilege; and only thus will God be honored by the praise and thanksgiving which must issue from such an individual.

The Subjects of Paul's Thanksgiving

Fourth, consider the *subjects* of Paul's thanksgiving: "for you all." This will appear strange to the natural man who is wrapped up so much in self. The carnal mind is quite incapable of appreciating the motives which activate and the principles which regulate those who are spiritual. Here was the apostle thanking God for those whom he had never met. They were not the fruits of his own labors, yet he rejoiced over them. How that condemns the narrow-minded bigotry and sectarian exclusiveness which have brought such a blight upon Christendom. Though these saints at Rome were not his own sons in the gospel, though he had never met them in the flesh, and as far as we know had not received any communication from them, yet he praised God for them. It was because of what *He* had wrought in them, because they were trees of His planting, the products of His husbandry (I Cor. 3:9). This principle is for our instruction. Do not expect the assurance of "my God" unless you have a love for and unless you pray for "all saints" (Eph. 6:18).

Fifth, observe the *occasion* of Paul's thanksgiving: "that your faith is spoken of throughout the whole world." These good tidings were spread abroad by travelers from Rome, the capital, telling of the humble reliance of the saints there on the Lord Jesus and their loving allegiance to Him. Wherever the apostle went this blessed information was given him. Not only had these people believed the gospel, but their faith was of such a character as to be everywhere spoken of, and Paul's thanksgiving for them was the recognition and acknowledgment that God was the Giver of their faith. Paul's notification of the same was not to induce complacency, but to quicken the saints in Rome to answer to the testimony borne to them and the expectations awakened thereby. Again we would remark, how blessed to behold the apostle praising God for what His grace had wrought in others. What an insight it gives us into his character. What a spirit of love for the brethren was here revealed. What gratitude and devotion for his Master. What an example for the servant of Christ today when tidings are received of the fruits of the Spirit in distant places.

A Personal Application

Before passing on to the next verse let us seek to make application to ourselves of what has been before us. It was not the doubting and unbelief of these Roman saints but their faith which was noised abroad. Is our faith known to others and talked about? Does it evoke praise and thanksgiving to God? Theirs was no formal and lifeless faith but a vigorous and fruitful one, which compelled others to take notice. It was a faith which transformed their character and conduct. Lest it be thought we have read into our verse more than is there, we refer the reader to 16:19: "your obedience is come abroad unto all." The two declarations are to be placed side by side, for the one explains and amplifies the other. If our faith is not productive of obedience such as others will take note of, there is something seriously wrong with us. We regard, then, the word *faith* in 1:8 as a generic expression for the graces of the Spirit, but the employment of this specific term was probably a prophetic rebuke of Romanism in which the chief thing lacking is saving faith!

"For God is my witness, whom I serve with my spirit in the gospel of his Son, that without ceasing I make mention of you always in my prayers" (1:9). "For God is my witness"; the opening "for" signifies that the One above knew how much these Christians were on Paul's heart. This was an act of worship, a due acknowledgment of God's omniscience. It was a reverent appeal to Him as the Searcher of hearts (cf. II Cor. 1:23; Gal. 1:20). "Whom I serve": Paul was at His entire disposal, subject to His orders. "With my spirit": not hypocritically from greed, nor formally, but from the very depths of Paul's being— willingly, heartily, joyously. "In the gospel of his Son" is the counterpart of "a servant of Jesus Christ . . . separated unto the gospel of God" (1:1). "That without ceasing I make mention of you always in my prayers" made known Paul's constancy. His rejoicing over and praying for them was no evanescent spasm but an enduring thing. Paul had called upon God as his Witness that his "without ceasing" was no exaggeration. Though these saints were in a flourishing condition, they still needed praying for.

We cannot do the saints a greater kindness, or exercise our love for them in a more practical and effective way, than by praying for them. Yet we do not regard the verses before us as establishing a precedent for Christians or ministers to proclaim abroad their praying. To parade our piety is but a species of Pharisaism. Praying is not a thing to advertise; as it is a secret exercise before God, it should as a rule be kept secret from men. True, there are exceptions: when believers are in trouble or isolated it is a comfort for them to know they are being remembered before the throne. Paul's mentioning of his praying was to inform the saints that his not having visited them (v. 13) was not due to indifference on his part, to assure them they had a constant place in his affections, and to pave the way for his coming to them by acquainting them of his deep solicitude for them.

Paul Desirous of Meeting the Roman Saints

"Making request, if by any means now at length I might have a prosperous journey by the will of God to come unto you" (v. 10). Paul's love for the Christians made him desirous of meeting them, and he prayed that God would make this possible. Let it be duly noted that he refused to take matters into his own hands and act upon an inward urge. Instead, he subordinated his own longings and impulses to the will of Him whom he served. This is very striking and blessed. Paul did not consider what many would regard as "the Spirit's prompting" a sufficient warrant. He must first be assured, by His providences, that this journey was ordered by his Master. Accordingly he spread his case before God, committing the matter to His decision and pleasure. Observe too that there was no "claiming," still less demanding, but a humble and submissive request—"if possible" or "if it may be." This was an acknowledgment that God is the Orderer of all events (Rom. 11:36).

"Now at length" shows that Paul was exercised about the timing of his journey and visit. "To everything there is a season, and a time to every purpose under the heaven" (Eccles. 3:1). It is of great practical importance for us to heed that fact, for it means the difference between success and failure in our undertakings. Unless we "rest in the Lord, and wait patiently for him" (Ps. 37:7) only confusion and trouble will ensue. We agree with Charles Hodge that the "prosperous journey" signified "that his circumstances should be so favorably ordered that he might be able to execute his long-cherished purpose of visiting Rome." It is blessed to note that a little later, before this epistle was completed, Paul was given divine assurance of his request being granted (Rom. 15:28-29). The journey itself is described in Acts 27 and 28. After a most trying and hazardous voyage Paul arrived in Rome a prisoner in chains! Yet see Acts 28:30-31 for the measure of liberty accorded him.

"For I long to see you, that I may impart unto you some spiritual gift, to the end ye may be established" (Rom. 1:11). This is not a part of Paul's prayer, yet it is intimately connected with it, for it makes known what prompted his request, why he was so desirous of seeing them. Paul's longing was that of spiritual affection, as a comparison with Philippians 2:26 and II Timothy 1:4 shows (the same Greek word occurs in all three). The word *long* tells how strong was Paul's desire to visit the Roman saints, and how real and commendable was his subjection to the will of God. We see the heart of an undershepherd in his burning zeal, yet at the same time we see his blessed submission to the chief Shepherd. Paul sought not to take a pleasure trip, nor to obtain variety in his labors, but to be made a blessing to these saints. Though their faith was well spoken of, yet he wished them to be established, strengthened, settled (I Peter 5:10). Paul's object was to expound the Way more perfectly to them, to add to their spiritual light and joy, to open to them more fully the unsearchable riches of Christ. Pastors, be not content with seeing sinners converted: seek their growth and establishment.

"That is, that I may be comforted together with you by the mutual faith both of you and me" (Rom. 1:12). This was to avoid giving offense lest they should feel he was reflecting upon their immaturity. Handley Moule has said, "Shall we call this a sentence of fine tact: beautifully conciliatory and endearing? Yes, but it is also perfectly sincere. True tact is certainly the skill of sympathetic love, but not the less genuine in its thought because that thought seeks to please and to win. He is glad to show himself as his disciples' brotherly friend: but then he first *is* such, and enjoys the character, and has continually found and felt his own soul made glad and strengthened by the witness for the Lord which far less gifted believers bore, as he and they talked together." It is beautiful to see Paul employing the passive form: "to the end ye may be established" (v. 11)—not "that I may establish you." He hides himself by expressing the result. Equally gracious is his "that I may be comforted together with you" (v. 12). Contact with kindred minds refreshes, and "he that watereth [others] shall be watered also himself" (Prov. 11:25).

Chapter 2

INSTRUCTION IN PRAYER

ROMANS 15:5-7

THE VERSES we are about to consider supply another illustration of how the apostle was wont to mingle prayer with instruction. He had just issued some practical exhortations; then he breathed a petition to God that He would make the same effectual. In order to enter into the spirit of this prayer it will be necessary to attend closely to its setting: the more so because not a few are very confused about the present-day bearing of the context. The section in which this passage is found begins at 14:1 and terminates at 15:13. In it the apostle gave directions relating to the maintenance of Christian fellowship and the mutual respect with which believers are to be regarded and treat one another, even where they are not entirely of one accord in matters pertaining to minor points of faith and practice. Those who do not see eye to eye with each other on things where no doctrine or principle is involved are to dwell together in unity, bearing and forbearing in a spirit of meekness and love.

Two Classes of Believers in Rome

In the Christian company at Rome, as in almost all the churches of God beyond the bounds of Judea at that time, there were two classes clearly distinguished from each other. The one was composed of Gentile converts and the more enlightened of their Jewish brethren, who (rightly) viewed the institutions of the Mosaic law as annulled by the new and better covenant. The other class comprised the great body of Jewish converts, who, while they believed in the Lord Jesus as the promised Messiah and Saviour, yet held that the Mosaic law was not and could not be repealed, and therefore continued zealous for it—not only observing its ceremonial requirements themselves but desirous of imposing the same on the Gentile Christians. The particular points here raised were abstinence from those "meats" which were prohibited under the old covenant, and the observance of certain "holy" days connected with the feasts of Judaism. The epistle of Hebrews had not then been written, and little explicit teaching was given on the subject. Until God allowed the overthrow of Judaism in A.D. 70, He tolerated slowness of understanding on the part of many Jewish Christians.

It can be easily understood, human nature being what it is, what evil tendencies such a situation threatened, and how real was the need for the apostle to address suitable exhortations to each party; for differences of opinion are liable

22

to lead to alienation of affections. The first party mentioned above was in danger of despising the other, looking down upon them as narrow-minded bigots, as superstitious. On the other hand, the party of the second part was in danger of judging the first harshly, viewing them as latitudinarians, lax, or as making unjust and unloving use of their Christian liberty. The apostle therefore made it clear that, where there is credible evidence of a genuine belief of saving truth, where the grand fundamentals of the faith are held, then such differences of opinion on minor matters should not in the slightest degree diminish brotherly love or mar spiritual and social fellowship. A spirit of bigotry, censoriousness, and intolerance is utterly foreign to Christianity.

The Particular Controversy

The particular controversy which existed in the apostle's time and the ill feelings it engendered have long since passed away, but the principles in human nature which gave rise to them are as powerful as ever. In companies of professing Christians there are diversities of endowment and acquirement (some have more light and grace than others), and there are differences of opinion and conduct. Therefore the things here recorded will, if rightly understood and legitimately applied, be found "written for our learning." Through *failure* to understand exactly what the apostle was dealing with, the most childish and unwarrantable applications of the passage have been made, many seeming to imagine that if their fellow Christians refuse to walk by *their* rules, they are guilty of acting uncharitably and of putting a stumbling block in their way. We know of a sect which deems it unscriptural for a married woman to wear a wedding ring, and of another that considers it wrong for a Christian man to shave. And these people condemn those who do not adhere to their ideas.

The cases just mentioned are not only entirely foreign to the scope of Romans 14 and 15 but they involve an evil which it is the duty of God's servants to resist and denounce. That such cases as the ones we have alluded to are in no wise analogous to what the apostle was dealing with should be clear to anyone who attentively considers these simple facts. Under Judaism certain meats were divinely prohibited and designated "unclean" (e.g., Lev. 11:4-8). But such prohibitions have been divinely removed (Acts 10:15; I Tim. 4:4), hence there is no point in abstaining from things which God has never forbidden. If some people wish to do so, if they think well to deprive themselves of some of the things which God has given us to enjoy (I Tim. 6:17), that is their privilege; but when they demand that others should do likewise out of respect to their ideas, they exceed their rights and attack the God-given liberty of their brethren.

But there are not a few who go yet farther. They not only insist that others should walk by the rule they have set up (or accept the particular interpretation of certain scriptures which they give *and* the specific application of the term "meat" which they make) but stigmatize as "unclean," "carnal," and "sinful" the conduct of those differing from them. This is a very serious matter, for it is a manifest and flagrant commission of that which this particular portion of God's Word expressly reprehends. "Let not him which eateth not judge him that eateth. . . . Who art thou that judgest another man's servant? . . . Why dost thou judge thy brother? . . . Let us not therefore judge one another any more" (Rom. 14:3-4, 10, 13). Thus the very ones who are so forward in judging their brethren are condemned by God. It is surely significant that there is no other portion of Holy Writ which so strongly and so repeatedly forbids passing judgment on others as this chapter to which appeal is so often (wrongly) made by those who condemn their fellows for things which Scripture has not prohibited.

The Right of Private Judgment

One of the grand blessings won for us by the fierce battle of the Reformation was the right of private judgment. Not only had the Word of God been withheld but no man had been at liberty to form any ideas on spiritual things for himself. If anyone dared to do so, he was anathematized; and if he remained firm in refusing bondage, he was cruelly tortured and then murdered. But in the mercy of God, Luther and his fellows defied Rome, and by divine providence the holy Scriptures were restored to the common people and translated into their own language. Every man then had the right to pray directly to God for enlightenment and to form his own judgment of what the Word taught. Alas that such an inestimable privilege is now so little prized, and that the vast majority of Protestants are too indolent to search the Scriptures for themselves, preferring to take their views from others.

Because many of those who enjoyed this dearly bought privilege had so little courage or wisdom to resist modern encroachments on personal liberty, those who sought to lord it over their brethren have made so much headway during the last two or three generations. The whirlwind has followed the "sowing of the wind," and that spirit which was allowed to domineer in the churches is now being more and more adumbrated in the world. We are aware of militant forces seeking to invade the right of conscience, the right each man has to interpret the Word according to the light God has given him.

When commenting on Romans 14, John Brown said, "It is to be hoped, notwithstanding much that still indicates, in some quarters, a disposition to exercise over the minds and consciences of men an authority and an influence which belong to God only, that the reign of spiritual tryanny—the worst of all tyrannies—is drawing to a close. Let us determine neither to exercise such domination, nor to submit to it even for an hour. Let us 'call no man master,' and let us not seek to be called masters by others. One is our Master, who is Christ the Lord, and we are His fellow servants. Let us help each other, but leave Him to judge us. He only has the capacity, as He only has the authority, for so doing." Let us heed that apostolic injunction "Stand fast therefore in the liberty wherewith Christ hath made us free, and be not entangled again with the yoke of bondage" (Gal. 5:1), refusing to heed the "touch not; taste not; handle not . . . after the commandments and doctrines of men" (Col. 2:21-22).

"Him that is weak in the faith receive ye, but not to doubtful disputations" (Rom. 14:1). The reference was not to one of feeble faith, beset by doubts, but rather to one who was imperfectly instructed in the faith, who had not yet grasped the real meaning of Christian liberty, who was still in bondage to the prohibitions of Judaism. Notwithstanding his lack of knowledge, the saints were to receive him into their affections, treat him kindly (cf. Acts 28:2 and Philemon 15, 17 for the force of the word *receive*). He was neither to be excommunicated from Christian circles nor looked upon with contempt because he had less light than others. "But not to doubtful disputations" means that he was not to be disturbed about his own conscientious views and practices, nor on the other hand was he to be allowed to pester his brethren by seeking to convert them to his views. There was to be a mutual forbearance and amity between believers. Matthew Henry stated, "Each Christian has and ought to have the judgment of discretion, and should have his senses exercised to the discerning between good and evil, truth and error."

But does the above verse mean that no effort is to be made to enlighten one who has failed to lay hold of and enter into the benefits Christ secured for His people? Certainly not; Rome may believe that "ignorance is the mother of devotion," but not so those who are guided by the Word. As Aquila and Priscilla took Apollos "and expounded unto him the way of God more perfectly" (Acts 18:26), so it is both our duty and privilege to pass on to fellow Christians the light God has given us. Yet that instruction must be given humbly and not censoriously, in a spirit of meekness and not with contention. Patience must be exercised. "He that winneth [not 'browbeateth'] souls is wise." The aim should be to enlighten his mind rather than force his will, for unless the conscience be convicted, uniformity of action would be mere hypocrisy. A spirit of moderation must temper zeal, and the right of private judgment must be fully respected: "Let every man be fully persuaded in his own mind." If we fail to win such a man it would be sinful to attribute it to his mulishness.

The Gospel Dispensation

Space will allow us to single out only one other weighty consideration: "The kingdom of God is not meat and drink; but righteousness, and peace, and joy in the Holy Ghost" (14:17). "The kingdom of God," or the gospel dispensation, does not consist of such comparative trivialities as using or abstaining from meat and drink (or other indifferent things); it gives no rule either one way or the other. The Jewish religion consisted much in such things (Heb. 9: 10), but Christianity consists of something infinitely more important and valuable. Let us not be guilty of the sin of the Pharisees, who paid tithes of "mint and anise" but "omitted the weightier matters of the law, judgment, mercy, and faith" (Matt. 23:23). John Brown stated, "You give a false and degrading view of Christianity by these contentions, leading men to think that freedom from ceremonial restrictions is its great privilege, while the truth is, justification, peace with God, and joy in God, produced by the Holy Spirit, are the characteristic privileges of the children of the kingdom."

But another principle is involved here, a most important and essential one, namely, the exercise of brotherly love. Suppose I fail to convince my weaker brother, and he claims to be stumbled by my allowing myself things he cannot conscientiously use? Then what is my duty? If he be unable to enter into the breadth of Christian liberty which I perceive and exercise, how far does the law of Christian charity require me to forgo my liberty and deny myself that which I feel free before God to use? That is not an easy question to answer, for there are many things which have to be taken into consideration. If it were nothing but a matter of deciding between pleasing myself and profiting my brethren, there would be no difficulty. But if it is merely a matter of yielding to their whims, where is the line to be drawn? We have met some who consider is wrong to drink tea or coffee because it is injurious. The one who sets out to try and please everybody is likely to end by pleasing nobody.

Moderation and Abstinence

A sharp distinction is to be drawn between moderation and abstinence. To be "temperate in all things" (I Cor. 9:25) is a dictate of prudence—to put it on the lowest ground. "Let your moderation be known unto all men" (Phil. 4:5) is a divine injunction. It is not the use but the abuse of many things which marks the difference between innocence and sin. But because many abuse certain of God's creatures, that is no sufficient reason why others should altogether shun them. As Spurgeon once said, "Shall I cease to use knives because some men cut their throats with them?" Shall, then, my wife remove her wedding ring because certain people profess to be "stumbled" at the sight of one on her finger? Does love to them require her to become fanatical? Would it really make for their profit, their edification, by conforming to their scruples? Or would it not be more likely to encourage a spirit of self-righteousness? We once lived for two years in a small place where there was a church of these people, but we saw few signs of humility in those who were constantly complaining of pride in others.

There are some professing Christians (by no means all of them Romanists) who would consider they grievously dishonored Christ if they partook of any animal meat on Friday. How far would the dictates of Christian love require me to join with them in such abstinence were I to reside in a community where these people preponderated? Answering for himself, the writer would say it depends upon their viewpoint. If it was nothing more than a sentiment he would probably yield, though he would endeavor to show them there was nothing in Scripture requiring such abstinence. But if they regarded it as a virtuous thing, as being necessary to salvation, he would unhesitatingly disregard their wishes, otherwise he would be encouraging them in fatal error. Or, if they said he too was sinning by eating animal meat on Friday, then he would deem it an unwarrantable exercise of brotherly love to countenance their mistake, and an unlawful trespassing upon his Christian liberty.

It is written, "Give none offence, neither to the Jews, nor to the Gentiles, nor to the church of God" (I Cor. 10:32); yet, like many another precept, that one cannot be taken absolutely without any qualification. For example, if I be invited to occupy an Arminian pulpit it would give great offense should I preach upon unconditional election; yet would that warrant my keeping silent thereon? Hyper-Calvinists do not like to hear about man's responsibility; but should I therefore withhold what is needful to and profitable for them? Would brotherly love require this of me? None was more pliable and adaptable than he who wrote, "Unto the Jews I became as a Jew, that I might gain the Jews. . . . To the weak became I as weak, that I might gain the weak" (I Cor. 9:20-22); yet when Peter was to be blamed because he acceded to those who condemned eating with the Gentiles, Paul "withstood him to the face" (Gal. 2:11-12); and when false brethren sought to bring Paul into bondage he refused to have Titus circumcised (Gal. 2:3-5).

Another incident much to the point before us is found in connection with our Lord and His disciples. "The Pharisees, and all the Jews, except they wash their hands oft, eat not, holding the tradition of the elders. And when they come from the market, except they wash, they eat not" (Mark 7:3-4). First a tradition, this had become a religious practice, a conscientious observance, among the Jews. Did our Lord then bid His disciples to respect the scruples of the Jews and conform to their standard? No, indeed; for when the Pharisees "saw some of his disciples eat bread with defiled [ceremonially defiled], that is to say, with unwashen hands, they found fault" (v. 2). On another occasion Christ Himself was invited by a certain Pharisee to dine with him, "and he went in, and sat down to meat. And when the Pharisee saw it, he marveled that he had not first washed before dinner" (Luke 11:37-38). Even though He knew it would give offense, Christ declined to be bound by man-made laws.

Christian Charity a Duty

The exercise of Christian charity is an essential duty, yet it is not to override everything else. God has not exercised love at the expense of righteousness. The exercising of love does not mean that the Christian himself is to become a nonentity, a mere straw blown hither and thither by every current of wind he encounters. He is never to please his brethren at the expense of displeasing God. Love is not to oust liberty. The exercise of love does not require the Christian to yield principle, to wound his own conscience, or to become the slave of every fanatic he meets. Love does enjoin the curbing of his own desires and seeking the good, the profit, the edification, of his brethren; but it does not call for subscribing to their errors and depriving himself of the right of personal judgment. There is a balance to be preserved here: a happy medium between cultivating unselfishness and becoming the victim of the selfishness of others.

Under the new covenant there is no longer any distinction in the sight of God between different kinds of "meat" or sacred "days" set apart for religious exercise which obtained under the Jewish economy. Some of the early Christians perceived this clearly; others either did not or would not acknowledge such liberty. This difference of opinion bred dissensions and disrupted fellowship. To remove this evil and to promote good, the apostle laid down certain rules which may be summed up thus. First, "Let every man be fully persuaded in his own mind" (Rom. 14:5) and not blindly swayed by the opinions or customs of others. Second, Be not censorious and condemn not those who differ from you (v. 13). Third, Be not occupied with mere trifles, but concentrate on the essentials (v. 17). Fourth, Follow after those things which make for peace and mutual edification (v. 19) and quibble not over matters which are to no profit. Fifth, Make not an ostentatious display of your liberty, nor exercise the same to the injury of others (vv. 19-21).

Variety and Diversity Among Saints

There is great variety and diversity among the saints. This is true of their natural makeup, temperament, manner, and thus in their likableness or unlikableness. This fact also holds good spiritually: Christians have received varying degrees of light, measures of grace, and different gifts. One reason why God has ordered things thus is to try their patience, give opportunity for the exercise of love, and provide occasion to display meekness and forbearance. All have their blemishes and infirmities. Some are proud, others peevish; some are censorious, and others backboneless, or in various ways difficult to get on with. Opinions differ and customs are by no means uniform. Much grace is needed if fellowship is to be maintained. If the rules above had been rightly interpreted and genuinely acted upon through the centuries, many dissensions would have been prevented, and much that has marred the Christian testimony in public would have been avoided.

"We then that are strong ought to bear the infirmities of the weak, and not to please ourselves" (15:1). The "then" is argumentative, pointing out a conclusion from the principles laid down in the foregoing chapter. The preceding chapter was necessary for some understanding of these principles. Let it be duly noted that the pronouns are in the *plural* number: it was not only individual differences of opinion and conduct, with the personal ill-feelings they bred, which the apostle had been reprehending, but also the development of the same collectively into party spirit and sectarian prejudice, which could rend asunder the Christian company. This too must be borne in mind when making a present-day application. "The weak" here signifies those who had a feeble grasp of that freedom which Christ obtained for His people, as reference to 14:1 makes clear; the "strong" indicates those who had a better apprehension of the extent of their Christian privileges, fully discerning their liberation from the restrictions imposed by the ceremonial law and the traditions of men—such as the austerities of the Essenes.

The Greek word here rendered "bear" signifies "to take up." It was used of porters carrying luggage, assisting travelers. It is found again in Galatians 6:2, only the apostle there mentioned "burdens" rather than infirmities (see also Luke 14:27). The term also helps to determine the interpretation of what is in view, and thus fixes the proper application. We are not here enjoined to bear with the petty whims or scruples of one another, but to render practical aid to those who lag behind the rest. A "burden" is something which is apt to cause its carrier to halt or faint by the way, incapacitating him in his pilgrimage. The strong are bidden to help these weak ones. As charity requires us to ascribe their weakness to lack of understanding, it becomes the duty of the better instructed to seek to enlighten them. No doubt it would be easier and nicer to leave them alone, but we are "not to please ourselves." Apparently the Gentile believers had failed on this point, for while the Jewish Christians were aggressive in seeking to impose their view on others, the Gentiles seem to have adopted a negative attitude.

It is ever thus: Fanatics and extremists are not content to deprive themselves of things which God has not prohibited but are zealous in endeavoring to press their will upon all; whereas others who use them temperately are content to mind their own business and leave in peace those who differ from them. For instance, it is not the use of wine but the intemperate abuse of the same which Scripture forbids (see John 2:1-11; Eph. 5:18; I Tim. 3:8). It was the ex-Pharisees "which believed" who insisted that "it was needful to circumcise" converted Gentiles and "to command them to keep the law of Moses" (Acts 15:5) and thereby bring them into bondage—a thing which the Apostle Paul steadfastly resisted and condemned.

Bearing the Infirmities of the Weak

In the passage before us the Roman saints were exhorted to desist from their negative attitude, however much easier and more congenial it might be to continue in the same. "And please not ourselves" (Rom. 15:1) signifies not an abstention from something they liked, but the performing of a duty which they disliked—how men do turn the things of God upside down! This is quite evident from the preceding part of the verse where the "strong" (or better instructed) were bidden to "bear the infirmities of the weak." How would their abstaining from certain "meats" be a compliance with such an injunction? No, it was not something they were told to forgo out of respect for others' scruples, but a bearing of their "infirmities," a rendering of assistance to their fellow pilgrims (Gal. 6:2) which they were called upon to do. And how was this to be done? Well, what were their "infirmities"? Why, self-imposed abstinences because of ignorance of the truth. Thus it was the duty of the Gentile Christians to expound to their Jewish bretheren "the way of God more perfectly" (Acts 18:26).

Try and place yourself in their position, my reader. Imagine yourself to be Lydia or the Philippian jailor. All your past life had been in the darkness and idolatry of heathenism; then, unsought by you, the sovereign grace of God opened your heart to receive the gospel. You are now a new creature in Christ Jesus, and have been enabled to perceive your standing and liberty in Him. Living next door to you, perhaps, is a family of converted Jews. All their past lives they have read the Scriptures and worshiped the true God; though they have now received Christ as the promised Messiah and as their personal Saviour, yet they are still in bondage to the restrictions of the Mosaic law. You marvel at their dullness, but consider it none of your concern to interfere. Then you receive a copy of this epistle and ponder 15:1. You now see that you have a duty toward your Jewish sister and brother, that God bids you make the effort to pass on to her or him the light He has granted you. The task is distasteful. Perhaps so, but we are "not to please ourselves"!

Pleasing Our Neighbor

The next verse unequivocally establishes that what we have sought to set forth above brings out, or at least points to, the real meaning of Romans 15:1. "Let every one of us please his neighbour for his good to edification" (v. 2). This is obviously the amplification in positive form of the negative clause in the verse before. To "edify" a brother—here called "neighbour" according to Jewish terminology—is to build him up in the faith; and the appointed means is to instruct him by and enlighten him with the truth. It should be carefully noted that this "pleasing our neighbor" is no mere yielding to his whims, but an industrious effort to promote his knowledge of divine things, particularly in the privileges which Christ has secured for him. It may prove a thankless task, but it ought to be undertaken, for concern for his good requires it. If he resents your efforts and insults you, your conscience is clear and you have the satisfaction of knowing that you have honestly attempted to discharge your duty.

"For even Christ pleased not himself; but, as it is written, The reproaches of them that reproached thee fell on me" (v. 3). This verse supplies further proof of the soundness of our interpretation of the previous verses. The meaning of "we . . . ought . . . not to please ourselves" is placed beyond all uncertainty by what is here said of our Lord. In His case it signifies something vastly different than abstaining from things that He liked, and certainly the very opposite of attempting to ingratiate Himself in the esteem of men by flattering their prejudices. Rather, Christ was in all things regulated by the divine rule: not His own will but the will of His Father was what governed Him. Not attempting to obtain the approval of His fellows, but rather seeking their "good" and the "edification" of His brethren was what uniformly actuated Christ. And in the exercise of disinterested charity, far from being appreciated for the same, He brought upon Himself "reproaches." And if the disciple follows His example he must not expect to fare any better.

Remarks by Charles Hodge

In his closing remarks on Romans 14, Charles Hodge pointed out, "It is often necessary to assert our Christian liberty at the expense of incurring censure and offending good men in order that right principles of duty may be preserved. Our Saviour consented to be regarded as a Sabbath-breaker and even a 'wine-bibber' and 'friend of publicans and sinners'; but wisdom was justified of her children. Christ did not in those cases see fit to accommodate His conduct to the rules of duty set up and conscientiously regarded as correct by those around Him. He saw that more good would arise from a practical disregard of the false opinion of the Jews as to the manner in which the Sabbath was to be kept and as to the degree of intercourse which was allowed with wicked men, than from concession to their prejudices." Better then to give offense or incur obloquy than sacrifice principle or disobey God.

"For whatsoever things were written aforetime were written for our learning, that we through patience and comfort of the scriptures might have hope" (v. 4). This statement seems to be made for a double reason. First, to inform the saints that though the Mosaic law was abrogated and the Old Testament treated of a past dispensation, they must not conclude that the Old Testament was now out of date. The uniform use which the New Testament writers made of it, frequently appealing to it in proof of what they advanced, proves otherwise. All of it is intended for our instruction today, and the examples of piety contained therein will stimulate us (see James 5:10). Second, a prayerful pondering of the Old Testament will nourish that very grace which will most need to be exercised when complying with the foregoing exhortations—"patience" in dealing with those who differ from us; further, it will minister "comfort" to us if we are reviled for performing our duty.

Prejudice of Heart to Be Overcome

"Now the God of patience and consolation grant you to be like-minded one toward another according to Christ Jesus" (v. 5). By his example the apostle here teaches us that if we are to discharge the aforesaid duty acceptably to God we must have recourse to prayer. God alone can grant success in it, and unless His aid be definitely and earnestly sought, failure is almost certain to be the outcome. There are few things which the majority of people more resent than to have their religious beliefs and ways called into question. More is involved than perfectly informed understanding: there is prejudice of heart to be overcome as well, for "convince a man against his will, and he is of the same opinion still." Moreover, much grace is required on the part of the one who undertakes to deal with the mistaken scruples of another lest, acting in the energy of the flesh, he gives place to the devil, sowing seeds of discord and causing "a root of bitterness" to spring up, thus making matters worse rather than better. Such grace needs to be personally and fervently sought.

Zeal Not According to Knowledge

There is a zeal which is not according to knowledge. There is an ardor which is merely of nature and not prompted by the Holy Spirit. If then it should become my duty to pass on to a brother a measure of that light which God has granted me and which I have reason to believe he does not enjoy, I need to ask help from Him for the execution of such a task. I need to ask Him to impress my heart afresh with the fact that I have nothing but what I received from Him (I Cor. 4:7) and to beg Him to subdue the workings of pride that I may approach my brother in a humble spirit. I need to ask for wisdom that I may be guided in what to say. I need to ask for love that I may truly seek the good of the other. I need to be shown the right time to approach him. Above all, I need to ask that God's glory may be my paramount concern. Furthermore, I need to request God to go before me and prepare the soil for the seed, graciously softening the heart of my brother, removing the prejudice, and making him receptive to the truth.

Observe the particular character in which the apostle addressed the Deity: as "the God of patience and consolation." He eyed those attributes in God which were most suited to the petition he presented, namely, that He would grant like-mindedness and mutual forbearance where there was a difference in judgment. The grace of patience was needed among dissenting brethren. Consolation too was required to bear the infirmities of the weak. As another has said, "If the heart be filled with the comforts of the Almighty, it will be as oil to the wheels of Christian charity." The Father is here contemplated as "the God of patience and consolation" because He is the Author of these graces, because He requires the exercise of the same in us (Eph. 5:1), and because we are to constantly seek the quickening and strengthening of these graces in us. In the preceding verse we are shown that "patience and comfort" are conveyed to believing souls through the Scriptures, which are the conduit; but here we are taught that God Himself is the Fountainhead.

The Mercy to Be Sought

Consider now the mercy sought: that the God of patience and consolation would "grant you to be like-minded one to another." As Charles Hodge rightly pointed out, the like-mindedness here "does not signify uniformity of opinion but harmony of feeling." This should be apparent to those who possess no knowledge of the Greek. How can "babes" in Christ be expected to have the same measure of light on spiritual things as mature Christians! No, the apostle's petition went deeper than that the saints might see eye to eye on every detail—which is neither to be expected nor desired in this life. It was that affection one toward another might obtain, even where difference of opinion upon minor matters persisted. Paul requested that quarreling should cease, ill feelings be set aside, patience and forbearance be exercised, and mutual love prevail. He requested that such a state of unity might obtain that notwithstanding difference of view the saints might enjoy together the delights and advantages of Christian fellowship.

"According to Christ Jesus" (v. 5). The margin renders it "after the example of," which is certainly included; yet the meaning is not to be restricted thereto. We regard this like-mindedness "according to Christ Jesus" as having a threefold force. First, according to the precept, command, or law of Christ: "By this shall all men know that ye are my disciples, if ye have love one to another" (John 13:35). "Bear ye one another's burdens, and so fulfil the law of Christ" (Gal. 6:2). Second, according to Christ's example. Remember how He dealt with the dullness and bickering of His disciples. Remember how He stooped to wash their feet. Third, by making Christ the Center of their unity. To quote Matthew Henry, "Agree in the truth, not in any error. It was a cursed concord and harmony of those who were of one mind to give their power and strength to the Beast (Rev. 17:13): that was not a like-mindedness *according* to Christ, but *against* Christ." Thus "according to Christ Jesus" signifies "in a Christian manner." Let the reader ponder carefully Philippians 2:2-5, for it furnishes an inspired comment on our present verse.

The Fullness of Scripture

Yet there is such a fullness in the words of Scripture that the threefold meaning of "according to Christ Jesus" given above by no means exhausts the scope of these words. They need also to be considered in the light of what immediately precedes, and pondered as a part of this prayer. The apostle made request that God would cause this Christian company (composed of such different elements as believing Jews and Gentiles) to be "like-minded," which, of course, implies that they were not so. Titus 3:3 describes what we are by nature. Observe that the blessing sought, however desirable, was not something to be claimed, but something to be hoped that God would "grant." By adding "according to Christ Jesus" we may therefore understand those words as the ground of appeal: grant it according to the merits of Christ. Finally, we may also regard this clause as a plea: grant it for the honor of Christ—that unity and concord may obtain for the glory of His name.

"That ye may with one mind and one mouth glorify God, even the Father of our Lord Jesus Christ" (v. 6). This is the grand end in view: that such brotherly love may be exercised, such mutual forbearance shown, such unity and concord maintained, that the spirit of worship be not quenched. The God who will not receive an offering while one is alienated from his brother (Matt. 5:23-24) will not accept the praise of a company of believers where there are divisions among them. Something more is required than coming together under the same roof and joining in the same ordinance (I Cor. 11:18-20). There cannot truly be "one mouth" unless there first be "one mind." Tongues which are used to backbite one another in private cannot blend together in singing God's praises. The "Father" is mentioned here as an emphatic reminder of the family relationship: all Christians are His children and therefore should dwell together in peace and amity as brethren and sisters. "Of our [not 'the'] Lord Jesus Christ" intensifies the same idea.

J. M. Stifler states, "They may be divided in their dietary views: this in itself is a small matter; but they must not be divided in their worship and praise of God. For the patient and comforted mind can join in praise with those from whom there is dissent of opinion. This is true Christian union." "Wherefore receive ye one another, as Christ also received us to the glory of God" (v. 7). This is not an exhortation to one class only, but to the "strong" and the "weak" alike. They are here bidden to ignore all minor differences. And inasmuch as Christ accepts all who genuinely believe His gospel, whether they be Jews or Gentiles, we are to receive into fellowship and favor all whom He has received. We again quote J. M. Stifler: "If He accepts men in all their weakness and without any regard to their views about secondary things, well may we." Thereby God is glorified, and for this we should pray and act.

Chapter 3

PRAYER IN HOPE

ROMANS 15:13

IN HIS PRECEDING PRAYER the Apostle Paul had made request that the God of patience and consolation would grant the saints at Rome to be "like-minded one toward another, according to Christ Jesus" (Rom. 15:5) so that amity and concord might prevail among them. He had followed this by reminding them that the Redeemer's mission embraced not only the Jews but also the Gentiles, that the eternal purpose of God respected an elect portion from both parts of the human race (vv. 8-9). In support of this statement he quoted no less than four Old Testament passages, taken respectively from the Law, the Psalms, and the Prophets (the principal sections into which the divine oracles were divided; see Luke 24:44), each of which foretold that the Gentiles would take their place alongside the Jews in worshiping the Lord. Thus the Hebrew Christians need have no hesitation in welcoming believing Gentiles into their midst. The apostle then concluded this section of his epistle, by again supplicating the throne of grace on their behalf, thereby evidencing his deep solicitude for them, and intimating that God alone could impart the grace necessary for obedience to the injunctions given them.

Vital instruction is to be obtained by attending closely to the connection between Romans 15:13 and the verses which immediately precede it. In the context Paul had cited a number of Old Testament passages which announced the salvation of the Gentiles and their union with believing Jews. Now the prophecies of Scripture are to be viewed in a threefold manner. First, as proofs of their divine inspiration, demonstrating as they do the omniscience of their Author in unerringly forecasting things to come. Second, as revelations of the will of God, announcements of what He has eternally decreed, which must therefore come to pass. Third, as possessing a moral and practical bearing upon us: where they are predictions of judgment, they are threatenings and therefore warnings of the objects to be avoided and the evils to be shunned—as the fore-announced destruction of the papacy bids us have nought to do with that system; but where they consist of predictions of divine blessing, they are promises for faith to lay hold of and for hope to anticipate before their actual fulfillment. Paul is viewing them in this third respect.

34

Our Use of the Divine Promises

Here the apostle shows us what use we are to make of the divine promises, namely, turn them into believing prayer, requesting God to make them good. As God draws near to us in promise, it is our privilege to draw near to Him in petition. Those prophecies were infallible assurances that God intended to show mercy to the Gentiles. No sooner had Paul quoted them than he bowed his knees before their Giver, thereby teaching the Roman saints—and us—how to turn the promises to practical account, instructing them what to ask for. In like manner when he would have the Ephesian saints beg God to enlighten their understandings, that they might know the great things of the gospel, he set them an example by praying for that very thing (1:17-18). So here; it was as though he said, "Thou hast promised that the Gentiles should hope in Thee [v. 12]. Thou art 'the God of hope.' Graciously work in these saints so that they 'may abound in hope, through the power of the Holy Ghost,' and that they too may from my example be constrained to supplicate Thee and plead this promise for the attainment of this very blessing."

That the reader may have a more definite view of the connection, we will now quote the verse before our prayer: "And again, Esaias [Isaiah] saith, There shall be a root of Jesse, and he that shall rise to reign over the Gentiles; in him shall the Gentiles trust." That is taken from one of the great Messianic prophecies, recorded in Isaiah 11. Whatever may or may not be its ultimate accomplishment, Paul was moved to make known to us that that prediction was even then receiving fulfillment. Literally the Greek reads, "In Him shall the Gentiles hope," and it is thus rendered correctly in the Revised Version. Though intimately connected, as Hebrews 11:1 shows, there is a real difference between faith and hope. Faith is more comprehensive in its range, for it believes all that God has said concerning the past, present, and future—the threatenings as well as the promises—but hope looks solely to a future good. Faith has to do with the Word promising; hope is engaged with the thing promised. Faith is a believing that God will do as He has said; hope is a confident looking forward to the fulfillment of the promise.

The Remote Context

Having sought to point out the instructive connection between the apostle's prayer and the verses immediately preceding, a word now on its remoter context. This prayer concludes that section of the epistle begun at 14:1, on unhappy division in the company of the Roman saints. Without taking sides and expressly declaring which was in the wrong, Paul had laid down broad and simple principles for each to act upon, so that if their conduct was regulated thereby, Christian love and Christian liberty would alike be conserved. He set before them the example of their Master, and then showed that both Jews and Gentiles were given equal place in the Word of prophecy. To borrow the lovely language of Moule, "He clasps them impartially to his own heart in this precious and pregnant benediction, beseeching for both sides, and for all their individuals, a wonderful fullness of those blessings in which most speedily and most surely the spirit of their strife would expire." The closer a company of Christians are drawn to their Lord, the closer they are drawn to one another.

"Now the God of hope fill you with all joy and peace in believing, that ye may abound in hope, through the power of the Holy Ghost." The "God of hope" is both the Object and the Author of hope. He is the One who has prepared the blessings which are to be the objects of our hope, who has set them before us in the gospel, and who by the power of the Spirit enables us to understand and believe the gospel, which awakens motives and sets in action principles that ensure hope. The burden of Paul's prayer was that the saints might abound in this spiritual grace, and therefore he addressed the Deity accordingly. As Matthew Henry pointed out, "It is good in prayer to fasten upon those names, titles and attributes of God which are most suitable to the errand we come upon and will best serve to encouragement concerning it." A further reason why the apostle thus addressed the Deity appears from the preceding verse, where it was announced of the Lord, "In him shall the Gentiles hope." More literally our verse reads, "Now the God of that [or 'the'] hope"—the One who is the Inspirer of all expectations of blessing.

"The God of Hope"

This expression "the God of [that] hope" had special pertinency and peculiar suitability to the Gentiles—who are mentioned by name no less than four times in the verses immediately preceding. Its force is the more apparent if we consider it in the light of Ephesians 2:11-12, where Gentile believers are reminded that in time past they "were without Christ [devoid of any claim upon Him], being aliens from the commonwealth of Israel, and strangers from the covenants of promise, having *no hope,* and without God in the world"—without any knowledge of Him, without a written revelation from Him. But the incarnation of Christ had radically altered this. The grand design of His mission was not restricted to Palestine but was worldwide, for He shed His atoning blood for sinners out of all peoples and tribes and, upon the triumphant conclusion of His mission, commissioned His servants to preach the gospel to all nations. Hence the apostle had reminded the Roman saints that God said, "Rejoice, ye Gentiles, with his people" (v. 10). He had now become *to them* "the God of hope."

If God had not revealed Himself in the Word of truth we should be without any foundation of hope. But the Scriptures are windows of hope to us. This is evident from the fourth verse of our chapter: "For whatsoever things were written aforetime were written for our learning, that we through patience and comfort of the scriptures might have *hope*" (v. 4). Thus the God of hope is revealed in His living oracles with the design of inspiring hope. If we would be filled with faith, joy, and peace it must be by believing what is presented to us in Holy Writ. Before we have any true inward ground of hope, God Himself as revealed in the Bible must be our confidence. Through God's Word the apostle discovered there was hope for the Gentiles; and so may the most burdened heart find solid consolation therein if he will search and believe its contents. Every divine promise is calculated to inspire the believer with hope. Therein is to be found a sure foundation, on which to rest.

Let us now consider the petition the apostle here presented to the God of hope: that He would "fill you with all joy and peace in believing." This is to be considered first in its local bearing. The phrase "in believing" looks back to those blessed portions of the Old Testament which had just been quoted. Paul prayed that God would graciously enable those saints to lay hold of such promises and conduct themselves in harmony therewith. We quote Charles Hodge: "In the fulfillment of that promise [v. 12] Christ came, and preached salvation to those who were near and to those who were afar off (Eph. 2:17). As both classes had been thus kindly received by the condescending Saviour and united into one community, they should receive and love each other as brethren, laying aside all censoriousness and contempt, neither judging nor despising one another." In other words, the apostle longed that both should be occupied alike with Christ. Let faith and hope be duly operative, and joy and peace would displace discord and strife.

Regarding this prayer of the Apostle Paul, Handley Moule wrote: "Let that prayer be granted, in its pure depth and height, and how could the 'weak brother' look with quite his old anxiety on the problems suggested by the dishes at a meal and by the dates of the Rabbinic calendar? And could 'the strong' bear any longer to lose his joy in God by an assertion, full of self, of his own insight and liberty? Profoundly happy and at rest in the Lord, whom they embraced by faith as their Righteousness and Life, and whom they anticipated in hope as their coming Glory; filled through their whole consciousness by the indwelling Spirit with a new insight into Christ, they would fall into each other's embrace, in Him. They would be much more ready when they met to speak 'concerning the King' than to begin a new stage of their not very elevating discussion. How many a church controversy now, as then, would die of inanition, leaving room for living truth, if the disputants could only gravitate, as to their always most beloved theme, to the praises and glories of their redeeming Lord Himself!"

As our Lord's prayer in John 17 was not confined to His disciples then but reached forward to "them also which shall believe" (v. 20), so this prayer of Paul's is suited to all the children of God. "The God of hope fill you with all joy and peace in believing." Let it be duly noted that Paul did not hesitate to ask for these particular blessings. We make that remark because we very much fear that some of our readers are well-nigh afraid to cry to God for such things; but they need not be. Fullness of spiritual joy does not unfit its possessor to live his life in this world, nor does fullness of peace produce presumption and carnal security. If such experiences were dangerous, as Satan would fain have us conclude, the apostle would not have sought them on behalf of his fellow Christians. From his making request for these very blessings we learn they are eminently desirable and furnished warrant for us to supplicate for the same, both for ourselves and our brethren.

The Apostle's Example

The example which the apostle has here set before us evidences not only that it is desirable for Christians to be filled with joy and peace, but also that such a delightful experience is attainable. C. H. Spurgeon stated, "We *may* be filled with joy and peace believing, and may abound in hope. There is no reason why we should hang our heads and live in perpetual doubt. We may not only be somewhat comforted, but we may be full of joy; we may not only have occasional quiet, but we may dwell in peace, and delight ourselves in the abundance of it. These great privileges are attainable or the apostle would not have made them the subject of prayer. . . . The sweetest delights are still grown in Zion's gardens, and are to be enjoyed by us; and shall they be within our reach and not be grasped? Shall a life of joy and peace be attainable, and shall we miss it through unbelief? God forbid. Let us as believers resolve that whatsoever of privilege is to be enjoyed we *will* enjoy it."

Once again we appeal to the context, for clear proof is found there that it *is* God's revealed will for His saints to be a *rejoicing* people. In verse 10 the apostle cited a verse from the Old Testament which says, "Rejoice, ye Gentiles, with his people." Israel had been given no monopoly of joy; those whom God had purposed to call from out the nations would also share therein. If there was joy for Israel when redeemed from the house of bondage and led through the Red Sea, much more so is there joy for those delivered from the power of Satan and translated into the kingdom of God's dear Son. Observe that the passage quoted is not in the form of a promise, but is a specific precept: regenerated Gentiles are expressly bidden to "rejoice." Nor did the apostle stop there. As though anticipating our slowness to enter into our privileges, he added, "And again, Praise the Lord, all ye Gentiles" (v. 11)—not merely the most eminent among them but all alike. Where there is praise there is joy, for joy is a component part of it. Thus one who professes to be a Christian and at the same time complains that he is devoid of joy and peace, acknowledges that he is failing to obey these precepts.

Degrees of Blessing

"The God of hope fill you with all joy and peace" intimates three things. First, there are degrees of these blessings. A few Christians enjoy them fully, but the great majority (to their shame) experience but a taste thereof. Each of us should look to God for the fullest communication of these privileges. Second, the breadth of the apostle's words, as also his "that ye may abound in hope," manifest how his heart was enlarged toward the saints and what comprehensive supplies of grace he sought for them. Third, thus we honor God in prayer: by counting on the freeness of His grace. There is no straitness in Him, and there should be none in us. Since we are coming to heaven's King, let us "large petitions with us bring." Has He not given us encouragement to do so? Having given His beloved Son for us and to us, "how shall he not with him also freely give us all things" (Rom. 8:32)! Has He not invited us to "drink, yea, drink abundantly" (Song of Sol: 5:1)! Then let our requests be in accord with His invitation; let us not approach Him as though He were circumscribed like ourselves.

Privileges and Duties

The fact that the apostle prayed for these blessings indicated not only that they are desirable and attainable, but also that it is incumbent upon us to enter into possession of them. We cannot now attempt proof, but will here state the fact that the things we may ask God to give us are, at the same time, obligations upon ourselves. Privileges and duties cannot be separated. It is the duty of the Christian to be joyous and peaceful. If any should question that statement, we would ask him to consider the opposite; surely none would affirm that it is a spiritual duty to be miserable and full of doubts! We do not at all deny that there is another side to the Christian's life, that there is much both within and without the believer to make him mourn. Nor is that at all inconsistent. The apostle avowed himself to be "sorrowful," yet in the very same breath he added "yet alway rejoicing" (II Cor. 6:10). Most assuredly those who claim to be accepted in the Beloved and journeying to everlasting bliss bring reproach on Him whose name they bear and cause His gospel to be evil spoken of, if they are doleful and dejected and spend most of their time in the slough of despond.

Blessings Obtained by Prayer

But we proceed one step further. The apostle here made known how these most desirable and requisite blessings may be obtained. First, they are to be sought in prayer, as is evident from Paul's example. Second, they can only be attained as the heart is occupied with "the God of hope," that is, the promising God, for the things we are to hope for are revealed in His promises. Third, these blessings come to us "in believing," in faith's laying hold of the things promised. "Fill you with all joy and peace *in believing*." Many seek, though vainly, to reverse that order. They will not believe God till they feel they have joy and peace, which is like requiring flowers before the bulb has been set in the ground. You ask, "But how can I have joy and peace while engaged in such a conflict— mostly a losing one—with indwelling sin?" Answer: You cannot successfully oppose indwelling sin if you are joyless and full of doubts, for "the joy of the Lord is your *strength*" (Neh. 8:10). There is no genuine joy and peace except "in believing," and in exact proportion to our faith will be joy and peace.

"That ye may abound in hope." This clause gave the Roman saints and us the reason why the apostle made the above request, or the design he had in view for them. They were established as to the past, joyous in the present. He would have them to be confident as to the future. The best is yet to be, for as yet the Christian has received but an earnest of his inheritance, and the more he is occupied with the inheritance itself the better equipped he will be to press forward to it, through all difficulties and obstacles, for hope is one of the most powerful motives or springs of action (Heb. 6:11-12). In our day some of the Lord's people need to be informed that the word *hope* has quite a different meaning in Scripture from that accorded to it in everyday speech. On the lips of most people "hope" signifies little more than a bare wish, and often with considerable fear that it will not be realized, being nothing better than a timid and hesitant desire that something may be obtained. But in Scripture (e.g., Rom. 8:25; Heb. 6:18-19) hope signifies a firm expectation and confident anticipation of the things God has promised. As joy and peace increase "in believing" so too does hope.

The Power of the Holy Spirit

"Through the power of the Holy Ghost." The Father is the Giver, but the Spirit is the Communicator of our graces. Though it is the Christian's duty to be filled with joy and peace in believing and to abound in hope, yet it is only by the Spirit's enablement such can be realized. Here, as everywhere in the Word, we find the kindred truths of our accountableness and dependency intimately connected. The joy, peace, and hope here are not carnal emotions or natural acquirements but spiritual graces, and therefore they must be divinely imparted. Even the promises of God will not produce these graces unless they be divinely applied to us. Note that it is not merely "through the operation" but "through the power" of the Holy Spirit, for there is much in us which opposes! Nor can these graces be increased or even maintained by us in our own strength—though they can be decreased by us, through grieving the Spirit. They are to be sought by prayer, by eyeing the promises, and by looking for the enablement of the Holy Spirit. That hope is but a vain fancy which is not fixed on God and inwrought by Him. "Remember the word unto thy servant, upon which thou hast caused me to hope" (Ps. 119:49).

Chapter 4

PRAYER FOR PEACE

ROMANS 15:33

"Now THE GOD OF PEACE be with you all. Amen." The "God of peace": Contrary to the general run of commentators, we regard this divine title as expressing first of all what God is in Himself, that is, as abstracted from relationship with His creatures and apart from His operations and bestowments. He is Himself the Fountain of peace. Perfect tranquillity reigns in His whole Being. He is never ruffled in the smallest measure, never perturbed by anything, either within or without Himself. How could He be? Nothing can possibly take Him by surprise, for "known unto God are all his works from the beginning of the world" (Acts 15:18). Nothing can ever disappoint Him, for "of him, and through him, and to him, are all things" (Rom. 11:36). Nothing can to the slightest degree disturb His perfect equanimity, for He is "the Father of lights, with whom is no variableness, neither shadow of turning" (James 1:17). Consequently perfect security ever fills Him: that is one component element of His essential glory. Ineffable peace is one of the jewels in the diadem of Deity.

The God of Peace

Let us for a season gird up the loins of our minds and endeavor to contemplate someone vastly different, someone infinitely more excellent, namely, the One who is a total stranger to unrest and disquietude, the One who enjoys undisturbed calm, "the God of peace." It seems strange that this glorious excellency of the divine character is so little dwelt upon by Christian writers. The sovereignty of God, the power of God, the holiness of God, the immutability of God, have frequently been made the theme of devout penmen; but the peace of God Himself has received scarcely any attention. Numerous sermons have been preached upon "the God of love" and "the God of all grace," but where shall we find any on "the God of peace" except as the reconciled God? Only once in all the Scriptures is He specifically designated "the God of love," and only once "the God of all grace," yet five times He is called "the God of peace." As such, a perpetual calm characterizes His whole being; He is infinitely blessed in Himself.

The names and titles of God make known to us His being and character. By meditating upon each one of them in turn, by mixing faith therewith, by giving all of them a place in our hearts and minds, we are enabled to form a better and fuller concept of who He is and what He is in Himself, His relationship to

41

and His attitude toward us. God is the Fountain of all good, the Sum of all excellency. Every grace and every virtue we perceive in the saints are but scattered rays which have emanated from Him who is Light. We not only do Him a great injustice but we are largely the losers ourselves if we habitually think and speak of God according to only one of His titles, be it "the Most High" on the one hand, or "our Father" on the other. Just as we need to read and ponder every part of the Word if we are to become acquainted with God's revealed will and be "throughly furnished unto all good works," so we need to meditate upon and make use of all the divine titles if we are to form a well-rounded and duly balanced concept of His perfections and realize what a God is ours—and what is the extent of His absolute sufficiency for us.

"The God of peace." According to the usage of this expression in the New Testament and in view of the teaching of Scripture as a whole concerning the triune Jehovah and peace, we believe it will be best opened up to the reader if we make use of the following outline. This title, "the God of peace," tells us first of all what He is essentially, namely, the Fountain of peace. Second, it announces what He is economically or dispensationally, namely, the Ordainer or Covenanter of peace. Third, it reveals what He is judicially, namely, the Provider of peace—the reconciled God. Fourth, it declares what He is paternally, namely, the Giver of peace to His children. Fifth, it proclaims what He is governmentally, namely, the Orderer of peace in all the churches and in the world. The meaning of these terms will become plainer—and simpler, we trust—as we fill in our outline.

The Triune Jehovah

First, "the God of peace" tells us what He is *essentially,* that is, what God is in Himself. As pointed out above, peace is one of grand perfections of the divine nature and character. We regard this title as referring not so much to what God is absolutely, nor only to the Father, but to the triune Jehovah. First, because there is nothing in the context or in the remainder of the verse which requires us to limit this prayer to any particular person in the Godhead. Second, because we should ever take the terms of Scripture in their widest latitude and most comprehensive meaning when there is nothing obliging us to restrict their scope. Third, because it is a fact, a divinely revealed truth, that the Father, the Son, and the Holy Spirit are alike "the God of peace." Nor could there be any force to the objection that since prayer is here made unto "the God of peace," we are obliged to regard the reference as being to the Father for, in Scripture, prayer is also made to the Son and to the Spirit. True, the reference in Hebrews 13:20 is to the Father, for He is there distinguished from the Lord Jesus, but since no such distinction is here made we decline to make any.

That this title belongs to God the Father scarcely needs any arguing, for the opening words of the salutation found at the beginning of most of the New Testament epistles will readily occur to the reader: "Grace to you and peace from God our Father" (Rom. 1:7; I Cor. 1:2, etc.)—grace from Him as He is "the God of all grace" (I Peter 5:10), peace from Him as "the God of peace." The added words of that salutation, "and the Lord Jesus Christ," establish the same fact concerning His Son, for grace and peace could not proceed from Him unless He were also the Fountain of both. It will be remembered that in Isaiah 9:6 He is expressly denominated "the Prince of peace," which—coming immediately after His other titles there ("the mighty God, the everlasting Father")— shows that He is "the Prince of peace" in His essential person. In II Thessalonians 3:16 Christ is designated "the Lord of peace." Hebrews 7:2 tells us that He is the "King of peace," typified as such by Melchizedek the priest-king. In Romans 16:20 the apostle announced, "The God of peace shall bruise Satan under your feet shortly," and in the light of Genesis 3:15 there can be no doubt that the reference is immediately to the incarnate Son.

Less is explicitly revealed in Scripture concerning the person of the Holy Spirit because He is not presented to us objectively like the Father and the Son, inasmuch as He works within and indwells the saints. Nevertheless, clear and full proof is given in the sacred oracles that He is God, coessential, coequal, and coglorious with the Father and the Son. As a careful examination of Scripture and a comparison of one passage with another will demonstrate, it is a most serious mistake to conclude from theologians referring to the Holy Spirit as the third person of the Godhead that He is in any wise inferior to the other two. If in Matthew 28:19 and II Corinthians 13:14 He is mentioned after the Father and Son, in Revelation 1:4-5 He is named (as "the seven Spirits," the Spirit in His fullness) before Jesus Christ, while in I Corinthians 12:4-6 and Ephesians 4:4-6 He is named before both the Son and the Father—such variation of order manifesting Their coequality. Thus, as equal with the Father and the Son the Holy Spirit must also be "the God of peace," which is evidenced by His communicating divine peace to the hearts of the redeemed. When He descended from heaven on our baptized Saviour it was in the form of a dove (Matt. 3:16), the bird of peace.

Second, "the God of peace" announces what He is *dispensationally,* in the economy of redemption, namely, the Ordainer or Covenantor of peace. This is clear from Hebrews 13:20-21, where the apostle prays, "Now the God of peace, that brought again from the dead our Lord Jesus, that great shepherd of the sheep, through the blood of the everlasting covenant, make you perfect in every good work to do His will." It was specifically as "the God of peace" that the Father delivered our Surety from the tomb, "through the blood of the everlasting covenant," that is, on the ground of that blood which ratified and sealed the great compact which had been made between Them before the foundation of the world. Reference is made to that compact in Psalm 89:3, which alludes to the antitypical David, the "Beloved," as verses 27 and 28 conclusively prove. In God's foreview of the entrance of sin into the world, with the fall of all men in Adam, and the breach that made between Him and them, alienating the One from the other, God graciously purposed to effect a reconciliation and secure a permanent peace on a righteous basis, a basis which paid homage to His authority and honored His law.

The Everlasting Covenant

A covenant is a mutual agreement between two parties wherein a certain work is proposed and a suitable reward promised in return. In the everlasting covenant the two parties were the Father and the Son. The task assigned the

Son was that He should become incarnate, render to the law a perfect obedience in thought, word, and deed, and then endure its penalty on behalf of His guilty people, thereby offering to the offended God (considered as Governor and Judge) an adequate atonement, satisfying His justice, magnifying His holiness, and bringing in an everlasting righteousness. The reward promised was that God would raise from the dead the Surety and Shepherd of His people, exalting Him to His own right hand high above all creatures, conforming them to the image of His Son, and having them with Himself in glory forever and ever. The Son's voluntary compliance with the proposal appears in His "Lo, I come ... to do thy will, O God" (Heb. 10:7); and all that He did and suffered was in fulfillment of His covenant agreement. The Father's fulfillment of His part of the contract, in bestowing the promised reward, is fully revealed in the New Testament. The Holy Spirit was the Witness and Recorder of that covenant.

Now that everlasting compact is expressly designated "the covenant of peace" in Isaiah 54:10; Ezekiel 34:25; 37:26. In that covenant Christ stood as the representative of His people, transacting in their name and on their behalf, holding all their interests dear to His heart. In that covenant, in compliance with the Father's will and from His wondrous love for them, Christ agreed to enter upon the most exacting engagement and to undergo the most fearful suffering in order that they might be delivered from the judicial wrath of God and have peace with Him, that there might be perfect amity and concord between God and them. That engagement was faithfully discharged by Christ, and the peace which God eternally ordained has been effected. And in due course the Father brings each of His elect into the good of it. It is to that same eternal compact that Zechariah 6:12-13 alludes: "The counsel of peace shall be between them both." That "counsel of peace" or mutual goodwill was "between them both," between "the man whose name is The BRANCH" and Jehovah "the LORD of hosts" (v. 12). The "counsel" concerned Christ's building of the Church (Eph. 2:21-22) and His exaltation to the throne of glory.

The God of Peace the Reconciled God

Third, "the God of peace" reveals what He is *judicially,* namely the Provider of peace, the reconciled God. That which here engages our attention is the actual outworking and accomplishment of what has been before us in the last division. Of old, God said concerning His people, "For I know the thoughts that I think toward you . . . thoughts of peace, and not of evil, to give you an expected end" (Jer. 29:11). Yes, despite the guilt that rested upon them for their legal participation in Adam's fall, and despite their own multiplied transgressions and apostasy against Him, there had been no change in His everlasting love for them. A real and fearful breach had been made, and as the moral Governor of the universe God would not ignore it; nay, as the Judge of all the earth His condemnation and curse rested upon them. Nevertheless His heart was toward them, and His wisdom found a way whereby the horrible breach might be healed and His banished people restored to Himself, and that not only without compromising His holiness and justice but by glorifying the one and satisfying the other.

"When the fulness of the time was come, God sent forth his Son, made of a woman, made under the law, to redeem them that were under the law" (Gal. 4:4-5). God sent forth His Son in order to carry out what had been agreed upon in the everlasting covenant, and to provide an adequate compensation to His law that God's Son was made of a woman, that in our nature He should satisfy the requirements of the law, put away our sins, and bring in everlasting righteousness. In order to redeem His people from the curse of the law, the Son lived and died and rose again. In order to make peace with God, to placate His wrath, to secure an equitable and stable peace, Christ obeyed and suffered. In His redemptive work through His Son, God provided peace. At Christ's birth the heavenly hosts, by anticipation, praised God, saying, "Glory to God in the highest, and on earth peace, good will toward men" (Luke 2:14). And at His death Christ "made peace [between God and His people] through the blood of his cross" (Col. 1:20), reconciling God (as the Judge) to them, establishing perfect and abiding amity and concord between them.

Fourth, "the God of peace" declares what He is *paternally,* namely, the Giver of peace to His children. This goes beyond what has been pointed out above. Before the foundation of the world God ordained there should be mutual peace between Himself and His people. As the immediate result of Christ's mediatorial work peace was made with God and provided for His people. Now we are to consider how the God of peace makes them the actual participants of this inestimable blessing. By nature they are utter strangers to it, for "there is no peace, saith my God, to the wicked" (Isa. 57:21). How could there be when they are engaged continually in active hostility against God? They are without peace in their conscience, in their minds, or in their hearts. "The way of peace have they not known" (Rom. 3:17).

The Work of the Holy Spirit

Before the sinner can be reconciled to God and enter into participation of the peace which Christ has made with Him, he must cease his rebellion, throw down the weapons of his warfare, and yield to God's rightful authority. But, in order to do that, a miracle of grace must be wrought in the sinner by the Holy Spirit. As the Father ordained peace, as the incarnate Son made peace, so the Holy Spirit brings us into the same. He convicts us of our awful sins, and makes us willing to forsake them. He communicates faith to the heart whereby we savingly believe in Christ. Then "being justified by faith, we have peace with God" (Rom. 5:1) objectively. We are brought into His favor. But more, we enjoy peace subjectively. The intolerable burden of guilt is removed from the conscience and we "find rest unto our souls." Then we know the meaning of that word "The peace of God, which passeth all understanding, shall keep your hearts and minds through Christ Jesus" (Phil. 4:7). By His Spirit, through Christ, the Father has now actually bestowed peace upon His believing child; and, in proportion as his mind is stayed on Him, by trusting in Him, the child of God will be kept in perfect peace (Isa. 26:3).

Fifth, "the God of peace" proclaims what He is *governmentally,* namely, the Orderer of peace in the churches and in the world. Though each Christian has peace with God, yet he is left in a world which lieth in the wicked one. Though the Christian has peace with God in his heart, yet the flesh remains, causing a continual conflict within and, unless restrained, breaking forth into strife with his brethren. Therefore, if God were not pleased to put forth His restraining power upon that which seeks to disturb and disrupt the believer's calm, he would enjoy little or no tranquillity within or rest without.

The Blessing of Peace

"Now the God of peace *be with you all*. Amen." By that petition the apostle requested that God would in this particular character manifest Himself among them so that His presence should be made known in their midst. Were it not for the overuling providence of the Lord His people would have no rest at any time in this world. But He rules in the midst of His enemies (Ps. 110:1-2) and gives His people a considerable measure of peace from their foes. This shows us that we ought to be constantly looking to God for His peace else assaults are likely to arise from every quarter. Peace is a blessing the churches greatly need. We ought to "pray for the peace of [the spiritual] Jerusalem" as our chief joy.

"Now the God of peace *be with you all*" implies that the saints must conduct themselves in harmony, that amity and concord must prevail among them, so that there be no grievous failure on their part that would offend God and cause Him to withdraw His manifested presence from them. "Those things, which ye have both learned, and received, and heard, and seen in me, do: *and* the God of peace shall be with you" (Phil. 4:9). Individuals as well as a corporate company of believers must be in subjection to the divine authority and maintain scriptural discipline if they would enjoy the peace of God (see II Cor. 13:11). Charles Hodge well said, "It is vain for us to pray for the presence of the God of love and peace unless we strive to free our hearts from all evil passions."

Chapter 5

PRAYER FOR INSIGHT

ROMANS 16:25-27

IN THIS STUDY we are endeavoring to give an interpretation as well as an application of those precious portions of Holy Writ being dealt with. The more closely we examine the wide range of the recorded prayers of the apostle, the more we are impressed with their deep importance—doctrinally as well as experimentally—as well as their great variety, their extensive scope; and the more we feel convinced that they need to be approached and dealt with expositionally as well as devotionally and practically. There has been far too much generalizing of the truth, and far too little painstaking and detailed instruction.

The passage before us is a case in point, though we admit it is rather an exceptional one, occurring as it does in what many regard as the profoundest epistle in the New Testament. We wonder how many of our readers, even after a careful reading and rereading of our present passage, will obtain any clear-cut and intelligent concept of the scope and subject of this prayer. We wonder how many of them could supply satisfactory answers to the following questions: (1) Why is the Diety here addressed as "him that is *of power* to establish you"? (2) What is the force of "according to *my* gospel"? (3) What is signified by "the *preaching* of Jesus Christ"? (4) What is this "mystery" which "was kept secret since the world began"? (5) How does one harmonize "kept secret" with "but now is made manifest by the scriptures of the prophets"? (6) Why is it "according to the commandment of the *everlasting* God"? (7) What is the special force of "to God *only* wise"? Is there not real need here for a teacher?

When one honestly faces and carefully ponders these questions, he is at once conscious of his dire need of wisdom from above. The central subject of these verses is something especially profound; this seems very obvious. Reader and writer alike should sense that they contain truth of the deepest importance. But if their meaning is not apparent from a cursory perusal, neither can it be conveyed to others through a hurriedly prepared article. Prayer and study, study and prayer, are called for; and *they* demand the exercise of faith and patience—graces in which the present generation of Christians are sadly deficient. While it has pleased God to grant us some insight into the contents of this portion of the Word of God, we doubt we shall ever plumb the depths in this life.

The Principal Subject

In his repeated studyings of this passage the writer felt that before he was ready to work out its details he must first ascertain its principal subject. Before he was prepared to identify the burden of this prayer, he needed to discover its leading theme. In setting about that task full consideration had to be given to the particular epistle in which the prayer was located and to the distinctive subject of that epsitle. Each separate detail had to be pondered in its relation to the whole; then parallel passages had to be sought and studied. This called for impartial investigation, focused attention, laborious and persevering effort and, above all, humbly seeking wisdom from God. The task of the expositor is no light one. That is why there are so few, for probably no generation ever detested hard work and mental toil more than ours.

This is not only a sublime prayer but one of the greatest doctrinal passages contained in Holy Writ. On the one hand it rises to unsurpassed heights of devotion; on the other it conducts us to the profoundest subject of divine revelation. Our passage speaks not only of a "mystery" but of "the mystery" which includes and is the sum of all others. The principal theme of the epistle is here epitomized as affording the special ground for the praise now offered to God. In Romans the gospel is expounded (see 1:1, 9, 16) in a more formal and systematic form than elsewhere in the Word. In the body of the epistle we are shown the blessings the gospel conveys to those who believe it; in their doxology we are taught how the gospel originated.

Excellence and Sufficiency of Divine Power

"Now to him that is of power to establish you" (v. 25). This is not a petitionary prayer, but the adoration of Deity. No request is made for the saints, but God is exalted before them. The apostle begins by reminding us of the excellency and sufficiency of the divine power. He had concluded his introduction to this epistle by affirming "the gospel of Christ . . . is the power of God unto salvation to every one that believeth" (1:16). Now he points out the believer is equally dependent upon God's power for his establishment. Christians cannot establish themselves, nor can their ministers establish them; the one or the other may use the appointed means, but they cannot ensure success. God alone can make them effectual to any of us. But blessed be His name, He *can* do so, for "God is able to make all grace abound toward you; that ye, always having all sufficiency in all things, may abound to every good work" (II Cor. 9:8). Note that the word *able* includes disposition as well as capacity: He *can*, He *will* (cf. Rom. 4:21; Eph. 3:20).

The Greek word translated "stablish" (*sterizo*) is rendered "set steadfastly" in Luke 9:51 and "strengthen" in Luke 22:32 and Revelation 3:2. It means "to thoroughly establish," "to make rooted and grounded in the faith" (Col. 1:27) both in heart (I Thess. 3:12) and in walk (II Thess. 2:17). This is a duty incumbent upon us, for we are expressly bidden, "Stablish your hearts" (James 5:8). But because we are not sufficient for such a task, God has graciously made the promise: "But the Lord is faithful [though we are unfaithful], who shall stablish you, and keep you from evil" (II Thess. 3:3). Though it be our privilege and obligation to study the Word, to grow in grace and in the knowledge of the Lord Jesus, yet so strongly are our hearts influenced by sin, so dull is our understanding and so feeble is our love, that the working of God's power is required to preserve us. Not only were we unable to bring ourselves into the faith but we cannot continue in it without divine strength. Because of our proneness to apostatize, the subtlety and strength of our spiritual enemies, the evil of the world in which we live, God's power alone can keep us (cf. Jude 24).

Christians Established in the Gospel

"According to my gospel." Here we are shown *what it is* in which Christians are established: namely, the gospel. God's own people are established in the truth—an inestimable favor, especially in such a day as this when God has given up the vast majority in Christendom to "believe a lie" (II Thess. 2:11). Second, the clause makes known to us not only the spiritual sphere in which Christians are established but also the *means* the Holy Spirit employs in this gracious work. Only as our hearts are divinely enabled to cleave to the grand substance of the gospel are we kept from being "tossed to and fro, . . . with every wind of doctrine, by the sleight of men, and cunning craftiness, whereby they lie in wait to deceive" (Eph. 4:14). Third, this clause signifies being established according to this divine rule—brought into accord with it both inwardly and outwardly so there is no swerving from it in belief or practice (cf. 6:17, marg.).

"According to my gospel." First, this is to be regarded as a discriminative expression because the gospel is that which Paul has proclaimed in contradistinction to the false gospel of the Judaizers. None of the other apostles made any reference to a spurious gospel, but Paul particularly warned the Corinthians against "another gospel" (II Cor. 11:4); and to the Galatians he wrote, "Though we, or an angel from heaven, preach any other gospel unto you than that which we have preached unto you, let him be accursed" (1:8). Paul was referring to his gospel, then, in opposition to all counterfeits, for none other can avail for the salvation of the soul. Second, the gospel was Paul's because he was the preeminent expounder of it, his first epistle being devoted to an unfolding of its grand contents. The term "gospel" occurs scores of times in Paul's writings, yet except for I Peter it is found nowhere else in the epistles. Third, Paul used the expression "my" because a special dispensation of the gospel was committed to him for the Gentiles (Gal. 2:7; Eph. 3:2). Finally, this expression accords with the special fervor which marked Paul: "*My* God shall . . ." (Phil. 4:9), "Christ Jesus *my* Lord" (Phil. 3:8).

"And the preaching of Jesus Christ." This clause is joined to the former in order to tell us the substance and contents of the gospel. Jesus Christ is the grand Object and Theme of all true evangelical ministry. The "*preaching* of Jesus Christ" is much more than making frequent use of His name in our discourses, or even telling of His wondrous love and work for sinners. The "preaching of Jesus Christ" is first and foremost the magnifying of His unique Person, the making known of who He is—the God-man. Second, it is the opening up of His mediatorial office in which He serves as Prophet, Priest, and Potentate. Third, it is the proclamation of His wondrous redemption. Fourth, it is the enforcing of His claims and the holding up of the perfect example He left us.

"According to the revelation of the mystery, which was kept secret since the world began." This is both an explanation and an amplification of the fore-going. The glorious gospel of Christ is no invention of human wit; it is the won-drous product of the consummate wisdom of God. As J. Evans well said of the gospel: "It has in it an inconceivable height and such an unfathomable depth as passes knowledge. It is a mystery which the angels desire to look into and cannot find the bottom of. And yet, blessed be God, there is as much of this mystery made plain as will suffice to bring us to heaven if we do not wilfully neglect so great salvation." The gospel infinitely surpasses man's skill to origi-nate. He was able to have no knowledge whatever of it until God was pleased to publish the same. Nor was the gospel any provision of His, devised in time, to meet some unforseen calamity, no mere imposed remedy for sin; it was that which engaged the divine mind before heaven and earth were created.

New Testament Mysteries

Mention is made in the New Testament of the "mysteries of the kingdom of heaven" (Matt. 13:11) and of the "mysteries of God" (I Cor. 4:1). The New Testament refers to the yet future restoration and salvation of Israel as a "mys-tery" (Rom. 11:25) and of the resurrection and bodily transformation of the saints as a "mystery" (I Cor. 15:51). We also read of the "mystery of iniquity" (II Thess. 2:7) which is in horrible contrast with "the mystery of godliness" (I Tim. 3:16). There is also the "mystery of the seven stars" in the right hand of Christ and the "seven golden candlesticks" among which He walks (Rev. 1:20; 2:1), which we interpret to mean Christ's local churches. Many regard the "mystery of God" as His ways in providence, particularly His governance of this world, and the mystery of Babylon the great, "the mother of harlots" (Rev. 17:5) as Romanism. That which is before us in Romans 16:25 is, we believe, elsewhere termed the "mystery of his will" (Eph. 1:9), the "great mys-tery" of Christ and His Church (Eph. 5:32), the "mystery of the gospel" (Eph. 6:19), the "mystery of God [the Spirit], and of the Father, and of Christ" (Col. 2:2).

According to the usage of the word in the New Testament a mystery is a concealed truth over which a veil is cast. It concerns something which tran-scends the powers of man to conceive, and is therefore beyond his ability to invent. It relates to something which is undiscoverable by the human mind, beyond human knowledge until divinely revealed.

In recent years those known as dispensationalists have substituted the term "secret," but we think it is a faulty alternative. True, these "mysteries" were secrets impenetrable by finite sagacity until brought to light by God, but they were still designated "mysteries" after their revelation! Even now that they are made known to us there remains a mysterious element that is beyond our ken. "Behold, I show you a mystery; We shall not all sleep" (I Cor. 15:51; cf. I Thess. 4:17). Before the Holy Spirit made such disclosures, who ever imagined a whole generation of God's people would enter heaven without pass-ing through the portals of death! "Great is the mystery of godliness: God was manifest in flesh" (I Tim. 3:16). Yet now that the miracle of the virgin birth has been recorded, there remains about the Divine incarnation that which passes our understanding. The divine mysteries, therefore, are addressed to faith and not to reason.

Definition of This Grand Mystery

In seeking to frame a definition of the grand mystery of our passage we will first appropriate the help supplied by the clauses which have already been before us. The mystery is something according to which God is able to establish His people. Contributory thereto—or as the means he employs in connection therewith—is what Paul styles "my gospel," that is that which he had expounded at length in this very epistle, the heart or central object of which is "the preaching of Jesus Christ." Next, we observe this mystery was "kept secret since the world began." By this we understand the mystery was hidden from all the wise men of this world (I Cor. 2:8); we understand also that the Old Testament saints had not such light upon the mystery of the gospel as Christians are now favored with (I Peter 1:10; Col. 1:26) and that even the holy angels were not permitted to enter into the gospel's wondrous contents until it was actualized historically (Eph. 3:9-10). In Romans 16:25 we are told further that this mystery is now "made known to all nations for the obedience of faith"—for Jew and Gentile alike to give themselves up to Christ to be accepted by God through Him, to be ruled by Him.

God's Revelation by His Spirit

Let us turn now to parallel passages. We find that this mystery has to do with that mystery which is mentioned in I Corinthians 2:7, 9-10. "We speak the wisdom of God in a mystery, even the hidden wisdom, which God ordained before the world unto our glory. But as it is written, Eye hath not seen, nor ear heard, neither have entered the heart of man, the things which God hath prepared for them that love him. But God hath revealed them unto us [especially in the New Testament] by his Spirit: for the Spirit searcheth all things [proof of His omniscience], yea, the deep things of God." This intimates the transcendent sublimity of the contents of the gospel mystery. The "mystery of his will" (Eph. 1:9) declares the origin of the gospel mystery and hints at its selective nature. The "mystery of Christ" (Eph. 3:4) signifies Christ mystical, for it is His body in which believing Jews and Gentiles are made "fellowheirs" (v. 6). This verse tells of the gospel's international scope. Colossians 1:26-27 speaks of "the riches of the glory of this mystery" and announces the plenitude of its bestowments. I Timothy 3:16 shows us the outworking of the gospel mystery centered around the incarnation, justification, and exaltation of God the Son.

This grand mystery of the gospel was, we believe, what is designated in other passages "the everlasting covenant" (Heb. 13:20), which concerned the divine plan of redemption, or the amazing scheme whereby lost and depraved sinners might be everlastingly saved to the glory of God. This seems clear not only from the other passages referred to above but more especially from the whole of I Corinthians 2. There Paul affirmed that his paramount concern was to preach "Jesus Christ and him crucified." Yet Paul spoke the, "wisdom of God in a mystery"—a message so unworldly, so incredible, so exacting that none

but the Holy Spirit could open human hearts to receive it to the salvation of
their souls.

The parallels between Romans 16:25-27 and I Corinthians 2 are more or
less obvious. In the one Paul adored "him that is of power to stablish you according to my gospel and the preaching of Jesus Christ." In the other he
averred that he had determined not to know anything among the Corinthians
save Jesus Christ and him crucified" (v. 2). In Romans 16 Paul affirmed his
preaching had been "according to the revelation of the mystery, which was kept
secret since the world began." And in I Corinthians 2 he affirmed, "We speak
the wisdom of God in a mystery, even the hidden wisdom, which God ordained
before the world unto our glory" (v. 2). In the former he announced the mystery
"now is made manifest, by the scriptures of the prophets." In the latter he
quoted one of the prophets and added, "But God hath revealed them [the inconceivable things mentioned in the previous verse] unto us by his Spirit"
(v. 10). In the doxology Paul ascribed glory unto "God only wise"; in the
doctrinal passage he expressly mentioned the wisdom of God. Thus one passage
serves to interpret the other.

Grand Mystery Made Manifest

"But now is made manifest" (Rom. 16:26). What is? Why, the grand mystery mentioned in the previous verse. And how is it "made manifest"? By the
"gospel and the preaching of Jesus Christ" (16:25). With this declaration of
the apostle's should be closely compared his earlier one: "But now the righteousness of God without the law is manifested" (3:21). And that in turn takes
us back to the thesis of this epistle: "For I am not ashamed of the gospel of
Christ, for it is the power of God unto salvation to everyone that believeth; to
the Jew first, and also to the Greek. For therein is the righteousness of God
revealed from faith to faith" (1:16-17). In the New Testament era (the "now"
of our text and of Romans 3:21) there has been a fuller and more glorious manifestation of God than there was in all the preceding eras. And that in a twofold sense: both in the degree of light given and in those who received it. God
was wondrously made known to Israel, yet nothing like He was when He became incarnate and tabernacled among men. God's perfections were exhibited
in His law, yet how much more clearly are they irradiated by His gospel!

Perhaps nothing more strikingly portrays the contrast between the two dispensations in connection with the manifestation of the divine excellency than
placing side by side what is recorded in Exodus 33 and a statement made in
II Corinthians 4. In the former we find Moses making request of Jehovah: "I
beseech thee, show me thy glory" (v. 18). Let the reader look up vv. 19-22
and then ponder the Lord's response, "Thou shalt see my back parts: but my
face shall not be seen" (v. 23). How well may a person be known by a passing
glance of his "back parts"! That was characteristic and emblematic of the Old
Testament economy. Now set over against that this most precious passage:
"For God, who commanded the light to shine out of darkness, hath shined in
our hearts, to give the light of the knowledge of the glory of God in *the face*
of Jesus Christ" (II Cor. 4:6). "The only begotten Son, which is in the bosom
of the Father, he hath declared him" (John 1:18)—revealed Him, made Him
known, fully told Him forth.

But there is another sense in which the mystery is now made manifest as it was not previously, namely, in the more extensive promulgation of it. Under the former economy the Psalmist declared, "He sheweth his word unto Jacob, his statutes and his judgments unto Israel. He hath not dealt so with any nation: and as for his judgments, they have not known them" (Ps. 147:19-20). For more than half the span of present human history the heathen world was left in darkness, for from the tower of Babel (Gen. 11) onward God "suffered all nations to walk in their own ways" (Acts 14:16) so that they were deprived of even the outward means of grace. But after His resurrection the Saviour bade His ambassadors, "Go ye therefore, and teach all nations, baptizing them in the name of the Father, and of the Son, and of the Holy Ghost" (Matt. 28:19). In accordance with this He gave a special commission unto Saul of Tarsus to bear His name "before the Gentiles" (Acts 9:15), and by and by through the gospel which Paul proclaimed the contents of the grand mystery were heralded far and wide.

That to which reference has been made receives express mention in all of the leading passages where this mystery is in view. In our present one it is specifically declared that the mystery is "made known to all nations" (Rom. 16:26). In II Corinthians we learn that in the past the mystery was that which "none of the princes of this world knew" (v. 8) but which God had revealed to the Corinthian saints (v. 10). In Ephesians 3:8 the apostle averred it had been given him to "preach among the Gentiles the unsearchable riches of Christ," which in the light of verses 2-5 signifies that therein was contained the very substance of the mystery.

In Colossians 1:25-27 Paul alluded again to the special dispensation God had given him to the Gentiles in connection with the mystery which he here speaks of as "Christ in you [or 'among you'] the hope of glory." While in what may perhaps be termed the classic passage of I Timothy 3:16, one of the items comprising the mystery is that it should be preached unto the Gentiles.

Gentiles Accorded a Prominent Place

The prominent place accorded the Gentiles in these passages has led some of the more extreme dispensationalists to draw an erroneous conclusion. They argue that the mystical Body of Christ is preeminently Gentile, that the Old Testament saints have no place in it, and that it not only had no historical existence before the call of the Apostle Paul but that no other reference to it is to be found in his epistles.

We shall not turn aside to refute this error, but would simply call attention to the fact that Old Testament prophecy clearly foretold that Christ should be a "light of the Gentiles" (Isa. 42:6-7; 49:6). The Saviour Himself announced, "Other sheep I have which are not of this fold: them also I must bring, . . . and there shall be one fold, and one shepherd" (John 10:16). Caiaphas prophesied that Christ would "gather together in one the children of God that were scattered abroad" (John 11:52). Not the simple purpose to call Gentiles into the Church nor to make them "joint-heirs" with the Jews, but rather the whole plan of redemption made that possible. The mystery is concerned with that.

"And by the scriptures of the prophets, according to the commandment of the everlasting God, made known to all nations for the obedience of faith" (Rom. 16:26). We will consider the subordinate clause first. This commandment respects the three things mentioned in the previous verse: it was by divine appointment that this gospel, this preaching of Jesus Christ, this revealed mystery, should be made known. The word rendered "commandment" may mean "decree," and then the reference is to Psalm 2:7 and those passages where the decree is declared, such as "all the ends of the earth have seen the salvation of our God" (Ps. 98:3). It may mean "law" or "statute," in which case the reference is to the words of our Lord: "Go ye therefore, and teach all nations" (Matt. 28:19). That was indeed the commandment of the everlasting God, both as the Father spake in Him and as He was and is, "over all God, blessed for ever" (Rom. 9:5). The reason for and the special propriety of here styling Deity "the everlasting God" lies in the dominant subject of this passage, namely, "the mystery" or "the everlasting covenant" in which was centralized His eternal purpose (Eph. 3:11), which concerned the salvation of His elect (II Tim. 1:9). This salvation God "promised [to Christ] before the world began" (Titus 1:2).

We regard the clause "and by the scriptures of the prophets" (Rom. 16:26) first, as looking back to the mystery of the previous verse; second, as being linked to "and now is made manifest"; and third, as connected with the final clause of this verse.

The mystery, or everlasting covenant, was the subject of Old Testament revelation (II Sam. 23:5; Ps. 89:34; Isa. 55:3), yet for the most part its wondrous contents were couched in obscure figures and mysterious prophecies. By means of the antitypes of those figures and the fulfillment of those prophecies, much light has been cast upon what was so heavily veiled throughout the old economy. The parable they contained has been explained and their symbols interpreted so that what was for many generations dark is "now made manifest." Israel's prophets announced the grace that should come to us and "searched diligently" (I Peter 1:10) in connection therewith. Yet Peter himself needed a special vision to convince him that salvation was designed for the Gentiles (Acts 10). Thus the Old Testament credits the New, and the New Testament illuminates the Old. What was latent in the one is not patent in the other.

Immediate Design of the Gospel

"Made known to all nations for the obedience of faith" (Rom. 16:26). This is the immediate design of the gospel, the preaching of Jesus Christ, the revelation of the mystery, the commandment of the everlasting God. It is that all who hear and read should both believe and obey, receive and be governed by it. Though saving faith and evangelical obedience may be distinguished, yet they are inseparable, the one never existing without the other. As has been said, the gospel commands us to give up ourselves to Christ, to be accepted through Him, and to be ruled by Him; for He is the "author of eternal salvation unto all them that obey him" (Heb. 5:9). Unspeakably solemn it is to know that He will yet come "in flaming fire taking vengeance on them that know not God, and that obey not the gospel" (II Thess. 1:8). Only that faith is of any value that produces sincere and loving obedience, and only that obedience is acceptable to God which issues from faith in His incarnate Son. The design of the gospel is to bring us to both. Faith is the vital principle, obedience the necessary product. Faith is the root; obedience the fruit.

"To God only wise, be glory" (v. 27). The reason why the apostle here adores the Deity in this way leads to a wide and wondrous subject which we trust will grip the reader as much as it has the writer. Though we propose to devote the balance of this chapter to a consideration of this verse, we shall not now attempt a complete outline of it. It is in the grand mystery to which the apostle had alluded in the previous verses, in the constitution and outworking of the everlasting covenant that the consummate wisdom of God is so illustriously and preeminently displayed and which drew out of the apostle's heart to give praise for this divine excellence. O that wisdom may be given us to hold up to view this perfection of Him whose "understanding is infinite" (Ps. 147:5).

"To God only wise." He is the only wise Being essentially, superlatively, eternally (cf. I Tim. 1:17; Jude 25). God is wise not by communication from another but originally and independently; whereas the wisdom of the creature is but a ray from the "Father of lights" (James 1:17). The wisdom of God is seen in all His ways and works, yet in some it appears more conspicuously than in others. "O LORD, how manifold are all thy works! in wisdom hast thou made them all: the earth is full of thy riches" (Ps. 104:24). The reference here is to His works in creation. The same adoring exclamation may be made of His works in providence, wherein He regulates all the complicated affairs of the universe and governs this world so that all things are made to redound unto His glory and work together for the good of His people. But it is the marvelous plan of redemption which may well be called the masterpiece of His wisdom. That is indeed the "wisdom of God in a mystery, even the hidden wisdom, which God ordained before the world unto our glory," containing as it does "the deep things of God" (I Cor. 2:7, 10). So many were the problems of redemption to be solved (humanly speaking), so many the ways and means required, so great the variety of its exercise, that it is designated "the manifold wisdom of God" (Eph. 3:10).

Wisdom of God Displayed in the Gospel

The consummate wisdom of God appears in devising salvation for sinners, which problem would have baffled forever the understanding of all finite intelligences. God contrived a way where they could have found none. Both the design of the everlasting covenant and the means ordained to be used are most worthy of God. "The mystery of his will" (Eph. 1:9) is the foundation of it. "I will have mercy on whom I will have mercy" (Rom. 9:15). "In whom also we have obtained an inheritance, being predestinated according to the purpose of him who worketh all things after the counsel of his own will" (Eph. 1:11). As one of the Puritans expressed it, "His will set His wisdom to work." During recent years Christian writers—when treating of God's so-great salvation— have thrown most of their emphasis on the grace which provided it and the power which effectuates it, and comparatively little attention has been given to the wisdom which planned it. God determined to work in a most glorious manner and the end and the means were equally admirable. So grand and marvelous is the work of redemption that when the angels were sent as ambassadors extraordinary to bring tidings of peace to the world, they burst forth in that moving adoration, "Glory to God in the highest" (Luke 2:14).

God's Glory His Supreme End

The supreme end which God had in view was His own glory, the subordinate end the recovery of His lapsed and ruined people. By the "glory of God" is meant the manifestation of Himself in the exercise of His attributes, the display of His perfections. In all the works of God His excellencies are evidenced. But as some stars shine more brightly than others, so His perfections are more manifest in certain of His works. And as there is one heavenly body which far surpasses all the planets, so the work of redemption greatly exceeds in wonder all the marvels of creation. It is here that wisdom and goodness, righteousness and mercy, holiness and grace, truth and peace, love and power, are united in their highest degree and beauty. On that account the apostle uses the expression "the glorious gospel of the blessed God" (I Tim. 1:11). That gospel is, as one has expressed it, "The unspotted mirror wherein the great and wonderful effects of Deity are set forth." It is the glorious work of redemption which evokes the praise and thanksgiving of all the inhabitants of heaven (Rev. 5: 12-13).

In contemplating the possibility of redemption the very attributes of God seem to be divided *against* it. Mercy was inclined to save, whereas justice demanded the death of the transgressor. The majesty of God seemed to render it unworthy of His exalted greatness that He should treat with defiled dust. The veracity of God required the infliction of the penalty which He had denounced against obedience; the honor of His truth must be preserved. The holiness of God appeared to preclude utterly any advance toward depraved creatures. Yet the love of God was set upon them. But how could it flow forth without compromising His other perfections? What finite intelligence could have found a solution to such a problem? Suppose this problem had been submitted to the angels and after due deliberation they had recognized that a mediator was necessary to heal the breach which sin had made, to reconcile God to sinners and sinners to God. Where was a suitable mediator to be found? Consider the qualifications he must possess.

Qualifications of a Suitable Mediator

In order to be eligible for such an undertaking, a mediator must be able to touch equally both extremes: he must be capable of the sentiments and affections of both the parties he would reconcile; he must be a just esteemer of the rights and injuries of the one and of the other. But for that he must possess the nature of both, so that he has in himself a common interest in both. Moreover, he must have sufficient merit as to secure the reward for many. But such an one was not to be found, either in heaven or in earth. Yet this absence did not defeat Omniscience. God determined to provide a Mediator, and that none other than His own Son. But how could that be seeing He was possessed of the divine nature only? Suppose *that* question had been submitted to the celestial spirits. Had they not been forever at a loss to unravel the difficulty? Suppose further that God had made known to them that His Son would become incarnate, taking unto Himself human nature, the Word becoming flesh. Would they not still have been completely baffled?

Admire then and adore the amazing wisdom of God in ordaining a Mediator fully qualified to reconcile God to men and men to God. Marvel at such exercise of omniscience that devised the virgin birth whereby the Son became partaker of our nature without contracting the least iota of defilement, whereby He was Immanuel both by nature and by office, whereby He was a fit Daysman (Job 9:33) to lay His hand on each of the estranged parties, whereby He had both zeal for God and compassion for men, and whereby He might serve as a substitute on behalf of the guilty and make full satisfaction to the divine justice in their stead. Moreover, divine wisdom resolved this difficulty in such a way that, far from the glory of the Son being tarnished by the incarnation, it has been enhanced thereby, for He receives throughout the endless ages of eternity such a revenue of praise from His redeemed which the holy angels are incapable of rendering Him, while they themselves have been afforded additional grounds for adoring Him.

Compass of Divine Wisdom

Consider also the *compass* of divine wisdom in taking occasion from the sin and fall of man to bring more glory to God and to raise man to a more excellent state. Sin, in its own nature, has no tendency to good; it is not an apt medium; it has no proper efficacy to promote the glory of God; so far is it from a direct contribution to God's glory that, on the contrary, it is the most real dishonor to Him. But as a black background in a picture, which in itself may be thought by some to detract, sets off the lighter colors and heightens their beauty, so the evil of sin, considered absolutely, obscures the glory of God. Yet by the overruling disposition of His providence sin serves to illustrate His name and to make it more glorious in the esteem of reasonable creatures. Without the sin of man there would be no place for the most perfect exercise of God's goodness. Happy fault, not in itself but by the wisdom and marvelous counsel of God, to be repaired in a way so advantageous that the salvation of the earth is the wonder of heaven.

Bates, in *The Harmony of the Divine Attributes*, said, "The wisdom of God appears in ordaining such contemptible and, in appearance, opposite means, to accomplish such glorious effects. The way is as wonderful as the work. That Christ by dying on the cross [as] a reputed malefactor should be made our everlasting righteousness; that descending to the grave, He should bring up a lost world to life and immortality, is so incredible to our narrow understandings that He saves us and astonishes us at once. In nothing is it more visible that the thoughts of God are far above our thoughts and His ways above our ways as heaven is above the earth (Isa. 55:8). It is a secret in physic to compound the most noble remedies of things destructible to nature, and thereby make one death victorious over another: but that eternal life should spring from death, glory from ignominy, blessedness from a curse, is so repugant to human sense that to render the belief of it easy, it was foretold by many prophets, that when it came to pass it might be looked on as the effect of God's eternal counsels."

"To God only wise, be glory through Jesus Christ for ever. Amen" (v. 27). The Greek is somewhat complex and the Revised Version states more literally, "To the only wise God, through Jesus Christ, to whom be the glory forever. Amen." As each translation is equally legitimate, we adopt them both, for each is in perfect harmony with other passages. The thought conveyed by the Authorized Version is this: Our adoration of God is possible only through the mediation of Jesus Christ. The concept expressed by the Revised Version is this: It is in and through Jesus Christ that God is superlatively manifested as both infinite in might and omniscient in knowledge. "Christ the power of God, and the wisdom of God" (I Cor. 1:24). In and by the person and work of Christ are these divine perfections supremely displayed. He is the "image of the invisible God" (Col. 1:15), "the brightness [or outshining] of his glory" (Heb. 1:3). The Object of this doxology is the omnipotent and omniscient God: the subject which gives rise to it is the mystery, or everlasting covenant; the substance of it is "glory for ever"; the Medium of it is Jesus Christ.

Chapter 6

PRAYER FOR WEAKER BROTHERS

I Corinthians 1:4-7

THE ORIGINAL CORINTH was the chief city of ancient Greece not only in authority but also in wealth and grandeur and, we may add, in luxury and licentiousness—the temple of Venus being situated there. Corinth was entirely destroyed by the Roman consul Mammius, 120 B.C. As one writer expresses it, "Its inhabitants were dispersed, and the conqueror carried with him to Rome the richest spoils that ever graced the triumphs of a Roman general." For a century after that Corinth lay desolate in ruins. But Julius Caesar, perceiving the military importance and commercial possibilities of its location, determined to rebuild it. For that purpose he sent to Corinth a colony consisting chiefly of freedmen. The Corinthian men Justus (Acts 19:7), Crispus and Gaius (I Cor. 1:4), Fortunatus and Achaicus (I Cor. 16:17) all had names of Roman origin. That colony however was little more than the nucleus of the new city. Merchants flocked to Corinth from all parts and many Jews were drawn to it by the lure of commerce. Art, literature, and luxury revived. The Isthmian Games were again celebrated there.

The New Corinth

The new Corinth was made the capital of Achaia. Under the fostering care of Augustus Caesar, Corinth regained much of its ancient splendor and by A.D. 50 had reached a preeminence which made it the glory of Greece. But it was a material and carnal glory, for it was the center of voluptuousness. Yet where sin abounded grace did much more abound, for God had ordained that this place of gross wickedness should witness some of the grandest triumphs of the Cross of Christ. From that viewpoint it is easy to perceive how well situated Corinth was to be a center from which the gospel might be diffused. Not only was it the political center of Greece, the seat of its commercial and intellectual life, a place of concourse of many citizens and nations, but it was a place from which influences of many kinds emanated in all directions. To this city Paul was sent. Though an ambassador of the King of kings he was attended by no retinue, and his approach was entirely unheralded and unaccompanied.

A complete stranger to the place, Paul sought out two of his own countrymen, Aquila and his wife Priscilla, who were employed in the same craft in which he was proficient. Paul lodged with them and worked with them in tent-

59

making (Acts 18:1-2). On the Sabbaths he went to the synagogue where he reasoned with and persuaded both Jews and Greeks. A little later Paul's hands were strengthened by Silas and Timothy joining with him, and he testified to the Jews that Jesus was the Christ. But they opposed and blasphemed. Nothing daunted, Paul shook his raiment and said to them, "Your blood be upon your own heads; I am clean: from henceforth I will go unto the Gentiles" (Acts 18:6). The Lord honored his decision, first saving Crispus, the chief ruler of the synagogue, and all his house. Then "many of the Corinthians hearing believed, and were baptized" (Acts 18:8). But they were only the firstfruits; a larger harvest was to be gathered. "Then spake the Lord to Paul in the night by a vision, Be not afraid, but speak, and hold not thy peace: For I am with thee, and no man shall set on thee to hurt thee: for I have much people in this city" (Acts 18:9-10).

Paul's Labors in Corinth

Note that they were the Lord's people, even though yet in a state of nature, dead in trespasses and sins—His by sovereign and eternal election. "And he continued there a year and six months, teaching the word of God among them" (Acts 18:11). Paul's labors were richly blessed, and the many monuments to divine grace that were raised up constituted the foundation members of the Church of God at Corinth.

After the apostle's departure trouble arose in the assembly and various evils broke out. It must be remembered that the membership of this church was a heterogeneous one, that many members had been reared in heathenism, that they were surrounded by all the incentives to self-indulgence, plied on every hand by vain philosophers, and that at this time no part of the New Testament was in circulation. Judaizers had propagated error and sown the seeds of dissension and a strong party spirit was at work. But considerable carnality prevailed and serious disorders were marring this Christian testimony.

Among the evils in the Corinthian church were cliques and factions, the violation of the seventh commandment in various forms, and the remissness of the assembly to exercise discipline in such matters. There was a disorderly and unbrotherly spirit in their meetings. Women were allowed to enter the congregation with uncovered heads and to speak in public, exercising the gift of prophecy and speaking in tongues without regard to order and edification. The Lord's supper was debased into a common meal. Brother went to law against brother before heathen magistrates, and some of them became rebellious against Paul. Tidings of these things had reached the apostle's ears. And though this epistle was written in answer to certain more specific inquiries he had received from them, he used the opportunity in his reply to take up all those things which needed correction. Though there were some things in this epistle which concerned local, evanescent, and special matters, yet fundamental doctrine and much of lasting importance was also interweaved.

It is most blessed to see how Paul commenced his letter to them. He had much more to say of blame than of praise, yet after the opening address and salutation he told them: "I thank my God always on your behalf" (I Cor. 1:4).

Before directly charging them with their disorderly conduct, he first assured them of the place they had in his affections. Though Paul was now absent from them, they held a warm place in his heart. He constantly remembered them before the throne of grace. A lesson here for those engaged in the pastoral office: When called of God to occupy another place in His vineyard, they are not to forget those they left in their former field of service. The "I thank my God *always* on your behalf" tells us that Paul did not regard prayer as a spiritual luxury to be enjoyed only on rare and special occasions. Rather it was a regular practice with him, a duty which he constantly discharged, and that, in seeking fresh supplies of grace not only for himself but on the behalf of others also. Prayer has been rightly termed "the pulse of the Christian's life," intimating his health or sickliness.

Paul Owns God as "My God"

Once more we find the apostle referring to the One to whom he returned thanks as "my God." Though we sought to bring out the force of that expression on a former occasion, it may be well for us to summarize the same here. Paul did not regard Deity as absolute and infinitely removed but as a living and personal reality to whom he was intimately related. "My God" was an avowal of covenant relationship, for the grand covenant promise was "I . . . will be your God, and ye shall be my people" (Lev. 26:12). "My God" was expressive of personal relationship: He was Paul's God by eternal election, by redemption, and by regenerating power. God communicated life to Paul and stamped the divine image on his heart, thereby making him manifestly His own dear child. "My God" was an acknowledgment of Paul's personal choice, for he had consciously and voluntarily taken God to be his absolute Lord, supreme Good, and everlasting Portion. "My God" was a confession of practical relationship. All Paul's talents and energies were devoted to the glory of God who had shown him such abundant mercy, who would keep that which Paul had committed to Him, who would supply all Paul's needs.

Such a God was an object of fervent adoration. His goodness had to be acknowledged, and Paul was continuously engaged in that holy exercise.

"I thank my God always *on your behalf*, for the grace of God which is given you by Jesus Christ" (I Cor. 1:4). In this Paul has set us all an example: "Be ye followers of me" (I Cor. 11:1). If we do not emulate him in this blessed practice of thanking God for others, then most certainly we shall suffer loss. Is not failure at this particular point one reason why some of the Lord's people find it so difficult to obtain assurance that "the grace of God" has been given them by Jesus Christ? Is it not because they were not and are not truly thankful when they have reason to believe He has bestowed His grace on *others?* Is there a tendency to be too much occupied with our own spiritual interests? God will not prosper self-centeredness. It is not without reason that the Lord has bidden His people, "Look not every man on his own things, but every man also on the things of others" (Phil. 2:4). There is such a thing as spiritual selfishness as well as natural selfishness. Then let us seek to heed that exhortation, "Rejoice with them that do rejoice" (Rom. 12:15).

An Important Practical Lesson

"I thank my God always on your behalf." That word *always* is very blessed when we call to mind the attendant circumstances. It points up an important practical lesson for us. There had been various changes in the Corinthian assembly during the apostle's absence, and none of those changes had been for the better. But there had been no alteration or lessening of Paul's affections for them. There had been that among them which must have dampened his joy, but he had not allowed it to chill his love. He gave thanks for them even then as frequently as he had done formerly; yes, even though some of them had become cool toward him. And do not the writer and reader need to keep close watch over their hearts that they do not allow any change in the conduct of their brethren to diminish their love for them? True, it may call for a variation of the expression (as in Paul's case; see 4:21), for love must ever be faithful; and the form taken by its outward manifestation is to be regulated for the good of its object, yet there is to be no lessening of its fervor.

Though Paul could not assure the Corinthians, "I thank my God through Jesus Christ for you all, that your faith is spoken of throughout the whole world" (Rom. 1:8), he did adore God for having effectually called them: "I thank my God always on your behalf, *for the grace* of God which is given you by Jesus Christ." And does not that inculcate another important lesson for us, namely, that we are not to despise the bruised reed nor the smoking flax? True, we shall thank God most ardently for those who most resemble His Son, yet we must not fail to thank Him also for those in whom as yet we can but faintly discern Him. If the name of Christ is fragrant to us, we shall rejoice wherever it is poured forth. If His image is precious to us, we should own it in whomsoever we see it—just as when His gospel is prized by us we shall be glad for whoever preaches it. Though as yet Christ's image can be only faintly detected in His babes, yet if we see it at all, we have the infallible assurance that He who has begun a good work in them will assuredly complete the same (Phil. 1:6).

It was this particular truth which sustained Paul's heart at this very time (I Cor. 1:8). At least three years had passed since he left Corinth, during which time he had labored hard in other fields. But he recalled with gratitude and joy how graciously and wondrously God had wrought in the notoriously wicked city of Corinth. That was what upheld him when he learned of the sad disorders among them. "I thank my God always on your behalf, for the grace of God which is given you by Jesus Christ." His memory went back to the "day of their espousals." Instead of being wholly absorbed with and weighted down by their sad failures, Paul held fast to the fact and kept foremost in his mind the truth that they had been both the objects and recipients of the sovereign and invincible grace of God. Since that grace had not been earned by them but "given by Jesus Christ," he knew that it could not be forfeited; they would grow in grace and in the knowledge of their Saviour. A careful reading of the second epistle which he later sent to the same church shows how blessedly his confidence was justified and his hope realized.

Important Instruction to God's Servants

Paul did not begin this epistle by rebuking the Corinthians for their waywardness but instead by enumerating certain things which evidenced them to be the special objects of divine favor. We are to see in this not only a lovely exemplification of the apostle's own magnanimity and graciousness but also important instruction as to how any servant of God is to proceed in his dealings with those—particularly his own children in the gospel—who have wandered out of the way. He must first seek to reach and melt their hearts with a renewed sense of God's goodness to them, for only then would they be capable of perceiving the exceeding sinfulness of sin and the dishonor done Him by a disorderly walk on the part of those who bore His name. By calling to remembrance the day of their salvation, Paul not only sought to recall to them the marvel of divine mercy that brought them out of darkness into His marvelous light but also to remind them that he himself had been the favored instrument used of God in their conversion. Therefore, since he was their spiritual father (I Cor. 4:15), they should more readily attend to the message he was about to give them.

The "grace of God" has reference first to His free and sovereign favor and then to the blessings which issue therefrom—as we speak of receiving favors from a person. It was in this second sense that the apostle used the term when he thanked God for the grace which had been given to the Corinthians. Observe how careful he was to honor the Saviour by according Him His due place as Mediator: "The grace of God which is given you *by Jesus Christ.*" God's grace was first given to His elect *in* Christ before the foundation of the world (II Tim. 1:9), and then it was given them *by* Christ at their regeneration and throughout their Christian course (John 1:14-16). All the grace of God flows to us through the Redeemer. It was, first, the grace of God by Jesus Christ that had been bestowed on the Corinthians at their conversion; then they were "enriched by him, in all utterance, and in all knowledge" (I Cor. 1:5). The same truth is emphasized here, gifts and attainments being expressly ascribed to Christ. Thus all ground for self-gratification and boasting was removed, and the honor was placed where it rightly belonged. There was no pandering to the creature here but a humbling of him.

Extraordinary Gifts of the Spirit

"Enriched by him, in all utterance, and in all knowledge." The order of those two things may strike us as strange. If so, it is through failure to understand the particular kind of utterance and knowledge to which Paul alluded. The reference was not to what is ordinary but to the extraordinary, not to the graces which the Spirit imparts but to His gifts. At the beginning of this dispensation there were not only officers extraordinary (apostles and prophets) but there were gifts extraordinary; and as successors were not appointed for the former so a continuance of the latter was never intended. In the early days of this era the Holy Spirit made His presence evident by sensible signs (see Acts 2:1-4; 10:44-46). Extraordinary gifts and signs were given in fulfillment of Christ's promise (Mark 16:17-18) for the establishing of Christianity and the infantile state of the Church, for certifying the truth of the gospel (Heb. 2:4), divinely attesting the doctrine taught by the apostles and evidencing God's approval of the same. We term these miraculous works of the Spirit extraordinary to distinguish them from His ordinary ones, or those gifts and graces which He has communicated to Christians all through this age.

Those supernatural gifts were designed to arrest the attention of outsiders (I Cor. 14:22), to command a hearing for the apostles, to authenticate the gospel in heathen countries. Of all the churches of God that we read of in the New Testament that at Corinth seems to have abounded most in these gifts— and to have abused them most. Those Corinthians who exhibited these spiritual gifts despised others of their number who had not their particular gift, and those without gifts envied those who had them.

The gift of utterance included prophesying, or speaking by divine afflatus, but more especially referred to a miraculous endowment which enabled its possessor to speak in divers languages (I Cor. 12:10; 14:4-5). The gift of knowledge was a supernatural endowment for interpreting the prophecies and strange tongues (I Cor. 12:10; 14:26). In the body of the epistle, Paul acquainted the Corinthians with the excellence of those gifts and how they were to be used. They were from the Spirit (12:4, 8); they were given for mutual profit (12:7); they were to be exercised in an orderly manner for edification (14:26-33). Paul also pointed out to the Corinthians something still more desirable and excellent—the way to exercise *love* (I Cor. 13).

Though these gifts were to render them more serviceable, they were not sanctifying ones (13:2). Though the Corinthians had been plenteously endowed, yet spiritually they were only babes (3:1). Though through their pride and forwardness those gifts had been much abused, yet the apostle adored God for the communicating of them. They were the purchase of Christ (Eph. 4:8) and the fruit of His ascension (Acts 2:33). Though the apostle could not (as yet) rejoice at the fruits of the Spirit being borne by them, yet he let them know he returned thanks for the extraordinary gifts bestowed on them. That too was calculated to have a conciliatory effect on the Corinthians and dispose them to heed what followed. Far from depreciating those gifts as valueless because they had not made better use of them, Paul traced them to God as their Source and Jesus Christ as their Bestower. There was no flattering of them because they were in possession of them, but a magnifying of Him to whom they were indebted (4:7).

The Extraordinary Gifts No Longer Prevalent

Though these extraordinary gifts are not exercised in most Christian assemblies, there are other gifts distinguishable from spiritual graces—natural endowments, intellectual capacity, readiness of speech, and so forth. While those gifts and the natural talents we have mentioned are far inferior to spiritual graces, yet from the example of the apostle here with reference to the former we may learn valuable lessons concerning the latter. First, the one as much as the other is the gift of God and is to be thankfully acknowledged as such. Grace is the most excellent thing of all, yet add gifts and it becomes more excellent. It was the temple which sanctified the gold; nevertheless the gold beautified the temple.

It is grace which sanctifies gifts, yet gifts adorn and render its possessors more useful. Second, the possessors of gifts have no reason to be puffed up thereby nor to look down upon those who do not have them, for it is God who makes one to differ from another. Third, we should not disparagingly contrast gifts with graces. Paul did not. If there is danger on the one hand there is no less on the other; one may be as proud of his faith or love as another of his utterance or knowledge.

After all that has been brought out above on I Corinthians 1:4-5 there is less need for us to say much on what follows. "Even as the testimony of Christ was confirmed in [or among] you" (v. 6). The "testimony of Christ" signifies the gospel. In I Corinthians 2:1 it is termed "the testimony of God." The former refers to its grand Object, the latter to its gracious Author. Mention is made of this testimony being confirmed as a proof that it did not come to them in the letter only but also in divine power. In other words, the testimony was an evidence they had received the gospel to their own salvation (cf. Col. 1:6). The gospel had been accepted by a God-given faith and was firmly established in their convictions and affections. If we translate it "confirmed *among* you" then the allusion is to the miraculous gifts which had been imparted to them (cf. Heb. 2:4). The opening "even as" looks back to both verses 4 and 5. Paul was saying, "As your conversion and your endowment with these gifts proceeded from the grace of God by Jesus Christ, equally so did this confirmation."

"So that ye come behind in no gift; waiting for the coming of our Lord Jesus Christ" (v. 7). This confirms the meaning we have given to the previous verse. The gospel had been so confirmed among them that no church was more plenteously endowed with gifts. It had been so confirmed in them that it produced this blessed fruit—they were eagerly awaiting the Redeemer's return. The reference is to the expectation they cherished of Christ's second advent, the promise of which was connected with the resurrection of His people and the consummation of His kingdom. So generally was Christ's return the blessed hope of all the early Christians that they were characterized as those who loved His appearing (II Tim. 4:8). How much more so should we love to contemplate His second advent now that that glorious event is two thousand years nearer! The gifts and graces of the Spirit are but the "firstfruits" (Rom. 8:23), and they should make us yearn for the coming of Christ, when we shall enter fully into the inheritance He purchased for us.

Chapter 7

PRAYER CONCERNING TRIBULATION

II Corinthians 1:3-5

The communication of news in ancient times was much slower business than it is today. How long an interval elapsed between Paul's sending his first epistle to the Corinthian church and his obtaining tidings from them we cannot be sure, but probably at least a year passed before he learned how they had received his communication and what effects, under God, it had produced in them. During that period of suspense he appears to have been in a state of unusual depression and anxiety. The fierce opposition he encountered in Asia where he was "pressed out of measure" (II Cor. 1:8) and the deep concern which he had for the Corinthians affected his peace of mind (II Cor. 7:5). His first epistle had been sent from Ephesus where he had expected to remain until the following Pentecost (I Cor. 16:8), evidently hoping to hear from the Corinthian Christians by then. From Ephesus Paul proposed to pass into Macedonia and from there to Corinth (I Cor. 16:5-7). But desiring to learn what had been their reactions to his letter, before he came to them he sent Timothy (I Cor. 4:17; 16:10), commissioning him to set things in order. He bade them to respond peacefully to Timothy's counsels.

Paul's Concern for the Corinthian Church

A little later on, Paul sent Titus to Corinth in order to ascertain how matters were progressing with instruction to return and make a report, for the manner and measure in which they had responded to his exhortations would regulate to a considerable extent his future movements. Momentous issues were at stake: the interests of the gospel in an important city, the prosperity of a church which Paul had planted, and the honor of his Master's name. Deeply exercised, Paul had left Ephesus and come to Troas on his way to Macedonia, where it seems he had arranged for Titus to meet him and make his report. But in this Paul was disappointed (II Cor. 2:13), and having no rest in his spirit he pressed forward to Macedonia. There again peace was denied him, for he "had no rest," being troubled on every side. "Without were fightings, within were fears" (II Cor. 7:5). Then God relieved the apostle's suspense by the arrival of the eagerly awaited Titus, who brought Paul a most favorable report, assuring him that his epistle had accomplished most of what he desired (II Cor. 7:6-16), and thereby Paul's heart was greatly comforted.

66

When Paul learned that the Corinthians had received his admonitions in Christian meekness, that they had been brought to repentance and had put out of fellowship the incestuous person (II Cor. 7:9; 2:6), and that the major portion of the assembly had expressed the warmest affection for him (II Cor. 1:14; 7:7), he at once sent this second epistle to them. The news brought by Titus not only greatly relieved his mind but also filled him with gratitude to God.

On the other hand, the boldness and influence of the false teachers there had increased, as had their charges against Paul, and their determined efforts to undermine his apostolic authority moved him to indignation (II Cor. 10:2; 11:2-6, 12-15). This explains the sudden change from one subject to another and the noticeable variation of tone in this second epistle. To the obedient section of the church Paul wrote with the tenderest affection, commending their penitence, assuring them he had forgiven and forgotten. But when he turned to the corrupters of the truth among them, he struck a note of severity which is not heard elsewhere in his epistles.

God Revealed Through His Titles

"Blessed be the God and Father of our Lord Jesus Christ, the Father of mercies and God of all comfort" (II Cor. 1:3 E.R.V.). This is an ascription of praise, for "blessed be" signifies "adored be." The Father is here adored under a threefold appellation, each phase of which views Him as related to us in Christ, that is, to Christ as the covenant Head and to us as God's elect in Him. As the first will come before us again in Ephesians 1:3, we will reserve our remarks on it until we come to that verse. The three titles are most intimately related, the one depending upon the other. He is "the Father of mercies" to His people because He is the God and Father of their Head. And because He is "the Father of mercies" to them, He is also their "God of all comfort." This threefold designation is worthy of our devoutest and closest meditation.

The Father of Mercies

Though it is blessedly true that God is "plenteous in mercy" (Ps. 86:5), the title "Father of Mercies" conveys more than the idea that He is our most merciful Father. It also connotes that these mercies issue from His very nature and that they are therefore both His offspring and His delights. The Hebrews used the word *father* for the author or first cause of anything, as Jabal is termed "the father of such as dwell in tents" and Jubal as "the father of all such as handle the harp and organ" (Gen. 4:20-21), that is, the originator or founder of such. For the same reason God is called the "Father of spirits" (Heb. 12:9) because He is the Begetter of them. In James 1:17 He is designated the "Father of lights" as He is the Author of all gifts coming to us from above. In this verse is a manifest allusion to the sun which is the author and giver of light to all the planets and may therefore be termed the "father," or first original, of light to the earth. God is appropriately termed "the Father of mercies," for without Him none of our mercies would have any existence. He sustains the same relation to His mercies as a father does to his dear children.

Thus there is at least a threefold reason why God is here styled the "Father of mercies." First, as "the God and Father of our Lord Jesus Christ" He is such to us: thus *covenant* mercies are here in view. Second, God is called the "Father of mercies" to signify that He is so far from begrudging these to us that mercies are regarded as the Father's offspring, as proceeding from His nature, therefore His *delights* (Micah 7:18). Third, the name "Father of mercies" was used because of its pertinency to the case of the Corinthians. It was His mercy which had moved Paul to deal so faithfully with them in his first letter, for—little as we may realize it and still less as we may prize it—it is a great mercy when we are rebuked for our faults instead of being abandoned by God. It was a further signal mercy which caused the Corinthians to be convicted by Paul's rebukes; for the most faithful admonitions are ignored by us unless God is pleased to sanctify them to us. Only in His light can we see ourselves. It was an additional mercy which wrought in them godly sorrow, which in turn caused them to mourn for their sins and put right what was wrong; it is the goodness of God which leads to repentance (Rom. 2:4).

The God of All Comfort

"And God of all comfort." This is an excellency peculiar to the true and living God. None of the false gods of heathendom have such a quality ascribed to them; rather they are represented as being cruel and ferocious. Consequently they are regarded, even by their worshipers, as objects of dread. But how different is the Lord God: "As one whom his mother comforteth, so will I comfort you" (Isa. 66:13), He declared. What a revelation of the divine character is that! Though inconceivable in majesty, almighty in power, inflexible in justice, He is also infinite in tenderness. How this should draw out our love for Him. How freely we should seek Him for relief in times of stress and sorrow. But alas, how slow most of us are in turning to God for consolation; how readily and eagerly we seek other creatures for the assuaging of our grief. Many believers seem to be as reluctant to go out of themselves to God alone for comfort as unbelievers are to go out of themselves to Christ alone for righteousness. Yes, are there not some who, in a petulant and rebellious mood, say by their actions, "My soul refused to be comforted" (Ps. 77:2), despising their own mercies?

"The God of all *comfort*." That term has come to have a narrower meaning than its derivatives, connoting little more today than consolation or soothing. Our English word is formed from the Latin *con fortis*, "with strength." Divine comfort is the effect produced by His mercies. Every genuine comfort is here traced back to its source. He is "the God of all comfort." In its lower sense comfort is the natural refreshment that we obtain, under God, from others. We say "under God," for apart from His blessing of them to us we can derive no enjoyment and no benefit even from temporal mercies. In its higher signification comfort has reference to support under trials. It is a divine strengthening of the mind when there is a danger of our being overwhelmed by fear or sorrow. "This is my comfort in my affliction: for thy word hath quickened me" (Ps. 119:50). It is blessed to remember how often the Holy Spirit is termed, in relation to God's people, the "Comforter." Sometimes He makes use of our fellow Christians to administer spiritual comfort to our fainting hearts, as Paul was comforted by the coming of Titus (II Cor. 7:6).

It is inexpressibly solemn to consider that in precisely these characters of "the Father of mercies and the God of all comfort" Christ was deserted by Him. As our Surety and not as His beloved Son (regarded as such) the Judge of all the earth dealt with Him in holy severity and inexorable justice, crying, "Awake, O sword, against my shepherd, and against the man that is my fellow, saith the LORD of hosts: smite the shepherd" (Zech. 13:7). That is why, amid all the indignities and inhumanities inflicted on Christ by *men*, He opened not His mouth; but when the Father of mercies withdrew from Him the light of His countenance, when His comforts were withheld, Christ broke forth into the mournful lamentation, "My God, my God, why hast thou forsaken me?" (Matt. 27:46). And it is just because God did not sustain those characteristics to the Saviour on the cross that Christ bears these relations to us. Let us ever remember that our cup is sweet because His was bitter, that God communes with us because He forsook Christ, that we are enlightened because He passed through those fearful hours of darkness.

"Who comforteth us in all our tribulation, that we may be able to comfort them which are in any trouble, by the comfort wherewith we ourselves are comforted of God" (II Cor. 1:4). The immediate reference is to the experiences through which Paul had recently passed. He had occasion personally to adore God as "the Father of mercies and God of all comfort" since he had been proving Him as such. For God had comforted Paul in all his troubles. Yet the apostle graciously and tenderly associated the Corinthians with himself, for they too had sorrowed and been comforted (II Cor. 7:9, 13).

How striking is the difference between these verses and those which occupied us in the previous discussion. There the apostle could thank God only for endowments of the Corinthians (I Cor. 1:4-7), for he could not rejoice in their condition. But now he adores Him for the grace which makes all things work together for good to His own and causes their very troubles to issue in their profit. There he had termed the One addressed "my God," but here he adores "the Father of mercies and God of all comfort." Only as we pass through the fires do we obtain a fuller experimental knowledge of God and become more intimately acquainted with Him.

"Who comforteth us in all our tribulation." The soul is more capable of receiving divine comfort during a season of trouble, for the things of time and sense then cease to charm it. Moreover, the Lord manifests more tenderness to His people on such occasions: "If ye be reproached for the name of Christ, happy are ye; for the Spirit of glory and of God resteth upon you" (I Peter 4:14). God has various designs in bringing His people into trouble and sustaining them under it: for their growth, for a fuller discovery of Himself to them, for them to learn the sufficiency of His grace.

Able to Comfort Others

Another reason for tribulation is here alluded to: "That we may be able to comfort them which are in any trouble, by the comfort wherewith we ourselves are comforted of God" (I Cor. 1:4). The favors which God bestows on us are intended to be made useful to others. If I have found the Lord "a very present help in trouble," it is both my privilege and duty to witness to my troubled brethren as to how I was enabled to overcome temptations, as to how I found the divine promises my support, as to how I obtained peace in Christ while in the midst of tribulation. The best place of training for the pastor is not a seminary but the school of adversity. Spiritual lessons can be learned only in the furnace of affliction.

This principle receives its highest exemplification in the person of our blessed Redeemer. "Wherefore in all things it behooved him to be made like unto his brethren, that he might be a merciful and faithful high priest" (Heb. 2:17). It is clear from these words that in order for the perfecting of Christ's character to serve in the office of High Priest He had first to know what actual trial and sorrow were. The "merciful" here signifies to lay to heart the miseries of His people and to care for them so as to sustain and relieve their distresses. Yet not His mercifulness in general is in view, for He possessed that as both God and man, but rather that which is drawn forth by the memory of the temptations and suffering through which He passed. Paul referred to the exercise of mercifulness and faithfulness in Christ's priestly work on high as excited and called into exercise by the sense of the afflictions He experienced on earth. Not only merciful but faithful also in His constant care and attention to the needs of His weak and weeping people here below. Filled with compassion toward them, He is ever ready to support and sustain, strengthen and cheer them.

"For in that he himself hath suffered being tempted, he is able to succour them that are tempted" (Heb. 2:18). Having trod the same path as His suffering people, Christ is qualified to enter into their afflictions. He is not like the holy angels who never experienced poverty or pain. No, during the season of His humiliation He knew what weakness and exhaustion were (John 4:6), what the hatred and persecution of enemies entailed, what it was to be misunderstood and then deserted by those nearest to Him. Then how well fitted is He to sympathize with His suffering Church! Ponder such a passage as Psalm 69:1-4. Is not the One who passed through such trials capacitated to enter into the exercises of His tried people? As Matthew Henry said, "the remembrance of *His own* sorrows and temptations makes Him mindful of the trials of His people, and ready to help them." The same heart that beat within the Lord Jesus when He shared the grief of Mary and Martha by the grave of Lazarus still beats today, for His sympathies have not been impaired by His exaltation to heaven (Heb. 13:8). Oh, what a Saviour is ours: the almighty God, the all-tender Man!

In All Our Afflictions He Is Afflicted

"For we have not an high priest which cannot be touched with the feeling of our infirmities; but was in all points tempted like as we are, yet without sin" (Heb. 4:15). Christ's temptation was not restricted to the evil solicitations of Satan. It included the whole of His condition, circumstances, and course during the days of His flesh, when He suffered the pangs of hunger, had not where to lay His head, encountered reproach and shame, endured the contradiction of sinners against Himself. Thereby He was prepared for the further discharge of His priestly office, fitted to be affected with a sense of our weakness and to suffer with us. Though so high above us, He is yet one with us in everything except our sins, and concerning them He is our Advocate with the Father. We too are tempted (tried) in many ways, but there is One who consoles us, yes, who is afflicted in all our afflictions and who helps our infirmities. But in remembering this, do not forget that He had to cry, "I looked for some to take pity, but there was none; and for comforters, but I found none" (Ps. 69:20).

"Who comforteth us in all our tribulation, that we may be able to comfort them which are in any trouble, by the comfort wherewith we ourselves are comforted of God." One can enter more fully and closely into the grief of another if he has passed through identical circumstances. The Israelites were reminded of this when the Lord said, "Thou shalt not oppress a stranger, for ye *know the heart of* a stranger, seeing ye were strangers in the land of Egypt" (Exodus 23:9). Thus it was with the Apostle Paul. God's design in so afflicting him was that he might be better qualified to minister to other afflicted souls. His afflictions are outlined in II Cor. 11:24-30. Yet, so wondrously had God sustained him that he said, "I am filled with comfort, I am exceeding joyful in all our tribulation" (7:6). God comforts by stilling the tumult of our mind, by assuaging the grief of our heart, and by filling the soul with peace and joy in believing. He does this so that we may be the comforters of others.

"For as the sufferings of Christ abound in us, so our consolation also aboundeth by Christ" (II Cor. 1:5). The Christian must expect sufferings in this world—such sufferings as non-Christians are free from. Faithfulness to Christ, instead of exempting the believer from sufferings, will rather intensify them. This is not always pointed out by preachers. It is true there is peace and joy for those who take Christ's yoke upon them, and such peace and joy as the worldling knows nothing of; yet it is true that each one who enlists under His banner will be called upon to "endure hardness as a good soldier of Jesus Christ" (II Tim. 2:3). "We must through much tribulation enter into the kingdom of God" (Acts 14:22). Therefore those contemplating taking upon them a Christian profession should be told to sit down first and count the cost (Luke 14:28-31). To be forewarned is to be forearmed, and those properly forearmed will not think it "strange" when the "fiery trial" comes upon them (I Peter 4:12).

Verse 5 supplies a confirmation of the preceding one, its force being: we *are* able to comfort others, for our consolation is equal to our sufferings. The particular afflictions to which the apostle here alluded are termed "the sufferings of Christ" because they are the same in kind (though rarely if ever so in degree) as He experienced at the hands of men; and because of our union with Him and in order to be conformed to His image we are required (in our measure) to have "fellowship" (Phil. 3:10) therein. They are also termed "the sufferings of Christ" because they are what His followers willingly endure for His sake (Phil. 1:29): since He is despised and rejected of the world, if we go forth unto Him without the camp it must inevitably entail "bearing his reproach" (Heb. 13:14). It may be well to point out that some Christians through their folly, fanaticism, haughtiness and other things, bring upon themselves needless suffering, but Christ gets no glory from them. But it is more necessary in this day to warn His people against a temporizing and compromising spirit which seeks to *escape* "the sufferings of Christ" at the price of unfaithfulness to Him.

"So our consolation also aboundeth by Christ." Here is rich compensation. As union with Christ is the source and cause of sufferings, so is it the source of our consolation (John 16:33). And it will be the source of our glorification (see Rom. 8:17; II Tim. 2:12). There is a due proportion between the sufferings and the consolation, and if we would experience more of the latter we must have more of the former. The more the world frowns on us the more we enjoy His smile. If material comforts are taken away, He supplies spiritual ones. If our bodies are cast into prison, our souls enjoy more of heaven. He graciously provides a sweetening tree for every Marah (Exodus 15:23-26).

Chapter 8

PRAYER IN AFFLICTION

II CORINTHIANS 12:7-10

FIRST WE SHALL CONSIDER the occasion of the prayer in II Corinthians 12:7-10 as we find it in the immediate context. False teachers had appeared at Corinth and had succeeded in sowing seeds of dissension in the assembly there. The saints were in danger of being turned away from Christ by having their confidence in Paul undermined by the misrepresentations of his enemies. This had obliged Paul to engage in the distasteful task of vindicating himself, presenting the grounds he had for claiming spiritual authority over them, and asserting his apostolic powers. So repugnant was this to his feelings that he apologized for thus speaking of himself and begged them to bear with him (II Cor. 11:1), pointing out it was solely for their good that he now appeared to indulge in self-laudation.

Paul a Divinely Called Apostle

Paul's enemies had insisted that he was greatly inferior to the eleven disciples, that he was not an apostle at all since he lacked all the essential qualifications stated in Acts 1:21-22. He had neither been one of the favored band who were most closely associated with Christ during His public ministry nor had he been a witness with them of His resurrection. That was an exceedingly grave charge, for if Paul was not a divinely called apostle he had no authority to oversee the churches and to regulate their concerns. This obliged him to indulge in what seemed like boasting and to affirm, "I was not a whit behind the very chiefest apostles" (II Cor. 11:5). Previously he had openly acknowledged his personal unworthiness to be numbered in their company (I Cor. 15:9), but now he was compelled to point out that in authority, knowledge, effective grace, none of them excelled him. Then Paul spread before the Corinthians his credentials (II Cor. 11:22-33).

To see the nature of the proofs Paul advanced to show that he was a true minister of the gospel is very blessed and touching. He did not boast of the success of his labors, the souls that had been saved under his preaching, or the number of churches he had planted; rather he mentioned the opposition he had met, the persecutions encountered and the sufferings he had gone through. He showed them as it were the scars he had received as a good soldier of Jesus Christ. He demonstrated he was a real servant of Christ by calling attention to the reproaches, the ignominy, the cruel treatment he had received.

His sufferings and his patient endurance of them made manifest that he was a genuine minister of Jesus Christ (cf. Gal. 1:10). Though great indeed was the honor attached to his office, yet the faithful discharge of it entailed that which no impostor, no self-seeker, no hireling would continue to bear meekly.

In chapter 11 the apostle first met his opponents on their own ground, and by comparing himself with them he answered the fool according to his folly (Prov. 26:5). Then he demonstrated that he was a genuine officer of the despised and rejected One. But then he came to that which was peculiar to himself and related an experience which far excelled any that the other apostles had been favored with. He continued his apology, but in an altered tone: "It is not expedient for me doubtless to glory. I will come to visions and revelations of the Lord" (II Cor. 12:1). To have seen the Lord was one of the requisites of valid apostleship (I Cor. 9:1), and Paul had done so by a heavenly vision (Acts 26:19). Moreover these Christians were probably aware that he had been the subject of a vision which especially concerned them (Acts 18:9-10). But over and above these Paul went on to relate an experience which afforded superlative evidence of the favor of God to him as an apostle.

Paul's Unparalleled Experience

"I knew a man in Christ above fourteen years ago, (whether in the body, I cannot tell; or whether out of the body, I cannot tell: God knoweth;) such an one caught up to the third heaven. How that he was caught up into paradise, and heard unspeakable words, which it is not lawful for man to utter" (II Cor. 12:2, 4). This was an experience unparalleled in the recorded history of men, an honor and privilege which far exceeded that bestowed upon any other mortal. It is impossible for us to adequately conceive of the extraordinary favor that was here granted the beloved apostle. He was personally transported to paradise, translated to the Father's house, permitted an entrance into the palace of the Sovereign of the universe. For a brief season he was taken to be with "the spirits of just men made perfect." He saw the glorified Lamb upon the throne, and he heard the seraphim exclaiming before Him, "Holy, holy, holy is the Lord of hosts." It is useless to indulge in speculation and impious to give rein to our imagination; we can but wonder and worship.

And note the following verses. "Of such an one will I glory: yet of myself I will not glory, but in mine infirmities. For though I would desire to glory, I shall not be a fool; for I will say the truth: but now I forbear, lest any man should think of me above that which he *seeth* me to be, or that he heareth of [not from] me" (II Cor. 12:5-6). This is exquisitely lovely. Paul could have boasted about the high favor which God had shown him, but he did not. Had he gloried, it would not have been as a fool or empty boaster but according to truth, to fact. But Paul restrained himself because he desired others not to think too highly of him! He preferred that men should judge him by what they saw and heard and not esteem him by the special revelations God had given him! He would glory in his "infirmities," for weakness, sustained by grace, is all that any saint may boast of in himself.

"And lest I should be exalted above measure through the abundance of the revelations, there was given to me a thorn in the flesh, the messenger of Satan to buffet me, lest I should be exalted above measure" (II Cor. 12:7). Having stated in the preceding verse that he did not wish others to think of him more highly than they should, he now tells us what means God used to prevent *him* from doing so. Paul was in danger of being unduly elated by the extraordinary manifestation of the divine favor he had received. This is quite understandable. For one who had visited paradise itself to be suddenly returned to this world of woe required a heavy ballast to keep his ship on an even keel. The third heaven was too dizzy a remembrance to be safely borne by one who had to walk again on earth in a body of sin and death. The Lord knew this and graciously dealt accordingly, bestowing on Paul that which kept him humble.

Pride a Besetting Sin

By nature Paul was just as proud and foolish as all other men. If his heart was kept lowly, it was not by his own unaided fidelity to the truth but because of the faithfulness of his Master who dealt so wisely with him.

We must distinguish between the cause and the occasion of pride: the former is the evil nature, or principle, from which it proceeds; the latter, the object on which it fastens and which it perverts to its use. The pride of life (I John 2:16) can feed on anything and turn temporal mercies and even spiritual gifts and graces into poison. Pride was the main ingredient in the sin of our first parents. They aspired to be as God. There is pride in every sin since it is the lifting up of the creature against the Creator. We are shown how God regards and abominates pride in Proverbs 6:16-19 where seven things are mentioned which the Lord hates. The list is headed with "a proud look!" The great work of grace is the subduing of our pride.

The celestial revelations which Paul had received had no tendency whatever in themselves to produce or promote pride, but like all other things they were capable of being abused by indwelling sin. Therefore lest he should be spiritually proud, become vain and self-confident, regarding himself as a special favorite of Christ, there was given to Paul "a thorn in the flesh." That it is termed a "thorn" intimates it was something that was painful. That it was a bodily affliction is signified, we feel, by the words "in the flesh." That it remained within him is seen from his prayer that it might depart. That Satan aggravated it appears from the next clause of the verse: "the messenger of Satan to buffet me." As to precisely what this thorn consisted of we are frank to say we have no idea.

Personally, we admire the divine wisdom in restraining the apostle from being more explicit, for the general statement is better suited to a far wider application. Human nature being what it now is, had the Holy Spirit made known the specific character of this particular "thorn in the flesh" certain afflicted and querulous souls would be most apt to say, "Paul might glory in *his*, but if he had had the painful distress which is *mine* he would have sung another tune." Suppose the apostle had mentioned any certain physical disorder (say, inflamed eyes) those free from it but having another (say, the gout) would consider that *their* thorn was much harder to endure. But since God has wisely left it undefined, each afflicted saint may take comfort from the possibility that his affliction is identical with Paul's. Whatever in our persons or our circumstances serves to mortify our pride may be regarded as our "thorn in the flesh."

Let us draw comfort from the blessed fact that Paul's thorn in the flesh was not sent but given by God as a divine favor! It is thus that we should regard each painful trial—as a merciful bestowment from God, the design of which is to hide pride from us. But the word *given* also connotes Paul's acceptance of the affliction; it shows that he meekly and thankfully regarded it as from the Lord. This thorn he also spoke of as "the messenger of Satan to buffet me." The cases of Job and his boils, the woman of Luke 13:16, and the demon-possessed man Christ healed show that the devil is given the power to cause bodily affliction. In Paul's case Satan desired to disqualify him from his work, but the Lord overruled Satan and made him render Paul a good service. This should teach us to look above Satan and seek from God the reason why He has permitted him to afflict us.

God's Merciful Design in Affliction

"Lest I should be exalted above measure" (II Cor. 12:7). Paul not only accepted this painful affliction as a gift from the Lord but he also perceived why it was given him. The thorn came to humble him. Is that not usually God's chief design in His disciplinary dealings with us? In Paul's case the affliction was not for correction but for prevention. Such may have been God's merciful design toward you: perhaps He turned a wealthy relative against you to will his money elsewhere, or perhaps he has withheld business prosperity from you lest you become proud. How effective Paul's thorn was appears from the fact that for fourteen years he never mentioned his rapture into paradise and would not have done so now but for exceptional circumstances.

"For this thing I besought the Lord thrice, that it might depart from me" (II Cor. 12:8). The thorn did not make Paul fret and fume; it caused him to pray! This brings us, second, to the Object of his prayer, namely, the Lord Jesus, as the next verse plainly shows. This is a decisive proof of the Godhood of Christ and also a clear intimation that petitions may be addressed to Him as well as to the Father. Prayer was made to the Son in Acts 1:24 and 4:24. As Stephen was being stoned he cried, "Lord Jesus, receive my spirit" and begged Him not to lay this sin to the charge of his slayers (Acts 7:59-60). After Paul's conversion before he received his sight, Ananias told the Lord that Paul had authority from the chief priests "to bind all that call upon thy name" (Acts 9:10-14). That it was the common practice of the Christians of the early Church to invoke the Saviour's name is very evident from I Corinthians 1:2. There was special propriety in Paul's here addressing Christ, for *He* is the One who admits into paradise (Acts 7:59; Rev. 1:18).

Paul's Petition

"I besought the Lord thrice, that it might depart from me" (II Cor. 12:8). We regard this request as being made before he had any perception of why the Lord had afflicted him, and we also regard it as manifesting Paul's native kinship with us. Thorns are far from pleasant, and we desire their prompt removal. Nor is it wrong for us to do so; we would not be rational and sentient creatures if we did not shrink from suffering. For us to ask for deliverance from pain and trouble is not sinful, neither is it spiritual. Then what is it? Why, the exercise of that instinct of self-preservation with which the Creator has endowed us. But it becomes sinful when we insist on deliverance, insubordinate to the divine will. In Paul's case, and in many others, we see how grace triumphed over nature, the heart gladly acquiescing to the Lord's design.

Some have argued from the example of Christ in Gethsemane and Paul's case here that we ought never to ask God more than three times for any particular thing and that if it is not then granted we must desist. But such an idea is contrary to the many scriptures where importunity in asking is inculcated, for example, in Isaiah 62:7; Luke 11:8; 18:7. God is often pleased to test our faith and patience, for He waits to be gracious (Isa. 30:18). The repeated request for deliverance shows how heavily the burden pressed upon Paul, as well as indicating how human he was—a man of "like passions as we are." But as God's dear Son learned obedience by the things which He suffered, so also on the behalf of Christ it was given His most eminent servant to tread a similar path and be perfected by a special process of affliction.

Mediatorial Grace Given by Christ to His People

Fourth, let us consider the answer Paul received: "And he said unto me, My grace is sufficient for thee: for my strength is made perfect in weakness" (II Cor. 12:9). God's answer is not always along the line that we think; how good for us that it is not. How little we are able to perceive what would be for our good. "We know not what we should pray for as we ought" (Rom. 8: 26). Often we ask for temporal things, and God gives us eternal; we ask for deliverance, and He grants us patience. He does not answer according to our will but according to our welfare and profit. Hence we must not be disheartened if our requests are not literally answered. Sometimes God answers by reconciling our minds to humiliating trials. "My grace is sufficient for thee." Sufficient to support under the severest and most protracted affliction, to enable the soul to lie submissively as clay in the hands of the Potter, to trust His wisdom and love, to be assured that He knows what is best for us.

"My grace." It is mediatorial grace, the grace given to Christ as the covenant Head of His people (John 1:16). It is the Head speaking to a member of His Body. It is not inherent grace or the new nature but freshly imparted, quickening grace. "My grace is sufficient" not simply "will prove to be." What Paul had known theoretically he was now to learn experimentally. A grace that can save a hell-deserving sinner must be sufficient for the petty trials of this life! He who gives the thorn also gives grace to bear it. Grace is given not only to resist temptations and strengthen graces but also to endure trials. Yet grace must be definitely and diligently sought (Heb. 4:16). "In the day when I cried thou answeredst me, and strengthenedst me with strength in my soul" (Ps. 138:3). "For my strength is made perfect in weakness," in supporting earthen vessels under the buffetings of Satan.

Glorying in Infirmities

Fifth, we will observe Paul's improvement of his weakness: "Most gladly therefore will I rather glory in my infirmities that the power of Christ may rest upon me" (II Cor. 12:9). Paul's statement was more than a sullen submission or even a meek acquiescence. The *rather* points a contrast from the removal of the thorn: to glory on account of infirmities went far beyond resignation in suffering, namely, to rejoicing. To this we should aspire and pray. "Souls that are rich in grace can bear burdens without a burden," said a Puritan. Here is a test by which we may measure the degree of grace we have: not by our speculative knowledge but by the ease with which we bear afflictions, the cheerfulness of our spirits under persecution. When the apostles had been beaten they departed "rejoicing that they were counted worthy to suffer shame for his name" (Acts 5:40-41).

"Therefore I take pleasure in infirmities, in reproaches, in necessities, in persecutions, in distresses for Christ's sake: for when I am weak, then am I strong" (II Cor. 12:10). This goes farther than the foregoing verse. Because Paul "took pleasure" in his infirmities he gloried in them; and because they were the occasion of manifesting the power of Christ to uphold and work through one so frail he was glad of them. What nature recoils from, an enlightened faith accepts and delights in for the sake of the ulterior blessing—another example of how God can bring a clean thing out of an unclean, another example of how He can make both the wrath of man and the enmity of the serpent to praise Him! In the same way, though on a lower plane, David said, "It is good for me that I have been afflicted; that I might learn thy statutes" (Ps. 119:71). By the power of Christ Paul triumphed over all obstacles.

What is meant by "when I am weak, then am I strong"? This needs to be correctly defined, for there is a weakness which does not result in strength, yes, a Christian's consciousness of weakness. Some are constantly talking about their inability and bemoaning their helplessness, and there it ends! But he who has a true and spiritual sense of his insufficiency to do anything as he ought is the one who is most earnest in crying to the Strong for strength and, other things being equal, he is the one who is most active in appropriating Christ's strength. To be weak is to be emptied of self; but to be all the time occupied with our inability is to be absorbed with self. To be spiritually weak is to be conscious that I "lack wisdom," and that makes me "ask of God" (James 1:5), feel my unbelief, and beg for an increase of faith.

Some say they are weak and then contradict their words by the way they act. Others are happy over the very realization of their impotency, which is like one smitten with a stroke rejoicing in his paralysis as such. It needs to be steadily borne in mind that "hands which hang down, and the feeble knees" bring no glory to God (Heb. 12:12). Second Kings 5:7 illustrates. The king used not the language of humility and piety but of unbelief and pride. A consciousness of my insufficiency is of value only when it moves me to turn to and lay hold of the Lord's sufficiency. Second Corinthians 3:5 gives *both* sides. The complement to "without me ye can do nothing" (John 15:5) is "I can do all things through Christ which strengtheneth me" (Phil. 4:13; cf. Eph. 6:10; II Tim. 2:1).

Chapter 9

PRAYER OF BENEDICTION

II CORINTHIANS 13:14

"THE GRACE OF THE LORD JESUS CHRIST, and the love of God, and the communion of the Holy Ghost, be with you all. Amen." This threefold invocation is familiarly known as the Christian benediction. God authorized this Old Testament formula of blessing to be used in the assemblies of Israel: "Speak unto Aaron and his sons, saying, On this wise shall ye bless the children of Israel, saying unto them, The LORD bless thee and keep thee: The LORD make his face shine upon thee, and be gracious unto thee: The LORD lift up his countenance upon thee, and give thee peace. And they shall [thus] put my name upon the children of Israel; and I will bless them" (Num. 6:23-27). But there is nothing to indicate that God required the benediction of II Corinthians 13:14 to be employed in the Christian churches; yet there is certainly nothing to show that it is incongruous to do so. As a fact, it has been made wide use of because of its deep importance doctrinally and because of its appropriateness, for those words are both a confession of the Christian faith and a declaration of Christian privilege.

The Christian Doctrine of God

The benediction in II Corinthians 13:14 contains a brief summary of the Christian doctrine of God. We say the *Christian* doctrine of God in contradistinction not only from the horrible delusions of the idolatrous heathen but also from the inadequate conception of Deity which was present in Judaism. By the Christian doctrine of God we mean the revelation which is given of Him in the New Testament more particularly. And that brings us to ground where we need to tread very carefully lest we disparage or underestimate what was revealed of Him in the Old Testament. If on the one hand we must guard against the fearful error that the God of the Old Testament is a very different character from the God of the New, on the other hand we need to be careful that we do not too fully read the clearer teaching of the New into the Old. At any rate we must not conclude that those under the legal dispensation perceived the same significance in some of those things in their Scriptures which we now interpret in the brighter light of the evangelical economy. Such a statement is "the darkness is past, and the true light now shineth" (I John 2:8) needs to be remembered in this connection.

79

It has been erroneously and blasphemously asserted by those who deny the real inspiration of the Scriptures that Jehovah was but a tribal God and that what is said of Him in the New Testament mirrors the views which the Hebrews entertained of Him. But it is greatly to be feared that many who reject such a Satanic crudity as that and who regard the Old Testament as being equally the Word of God with the New nevertheless hold the idea, with varying degrees of consciousness, that the revelation which we have of the divine character in the New Testament is much to be preferred above that in the Old. Such is a serious misconception. The severity of God appears as plainly in the book of Revelation as it does in Joshua. In fact, the vials of His wrath there are more fearful in their nature than the plagues which He inflicted upon Egypt and Canaan. On the other hand, the goodness of God as made known in the epistles in no wise surpasses His benevolence as depicted in the Psalms. The God of Sinai and Calvary is one and the same, as He is also the Author of both the law and the gospel.

As has been said, we need to be careful not to read too fully into the Old Testament Scriptures the clearer teaching of the New. We who now have the completed Word of God in our hands are thereby enabled to recognize more plainly that the substance of the truth of the Triunity of God is found in the earlier books of the Bible. Yet it has to be granted that there is no statement in them which is quite as explicit as the one in Matthew 28:19. Certainly it is much to be doubted if the Jewish nation recognized that there were three distinct Persons in the Godhead. The grand truth made known under the old economy was rather the unity of God: "Hear, O Israel: the LORD our God is one LORD" (Deut. 6:4). This truth was in sharp contrast with the polytheism of the idolatries of the heathen. On the other hand, we have no doubt that individual saints in those times had a saving knowledge of the triune God, yet not so fully perhaps as we have. Concerning this Calvin said, "As God afforded a clearer manifestation of Himself at the advent of Christ, the three Persons became better known." We add, especially in Their covenant offices and distinct operations.

Old Testament Revelation

"The path of the just is as the shining light, that shineth more and more unto the perfect day" (Prov. 4:18). These words have a corporate fulfillment as well as a personal; they apply to the Church collectively as well as individually. The light of divine revelation broke forth "here a little and there a little" and did not shine in midday splendor until Emmanuel Himself tabernacled among men. The degree in which the doctrine of the Trinity was made known in the Old Testament Scriptures no doubt bore a proportion to the discovery of other mysteries of the faith. It was definitely revealed from the beginning, yet hardly with the same explicitness and perspicuity as now. "God, who at sundry times and in divers manners spake in time past unto the fathers by the prophets, hath in these last days spoken unto us by his Son" (Heb. 1:1-2). This is the first contrast given in Hebrews, the theme of which is the superiority of Christianity over Judaism. Under the former era God's revelation of Himself was fragmentary and incomplete, but in this final dispensation His mind and heart have been fully revealed. There it was through such instruments as the prophets; now it is by the person of His own Son.

Christian revelation comes to us through the Lord Jesus Christ. God is manifested in and by the incarnate Son, for He can be approached only through the Mediator. God can be vitally known only in Him. Only through Him can we have a saving knowledge of God. The grand mission of Christ as the Prophet of His Church was to make known the character and perfections of God. This is signified by His title "the Word." "In the beginning was the Word, and the Word was with God, and the Word was God. And the Word was made flesh and dwelt among us, (and we beheld his glory, the glory as of the only begotten of the Father,) full of grace and truth" (John 1:1, 14). A word is a medium of manifestation. I have a thought in my mind, yet others do not know it. But the moment I clothe that thought in words it becomes cognizable. Words then make unseen thoughts objective. This is precisely what the Lord Jesus has done; He has made manifest the invisible God. A word is also a means of communication. By my words I transmit information to others. By words I express myself, make known my will, and impart knowledge. So Christ, as the Word, is the divine Transmitter, expressing to us God's full mind and will, communicating to us His life and love.

Christ Reveals the Attributes and Perfections of God

A word is also a means of revelation. By his words a speaker or writer exhibits both his intellectual caliber and his moral character. Out of the abundance of our hearts our mouths speak, and our very language betrays what we are within. By our words we shall be justified or condemned in the judgment, for they will reveal and attest what we were and are. And Christ as the Word reveals the attributes and perfections of God. How fully Christ has revealed God! Christ displayed God's power, illustrated His patience, manifested His wisdom, exhibited His holiness, showed forth His faithfulness, demonstrated His righteousness, made known His grace, and unveiled His heart. In Christ, and nowhere else, is God fully and finally manifested. That is why He is designated the "image of the invisible God" (Col. 1:15). He has set before our eyes and hearts a visible, tangible, and cognizable representation of Him. Though "no man hath seen God at any time," yet "the only begotten Son, which is in the bosom of the Father, he hath declared him" (John 1:18). That is, Christ has faithfully and fully proclaimed Him. The same Greek word that is translated "declared" here is translated "told" in Luke 24:35.

Christ the Revealer of the Father

It was infinitely suitable that He who was in the bosom of the Father, even when He walked this earth, should declare Him, for only One who was God's coequal could tell Him forth. So perfectly did Christ reveal God the Father that at the close of His ministry He said to Philip, "He that hath seen me hath seen the Father" (John 14:9). And to the Father He affirmed, "I have manifested thy name unto the men which thou gavest me out of the world: . . . I have declared unto them thy name" (John 17:6, 26). By the name of God is meant all that He is in a demonstrative and communicative way. For what God is essentially in His absoluteness, in His ineffable majesty, in His incomprehensible boundlessness, in His self-existing essence, as three in one and one in three, the infinite Jehovah, He cannot be made fully known to any finite intelligence, however spiritual. No, not until eternity. In His love to His Church, in His covenant relationship to His people in Christ, in His everlasting delight to them in His Beloved, as the Medium and Mediator of all union and communion with them, God has been graciously pleased to reveal and make Himself known.

God is revealed to us in and by and through the Lord Jesus Christ. The writer of Hebrews declared Him to be "the brightness of his [the Triune God's] glory, and the express image of his person" (Heb. 1:3). He was certainly speaking of Christ as the God-man, that is, of the Son as incarnate as the same verse goes on to show: "When he had by himself purged our sins." By that blessed statement we understand that through Christ a clear and full exhibition has been made of the Father's personality. In the Mediator all the glory of the Godhead is realized and manifested in order for it to be reflected on the Church and thereby be made known and enjoyed and in order for God to be glorified. Manifestation consists in revealing, so our Lord revealed and made known the "name" of God. He did so by His incarnation, by His holy life, by His magnifying the law, by His preaching, by His miracles, by His sufferings and death, by His triumphant resurrection, by His ascension. He did so by His Spirit, for it was more than an external manifestation of God which Christ made to His own —namely, an internal—by supernatural revelation, just as He "opened . . . their understanding, that they might understand the scriptures" (Luke 24:45).

We are grateful to the Lord Jesus Christ for the revelation of the Christian doctrine of God which we have dwelt on above. We deemed it best to make clear what we owe to our Redeemer in making known to us the character of God Himself and the relations which He sustains to us instead of entering at once into a detailed exposition of II Corinthians 13:14. As Christ averred, "All things are delivered unto me of my Father: and no one knoweth the Son, but the Father; neither knoweth any man the Father, save the Son, and he to whomsoever the Son will reveal him" (Matt. 11:27). No one can approach the Father except by Christ's mediation and none can have any vital and spiritual knowledge of the Father except by Christ's supernatural revelation of Him to the soul.

When our Lord declared, "He that hath seen me hath seen the Father", He uttered words with a far deeper significance than appears on the surface. Locally they were spoken more by way of reproof, for Philip had said to Him, "Shew us the Father and it sufficeth us" (John 14:8). To this the Saviour replied, "Have I been so long time with you, and yet hast thou not known me, Philip?" His life, His teaching, His works revealed plainly enough who He was. And then Jesus added, "He that hath seen me hath seen the Father; and how sayest thou, Shew us the Father?" But remember that the Spirit was not then given as He is now and that the hearts of these apostles were troubled at the prospect of Christ's death and His subsequent departure from them (John 14:1). But in its deeper meaning "he that hath seen me" refers not to any physical sight of Him but to a spiritual view of Him which one can see with the eyes of a divinely-enlightened understanding. Such an one is enabled to recognize His oneness with the Father and to exclaim, "My Lord and my God!"

God Clearly Revealed in Christ

The two things we have mentioned above are brought together in that familiar statement, "For God, who commanded the light to shine out of darkness, hath shined in our hearts, to give the light of the knowledge of the glory of God in the face of Jesus Christ" (II Cor. 4:6). First, the clearest revelation that God is and what He is, is made in the person of Christ, so that those who refuse to see God in the Redeemer lose all true knowledge of Him. Second, as the glory of God is spiritual, it can only be spiritually discerned. Only in God's light can we see Him who is light, and therefore God must shine in our hearts to give us a real and experimental knowledge of Himself. Such knowledge of Him is not by mental apprehension nor that which one man can communicate to another. Our reception of that light is not the result of our will or any effort put forth by us but is the immediate effect of a divine fiat, as when at the beginning of this world God said, "Let there be light: and there was light" (Gen. 1:3). God created light, and He awakens the dead souls of His elect, thereby calling them out of darkness into His own marvelous light, whereby they behold Himself shining in the perfection of grace and truth in the face or person of Jesus Christ. Nothing but the exercise of omnipotence can produce a miracle so wondrous and so blessed. God shines in our hearts by the power and operation of the Holy Spirit.

Here then is found the answer to that all-important question, "How may I obtain a better, deeper, fuller, and more influential knowledge of God?" By the heart's occupation with the Lord Jesus. By studying and meditating upon all that is revealed in the Bible concerning His wondrous person and work. By realizing my complete dependence upon the Holy Spirit and begging Him to take of the things of Christ and show them to me (John 16:14) and thereby abstaining from everything which grieves the Spirit and would (morally) hinder Him from performing this work of His. Nothing can make up for or take the place of personal intercourse with the Redeemer. It is only as we behold, with the eyes of faith and love, the glory of the Lord in the mirror of the Word that we are "changed into the same image from glory to glory, even as by the Spirit of the Lord" (II Cor. 3:18). Let us then emulate the apostle and make it our chief ambition and endeavor that we may know Him, for in knowing Him we arrive at the knowledge of the triune God.

Christ Anointed for His Priestly Work

The Christian benediction stands closely linked with both the baptism of Christ and the baptismal formula which He gave to His disciples. The former presents to us a most remarkable scene, for at the baptism of Christ the three Persons of the Godhead were openly manifested together in connection with that which gave a symbolical showing forth of the work of redemption. John the Baptist had come preaching repentance toward God and faith in His Lamb who should take away the sin of the world. But he also made definite mention of the Holy Spirit (Matt. 3:11). When the Saviour presented Himself for baptism in the Jordan at the hands of His forerunner, He came as our Surety acknowledging that death was His due. It was there He entered upon that path which was to terminate at the cross. As Christ rose from that symbolical grave the heavens were opened and the Spirit of God in form as a dove descended and alighted on Him, thereby anointing Him for His priestly work (Acts 10:38). At the same time the Father's voice was audibly heard saying, "This is my beloved Son, in whom I am well pleased" (Matt. 3:17). "Therefore doth my Father love me, because I lay down my life, that I might take it again" (John 10:17). At Christ's baptism while He emblematically pledged Himself to death on the cross, the Father attested His pleasure in the Son and the acceptance of His offering.

Christ's reception of the Spirit at the Jordan was the equipment for His Messianic ministry. As He was sent and anointed by the Spirit, so He commissions and endows His ambassadors: "As my Father hath sent me, even so send I you. And when he had said this, he breathed on them, and saith unto them, Receive ye the Holy Ghost" (John 20:21-22). Later Christ gave the great commission to His disciples: "All power is given unto me in heaven and in earth. Go ye therefore, and teach all nations, baptizing them [after they have been taught and have become disciples or Christians] in the name of the Father, and of the Son, and of the Holy Ghost" (Matt. 28:18-20). Baptism into "the name" means baptism unto God, and the names of God in the New Covenant are "the Father, and the Son, and the Holy Spirit." The triune God is now fully revealed. That was the consummation and culmination of Christ's teaching concerning God. He ordained baptism for all time to be the initiating avowal of faith for all who enter His kingdom. And the names of God, in which believers are to be baptized, set forth the Trinity of God, a fundamental doctrine of the Christian Church.

The Divine Trinity

The Christian benediction, then, enunciates one of the foundational doctrines of Christianity, for no one is entitled to be regarded as a Christian who does not believe and acknowledge the triune God. That is why Scripture bids all who avow themselves Christians to be baptized in "the name of the Father, and of the Son, and of the Holy Ghost." The divine Trinity lies at the basis of all New Testament teaching. The Redeemer claimed to be equal with God, one with the Father, and ever spoke of the Spirit as being both personal and divine. The apostles everywhere proclaimed His doctrine and recognized the threefold distinction in the Persons of the Godhead. The equal deity (and honor) of the Son and the Spirit with the Father is the mystery and glory of the gospel they preached. "This is life eternal, that they might know thee the only true God, and Jesus Christ, whom thou hast sent" (John 17:3). The "only true God" is revealed as Father, Son, and Holy Spirit and is known in and through Jesus Christ, the one Mediator.

That the revelation of the triune God constitutes the doctrinal foundation of Christianity is easily capable of demonstration. First, as pointed out above, the true God subsists in three coessential and coeternal Persons, and therefore he who worships any but the triune God is merely rendering homage to a figment of his own imagination. He who denies the personality and absolute deity of either the Father, the Son, or the Spirit cannot be a true Christian. Second, no salvation is possible for any sinner save that of which the triune God is the Author. To regard the Lord Jesus Christ as our Saviour to the exclusion of the saving operations of both the Father and the Spirit is a serious mistake. The Father eternally purposed the salvation of His elect in Christ (Eph. 1:3-6). The Father, Son, and Holy Spirit entered into an everlasting covenant with each other for the Son to become incarnate in order to redeem sinners.

The salvation of the Church is ascribed to the Father: "Who hath saved us, and called us with an holy calling, . . . according to his own purpose and grace, which was given us in Christ Jesus before the world began" (II Tim. 1:9). The Father, then, was our Saviour long before Christ died to become such, and thanksgiving is due Him for the same. Equally necessary are the operations of the Spirit to actually apply to the hearts of God's elect the good of what Christ did for them. It is the Spirit who convicts men of sin and who imparts saving faith to them. Therefore is our salvation also ascribed to Him: "God hath from the beginning chosen you to salvation through sanctification of the Spirit and belief of the truth" (II Thess. 2:13). A careful reading of Titus 3:4-6 shows the three Persons together in this connection, for "God our Saviour" is plainly the Father; "*he* saved us, *by* the washing of regeneration, and renewing of the *Holy Ghost;* Which he shed on us abundantly through Jesus Christ our Saviour" (v. 6).

Third, the doctrine of the Trinity is a foundational doctrine because it is by the distinctive operations of the Holy Three that our varied needs are supplied. Do we not need "the grace of the Lord Jesus Christ"? Is not our most urgent experimental requirement to come to Him constantly and draw from the fullness of grace which is treasured up for us in Him? (John 1:16). If we would obtain "grace to help in time of need" then we must go to that throne on which the Mediator sits. And do we not also need "the love of God", that is, fresh manifestations of it, new apprehensions thereof? Are we not bidden to keep ourselves "in the love of God"? (Jude 21); And do we not equally need "the communion of the Holy Spirit"? What would become of us if He did not renew day by day in the inner man? (See II Corinthians 4:16; Ephesians 3:16.) What would be our prayer-life if He no longer helped "our infirmities" and made "intercession for the saints according to the will of God"? (Rom. 8:26-27).

The Holy Trinity

Like the virgin birth of Christ and the resurrection of our bodies, the doctrine of the Holy Trinity is one of the mysteries of the faith. The first truth presented to faith is the Being of the true and living God, and this we know not from any discovery of reason but because He has revealed it in His Word. The next grand truth is that the one living and true God has made Himself known to us under the threefold relation of Father, Son, and Holy Spirit; and this we know on the same authority as the first. They are equally above reason, and real Christians do not attempt to fathom them; yet their incomprehensibility so far from being an objection is a necessary condition of confidence in revelation and faith in Him who is revealed. If the Bible presented no heights beyond the powers of reason to scale, if it contained no depths unfathomable to the keenest mental acumen, this writer for one would have discarded it as being nothing more than a human production and imposture. For our part we would no more worship a "god" that we could measure by our intellect than we would honor an image that our hands fashioned.

Whenever we attempt to discuss the revelation God has made of His three Persons we should do so with bowed heads and reverent hearts, for the ground we tread is ineffably holy. The subject is one of transcendent sacredness for it concerns the infinitely majestic and glorious One. For the whole of our knowledge on this subject we are entirely shut up to what it has pleased God to reveal of Himself in His Oracles. Science, philosophy, experience, observation, or speculation cannot in this exalted sphere increase our knowledge one iota.

Trinity in Unity

The divine Trinity is a Trinity in Unity: that is to say, there are not three Gods but three Persons as coexisting by essential union in the divine essence as being the one true God. Those three Persons are coequal and coglorious so that one is not before or after the other, neither greater nor less than the other. It is in and by Their covenant offices They are manifested to us, and it is our privilege and duty to believe and know how these three Persons stand committed to us and are interested in us by the everlasting covenant; but we cannot understand the mystery of Their subsistence. Any teaching which does not equally honor all the Persons of the Godhead, distinctively and unitedly, is of no value to the soul. As one has said, "There is not a vestige of Christianity where the truth of the Trinity is not known and acknowledged. Not a vestige of godliness in the heart where the Father, Son, and Spirit do not officially dwell. There is not a clear view of any doctrine of God's grace to be obtained unless (so to speak) the telescope of the truth of the Trinity be applied to the eye of faith and that doctrine be viewed through it."

In view of what has just been pointed out, it constitutes one of the gravest signs of the times that in professedly "Christian" countries the Triune God is no longer officially acknowledged. While some of our national leaders still give thanks to "God" and own our dependence upon "the Almighty," that is no more than any Orthodox Jew or Muhammadan would do. There is a studied avoidance of any reference to the Lord Jesus Christ and to the Holy Spirit. Though that is sad, it is not to be wondered at; it is simply the shadowing forth in the civil realm of what has long obtained in the religious. For several generations past the absolute deity of Christ and of the Spirit has been openly denied in most of the theological seminaries, and thereby the triunity of God was repudiated. Even in most of the "orthodox churches" the eternal Three have not been accorded Their rightful place either in the doctrinal teaching of the pulpit or the devotional life of the pew.

In this benediction the apostle invokes the Trinity as the Source of grace, love, and communion. Its unique features must not be overlooked: the order is unusual, and the Names used informally. The Son is placed before the Father. The divine Persons are not here spoken of as the Son, the Father, and the Spirit, but as the Lord Jesus Christ, God, and the Holy Spirit. The reason for this is because what we have in our text is not primarily a confession of faith (as is Matthew 28:19), nor a doxology (as is Jude 24-25), but a benediction. A doxology is an ascription of praise, a benediction is a word of blessing; the one ascends from the heart of the saint to God, the other descends from God to the saint. Samuel Chadwick wrote, "Consequently the benediction does not approach the subject from the standpoint of theology but of *experience*. It is not concerned with definition, nor does it contemplate the glory of God in the absoluteness of His deity; but it sets Him forth as He is realized in the soul."

The Doctrine of the Trinity of Great Importance

The Christian benediction therefore intimates that the doctrine of the Trinity is one of great importance to the existence and progress of vital godliness: that it is not a subject of mere speculation but one on which depends all the communications of grace and peace to the saints. It is a striking and solemn fact that those who reject the truth of the Trinity are seldom known to even profess having spiritual communion with God but instead treat the same as a species of enthusiasm and fanaticism, as a perusal of the writings of Unitarians will show. The benediction, then, sums up the blessings of Christian privilege in the three great words of the gospel: *grace, love, communion*. Those three divine gifts are attributed to different Persons in the Godhead. Each takes precedence in His own peculiar work, though we cannot trace the limits of such, and must be careful lest we conceive of God as three Gods rather than one. Each belongs to all. Grace is of God and of the Spirit as well as of the Son. Love is of the Son and Spirit as well as the Father. And our communion is with the Father and the Son as well as with the Spirit.

Grace a Great Word of the Gospel

"The grace of the Lord Jesus Christ." Why distinctively ascribe grace to *Him* if it is of God and the Spirit as well? Because in the economy of redemption all grace comes to us through Him. The word *grace* is the special token of Paul in every epistle: eight close with "the grace of our Lord Jesus Christ be with you," sometimes varying the formula to "with your spirit." *Grace* is one of the outstanding words of the gospel. Again quoting Chadwick: "It is more than mercy and greater than love. Justice demands integrity, and mercy is the ministry of pity; love seeks correspondence, appreciation, and response; but grace demands no merit. Grace flows unrestrained and unreserved upon those who have no goodness to plead and no claim to advance. Grace seeks the unfit and the unworthy. It is love, mercy, and compassion combined, stretching out toward the guilty, ungracious, and rebellious. It is the only hope for sinful men. If salvation comes not by grace, it can never be ours. Without grace there can be no reconciliation, no pardon, no peace."

"The grace of the Lord Jesus Christ." That is His designation as the God-man Mediator. It includes and indicates His divine nature: He is "the Lord," yes, "the Lord of lords." His human nature: He is "Jesus"; His office: He is "Christ," the anointed One, the long-promised Messiah, the Mediator. It is the favor of His divine person clothed with our nature and made the Head of His people which the apostle invokes for all his believing brethren. *"His* grace be with you all." That comes first in the benediction because it is our initial need.

"For ye know the grace of our Lord Jesus Christ, that, though he was rich, yet for your sakes he became poor, that ye through his poverty might be rich" (II Cor. 8:9). There it is His infinite condescension in submitting to such a mean condition for our sakes.

When He became incarnate the only begotten of the Father was beheld by His own as "full of grace and truth," and as the apostle added, "And of his fulness have all we received, and grace for grace" (John 1:14, 16). Here the meaning of grace passes from an attribute of the divine character to an active energy in the souls of the redeemed. At the throne of grace we "find grace to help in time of need" (Heb. 4:16). The heart is "established with grace" (Heb. 13:9) and by that grace we are enabled to "serve God acceptably with reverence and godly fear" (Heb. 12:28). It is in "the grace that is in Christ Jesus" (II Tim. 2:1) that we find our strength, and He assures us of its competency to support us under all afflictions and persecutions by the promise "My grace is sufficient for thee" (II Cor. 12:9). Therefore we are exhorted to "grow in grace, and in the knowledge of our Lord and Saviour Jesus Christ" (II Pet. 3:18). Those passages all speak of the divine power in the soul as the operation of grace in connection with the Lord Jesus Christ as its Fountain.

The Love of God

"And the love of God." There are two reasons why this comes second: because this is the order both in the economy of redemption and in Christian experience. First, it was the mediatorial grace or work of Christ which procured the love of God for His people, which turned away His wrath from them and reconciled Him to them. Hence it is referred to not as "the love of the Father," which never changed or diminished to His people, but as the love or goodwill of God considered as their Governor and Judge. Second, it is by the grace of the Lord Jesus Christ in saving us that we are brought to the knowledge and enjoyment of the love of God. The love of the Father is indeed the source and originating cause of redemption, but that is not the particular love of God which is here in view. The death of Christ as a satisfaction for our sins was necessary in order to bring us to God and into participation of His love. The manifestation of the love of God toward us in the pardon of our sins and the justification of our persons was conditioned on the atoning blood.

The Communion of the Holy Spirit

"And the communion of the Holy Spirit." As the grand design of Christ's work Godward was to appease His judicial wrath and procure for us His love and favor, so the grand effect saintward was the procuring of the gift of the Holy Spirit. The Greek word may be rendered either "communion" or "communication." By the communication of the Holy Spirit we are regenerated, faith is given, holiness is wrought in us. Life, light, love, and liberty are the special benefits He bestows on us. Without the Spirit being communicated to us we could never enter, personally and experimentally, into the benefits of Christ's mediation. "Christ hath redeemed us from the curse of the law, being made a curse for us . . . that the blessing of Abraham might come on the Gentiles through Jesus Christ; that we might receive the promise of the Spirit through faith" (Gal. 3:13-14). Thus, the communicating of the Spirit to His people was one of the chief objects of Christ's death.

But the Greek also signifies the *communion* of the Holy Spirit, a word which means "partnership, companionship." He shares with us the things of God. Grace tends to love, and love to communion. Hence we see again that the order here is that of Christian experience. Only as grace is consciously received and the love of God is realized in the soul can there be any intelligent and real communion. Through Christ to God, the Father, and through Both to the abiding presence of the Comforter. This expression "the communion of the Holy Spirit" shows He is a person, for it is meaningless to talk of communion with an impersonal principle or influence. United as He is in this verse with "the Lord Jesus Christ and God" it evidences Him to be a divine Person. Further, it denotes He is an Object of intercourse and converse, and hence we must be on our guard against grieving Him (Eph. 4:30). The separate mention of each of the eternal Three teaches us that They are to be accorded equal honor, glory, and praise from us.

What is signified by "The grace of the Lord Jesus Christ, and the love of God, and the communion of the Holy Ghost, *be with you all*"? It cannot mean less than a consciousness of God's presence. The apostle was not praying for the gifts of grace, love, and communion apart from the Persons in whom alone they are to be found. He requested that the presence of the triune God might be realized in the souls of His people. The New Testament teaches that the divine Three are equally present in the heart of the believer. Speaking of the Spirit Christ said, "He dwelleth with you, and shall be in you," and of Himself and the Father, "If a man love me, he will keep my words: and my Father will love him, and *we* will come unto him, and make our abode with him" (John 14:17, 23). The Christian is indwelt by the triune God: the Lord Jesus dwells in him as the source of all grace, God the Father abides in him as the spring of all love, and the Holy Spirit communes with him and energizes him for all spiritual service.

What is the *purpose* of that indwelling? God the Father abides in the believer to conform him to His image, that he may become one with Him: one with Him in mind and heart, in character and purpose. The Christian reflects his God. The grace by which the Lord Jesus tasted death for His people is designed to produce a like spirit of sacrifice in them: "Because he laid down his life for us . . . we ought to lay down our lives for the brethren" (I John 3:16). They that know the love of God must live the life of love. If we say the love of God is "with us" and we walk contrary to love, we are liars. The God of love dwells in His people that they may live the life of Godlike love. So it is with the communion of the Holy Spirit: He does not share with us His riches that we may spend them upon ourselves. Chadwick averred: "The threefold benediction is to abide with us that its threefold grace may be manifested by us, and the presence of the three-one God demonstrated through us."

Chapter 10

PRAYER OF GRATITUDE

EPHESIANS 1:3

EPHESIANS PRESENTS the inestimable treasures of divine wisdom, the knowledge-surpassing manifestations of God's love to His people. The book sets forth "the riches of his grace" (1:7), yes, "the exceeding riches of his grace" (2:7), "the riches of his glory" (3:16), and "the unsearchable riches of Christ" (3:8). Ephesians contains the fullest opening up of the mystery, or the contents of the everlasting covenant. Here we are shown in greater detail than elsewhere the intimate and ineffable relation of the Church to Christ. Here as nowhere else we are conducted unto and into the "heavenlies." Here are revealed depths which no finite mind can fathom and heights which no imagination can scale.

Paul Bows in Worship

Before Paul proceeded to the orderly development of his wonderful theme, he bowed in worship. As his mind was absorbed with the transcendentally glorious subject on which he was to write, as he contemplated the exceeding riches of God's grace to His people, his soul was overwhelmed—"lost in wonder, love, and praise." The heart of Paul was too full to contain itself and overflowed in adoring gratitude. *That* is the highest form of worship, and only in such a spirit can we truly enter into the contents of this epistle. "Blessed be the God and Father of our Lord Jesus Christ, who hath blessed us with all spiritual blessings in heavenly places in Christ" (Eph. 1:3). As a prayer those words may be viewed thus: first, its *nature*—an ascription of praise; second, its *Object*—the God and Father of Christ; third, its *incitement*—our enrichment in Him. Were we to sermonize the verse, our divisions would be (1) The believer's excellent portion: blessed with all spiritual blessings. (2) The believer's exalted position: in the heavenlies in Christ. (3) The believer's exultant praise: "blessed be the God and Father."

What It Means to Bless God

"Blessed be the God and Father." That those words signify an act of prayer is clear from many passages. "I will bless the LORD at all times: his praise shall continually be in my mouth" (Ps. 34:1). "Thus will I bless thee while I live: I will lift up my hands in thy name" (Ps. 63:4; cf. I Tim. 2:8). "Sing unto the

90

LORD, bless his name" (Ps. 96:2). "Lift up your hands in the sanctuary, and bless the LORD" (Ps. 134:2). To bless God is to adore Him, to acknowledge His excellency, to express the highest veneration and gratitude. To bless God is to render Him the homage of our hearts as the Giver of every good and perfect gift. The three principal branches of prayer are humiliation, supplication, and adoration. Included in the first is confession of sin; in the second, making known our requests and interceding on behalf of others; in the third, thanksgiving and praise. Paul's action here is a summons to all believers to unite with him in magnifying the Source of all our spiritual blessings: "Adored be God the Father."

By way of infinite eminency God is the "blessed" One (Mark 14:61)—a title which is peculiar and solely proper to Himself. Nevertheless, He is graciously pleased to hear His saints attest to His blessedness. This was intimated by Paul when, after declaring Him to be "God blessed for ever" he at once added his "Amen" to the statement (Rom. 1:25). This amen, "so be it," was added not to a blessing of invocation but to a joyful acclamation that expressed Paul's own satisfaction and joy. "All thy works shall praise thee" (Ps. 145:10). His works alone bless Him, for they alone bear Him goodwill. They bless Him not only for what He is to them and for what He has done for them but for what He is in Himself.

The nature of this prayer, then, is not a petitionary one like those which come later in Ephesians, but it is an ascription of praise, evoked by an apprehension of the spiritual blessings with which God the Father has blessed His people. The principal blessings are described in the verses which immediately follow Ephesians 1:3. The prayer was an adoring of God for such an amazing portion, such inestimable treasure, such a glorious inheritance. The apostle was filled with overwhelming gratitude for such infinite love and grace, and like new wine bursting out of the old bottle into which it was poured, fervent thanksgiving flowed forth from him. Someone has beautifully said, "The first notes of the everlasting song of the heavenly world are sounded here below, and are produced and drawn forth by a sense of God's goodness and mercy as revealed to the soul, and especially when the love of God is shed abroad in the heart by the Holy Spirit." It was this which made David exclaim, "Bless the LORD, O my soul: and all that is within me, bless his holy name" (Ps. 103:1). He blessed God for having so richly blessed him.

The Object Adored

We turn now to consider the Object adored. God the Father is not absolutely considered, for as such—apart from Christ—He is "a consuming fire" to sinners such as we. Nor is the Object simply the God and Father of *the* Lord Jesus, for we could have no approach to Him as such. Rather the Object is "the God and Father of *our* Lord Jesus Christ," the One who has blessed us with all spiritual blessings in Him. A wealth of theological instruction is in the divine titles, and we are greatly the losers if we fail to pay due attention to them. This title is the peculiar and characteristic designation of the Father as the God of accomplished redemption (cf. II Cor. 1:3; I Peter 1:3). *This* blessed relationship is the ground of our confidence. We stand related not to the absolute Jehovah but to the God of redemption as He is revealed in Jesus Christ, the One whom the Saviour declared, whose will He perfectly accomplished. Because God spared not His own dear Son but "delivered him up for us all," He is our God and Father, and through Christ and by the Spirit we have access to Him.

God Our Covenant God

When the Deity is said to be "the God" of any person, He is his covenant God. Thus, after the first covenant described in Genesis, we find Noah speaking of "the LORD God of Shem" (Gen. 9:26), for through that son God's covenant with Noah was to be accomplished. Later, He became known as "the God of Abraham, the God of Isaac, and the God of Jacob" (Exodus 3:6). These patriarchs' names conveyed the covenant blessings and consequently redounded to praise and blessing to God. Thus Noah exclaimed, "Blessed be the LORD God of Shem." Later, as in a parallel case, the Prophet Jeremiah declared, "Behold, the days come, saith the LORD, that it shall no more be said, The LORD liveth, that brought up the children of Israel out of the land of Egypt. Behold, the days come, saith the LORD, that I will make a new covenant with the house of Israel" (Jer. 16:14; 31:31). So we may say that, under the fuller revelation of the gospel, God has said, "I will no longer be known as the God of Abraham, but as the God and Father of our Lord Jesus Christ; and I will be owned and adored as such."

"Blessed be the God and Father of our Lord Jesus Christ." This unspeakably precious title views God as He is related to us in Christ, that is, to Christ as the covenant Head and to His elect in Him; He was, is, and ever will be the God and Father of the Lord Jesus. We question whether there is here any direct reference to the miraculous begetting of our Lord. Rather do we consider that He is contemplated in His mediatorial character, that is, as the eternal Son invested with our nature. In view of our Lord's own utterances it is abundantly clear that He owned the Father as *His* God. "I was cast upon thee from the womb: thou art my God from my mother's belly" (Ps. 22:10). "I delight to do thy will, O my God" (Ps. 40:8). On the cross Christ owned the Father as His God (Matt. 27:46). After His resurrection He spoke of the Father as "my God" (John 20:17). Enthroned in heaven, Jesus Christ still declares the Father to be His God four times over in a single verse (Rev. 3:12). Though God the Son, coequal and coeternal with the Father, Christ assumed the form of a servant.

The Father is the God of Christ in the following respects: (1) In regard to His human nature. Being a creature (" a body hast thou prepared me," Heb. 10:5), Christ was subject to God. (2) In regard to His human nature being predestinated to union with His divine person. Goodwin said, "Christ as man was 'predestinated' (I Peter 1:20) as well as we, and so hath God to be His God by predestination, and so by free grace, as well as He is our God in that respect." (3) In regard to His well-being. Goodwin again said, "God is the Author and immediately the matter of Christ's blessedness (as He is man) and therefore blessed be God as the God of Christ, who hath 'blessed Him forever' as appears in what follows: 'God, thy God, hath anointed thee with the oil of gladness above thy fellows' (Ps. 45:2, 7)." (4) In regard to the covenant between the Father and the Son. "Thus saith God the LORD, . . . I the LORD have called thee . . ., and will keep thee, and give thee for a covenant of the people, for a light of the Gentiles" (Isa. 42:5-6). (5) In regard to His relation to the Church as the Head and Representative of His people. "For both he that sanctifieth and they who are sanctified are all of one" (Heb. 2:11).

God must be the God and Father of the Lord Jesus Christ in order to be the God and Father of His people whom He chose in Christ. The relation which the Church sustains to God is determined by Christ's own relation to God, for she is Christ's and Christ is God's (I Cor. 3:23). The general principle of this is established by those words, "God sent forth his Son, . . . that we might receive the adoption of sons" (Gal. 4:4-5). Still more explicitly it is found in Christ's own words, "I ascend unto my Father, and your Father; and to my God, and your God" (John 20:17). Not "our," be it carefully noted, but "my"; first His and then ours—His originally, and ours by participation.

In view of all that follows in Ephesians 1 it is clear that Paul's design here in 1:3 was to show us that those "spiritual blessings" issue from God the Father through our Lord Jesus Christ. Thus in 1:5 God the Father "predestinated us unto the adoption of children by Jesus Christ to himself." It should also be pointed out that *"our* Lord Jesus Christ" pertains only to His people. In a special way He is Lord of the saints, as He is called "King of the nations" (Jer. 10:7); and certainly He is the Saviour of those alone who acknowledge Him as their Saviour.

God Alone Can Bless

What was it that occasioned Paul's outburst of joyous praise to the God and Father of our Lord Jesus Christ? This: "Who hath blessed us with all spiritual blessings in heavenly places in Christ." As God alone is styled the "Blessed" One (Mark 14:61) so, as Goodwin points out, He alone blesses or is able to do so. When creatures bless, they can only do so "in the name of the LORD" (Ps. 129:8). When man is made an instrument to convey good things to us, he cannot make them blessings. We are to have recourse to God for those. God has blessed us under the relation of His being our covenant God and our Father through Christ.

"God [even our own God] shall bless us" (Ps. 67:6), for having taken upon Himself to be such to us, He cannot but bless us. This is obviously the force of the duplication which immediately follows: "God *shall* bless us" (v. 7). He has blessed us by giving Himself to us. And how is it that He has become "our *own* God"? Why, by choosing us to be His. Therefore we are termed "his own elect" (Luke 18:7)—made His own by sovereign choice.

As "Our Father," God Blesses Us

Likewise God blesses us under the relation of "our Father." This was purposely foretold of old, for the first human beings who pronounced blessing upon others were those who bore the relation of *fathers*. Having love and goodwill to their children, it was natural to wish them well. Therefore the fathers sought God to perform their desire as that which was not in their own power to do. Thus we find the patriarchs blessing their children and posterity (Gen. 27:1-36; 48:9). So too we recall that utterance of our Lord's, "If ye then, being evil [filled with self-love, yet moved by natural affection], know how to give good gifts unto your children, how much more shall your Father which is in heaven give good things?" (Matt. 7:11). To this very end He was pleased to become a Father to us. Being the Blessed One He is in Himself an ocean of all blessings, which seeks an outlet for itself to communicate to those whom He has loved and chosen. He has become our Father for the very purpose of lavishing His love and grace upon His dear children.

Let us notice carefully the tense of the verb in Ephesians 1:3. It is not "who will bless us," nor "who is blessing us" but "who *hath* blessed us." The time when God bestowed all spiritual blessings upon His people in Christ was when He chose them in Him, even before heaven and earth were called into existence. Supercreation blessings are here in view. In His eternal decree God the Father gave to His people both being and well-being in Christ. In the order of His counsels, that was prior to His foreview of their fall in Adam. This is evident from what follows: "According as he hath chosen us in him [Christ] before the foundation of the world, that we should be holy and without blame before him" (Eph. 1:4). Note the "having predestinated" in verse 5 and the "hath made us" in verse 6 and contrast with "in whom we *have* redemption" in verse 7, which harmonizes with II Timothy 1:9: which "according to his own purpose and grace, which was given us in Christ Jesus before the world began." The purpose in that verse is all one with the blessing of Ephesians 1:3.

"Who hath blessed us with all spiritual *blessings*." Each word is selected with divine precision and propriety. It is not all spiritual "gifts" or "enrichments" but "blessings," because the word *blessing* accords with God's new-covenant title here and emphasizes that these are *covenant* bestowments. As Goodwin reminds us, this is "that original word under which the promise of the covenant of grace was at the first given to Abraham the father of the faithful, as that which contained all particular good things—as his loins did [contain] that 'seed' to whom that promise was made."

"In blessing I will bless thee" (Gen. 22:17). Though the New Testament uses higher terms than the Old to express spiritual things, it did not alter this expression, for no better was to be found. In His first public sermon Christ repeatedly declared, "Blessed are . . ." When He ascended, His last act was to bless (Luke 24:50), and at the last day—when heaven's doors are opened to all the righteous—their eternal happiness is expressed by, "Come, ye blessed of my Father" (Matt. 25:34).

Our Spiritual Blessings

"Who hath blessed us with all *spiritual* blessings." (1) In contrast with the blessings promised to the nation of Israel under the old covenant, which were material and temporal (Deut. 28:1-8). (2) In contrast with the common blessings of creation and providence which the nonelect share with the people of God, for He "maketh his sun to rise on the evil and the good, and sendeth the rain on the just and on the unjust" (Matt. 5:45). (3) In explanation of His promise to Abraham: "That the blessing of Abraham might come on the Gentiles through Jesus Christ; that we might receive the promise of the Spirit through faith" (Gal. 3:14). The second clause of this verse is an exposition of the first showing what sort of blessing was meant. (4) Spiritual blessings are withheld from the reprobate and are tokens of our eternal heritage. (5) Spiritual blessings are actually what dispose the heart to thanksgiving. Temporal mercies simply furnish motives to give thanks.

Universality of the Blessings

"Who hath blessed us with *all* spiritual blessings." Note well it is not simply "who hath blessed me" but "us." The spiritual blessings which God bestows upon one of His people He bestows upon them all. "Whom he did predestinate, them he also called: and whom he called, them he also justified; and whom he justified, them he also glorified" (Rom. 8:30). Some believers think they can be justified and yet not be sanctified.

However Romans 8:32 says, "He that spared not his own Son, but delivered him up for us all, how shall he not with him also freely give us all things?" If Christ be mine, then all spiritual blessings are mine. As Paul declared in another epistle, "All things are your's," and the proof he gave was "And ye are Christ's; and Christ is God's" (I Cor. 3:21-23). As Goodwin puts it, "If any one blessing, then . . . all; they hang together and go in a cluster." Everything necessary to give each Christian title and fitness for heaven is his.

Our Heavenly Blessings

"Who hath blessed us with all spiritual blessings in *heavenly* places in Christ." The Greek New Testament has the article before *heavenly* and nothing to warrant the word *places* supplied by our translators. Bagster's Interlinear is much to be preferred—"in the heavenlies." Nor need the English reader have any difficulty: the same expression occurs again in Ephesians 1:20, where its meaning is plain. Our spiritual blessings are said to be "in the heavenlies" to mark the distinction between them and the blessings Israel enjoyed in Canaan. More remotely still, they point a contrast with those blessings God blessed us with in Adam while he was in Eden (Gen. 1:27-28). Christians have their "citizenship" in heaven (rendered "conversation" in Philippians 3:20). They are "partakers of the heavenly calling" (Heb. 3:1). They have been begotten to an inheritance which is "reserved in heaven" for them (I Peter 1:4). Again quoting Goodwin: "Christ is the Lord from heaven, a heavenly man (I Cor. 15:47-48); therefore being blessed in and together with Him we are blessed with heavenly blessings and raised up to heavenly places in Him (2:6)."

"Who hath blessed us with all spiritual blessings in the heavenlies *in Christ*." Out of Christ there is no spiritual blessing whatever for any soul, but in Him there is blessing abundant for all eternity. The words "in Christ" signify "in union with Him": a mystical, legal, and vital union. It is in Christ we are loved by God (Rom. 8:39). It was in Christ he drew us nigh to Himself (Eph.

2:13). In Him we are "complete" (Col. 2:10). We are "all one in Christ" (Gal. 3:28). The departed saints are still "in Christ" (I Thess. 4:16). And it is of the Father that we are "in Christ" (I Cor. 1:30). But though all our blessings are in Him we can only live in the power and enjoyment of them as *faith* looks away from self and all its concerns and is occupied entirely with Him. "Thanks be unto God for his unspeakable gift" (II Cor. 9:15).

Chapter 11

PRAYER FOR FAITH AND KNOWLEDGE

EPHESIANS 1:15-17

IN THE FIRST HALF OF EPHESIANS 1 we have what is probably the profoundest and most comprehensive doctrinal summary to be found in Holy Writ; in the second half of the chapter we are shown, by implication, what our response should be to that doctrine. In view of the wondrous spiritual blessings with which God has blessed us, His people in Christ, we should go to Him in praise and prayer. Those duties are clearly suggested by the example which the apostle sets before us here. His prayer on this occasion is the longest one recorded in the New Testament. It reaches depths and points to heights which faith alone can sound and scale. For the purpose of analysis we may outline the prayer thus. First, its occasion, when the apostle had heard of the faith and love of the Ephesian saints (v. 15). Second, its nature, namely, praise and petition (vv. 15-16). Third, its Object, "the God of our Lord Jesus Christ, the Father of glory" (v. 17). Fourth, its requests (vv. 17-19), which we consider to be four in number. Fifth, its revelation, concerning Christ and the Church (vv. 20-23).

Occasion of the Prayer

First, the occasion for the prayer. "Wherefore I also, after I heard of your faith in the Lord Jesus, and love unto all the saints, cease not to give thanks for you, making mention of you in my prayers" (Eph. 1:15-16). The opening "wherefore" intimates to us why the apostle prayed as he did here. Most writers restrict Paul's reason for writing to what immediately follows. He had received tidings of their spiritual prosperity and that caused him to bless God for His goodness to them and to seek further favors for them. While that is undoubtedly to be included, yet we see no reason why the "wherefore" should be severed from what precedes. In the previous verses a description is given of the inestimable benefits which had been conferred on them. As Paul considered how God had chosen, predestinated, redeemed them by the blood of His Son, given them faith, sealed them by His Spirit, he could not forbear to give thanks for them, and he ceased not to do so. After a most precise doctrinal enumeration of the rich blessings which God's people have in and from Christ, Paul rejoiced as he was assured these Ephesians had a personal interest and participation in those blessings.

More immediately still, in the verse preceding, the apostle had pointed out that the climax of those blessings lay in the Holy Spirit of promise, wherewith they had been sealed (identified and secured). This sealing was the "earnest of . . . [their] inheritance, until the redemption of the purchased possession, unto the praise of his glory" (Eph. 1:14). The grand end of God in all the blessings of His so-great salvation was that He should be glorified by and for them. This end had been mentioned in verse 6: "to the praise of the glory of his grace." And in verse 12 in its application to the Jews: "that we should be to the praise of his glory, who first trusted in Christ." And it is mentioned again here in its application to all the Gentiles: "in whom ye also trusted, . . . unto the praise of his glory" (Eph. 1:13-14). *"Wherefore,"* says the apostle, "I . . . cease not to give thanks for you" (Eph. 1:15-16). God is not to lose the revenue of praise due Him. Paul therefore feels it his duty to glorify Him on their behalf. If God glorify us, the least we can do is to act and live to His glory.

Paul a Prisoner in Rome

It is to be remembered that at the time Paul offered up this prayer he was in detention by the Romans, but it is most blessed to mark how he viewed his incarceration: "I therefore, the prisoner of the Lord" (Eph. 4:1). Note that well, my reader. Not the prisoner of Caesar but of the Lord. Paul knew full well that none could lay hands on him except as it was ordered by the One who regulates every creature and every event, "For of him, and through him, and to him are all things: to whom be glory for ever. Amen" (Rom. 11:36). Equally blessed it is to behold how this "ambassador in bonds" (Eph. 6:20) occupied himself: not in repining at the unkindness of Providence, asking "What have I done to deserve such treatment?" but rather in praising and petitioning God. And do you not think there is an intimate connection between the two things? Most assuredly. There can be no peace for the mind, no joy of heart, if we fail to recognize that our lot—our circumstances, our condition—is fully ordered by a sovereign and gracious God.

Paul said he *also* gave thanks, meaning in addition to the thanks of the Ephesian believers themselves and those who had communicated to Paul the latest tidings of their case. Doubtless those saints were full of gratitude to God because he brought them out of darkness into his marvelous light. And here the apostle assured them that he joined with them in fervent thanksgiving for that glorious event. He also assured them that he continued to bless God as he received word that their lives gave evidence of the genuineness of their conversion. Nothing affords the servant of Christ such happiness as hearing of the salvation of sinners and the accompanying transformation in their lives "I have no greater joy than to hear that my children walk in the truth" (III John 4). Paul himself was the founder of the Ephesian assembly (Act 19:1-10; 20:17-38), but he had been away from them now for several years Therefore the statement "after I *heard* of your faith" is not to be understood as meaning for the first time. Paul continued to receive most favorable reports of their spiritual health and prosperity.

Praise Belongs to God

By making known his thanksgiving to God on their behalf the apostle also intimated their own privilege and duty. Paul would by his example stir up their hearts to the renewed praising of God for His sovereign and amazing goodness to them. Nothing is more acceptable to Him; "whoso offereth praise glorifieth me" (Ps. 50:23). Nothing is more becoming in us; "rejoice in the LORD, O ye righteous: for praise is comely for the upright" (Ps. 33:1). Nothing is more conducive to stirring us up to this God-honoring and delightful exercise than considering the greatness of His benefits to us, named in the verses preceding this prayer. If the Christian takes a believing view of all his blessings in Christ, labors to see his own personal interest in the same, and then considers how God has ordered this not only for his salvation but for "the praise of his glory," his heart cannot but be moved to pour out itself in adoration and gratitude. Nor is such thanksgiving to be confined to his own case but rendered for all who give evidence that they are new creatures in Christ.

"Faith Worketh"

"After I heard of your faith in the Lord Jesus, and love unto all the saints" (Eph. 1:15). Faith and love are the best evidences of a genuine conversion, for they are the fruits brought forth by the two principal graces communicated to us at the new birth. Faith is known by what it effects and produces. It was not the Ephesians' first believing in Christ that the apostle alluded to, for he had witnessed that for himself, but rather the working and constancy of their faith of which he had heard—the influence it had on their daily walk. The faith of God's elect is active in purifying the heart (Acts 15:9) by engaging it with holy objects. The faith of God's elect brings forth good works (James 2:14-22), such as those described in Hebrews 11. This faith "overcometh the world" (I John 5:4), enabling its possessor to resist the world's seduction, scorn its principles and policy, and be "not of it" in his affections and ways.*

Another mark of the faith of God's elect is that it "worketh by love" (Gal. 5:6): love for the truth, for Christ, and for His redeemed. Faith is but an empty name if it does not fructify in love. Faith in Christ is only a delusion if it issues not in love for those who are His. Scripture is too plain on this point to admit any uncertainty: "If a man say, I love God, and hateth his brother, he is a liar: for he that loveth not his brother whom he hath seen, how can he love God whom he hath not seen?" (I John 4:20). Saving faith in Christ and spiritual love for all whom He loves are inseparably connected (see Col. 1:4; Philemon 5; I John 3:23). "We know that we have passed from death unto life, because we love the brethren" (I John 3:14). If we love one saint as a "saint"—for what we see of Christ in him—we shall love *all* saints. Faith in Christ and love for His people are inseparable, and as one waxes or wanes so does the other. If my love for Christians is cooling (if I pray less for them and am less active in seeking to promote their highest good), my faith in Christ is declining.

*[Editor's Note: Some Greek scholars believe the word here translated "faith" (*pistis*) to mean "faithfulness" in the original.]

The Nature of Faith

Second, the nature of the prayer. The character of this particular prayer was twofold: it consisted of thanksgiving and requests—praise for what God had done for the Ephesians and wrought in and through them, petitions for further blessings for them. The order of these two things is something we need to lay carefully to heart, for there is much failure at this very point. Scripture is very explicit on this: "In everything by prayer and supplication with thanksgiving let your requests be made known unto God" (Phil. 4:6). "Continue in prayer, and watch in the same with thanksgiving" (Col. 4:2). Here we see how the apostle set us an example. Praise gives wings to our petitions. The more my heart is occupied with God's goodness, the more thankful I am for the favors already bestowed on me, the more will my soul be stirred up in seeking further mercies, the more liberty shall I experience in making requests for them, and the more expectation shall I have to receive the same. Cultivate the habit of gratitude, reader, if you would be more successful at the throne of grace. "I sought the LORD, and he heard me" is preceded by "I will bless the LORD at all times: his praise shall continually be in my mouth" (Ps. 34:4, 1).

We should thank God not only for His mercies to us personally but also for His grace to fellow saints, which is more especially in view in our present passage. Said Paul on another occasion, "But we are bound [as a matter of duty] to give thanks alway to God for you, brethren beloved of the Lord, because God hath from the beginning chosen you to salvation" (II Thess. 2:13). "For what thanks can we render to God again for you, for all the joy wherewith we joy for your sakes before our God?" (I Thess. 3:9). There is so little of this unselfish affection in our day.

But Paul did more than give thanks for what God had done for the Ephesians and wrought in them; he requested *further* blessings on their behalf. Carnal wisdom would draw the very opposite conclusion from that opening "wherefore"; it would have inferred that since they were so highly favored of the Lord there was no need to seek additional mercies for them. But the spiritual mind sees in the smile of God on a people an encouragement to ask for further benefits to be vouchsafed them. Similarly should we argue in our own case, regarding each fresh token of love from God as merely a down payment of more. Note that Paul did not pray that God would exempt them from persecution or give them a smooth passage through this world. Nor did he beg God to make them eminent winners of souls. Nor did he ask that they might be given a deep insight into the mysteries of prophecy or skill in "rightly dividing the word of truth," as might be expected if many of our moderns were right. What he *did* pray for we hope to consider in due course.

The Object of Faith

Third, the Object of the prayer: "the God of our Lord Jesus Christ, the Father of glory" (Eph. 1:17). As we dwelt at some length upon God as "the God of our Lord Jesus Christ" when we expounded on Ephesians 1:3, we will confine ourselves now to "the Father of glory." With this phrase should be compared "the Lord of glory" (I Cor. 2:8) and "the Spirit of glory" (I Peter 4:14) which bring out the coequality of the three Persons in the Godhead.

"The Father of glory." Ah, who is competent to write thereon! To describe or even define the meaning of that ineffable title transcends the power of any mortal tongue or pen. At most we can but offer a few notes. We are told that the Father is "glorious in holiness" (Exodus 15:11), that "his work is honourable and glorious" (Ps. 111:3), that he is seated upon a "glorious high throne" (Jer. 17:12). We read of His "glorious voice" (Isa. 30:30), His glorious apparel 'Isa. 63:1), His "glorious arm" (Isa. 63:12), the "glorious honour of . . . [His] majesty," and the "glorious majesty of his kingdom" (Ps. 145:5, 12). Well may we exclaim, "Blessed be thy glorious name, which is exalted above all blessing and praise" (Neh. 9:5), for "his glory is above the earth and heaven" (Ps. 148:13).

When we have affirmed that "the glory of God is the excellency of His being or character, that it is the sum of His perfections or the outshining of all His attributes in resplendent combination," we are conscious of the paucity of human language and of the incapability of the finite to comprehend the Infinite. But if we have experimentally tasted of "the glory of his grace" (Eph. 1:6), if we have felt in our souls "his glorious power" (Col. 1:11), if our sin-blinded eyes have been opened to see Him "glorious in holiness" (Exodus 15:11), then we *know* He is the glorious God, even though we can only lisp out what He has made known to our hearts. All the regenerate have such a knowledge (though only a foretaste). "For God, who commanded the light to shine out of darkness, hath shined in our hearts, to give the light of the knowledge of the glory of God in the face of Jesus Christ" (II Cor. 4:6). By supernatural illumination and inward revelation (cf. Matt. 16:17; Gal. 1:16) the saints are given spiritual discernment and a view of the divine glory, such as no creature can communicate to another and which no mere mental acumen can ever attain. They know without any uncertainty that He *is* "the Father of glory."

The Father of Glory

Thomas Goodwin states: "He is called 'the Father of glory.' First, by way of *eminency of fatherhood*: there is no such father as He is. He is a glorious Father, and by a Hebrewism He is a Father of glory: that is, a glorious Father, such as no father else is. He is called 'the King of glory': there are other kings, but He only is the glorious king. There are other fathers: he only is the Father of glory; He is therefore called the 'heavenly Father.' . . . Heaven and glory are the highest things we can conceive of, and therefore when He would put forth how great a God, how glorious a Father, He is, He calleth Himself the heavenly Father, the Father of glory, in distinction from all fatherhoods. The use of this is: Never be ashamed of your Father, you that are the sons of God, for you are the highest born in the world—no nobility rises up to *glory*. Therefore walk worthy of Him, and let your light so shine before men that you may glorify your Father, the Father of glory, which is in Heaven." As the God of glory, the Father first appeared to the father of the faithful, when He called him to leave Chaldea and go forth to Canaan (Acts 7:2). And as the most glorious God He reveals Himself to the newly born soul.

Second, God is designated "the Father of glory" not only because He is infinitely glorious in Himself, but also because He is the Bestower of glory upon His dear children: "The LORD will give grace and glory" (Ps. 84:11). He is the Author of all the glory with which His saints are or ever will be invested. There is what we may call (for want of a better term) the *official* glory of God, which is incommunicable; and there is His *moral* glory, of which He makes His people partakers. That distinction is observed in those words of Christ's: "The glory which thou gavest me I have given them"; on the other hand, "Father, I will that they also, whom thou hast given me, be with me where I am; that they may behold my [mediatorial and incommunicable] glory, which thou hast given me" (John 17:22, 24). A measure of His moral glory is communicated to us in this life: "But we all with open face beholding as in a glass the glory of the Lord, are changed into the same image from glory to glory, even as by the Spirit of the Lord" (II Cor. 3:18). Utterly unable as we are to explain the mystery of that spiritual alchemy, yet the fact is clearly stated. And the fact receives verification in the experience of the saints, for as faith is exercised that divine glory has a transforming efficacy on their souls.

Third, there was a particular propriety in addressing God on this occasion as "the Father of glory." As we have pointed out in former chapters, the titles given to God when approaching Him in prayer were not selected at random, nor were different ones used merely for the sake of variety. Rather was the particular character in which God was viewed most in accord with the special exercises of Paul's heart and the specific nature of the requests he was about to make. Such was the case here. He was about to pray for spiritual knowledge of glorious things, an apprehension of the riches of the glory of God's inheritance in the saints and of the exceeding greatness of His power. Suitably, therefore, he called on the Father of glory just as he addressed Him as "the God of hope" when making request that the saints might "abound in hope, through the power of the Holy Ghost" (Rom. 15:13).

We cannot anticipate too much that which immediately follows in this prayer, but we may at least point out that each of its petitions is closely related to the particular title which is here ascribed to the Father. Paul asked God to give His people "the spirit of wisdom and revelation in the knowledge of him"— a knowledge of Him as the glorious One. Paul also requested that they might know "what is the hope of his calling." From I Peter 5:10 we learn that, among other things, this calling is "unto his eternal glory." Yes, we are called to glory itself (II Peter 1:3). The phrase "riches of the glory of his inheritance in the saints" (Eph. 1:18) signifies a glorious inheritance, an inheritance in the Glory. In making request that we might know "what is the exceeding greatness of his power to us-ward" something more than the bare exercise of Omnipotence is included, namely, the putting forth in a special manner of "his glorious power" (Col. 1:11). Thus we may better perceive why the apostle here addressed God as "the Father of glory," this title being most consistent to the particular favors he was about to ask for.

What We Should Pray For

Our fathers used to say, "A word to the wise is sufficient." And so it ought to be. To a receptive mind and responsive heart a hint should be enough. Thus, if a godly and mature saint who was deeply interested in my spiritual welfare wrote to say he was praying unceasingly that God would grant me a larger measure of patience or that He would make me more humble, then—if I value his judgment—I would at once regard that as a gracious word from God, informing me what I especially need to be petitioning Him for. We should look in this way on this prayer we are now considering. In making known to these saints what he sought from the throne of grace on their behalf, the apostle intimated indirectly what they needed to make the particular burden of *their* supplications. If the Ephesian saints needed to ask these blessings, most certainly God's people today need to do so. Let us then view this prayer as divine instruction regarding what we most need to pray for.

The Spirit of Wisdom and Revelation

"That the God of our Lord Jesus Christ, the Father of glory, may give unto you the spirit of wisdom and revelation in the knowledge of him" (Eph. 1:17). We believe that God is here viewed in this way to strengthen our faith and to fire our hearts. Request is to be made for a fuller knowledge and a closer communion with God. To encourage us to ask for this knowledge with confidence, we are assured that the "God of our Lord Jesus Christ" gives this knowledge to those who seek it. To stimulate our aspirations we are reminded that He is "the Father of glory." Then with what trustful reliance we should present these petitions! With what ardor we should seek for their fulfillment! If we view God in this character, our view will have a most animating effect upon the soul. This God is the One who so loved us that He gave His only begotten Son for us, the One who was the all-absorbing Portion of our Saviour during the days of His flesh. He is His and our covenant God. Further, He is the most glorious Father whom Christ revealed and of whom we have already obtained a glimpse in the face of the Redeemer.

We are living in a day of such appalling ignorance that nothing may be taken for granted. Therefore we need to point out that in asking God for these particular things Paul did not signify the Ephesians were totally devoid of them any more than his opening "grace be unto you and peace" (1:2) implied they possessed neither the one nor the other; rather he desired for them an increase of both. Thus it is here. They already had a saving knowledge of God or he would not have addressed them as "saints" and "faithful in Christ Jesus" (1:1). In asking God to grant them the "Spirit of wisdom and revelation," Paul most certainly was not making request for the Spirit to be given them for the first time, for he had just affirmed in the context that they were "sealed with that Holy Spirit of promise" (v. 13). No, rather he was making request for further supplies and a richer outpouring of the Spirit upon them. In this way we must view the words "in the knowledge of him." Paul prayed for a fuller, deeper, closer acquaintance and fellowship with Him, an "increasing in the knowledge of God" as Colossians 1:10 expresses it. So too must we regard each of the other things prayed for.

"That the God of our Lord Jesus Christ, the Father of glory, may give unto you the Spirit of wisdom and revelation." The careful reader will note that the word *Spirit* is spelled with a small *s* in his Bible, and our capitalizing of it calls for an explanation. The original Greek manuscripts were written in capitals throughout so that there is nothing to distinguish between "the Spirit" and "the spirit." Thus it is entirely a matter of interpretation on the part of the translators in using the small or capital letter. Where it is the "Holy Spirit" or the "Spirit of God" all is quite clear. But when it reads, "That which is born of the Spirit is *spirit*" (John 3:6), the principle of grace or "new nature" which is imparted to the regenerate partakes of the character of its Begetter or Communicator and is named after Him. Consequently there are some passages where it is rather difficult to determine whether it is the Giver of His gift which is in view, whether the reference is to the person of the Spirit or to His gracious operations, the one being so inseparably connected with the other. In such cases, this writer includes *both*.

The word *spirit* is sometimes used as expressive of such mental states and acts as the new nature brings forth in the believer yet under the influence of the Holy Spirit. Thus we read of the "spirit of meekness" (I Cor. 4:21), the "same spirit of faith" (II Cor. 4:13), the "spirit of your mind" (Eph. 4:23). On the other hand when we read of the "Spirit of truth" (John 15:26), the "Spirit of holiness" (Rom. 1:4), the "Spirit of Christ" (Rom. 8:9) it is obvious that the person of the Spirit is in view. But when we are told, "The fruit of the Spirit is love, joy, peace," and so on (Gal. 5:22), what are we to understand? In the context Paul has described some of the "works of the flesh," or old nature (Eph. 5:19-21). Therefore we conclude that the products of the new nature, or "spirit," are set over in contrast with the products of the flesh. Yet, since the new nature bears fruit only as it is energized by the indwelling Spirit, He is the real Author of that fruit and is to be acknowledged as such. Thus, this writer would give the twofold meaning to "the Spirit" in Galatians 5:22, namely, what the Spirit of God produces through the principle of grace in the regenerate. And it is thus he regards the expression in the verse now before us.

It is true that the saint received the "spirit of wisdom" at the time of his regeneration (symbolized by the case of the one described in Mark 5:15), and it was the Holy Spirit who imparted that wisdom to him and who was also the Author of its development and activities.

But something more than the spirit of wisdom is here included, namely, revelation, which cannot be understood as an inherent gift. Had the verse only named the "spirit of wisdom" we would have regarded it as referring to a principle infused into Christians. But "revelation" necessarily implies a Revealer, for revealing is an act of one without us, of a person distinct from us, and Scripture leaves us in no doubt as to who that person is. "Eye hath not seen, nor ear heard, neither have entered into the heart of man, the things which God hath prepared for them that love him. But God hath *revealed* them unto us *by his Spirit*. . . . Now we have received, not the spirit of the world, but the spirit which is of God; that we might know the things that are freely given to us of God" (I Cor. 2:9-10, 12).

Our understanding then of this opening petition is that the apostle first sought from God an increased measure of the Spirit, from whom all spiritual wisdom comes and who reveals the certainty, the reality, the surpassing blessedness of divine things. Second, Paul sought for an enlargement of the gift of wisdom to be bestowed upon the Ephesians, a fuller capacity to take in the things of God, that He would further manifest Himself to them (John 14:21), that they might perceive more clearly His ineffable and soul-satisfying glory. Paul prayed that God would make good His promise that all their children would be taught of the Lord (Isa. 54:13), for it is in such ways that we obtain knowledge of Him. And that leads us to ask more distinctly: "Knowledge *of whom?* Of the Father or of Christ?" Some believe the former to be true, but the majority hold to the latter, being unduly influenced by Philippians 3:8. The "Father of glory" is the One spoken of in the immediate context of Ephesians 1:15-23, and it is to Him that the "his calling," "his inheritance," and "his power" of verses 18-19 clearly refer. Yet He was specifically viewed as the "God of our Lord Jesus Christ." So, putting the two together, it is the knowledge of God in Christ which is here referred to.

The Knowledge of God

Coming to the substance of this petition, what is meant by the "knowledge of Him"? As more than one kind of faith is spoken of in Scripture, so there are several species of "knowledge"—not only of different objects and subjects known but of ways of knowing the same. One may know or be fully assured from the testimony of reliable witnesses that fire produces most unpleasant effects if an unprotected hand is thrust into it. But if I have personally felt the consequences of being burned, I have quite a different order of knowledge. The one may be termed notional, the other experiential—usually wrongfully termed "experimental." The distinction frequently drawn between real and assumed knowledge does not define the difference. When the unclean spirit said to Christ, "I *know thee* who thou art" (Mark 1:24), his knowledge was both real and accurate, but it profited him nothing spiritually. On the other hand, "they that know thy name will put their trust in thee" (Ps. 9:10) speaks of a knowledge which inspires such confidence that its possessor cannot help but believe.

As there are degrees of trusting God, so there are degrees in our knowledge of Him, and the measure in which we know Him will determine the extent to which we love, trust, and obey Him. Since that is the case, we may at once perceive the vital importance of obtaining a fuller knowledge of God and why this is the *first* petition of the four. The defectiveness of our faith, love, and obedience is to be traced to the inadequacy of our knowledge of God. If we were more intimately and influentially acquainted with Him, we would love Him more fervently, trust Him more implicitly, and obey Him more freely. We cannot sufficiently realize the value of a better knowledge of God. But let us again remark it is not a mere notional knowledge of Him but a visual and vital one that is needed. The former kind is one in which ideas or mental images are presented to the understanding to work upon, but the latter brings the reality of them down into the heart. By such a knowledge we behold the glory of the Lord and are "changed into the same image" (II Cor. 3:18).

There is also a knowledge by way of special gifts which is quite distinct from this spiritual knowledge. One may have much of the former and very little of the latter, as with the Corinthians. They came behind "in no gift," being "enriched by him, in all utterance, and in all knowledge" (I Cor. 1:7, 5). They were not only well informed but also able to so express themselves on spiritual things as to stamp upon the minds of their hearers an accurate image of them. Yet of those same highly gifted and talented Christians Paul said, "And I, brethren, could not speak unto you as unto spiritual, but as unto carnal, even as unto babes" (I Cor. 3:1). Thus they were largely deficient in spiritual knowledge. But there are other saints with a much deeper and closer acquaintance of God, who are incapable of expressing themselves so freely and fluently as the Corinthians. A heart knowledge, not a head knowledge, of God makes a person more holy.

The opening petition in these verses in Ephesians 1 was that the saints might be granted through the operations of the Spirit a fuller entry into that knowledge of God in which eternal life primarily consists. It was a request that they might perceive more clearly the glory of God, to give them an inward realization of His ineffable perfections, to make their hearts so in love with these perfections that their wills would choose them for their chief delight. God first prepares the mind by an act of renewal to receive spiritual instruction, giving His people an understanding that they might know Him (I John 5:20), and then He imparts to them a larger measure of "the spirit of wisdom and revelation." At the new birth we are called out of darkness into God's marvelous light, yet further light, fuller manifestations of Himself to us are needed if we are to know Him better.

God has promised, "All *shall* know me" (Heb. 8:11). Isaiah prophesied, "All thy children shall be taught of the LORD" (Isa. 54:13). Those promises are for faith to lay hold of and plead before God. Neither the arts nor the sciences can impart one eternal idea to the soul; still less can they impart any vital knowledge of God Himself. It is only in His light that we can see light. It is only as He shines upon our understandings and reveals Himself to our hearts that we can become better acquainted with Him. It is by means of the Word that the Holy Spirit carries on the work of God in the soul; therefore whenever we read or meditate upon it we need to beg Him to take of the things of God and of Christ and show them to us, apply them to our hearts, that we may be more and more changed into their very image. But it is one thing to be convinced of that need and another to put it into practice. Pride, or self-sufficiency, is the chief deterrent. The things of God are only revealed to those who preserve this humble characteristic of the "babes" (Matt. 11:25).

The Greek word rendered "knowledge" in Ephesians 1:17 is *epignōsei*. *Gnosis* signifies "knowledge" and *epi* "*upon*." So as our moderns would express it, it is "knowledge plus," or as the lexicons define it "full knowledge." The word occurs in Romans 3:20, which will enable the average reader to better perceive its force: "By the law is the knowledge [or full knowledge] of sin." A man knows something of what sin is by the light of nature; but only as sin is viewed and measured in the light of the authority, the spirituality, the strictness of the divine law, does he obtain a full and adequate knowledge of the sinfulness of sin. Thus something more than a bare, fragmentary inchoate acquaintance with God was here prayed for—a full knowledge of Him. Not a *perfect* knowledge but a firsthand, well-rounded, intimate, and thorough knowledge of His person, His character, His perfections, especially as He is revealed in and by Christ.

The margin of some of our Bibles gives "for the acknowledgment of him," as the Greek may be thus rendered. To acknowledge is to own a knowledge of, to admit the same, and this we do of God first in our secret communion with Him and then outwardly by confessing Him before men with our lips and lives. Goodwin pointed out this distinction thus: "One knoweth a stranger, but he doth 'acknowledge' he knew before his *friend*. So that the intimate knowledge of God as of a friend is the thing which the apostle meant. As He said of Moses 'I know thee by name' and Moses knew God in turn: and as John 10:14 'I know my sheep, and am known of mine.' It is to have this mutual knowledge, God knowing me and I knowing God so as to converse daily with Him and to have communion with Him as with a friend." Thus we see the excellence of this particular knowledge. It is not only a more enlarged knowledge about the things of God such as Christ communicated to His disciples in Luke 24:27 but also the end or issue of such knowledge, namely, such a knowledge as leads to real fellowship with Him, intimate communion with Him as with a friend. This is the ultimate intent of God in His grace and favor to us: that we may so know Him as to acquaint ourselves with Him, delight ourselves in Him, be free with Him, enjoy mutual converse with Him. "Our fellowship is with the Father, and with his Son Jesus Christ" (I John 1:3), so that He knows us and we know Him, He owns us and we own Him, and as the consequence— we cleave to Him as our supreme Good, give up ourselves to Him as our absolute Lord, delight ourselves in Him as our everlasting Portion. That acknowledgment will be evidenced in our daily walk by submitting to His authority, seeking to please Him in all things, and thus becoming more and more lively toward Him. Then obedience will be spontaneous and joyful. The more we increase in this knowledge of God the easier shall we find it to acknowledge Him in all our ways (Prov. 3:6).

Spiritual Knowledge a Divine Revelation

Now this spiritual knowledge of God which leads to the practical acknowledgment of Him comes to us in a way of wisdom (that is, faith exercising itself on the Word) and of revelation (that is, the Spirit operating by the Word). The word *revelation* in this connection signifies the particularity of it; something is made known by the Spirit to the saints which is hidden from the wise and prudent of this world, as is clear from Matthew 11:25 and 27. It is a knowledge which is peculiar to the regenerate. *Revelation* also connotes a knowledge which is additional to what "wisdom" or the workings of faith produce; not a different kind of knowledge but a different degree of it. Faith obtains clear apprehension of God, but when the Spirit shines through the Word upon the understanding, God's glory is more awe-inspiring to the soul.

Revelation also emphasizes the excellency of this knowledge; that of wisdom is discoursive or acquired by information, but that of revelation is intuitive. That difference has to be experienced in order to be understood. But has not the Christian reader, when at prayer, been favored at times with an unusual revelation of God to his soul which at other seasons was not the case!

In conclusion we will summarize the exposition of Goodwin, who pointed out the bearing of each word of the text on its central theme. An increased, more intimate knowledge of God may be obtained *in a way* of wisdom, that is, by faith making sanctified use of reason, by meditating on the various parts of truth where God's excellencies are revealed. That is the ordinary way, for wisdom is a rational laying of things together, perceiving their harmony. But there is also a way of revelation whereby the Holy Spirit comes down into the heart with a beam from heaven, enabling us to discern the glory of God such as no cognition can produce. It was thus with Job when he said, "But now mine eye seeth thee" (Job 42:5). It is thus when Christ makes good that word "I will come in to him and sup with him" (Rev. 3:20). This is not done apart from the Word but by God causing a beam of light from that Word to suddenly and powerfully strike into the heart.

Chapter 12

PRAYER FOR UNDERSTANDING

EPHESIANS 1:18

"THE EYES OF YOUR UNDERSTANDING being enlightened, that ye may know what is the hope of his calling" (Eph. 1:18). In taking up this second petition in the apostle's prayer we shall endeavor to supply answers to the following questions: What relation does the opening clause of our verse bear to that which precedes and that which follows? Exactly what is signified by the "hope of his calling"? What is meant by a knowledge of the same? It is one thing to be familiar with the *sound* of a verse, but it is quite another to ascertain its *sense,* as there is much difference between answering these questions and proving them to be correct. It is just because so many people assume they understand the meaning of various passages that they never obtain a clear insight of the passages' purport. Because the wording of a verse is simple, it does not follow that we understand its connections or even its connotations. The mere fact that either "hope" or "calling" signifies a certain thing in some verses gives no guarantee that it means precisely the same thing when used in others. We are only on safe ground when we plead ignorance and prayerfully study each verse for ourselves.

"The eyes of your understanding being enlightened." Four different views have been taken on the relation of this clause. First, that it is to be taken absolutely and regarded as a separate petition. This appears to have been the idea entertained by our translators, as their punctuation suggests. Second, that it is in apposition to and explanatory of the verse preceding—the view adopted by Charles Hodge. Third, that it states an effect of the gift of "the spirit of wisdom and revelation in the knowledge of him"—the concept of J. C. Philpot. Fourth, that it is separate from the preceding petition and introductory to this second one. This is the way Thomas Goodwin expounds it and the way we personally understand it. No difference in doctrine is involved whichever view is taken. According to the hermeneutical principle of the analogy of faith, it is equally permissible to link this clause with what precedes or with what follows, or even with both. Because we are addressing ourselves to critical students as well as the more ordinary reader, we have penned this paragraph, for a word of explanation was required as to why we have deviated from the common course.

109

The Glory of God

Goodwin has well pointed out that there are two things to be considered in connection with our blessedness in heaven: "the happiness that the saints themselves shall enjoy" there and their "communion with God, which is the cause of their happiness." As to which is the greater of them there can be no room for doubt: the Fountain of all blessedness infinitely surpasses our draught therefrom, no matter how abundantly we may drink. Hence Paul began his prayer with a request for a fuller measure of the Spirit that the Ephesians might be brought into a closer communion with God, and then he asked for illumination of understanding that they might obtain a better apprehension and enter into a fuller enjoyment of those things which belonged to their peace. The same two things are kept distinct in Romans 5. First, Paul said that by faith we "rejoice in hope of the glory of God" (v. 2), that is, of the glory we expect to receive from God. This expectation makes us "glory in tribulations also" (v. 3) despite the unpleasantness thereof. But blessed as that is, when Paul reached the climax, he said, "Not only so: we also joy *in God*" (v. 11)—in God Himself.

Two things are indispensable to vision, whether it be physical or spiritual: sight and light. A blind man is incapable of perceiving objects even when the midday sun is shining. The strongest eyes are useless when a person is in total darkness. Now the natural man is without either spiritual sight or spiritual light. He has eyes, but they do not see, perceiving no beauty in Christ that he should desire Him. He is alienated from Him who is Light and therefore dwells and walks in darkness. Hence the natural man receives not the things of the Spirit of God. They are foolishness to him, for he is devoid of spiritual discernment (I Cor. 2:14). But at regeneration the objects of sovereign grace are brought out of darkness into God's marvelous light and are "given an understanding, that they may know him that is true" (I John 5:20), so that they are now capacitated to discern, understand, and enjoy spiritual things. Nevertheless, because ignorance, prejudice, pride, and carnality ever tend to becloud his vision so long as he remains in this world, the Christian is in constant need of having the eyes of his understanding enlightened afresh and of praying with David, "Open thou mine eyes, that I may behold wondrous things out of thy law" (Ps. 119:18).

As the eye is the organ of the body by which we see physical objects, so the understanding is the faculty by which truth is perceived. Yet far more than a mental perception is involved in the apprehension of truth. God's Word is very much more than a species of intellectual propositions; it is a divine revelation, an unveiling of spiritual things, requiring a spiritual faculty to take them in, producing spiritual effects where the revelation is received. Therefore "the eyes of your understanding being enlightened" must not be narrowed down to "your minds being furnished with new ideas." In the Scriptures "light," when used with reference to spiritual things, includes both holiness and happiness. When the Lord Jesus said, "I am the light of the world: he that followeth me shall not walk in darkness, but shall have the light of life" (John 8:12), He signified much more than intellectual illumination. Saints are the "children of light" (I Thess. 5:5) because they have been renewed in the image of Him that is Light; and therefore they are bidden to conduct themselves as such (Eph. 5:8). Thus, "the eyes of your understanding being enlightened" signifies their being divinely anointed, spiritualized, made "single" (Matt. 6:22) and more holy.

Among the high and honorable titles of God, this is used to describe His goodness to the children of men: "He that teacheth man knowledge" (Ps. 94:10). Therefore David added, "Blessed is the man whom thou . . . teachest . . . out of thy law" (v. 12). It is this divine teaching of the saints that is signified by "eyes of your understanding being enlightened," namely, bestowing upon them a teachable disposition, a humble desire to be instructed of God. That teaching consists of God's enabling the mind to perceive spiritual and divine objects and to see their importance and value in such a way as to incline the affections to love them and the will to choose them. God first prepares the heart to receive His truth (Prov. 16:1) and then fills it with the "knowledge of his will in all wisdom and spiritual understanding" (Col. 1:9). His established method is by the Word and by the Spirit, for these two always go together, the Word explaining and the Spirit applying the Word. When the Spirit works by the Word He makes it effectual, through His operations, to build up and perfect the saint.

"Hope" in Scripture

But we must now inquire, "What is meant by 'the hope of His calling'?" This is really a double question: What is meant by the word *hope* in this passage, and what is meant by "his calling"? Before supplying answers may we remind our friends that we are seeking to furnish something more than mere generalizations or even topical chapters, namely, *studies* in the Scriptures. We are not just jotting down the first thoughts on this verse which come to mind but desire to open its meaning, to *expound* it.

In Scripture "hope" always respects something future, and signifies far more than a mere wish that it *may* be realized. It sets forth a confident expectation that it *will* be realized (Ps. 16:9). In many passages "hope" has reference to its *object*, that is, to the thing expected (Rom. 8:25), the One looked to: "O LORD, the hope of Israel" (Jer. 17:13; cf. 50:7). In other passages "hope" refers to the *grace* of hope, that is, the faculty by which we expect. Hope is used in this sense in I Corinthians 13:13: "Now abideth faith, hope, charity." Sometimes "hope" expresses the *assurance* we have of our personal interest in the thing hoped for: "Tribulation worketh patience; and patience, experience; and experience, hope: And hope maketh not ashamed" (Rom. 5:3-5). That is, hope deepens our assurance of our personal confidence in God. In still other cases "hope" has reference to the *ground* of our expectation. The clause "there is hope in Israel concerning this thing" (Ezra 10:2) means there were good grounds to hope for it. "Who against hope believed in hope" (Rom. 4:18): though contrary to nature, Abraham was persuaded he had good and sufficient ground to expect God to make good His promise. The unregenerate are "without hope" (Eph. 2:12). They have hope, but it is based on no solid foundation.

Now in the last mentioned sense we regard the word *hope* as being used in our present passage: that you may know the *ground* on which rests your expectation of His calling, that you may be assured of your personal interest therein, that you may stand in no doubt regarding the same, that you may be so enlightened from above as to be able to clearly perceive that you have both part and lot therein. In other words, that your evidence of this ground of faith may be clear and unmistakable. First, Paul prayed for an increased knowledge of God, that is, such spiritual sights and apprehensions of Him as led to more real and intimate fellowship with Him, which is the basic longing of every renewed soul. And what did he desire next to that? Was it not that which contributed most to his peace and comfort, namely, to be *assured* of his own filial relation to God? What does it avail my soul to perceive the excellency of the divine character unless I have scriptural warrant to view Him as *my* God? *That* is what I need to have continually kept fresh in my heart. This, then, is the second thing which the apostle sought for these saints.

The Gospel's Twofold Call

What is meant by "his calling"? Here is another term which is used by no means uniformly in the Scriptures. Broadly speaking, there is a twofold calling of God or call from God: an external one and an internal one. The former is made to all who hear the gospel: "Unto you, O men, I call; and my voice is to the sons of man" (Prov. 8:4). "Many be called, but few chosen" (Matt. 20:16). That external call through the Scriptures is addressed to human responsibility and meets with universal rejection. "I have called, and ye refused; I have stretched out my hand, and no man regarded" (Prov. 1:24); "Come, for all things are now ready; and they all with one consent began to make excuse" (Luke 14:18).

But God gives another call to His elect: a quickening call, an inward call, an invincible call, what the theologians term His "effectual call." "Whom he did predestinate, them he also called: and whom he called, them he also justified" (Rom. 8:30). *This* is calling from death to life, out of darkness into God's "marvellous light" (I Peter 2:9). As the closing verses of I Corinthians 1 tell us, not many receive *this* call; it is one of mercy and discriminating grace.

Our text then speaks of the effectual call, and it is termed *"his* calling" because God is the Author of it. The regenerate are "the called according to his [eternal] purpose" (Rom. 8:28), because God is the Caller. Yet, having said that much, we have only generalized, and the expositor must particularize if he is to bring out the various shades of meaning which the same word bears in different verses. In some passages the effectual call which God gives His people refers to that work of grace *itself,* as in I Peter 2:9. In others, it concerns more especially that *to which* God has called them—"unto his kingdom and glory," (I Thess. 2:12), "unto holiness" (I Thess. 4:7). As there seems to be nothing in our present verse which requires us to restrict the scope of the word, we shall interpret it in its double sense: "that ye may be assured ye have been made partakers of God's effectual or regenerative call; that ye may perceive the sure grounds of hope which God has called you unto."

Take the calling itself first. Paul desired that the Ephesians might have a better knowledge, or assurance, that they had been supernaturally quickened, personally called out of darkness into God's light. If the Christian measures himself impartially by the Word, he should have no difficulty on that score. He should be certain of his salvation. He ought to be able to say, humbly yet confidently, "One thing I *know,* that, whereas I was blind, now I see" (John 9:25). If I see, with a feeling sense in my heart, what a heinous and filthy thing all sin is, what a depraved and loathsome creature I am by nature, what a sink of iniquity still remains within me, what a suitable and sufficient Saviour Christ is for such a wretch as me, what a lovely and desirable thing holiness is, then I must have been called to life. If I am now conscious of holy desires and endeavors to which I was previously a stranger, then I must be alive in Christ.

Take, second, that to which the Christian is called—in this verse, an assured expectation: "that ye may know what is the hope of his calling." As God has called His people to holiness, so also He has called them to be full of hope and good cheer. The apostle prayed in another place, "Now the God of hope fill you with all joy and peace in believing, that ye may abound in hope, through the power of the Holy Ghost" (Rom. 15:13). Thus, we may understand that by His calling we may know that hope which God has commanded us as Christians to have. First Thessalonians 4:7, "God hath called us not to uncleanness, but unto holiness," means that He *bids* us to be holy, for the third verse of that same chapter declares, "This is the will of God, even your sanctification." In that passage the "will" and "calling" of God are one and the same thing. Thus it may also be understood here: "That ye may know the hope of His revealed will," which He requires us to have.

"That ye may know," not being ignorant or doubtful. This denies one of the doctrines of the Council of Trent: "If any one affirm that a regenerate and justified man is bound to believe that he is *certainly* in the number of the elect, let such an one be accursed." The very fact that Paul was inspired to place on record this petition shows clearly that it is God's will for His people to have assurance, that it is both their privilege and duty to earnestly seek it, and that an increased experience of assurance should be theirs. A doubting Thomas does not honor God.

Assurance of Salvation

Now let us put the whole together. Only as the eyes of our understanding are divinely enlightened are we able to know "what is the hope of his calling"— know it, not by carnal presumption nor by mental acumen but perceive it with anointed vision. Nevertheless, if our eyes are not enlightened, the fault is entirely our own, for it is the revealed will of God that each regenerate person should have assurance that he is a new creature in Christ Jesus. The Holy Spirit has given us one whole epistle to that very end: "These things have I written unto you that believe on the name of the Son of God; that ye may *know* that ye *have* eternal life" (I John 5:13). Hence, those who would have the Christian believe that a firm and abiding assurance is not desirable are standing on an unscriptural doctrine.

Note how emphatic it is: "the eyes of *your* understanding being enlightened that *ye* may know." That cannot signify less than that your *own* eyes should see what grounds of assurance the Christian really has to know that eternal life is his, that his own heart may realize the hope which God has bidden him to exercise. Not to see with someone else's eyes, not to read through creedal spectacles, not to take any man's say-so for it, but to live by your own God-given faith and read in the light of Holy Writ your own clear evidences. The apostle prayed here that they might know what great, infallible, multitudinous grounds of hope God had called them to; that they might appreciate what grounds of assurance and evidence they had that heaven was theirs; that they might have assurance of their own interest in heaven! Every time I truly mourn over my sins, feel my poverty of spirit, hunger and thirst after righteousness, I have an indubitable evidence that I am among the "blessed."

Precepts and petitions are complementary one to the other. The precepts tell me what God requires and therefore what I need to ask Him for most, that enabling grace may be given me to perform the same. The prayers intimate what it is my privilege and duty to make request for, thus they indirectly reveal my duty. "Give diligence to make your calling and election sure" (II Peter 1:10) is the divine precept making known my duty. That "the Father of glory, may give unto you . . . wisdom and revelation in the knowledge of him: The eyes of your understanding enlightened; that ye may know what is the hope of his calling" is a request that I may be enabled to successfully carry out that task of making my election sure. This petition tells us we ought to labor after and pray earnestly for a clearer insight into and a fuller acquaintance with the great objects of the Christian's hopes and expectations.

We have endeavored to show that the opening clause of this verse is not a separate petition for a distinct blessing but rather the stating of an essential spiritual qualification. We cannot obtain a true and influential knowledge of the grounds which regeneration gives its subject to hope that he has passed from death to life, nor realize what confidence of God has bidden him to have (for both things are included) unless our eyes are divinely anointed. This essential qualification applies with equal force to the following clause. The grammatical construction of our passage makes it quite clear that an enlightened understanding is also indispensable for a spiritual knowledge of both "the riches of the glory of his inheritance in the saints" and "the exceeding greatness of his power to usward." Thus, that opening clause governs all the petitions that follow it.

Having pondered the opening request of this prayer in verse 17 and the first request mentioned in verse 18, we turn now to consider the prayer's third petition. We propose to concentrate on these three things: First, what is the relation of this petition to what precedes? Second, what is the precise meaning of its terms? Third, what use is the Christian to make of knowing what are the riches of the glory of God's inheritance in the saints? We shall devote most of our space to the second. First, the apostle prayed that the saints might experience and enjoy closer and fuller communion with God. Then he asked that the grace of hope might be more operative within them; that they should realize God's revealed will for them to "abound in hope" (Rom. 15:13) and not to live in a state of uncertainty. That they might perceive how many sure grounds they had for believing they *were* recipients of an effectual call, as when we ask a doctor concerning a loved one who is seriously ill, "What hope is there?" We mean, "What ground is there to expect his recovery?"

Spiritual Discernment Required

No matter how clearly and vividly the landscape appears when the sun is shining, a blind man does not behold it. Christ is manifestly set forth in the gospel, but the hearer must be given spiritual sight before he will perceive the absolute suitability of such a Saviour to his own desperate case. Even after regeneration, the Christian is still completely dependent on divine illumination in order for him to continue apprehending spiritual things. That was exemplified in the case of Peter. Some time after he had become a disciple of Christ, he made his memorable confession of Christ's deity. Then the Lord Jesus informed him, "Flesh and blood hath not revealed it unto thee, but my Father which is in heaven" (Matt. 16:17). The same thing is repeatedly illustrated in the experience of every saint. At one time he will read a portion of Scripture and perceive little in it which impresses his heart or stirs his soul; at another time the same passage appears scintillating with divine beauty and glory. The difference is that at the latter time his eyes are divinely anointed.

No reading of commentaries can secure an answer to this petition, and even a searching or study of the Scriptures will not of itself convey to the believer a spiritual and influential knowledge of what are the riches of the glory of God's inheritance in the saints. Only as and when the eyes of his understanding are enlightened will that delightful and wondrous experience be his. Thus Paul asked for such illumination to be granted them so that the Ephesians might know not only the hope of God's calling but also the excellency of His inheritance, that they might apprehend more clearly and comprehensively the greatness of that glory which they had a personal interest in, for when the God of all grace quickens His elect they are "called unto his eternal glory by Jesus Christ" (I Peter 5:10). The Father has "begotten us again unto a lively [living] hope by the resurrection of Jesus Christ from the dead, to an inheritance incorruptible and undefiled, and that fadeth not away, reserved in heaven for us" (I Peter 1:3-4). The one is preparatory to and ensures the other: begetting and inheritance, calling and eternal glory. But some who have been spiritually begotten of the Father are doubtful of that birth; they should not be. Instead, their duty and privilege are to know what is "the hope of his calling."

Now the apostle goes further. He desires that they might enjoy a better apprehension of the hope itself, that is, of its *object*. This is what we understand to be the relation between the second and third petitions. That the two things are not to be separated is intimated by their connecting "and," but that they relate to distinct blessings is clear from the "what is." This consideration determines the meaning of the word *hope* in the second petition, namely, that it is not the thing hoped for (which is named in the third) but rather the confidence and assurance which God commands His called people to have. The third petition announces what a great and glorious inheritance they have a personal interest in, and the fourth tells of the exceeding greatness of God's power which works in those who believe and which preserves them unto that glorious inheritance.

First, the apostle prayed for communion with God. Next he prayed that they would have the grounds of their assurance kept continually fresh in their hearts, that they would know the hope of their calling. And then he prayed that they would know the greatness of that glory in which they had an interest. Link those three things together, and this makes a perfect Christian: full of comfort, full of peace and joy in believing. And for the Christian to enter into experimental enjoyment of each and all of those ineffable favors he is dependent upon the Spirit of wisdom and revelation for the eyes of his understanding to be divinely enlightened. It utterly transcends the powers of the human mind to so much as conceive of the "things which God hath prepared for them that love him." Yet in response to earnest and expectant prayer, real and satisfying thoughts on the subject may be obtained even in this life, for "God hath revealed them unto us by his Spirit" (I Cor. 2:9-10).

When Paul was commissioned to preach to the Gentiles, it was "to open their eyes, and to turn them from darkness to light, and from the power of Satan unto God, that they might receive forgiveness of sins, and *inheritance* among them which are sanctified by faith that is in me [God]" (Acts 26:18). To the Hebrews Paul declared that Christ was the Mediator of the new covenant so that they who were called might receive the "promise of eternal inheritance" (9:15). Thus we see again how closely connected and yet distinct are the effectual call of God and the inheritance to which the called are begotten. That inheritance is described in part in I Peter 1:4. But in Ephesians 1:18 it is designated God's "inheritance in the saints," which at once brings to mind that remarkable statement: "For the LORD's portion is his people; Jacob is the lot of his inheritance" (Deut. 32:9; cf. Ps. 78:70-72; "my jewels" in Mal. 3:17). The one is complementary to the other. God has an inheritance in the saints, and they have an inheritance in and from God; for if they are His children, then they are also heirs—"heirs of God, and joint-heirs with Christ" (Rom. 8:17).

A Glorious Inheritance

Now this inheritance is a glorious one. Nothing is in heaven but that which is glorious. The central and all-absorbing Object there is the God of glory, particularly as He shines forth in the person of our glorious Redeemer. There our souls and bodies will be glorious (Rom. 8:30; Phil. 3:20). Our employments will be glorious—praising and glorifying God forever and ever. We shall be surrounded by the glorious angels. Nothing shall ever enter there which can defile. For a brief season Paul himself had been caught up into paradise, where he had received "revelations of the Lord" and heard "unspeakable words, which it is not lawful [nor possible] for a man [returned to earth] to utter" (II Cor. 12:1-4). Little wonder then that he longed so vehemently that the saints in general might be admitted into a clearer and enlarged apprehension of the things which God had prepared for them that love Him. Little wonder that in Ephesians 1 he should be found laboring for words to express the same to us: an "inheritance," "his inheritance," "the glory of his inheritance," "the riches of the glory of his inheritance."

Our ideas of heaven, of glory, of perfection—even after the partial revelation of them in the Scriptures—is at very best defective. Yet enough is revealed to fill us with admiration, astonishment, and adoration; and in proportion as the eyes of our understanding are enlightened and as faith is exercised on what God has made known to us thereon in His Word, our hearts will be affected and our lives influenced. The term "God's inheritance in the saints" is used to show the greatness and grandeur of it. It is "his inheritance" because He is the Deviser and Author of it. And let it not be overlooked that "his inheritance" as the "Father of glory" (Eph. 1:17) emphasizes the surpassing excellence of it.

It is God's inheritance, yet the saints are the "heirs" of it. That it is designated an "inheritance" announces that it is a free gift which we can do nothing to earn or merit. It is an inheritance of God's own planning, preparing, and bestowing. Such an inheritance must be inexpressibly grand, inconceivably wonderful, unspeakably glorious. It is the "inheritance of the saints in light" (Col. 1:12).

Let us now observe the qualities by which the inheritance is described in our text: "the *riches* of the glory of his inheritance." In human speech that word is applied to things which men value most highly, in order to attain which the majority are prepared to sell their souls. In Scripture, when "riches" is employed in connection with spiritual and divine things, it is for the purpose of emphasizing the excellency and copiousness of them. Thus we read of God being "rich in mercy" (Eph. 2:4), of the "riches of his grace," of the "unsearchable riches of Christ" (Eph. 3:8), and of the "riches both of the wisdom and knowledge of God" (Rom. 11:33).

It should enable us to form a better concept of this rich inheritance by recalling that verse "Ye know the grace of our Lord Jesus Christ, that, though he was rich, yet for your sakes he became poor, that ye through his poverty might be rich" (II Cor. 8:9). Christ was the Beloved of the Father, the Lord of glory, the Heir of all things, and therefore "thought it not robbery to be equal with God" (Phil. 2:6). Yet He laid aside His glory, became incarnate, was born in a manger, and entered into such poverty that He had nowhere to lay His head. He voluntarily endured such unspeakable humiliation for the express purpose that His people "might be rich." *How* rich then are they? How rich will they become? Those riches will bear a proportion to the unparalleled shame and penury into which the Son of God descended for our sakes.

"The Riches of His Glory"

But not only "riches" and "*the* riches" are meant but "the riches of his *glory*." How little are we capable of entering into the meaning and blessedness of that! Goodwin has pointed out that if "riches" connote excellency, the "glory" of them imports superexcellency. Thus we read of the "excellent glory" (II Peter 1:17), or height of excellency, and of the "glory that excelleth" (II Cor. 3:10). That gives perhaps as full a definition as can be furnished. It signifies all excellencies, and all excellencies in the height, and such a weight of excellencies which the ordinary understanding of a man cannot bear. Joy, when it excels, is called "joy unspeakable and full of glory" (I Peter 1:8). Now put the two together: the "riches of his glory," that is, of "the Father of glory!"

The two things are combined again in that familiar verse "My God shall supply all your need according to his riches in glory by Christ Jesus" (Phil. 4:19). Not "out of" but "according to" His riches. It is the standard of measurement rather than the source of supply. God is a rich and glorious God: nor will He have those riches of glory lie idle. When Abraham had no son, he said, "Lord, Thou hast given me these riches, but to me Thou hast given no seed—no son to *inherit*." Therefore God gave him Isaac, on whom he might bestow his riches and inheritance (Gen. 15:1-4). God had riches of glory lying by, and therefore He chose His sons to inherit them.

When Alexander the Great gave a city to a mean man, he said, " I do not give a city away according to the proportion of the man, but as it is fit for *me* to give."

In showing how glorious must be the inheritance which the saints shall have, Goodwin called attention to Psalm 115:15-16 where we read, "Ye are blessed of the LORD which made heaven and earth. The heaven, even the heavens, are the LORD's; but the earth hath he given to the children of men." The earth, and all the good things in it, God has given to the human family, but heaven and the heaven of heavens He has reserved for Himself as *His* possession. The earth He has given away to the children of men, but the celestial courts are His own inheritance. Now this is mentioned in order to show how favored the saints are: "Ye are the blessed of the LORD." God does not prize the earth, but gives it away; but the heavens He has set apart for Himself. Then how happy the saints must be that they are taken up to heaven to share God's own inheritance! The earth is not good enough for Him, nor does He deem it to be so for them. The Lord is the Possessor of heaven, and blessed indeed must those be who are predestinated to be partakers of God's own inheritance.

"The riches of the glory of *his inheritance in the saints*." In an allusion to this verse Calvin remarked, "The eyes of our understanding are not truly 'enlightened' unless we discover what is the hope of the eternal inheritance to which we are called." Manton understood it as the inheritance "appointed for those who are renewed by the Spirit of God, . . . that they might more clearly see and fully believe those good things which they shall enjoy hereafter." Hodge defined it as the "abundance and greatness of that inheritance of which God is the Author." Whether we regard it as God's inheritance or the Christian's, it comes to the same thing in effect, for it is displayed *in* the saints. According as God has glory in the saints, they must be glorious just as the glory of a king is exhibited in the glory of his attendants. God regards the glory which the saints shall have as His inheritance. Moreover, there is a revenue of glory which He receives from them in their worship and thanksgiving.

The Greek may also be fairly rendered "What is the riches of the glory of the inheritance *of Him by* the saints," meaning that God Himself is the inheritance of the saints. This will constitute the ineffable bliss and blessedness of heaven—that God Himself will be our all-absorbing and eternally satisfying portion and heritage. When the mind soars that high it finds an all-sufficient resting place: "He that overcometh shall inherit all things; and I will be his God" (Rev. 21:7). O what a marvelous and inconceivable prospect: that the saints will possess God Himself; that the Redeemer will yet say to His people, "Enter thou into the joy of thy Lord"; and that word *enter* is couched in the language of this very figure, for a man enters into his inheritance when he actually takes possession of the same. Then each saint will exclaim, "The LORD is the portion of mine inheritance. . . . In thy presence is fulness of joy" (Ps. 16:5, 11).

The Fullness of Scripture

Yet so full are the words of Scripture that no single definition can exhaust their scope. Our text not only includes the inheritance which God has provided *for* His saints and which they have *in* Him but it also refers to what God Himself has *in them*. Second Thessalonians 1:10 says that Christ "shall come to be glorified in his saints, and to be admired in all them that believe." How will they be glorified? Why, so that *He* will be admired *in them*. God makes known the "riches of his glory on the vessels of mercy, which he hath afore prepared unto glory" (Rom. 9:23). Bringing vessels of mercy to glory is to make known the riches of *His glory*. His glory shall arise out of theirs, and therefore it is said to be "his inheritance in the saints." When the saints are glorified and with Him in heaven, then "he will rejoice over . . . [them] with joy; he will rest in his love, he will joy over . . . [them] with singing" (Zeph. 3:17). What glory must that consist of to be an inheritance for God to rest in forever!

Now Paul prayed the saints might have a better knowledge of that glorious inheritance, in order that the eyes of their understanding should be enlightened in regard to that inheritance. As a well-trained mind is required in order to grapple with an intricate problem in philosophy, as a musical temperament and ear are needed to fully appreciate a master production of melody, so spiritual vision and the eyes of faith are indispensable in order to take in spiritual views of heavenly objects. Certainly Paul would not have prayed for this blessing unless it was of great value and importance. We are bidden to set our affection on things above, and the more real and glorious they appear to us the easier it will be to comply with such a precept. And obviously the more our hearts are set on heavenly objects the less power will the perishing things of time and sense have to enthrall or even influence us.

If we perceived more clearly the riches of the glory of the inheritance to which we are called, we would be well content with "food and raiment" and a covering over our heads while here. We would have more of the spirit of those who took joyfully the spoiling of their goods, knowing that they had in heaven a *"better* and an enduring substance" (Heb. 10:34). "For the joy that was set before him" the Lord Jesus "endured the cross, despising [treating with contempt] the shame" (Heb. 12:2). If we were more occupied with those "pleasures for evermore" which are at God's right hand (Ps. 16:11), we would run with patience the race set before us and be less cast down by the petty sufferings and sorrows of the way. If heaven were more real to us, we would be more earnest in seeking to walk as those journeying to it, and we would long more ardently for Christ to come and take us there.

Chapter 13

PRAYER FOR SPIRITUAL APPREHENSION

EPHESIANS 1: 19-20

WE HAVE NOW ARRIVED at the fourth petition in this prayer. In pondering the petition it is both important and necessary to realize that, equally with the two preceding requests, this final one is based upon and governed by the initial blessing. We can no more know spiritually and experimentally the "exceeding greatness of his [God's] power to us-ward" without first having the "spirit of wisdom and revelation in the knowledge of him." As a result, the eyes of our understanding are enlightened so that we can know "what is the hope of his calling and what the riches of the glory of his inheritance in the saints." We are as entirely dependent upon the gracious operations of the Spirit for the one as we are for the other. Grammatically, logically, doctrinally, and experimentally the one is governed by and follows from the other. Something far more than a mere speculative or intellectual knowledge of God's mighty power is here supplicated, namely, a personal acquaintance, a heart apprehension. For *that* anointed eyes—as the consequence of an increased measure of the "spirit of wisdom and revelation"—are indispensable.

"And what is the exceeding greatness of his power to us-ward" (Eph. 1:19). It may not be so apparent to some of us why Paul felt the need to make this particular petition. To a greater or less degree all Christians are conscious of their need for a fuller supply of the "spirit of wisdom and revelation" in the knowledge of God and of their being granted a clearer and enlarged apprehension of "what is the hope of his calling, and what the riches of the glory of his inheritance in the saints." But probably many Christians are less aware that it is equally desirous and essential for them to know more about the mighty operations of God to them. If they have good grounds for believing they have received an effectual call, then they *do* realize that a miracle of grace must have been wrought in them, that nothing short of omnipotence could have brought them from death to life. Yet much more than that is included in this petition. We shall therefore begin our study of it by suggesting several reasons why the apostle should have made this particular request.

Spiritual Helplessness of Fallen Man

First, Paul probably made this request because it would *stain human pride.* The natural man is so self-confident and self-sufficient that he deems himself

120

quite competent to determine his own destiny. But over all his fancied efficiency, egotism, and independence, God has written "without strength" (Rom. 5:6). Not without physical, mental, or moral strength but without *spiritual*. Fallen man is spiritually dead. Therefore he is not only utterly unable to perform a spiritual act in a spiritual way and from a spiritual principle but also devoid of any spiritual desires or aspirations, though he may be very devout as the world conceives of "religion." "Without strength" Godward. But who believes this today? Few indeed, and fewer still have confirmed it by actual experience. The boast of Christendom is, "I am rich, and increased with goods, and have need of nothing"—ignorant of her true condition, for the divine Judge says to her," [Thou] knowest not that thou are wretched, and miserable, and poor, and blind, and naked" (Rev. 3:17). Nothing but God's great power can subdue the workings of such pride and bring the sinner as a humble suppliant and empty-handed beggar to the throne of grace.

To believe on Jesus Christ with all our hearts appears to be one of the simplest acts imaginable, and to receive Him as our personal Lord and Saviour seems to present no great difficulty. Yet, in reality, before any soul actually submits to the Saviour, there has to be the working of God's mighty power. In other words, a miracle of grace must be wrought in him. Before a fallen and depraved creature will voluntarily and unreservedly surrender to the just claims of Christ, before he will forsake his cherished sins and abandon his beloved idols, before his proud heart is brought to repudiate all his righteousnesses as filthy rags, before he is willing to be saved by grace alone, before he is ready to whole-heartedly receive Christ as his Prophet, Priest, and King, God must draw him by His mighty power. Nothing short of the exercise of omnipotence is sufficient.

The Fall has wrought fearful havoc in the whole of man's nature and constitution. Every descendant of Adam was "shapen in iniquity" and born into the world the slave of sin; no efforts of his own nor any attempts by his fellow-men can, to the slightest degree, deliver him from his fearful bondage. It is apparent that a supernatural power must intervene if the sinner is ever to be emancipated from his captivity, that none but the hand of God can smite off his fetters and bring him out of prison. If the spiritual darkness of man's understanding, the perversity of his will, the disorderliness of his affections and passions were better understood, then it would be more evident that no mere reformation could suffice, that nothing short of personal regeneration—the communication to him of a new nature and life—could be of any avail.

Slavery of the Natural Man to Sin and Satan

Second, Paul requested knowledge of God's power *because men are so ignorant of the terrible powers arrayed against them.* When engaged in a serious conflict, nothing is so fatal to success as to underestimate the strength of our opponents. Only as our judgment of the might and malignity of our spiritual foes is formed by the teaching of Scripture can we really assess the same. Unless our thoughts concerning the enemies of our souls are regulated by what God's Word reveals about them, we are certain to err. Above we have referred to the potency of indwelling sin, but how little its awful dominion and preva-

lence is realized! "Can the Ethiopian change his skin, or the leopard his spots?"
then may ye also do good, that are accustomed to do evil" (Jer. 13:23). The
natural man cannot improve his sinful nature and make himself love God. As
neither external applications nor internal potions could whiten the Ethiopian's
dark complexion, so neither education, culture, nor reformation can change the
sinner's nature and bring him to hate what he now loves or love that to which
he is inveterately averse.

Not only is the natural man the slave of sin but he is also the captive of
the devil. Immediately after praying the prayer we are now pondering, Paul
reminded the saints: "In time past ye walked according to the course of this
world, according to the prince of the power of the air, the spirit that now
worketh in the children of disobedience" (Eph. 2:2). So complete is Satan's
dominion over the unregenerate that he not only tempts them from without but
works *within* them so that they are made both to will and to do of his evil
pleasure. Therefore he is termed their father, and as Christ declared to the
Pharisees, "The lusts [desires] of your father ye will do" (John 8:44). Unregenerate men fondly imagine they are "free agents," pleasing themselves, but
in concluding this they are deceived by their archenemy, their master and king,
for they are held fast in the "snare of the devil, . . . taken captive by him at
his will" (II Tim. 2:26). They are no more able to escape from his toils than
they are to create a world; indeed, they have no desire to do so.

"But if our gospel be hid, it is hid to them that are lost: In whom the god
of this world hath blinded the minds of them which believe not, lest the light
of the glorious gospel of Christ, who is the image of God, should shine unto
them" (II Cor. 4:3-4). What then can Satan's victims do? As the "prince of
this world" he influences its politics and policies. As the "god of this world"
he controls its superstitions and religions. In this way he maintains his "kingdom" (Matt. 12:26) and governs his subjects. In our Lord's parable of the
wheat He intimated something of the fearful dominion of our great foe: "When
any one heareth the word of the kingdom, and understandeth it not, then cometh
the wicked one and catcheth away that which was sown in his heart" (Matt
13:19). How helpless then are his victims! One has but to read in Mark 5
the case of the poor demoniac whom "no man could bind, . . . no, not with
chains" (v. 3) to ascertain how thoroughly unavailing are all human attempts
to escape Satan's thralldom. Yet how little this is realized!

When the Lord saves a person He delivers him from Satan's control, and
that is a work of exceeding great power such as He alone is capable of putting
forth. This was clearly made known by Christ's statement "When a strong
man armed keepeth his palace, his goods are in peace [i.e., secure]: But when
a stronger than he shall come upon him, and overcome him, he taketh from him
all his armour wherein he trusted, and divideth his spoils" (Luke 11:21-22)
Only divine omnipotence can turn souls "from the power of Satan unto God'
(Acts 26:18). Nor does the devil admit defeat even when any of his captives
are taken from him by force. No, he makes the most relentless and persevering
efforts to recapture them, employing his powerful and numerous emissaries to
reach that end. Therefore are the saints warned, "For we wrestle not against
flesh and blood [merely human beings], but against principalities, against pow

ers, against the rulers of the darkness of this world, against spiritual wickedness in high places" (Eph. 6:12). Hence they are bidden to be "strong in the Lord, and in the power of his might. Put on the whole armour of God" (Eph. 6:10-11).

Third, Paul made his request because of *the unbelief and timidity of the saints*. We are creatures of extremes. When our self-confidence and self-sufficiency are subdued, we are prone to become occupied with our weakness and insufficiency instead of keeping our eyes fixed steadily on the One who began a good work in us. As we learn something of the might of our foes—both within and without—and of our feebleness and incompetence to resist them, we are apt to become thoroughly discouraged and give way to despair. This explains why Paul reserved this petition for God's power for the last. He had just asked that the saints might know what were the "riches of the glory of his inheritance in the saints," and then it was as though he anticipated their inevitable objection: "How shall vile creatures as we ever come to be made glorious? Even though we have been delivered from a bondage worse than Egyptian bondage, are we not likely, as the Israelites of old, to perish in the wilderness before we reach the promised land?" It was to quiet such fears that Paul reminded the Ephesians of the exceeding greatness of God's power.

Divine Omnipotence

In the early part of Ephesians 1 Paul spoke much about the goodwill of God toward His people. In the second part of the chapter, in order to warm their hearts and strengthen their faith, Paul had the Ephesians contemplate divine omnipotence. The power of God executes His counsels. That power has ever been the confidence and glory of His saints. His "mighty arm" is the security of their salvation. It is inexpressibly blessed to see that the power of God is exactly proportioned to His promises. Has He given us "exceeding great and precious promises" (II Peter 1:4)? Then there is the "exceeding greatness of his power" to make them good! That was the ground of Abraham's assurance when God declared he should have a son in his old age: "Being not weak in faith, he considered not his own body now dead . . ., neither yet the deadness of Sarah's womb: He staggered not at the promise of God through unbelief; but was strong in faith, giving glory to God; and being fully persuaded that, what he had promised, he was able also to perform" (Rom. 4:19-21). When we remember the power of God, weakness and readiness to faint are changed into confidence and joy (Ps. 77:7-15).

"That ye may know . . . what is the exceeding greatness of his power *to usward*." That petition only meets with a suitable response from us when we remember that divine omnipotence is engaged to uphold, strengthen, and defend God's people, to complete the good work which it has begun in them, to fully redeem them from sin, Satan, and death, to conform them perfectly to the image of His dear Son. Just in proportion as believers realize that the infinite power of God is available for them to lay hold of and draw from do they answer to Paul's design in placing on record this request for them. When we are most conscious of our weakness and the might of our enemies, our privilege is to come boldly to the throne of grace and there find "grace to help in time of need" (Heb. 4:16). It is one thing to believe intellectually in the exceeding greatness of God's power, but it is quite another for us to personally and experimentally take hold of His strength (Isa. 27:5). Then it is that we prove for ourselves the meaning of those words "out of weakness were made strong" (Heb. 11:34); then we know what it is to be "strong in the grace that is in Christ Jesus" (II Tim. 2:1).

Fourth, Paul made request that the Ephesians might know God's power because *only thus is He honored*. To give place to fear as David did when he said, "I shall now perish one day by the hand of Saul" is most dishonoring to God. It is the consequence of being absorbed with our enemies rather than with the Lord. Let self-diffidence be accompanied with confidence in God, and all will be well. Since the glory of God is concerned in the salvation and preservation of His people and since Paul was about to make requests concerning the furtherance of the same, he here addressed Deity as "the Father of glory" (Eph. 1:17). It is blessed to realize the import of that. Since the Father of glory is the Author of our salvation, He will certainly be the Guardian of it. The same motive which disposed Him to contrive and effect our salvation will also move Him to ripen all the fruits of it. It is for this reason chiefly that He who has begun a good work in us will finish it (Phil. 1:6). His glory requires our perseverance and His power will secure it; therefore it is termed "his glorious power" (Col. 1:11).

To God Be the Glory

"That ye may know . . . what is the exceeding greatness of his power to us-ward" in removing our enmity against Him, in dispelling the native darkness of our understanding, in subduing our rebellious wills, in drawing our hearts to Himself, in giving us a love for His law and a longing for holiness, in delivering us from the power of Satan. It is most necessary for us to know all that if all the praise and glory are to be ascribed to Him to whom alone it is due. As we compare ourselves with the unregenerate—who naturally may shame us in many respects but who spiritually are on the broad road that leads to destruction, unconcerned about their eternal interests—we do well to ponder that question: *"Who* maketh thee to differ?" (I Cor. 4:7). The answer is, and only can be "A sovereign God who puts forth His omnipotence and makes us willing to receive Christ as our *Lord* in the day of His power." And if we can now perceive any good thing, the root of the matter in us, the fruits of a new nature, then we must exclaim, "Not unto us, O LORD, not unto us, but unto thy name give glory" (Ps. 115:1).

This fourth petition then was a request that the saints might have a clearer understanding and a better apprehension of how that miraculous change within them had been brought about and of what that initial change was the sure down payment. The change was not produced by rational considerations, by moral suasion, nor by the power of the preacher, for he can no more quicken dead souls than he can dead bodies. It did not originate in any act of our wills; it was not effected by any human agency. There was something *prior* to the consent of our wills, namely, a radical and permanent inward transformation wrought by the hand of the Most High. And observe how energetic and impressive is the language used: not only the power of God or the greatness of that power but the "exceeding greatness of his power to us-ward." So weighty and emphatic is the language of the Greek that it is difficult to reproduce in English: "the super-excellent, sublime, and overcoming, or triumphant, greatness of His power" is how one rendered it.

J. C. Philpot gave an excellent definition of that power: "The power put forth in first communicating; second, in subsequent maintaining; third, in completing and consummating the work of grace in the heart." We would include God's power in working on our behalf and in the resurrection of our bodies as well. But what we most desire to impress upon and leave with the Christian reader is that the exceeding greatness of God's power is toward us. It is not merely latent in Himself; still less is it against us—as was the case with Pharaoh—but is engaged on our behalf, making all things work together for our good. Then what is there to fear! Join the apostle in praying for an enlarged heart apprehension of God's power.

"That ye may know . . . what is the exceeding greatness of His power to us-ward" (vv. 18-19). In our last chapter we suggested several reasons why it is necessary that such a request should be made. It is of no small importance, both for our own good and for the glory of God, that we should obtain a better understanding and clearer apprehension of *how* the wondrous change within us has been brought about, for our ignorance concerning the same is very great. Nevertheless, the workings of omnipotence toward us must by no means be restricted to the initial miracle of regeneration, amazing and blessed though that is, for it was but the forerunner, the sure earnest, of further marvels of grace. None but God can save a sinner, and He alone can *preserve* him in such a world as this. If the exceedingly great power of God is required to deliver a soul from spiritual death, the continued exercise of it is equally essential in bringing him safe home to heaven. If nothing short of the infinite strength of the Almighty was sufficient to free one of Satan's captives, anything less would be quite inadequate to prevent the archenemy of man from recovering his former victim.

The Lord Our Keeper

"Who are kept by the *power of God* through faith unto salvation ready to be revealed in the last time" (I Peter 1:5). "He that keepth Israel shall neither slumber nor sleep. The LORD is thy keeper" (Ps. 121:4-5). Of His vineyard it is said, "I the LORD do keep it; I will water it every moment: lest any hurt it, I will keep it night and day" (Isa. 27:3). Such blessed assurances are not given to encourage carnal confidence and presumptuous carelessness but are recorded for the comfort and heartening of those who have been brought to realize they have "no might" of their own and would certainly make shipwreck of the faith were they left to themselves and their own resources. But, thank God, the same mighty power which was put forth at first to make them new creatures in Christ is engaged to carry forward the work of grace within them, to defend from all enemies, to supply their every need while left in this "howling wilderness." Thus, their eternal security is infallibly guaranteed and the

Lord of hosts is their sole but all-sufficient confidence, the might of His omnipotence their ever available resource.

The exceeding greatness of God's power *to* us not only includes all the operations of His grace to and within His people but also comprehends His wondrous providences to them in meeting every need and making all things work together for their good. There is also one other exercise of the divine omnipotence to the saints which we must at least mention, and that is their *glorification,* when in spirit and soul and body they shall be perfectly and permanently conformed to the image of God's Son. Their very bodies which were sown in dishonor will be raised in glory, and what before was natural will then be made spiritual. Whatever difficulties carnal reason and unbelief may advance about the supposed change of the particles which comprise our present bodies and the alleged impossibility of the same bodies coming forth on the resurrection morning, faith disposes of them all by a confident appeal to God's promise: "Who shall change our vile body, that it may be like unto his glorious body, according to the working whereby *he is able* even to subdue all things unto himself" (Phil. 3:21). The regeneration of the soul is a great miracle as is the resurrection of the body. The same mighty power which effected the one will accomplish the other.

We turn now to a technical detail, yet it is not devoid of interest and importance. Careful readers will have observed that in our quoting of Ephesians 1:19a we stopped at the word *usward* rather than *believe* as in the Authorized Version. Two things must be determined, namely, the precise point at which the petitionary part of the prayer ends and the punctuation of verse 19. Really the two things are one, for as soon as the former is settled, the latter is at once determined. In chapter 11 we outlined the prayer thus: first, its occasion (v. 15); second, its nature (vv. 15-16); third, its object (v. 17); fourth, its requests (vv. 17-19); fifth, its revelation (vv. 19-23)—our reason for so designating its last section, we give below. Now it is our impression that we have already reached the conclusion of the petitionary portion of this prayer at the word *usward* and that a colon should follow it; therefore we believe that the "who believe" is to be connected and considered with what immediately follows.

It is quite clear that the requests begin at the words "may give unto you" (v. 17). Whether they end at the word *usward* or at *believe* is a point on which the commentators differ, the great majority favoring the latter as our translators did. Yet personally we much prefer the former, for the following reasons. First, the added "who believe" is not necessary for the purpose of defining the "us-ward"—the subject or beneficiaries of God's power—for they are manifestly the "saints" of the preceding clause. Second, to say that God's power is "to us-ward who believe" unwarrantably *restricts* the idea, for God's omnipotence wrought in the saints *previously,* and had it not done so they never would have believed! Third, if the "who believe" is linked to the preceding clause, the final section of the prayer begins too abruptly—"according to." Fourth, if the "who believe" commences a new clause the words present a most important truth which our passage would otherwise omit, namely, that our believing is itself the immediate result of the divine operations.

"Who believe according to the working of his mighty power." Before attempting to open up the meaning of those words let us seek to point out their wider scope or the relation which they bear to what follows. True prayer is something more than making our requests known to God, even with thanksgiving: it is something more than an act of adoration, wherein the believer praises and adores Deity. It is also *communing* with God, and communing, or fellowship, is *mutual*. When the redeemed soul is favored to have an audience with the divine Majesty, not only does He hearken to his petitions but He graciously condescends to speak with him. A beautiful illustration of that is found in Numbers 7:89: "When Moses was gone into the tabernacle of the congregation to speak with . . . [God], then he heard the voice of one speaking unto him from off the mercy seat" (cf. Exodus 33:11). This was the case here in Ephesians 1: while the apostle was making known his requests to the Father of glory, he received a revelation from Him, which is recorded in the closing verses of our chapter.

Wondrous things were here made known, things which had not been disclosed before. In the closing verses of Ephesians 1 certain aspects of truth are revealed which are nowhere else set forth in the Scriptures. Psalm 110:3 plainly intimated that there must be a putting forth of divine power before the people of God are made willing to abandon their prejudices and idols. Once and again Christ affirmed the natural man to be incapable of exercising faith (John 5:44; 8:43; 10:26), but here alone we learn that God puts forth the *same* power in working faith in us as He wrought in Christ when He raised Him from the dead. On the day of Pentecost Peter declared that God had raised the crucified Jesus and made Him "both Lord and Christ" (Acts 2:36), but here alone it is formally stated that the Redeemer has been exalted "far above all principality and power, and might and dominion." In I Corinthians 15:27 we read that God has "put all things under" Christ, but here alone do we discover that God "gave him to be the head over all things *to* the church" (v. 22). In I Corinthians 12:27 the Church is designated "the body of Christ," but here alone she is called *His* "fulness."

Wondrous indeed are those things to which we have just called attention, things which it should be our joy to carefully contemplate and not carelessly dismiss with a passing glance. Some readers may chafe at the slowness of our progress, but why should we hurry over such a passage as this? Is there anything more sublime or precious in the prayers yet to follow that we should get through with this one as quickly as possible? If the writer followed his own inclinations, he would write another twelve chapters on these closing verses of Ephesians 1, but he realizes that would unduly tax the patience of many. On the other hand, not a few welcome a detailed exposition and sermonizing of such a passage, desiring something more instructive and edifying than the superficial generalizations which characterize most of the productions of our day. May the Spirit of truth graciously shine upon our understanding and enable us to so "open" these verses that faith may be instructed, souls fed, God glorified, and His Son endeared to His redeemed.

The Natural Man's Will Ruined and Depraved

"Who believe according to the working of His mighty power." To savingly believe in the Lord Jesus Christ does not lie within the ability of the natural man's will, for his will, like every other faculty of his being, has been depraved and ruined by the fall. The will follows the dictates of the mind and the inclinations of the affections; in other words, we will or choose that which is most agreeable to us. We do not choose that to which we are averse. Now the heart of the natural man is averse to the thrice holy God and his carnal mind is enmity against Him. How then can he voluntarily and gladly choose Him for his Lord and Portion? The bent of his desires must be changed before his will embraces God as his absolute End. No man by a mere act of his will can make himself love any person or thing that he hates. If then I have been brought to esteem and receive as my Lord the One whom I formerly despised and rejected, a radical change must have been wrought within me. Hence we read of "the faith of the operation of *God*" (Col. 2:12).

"Who *believe*." That word must be understood here in its widest scope, as including repentance and as issuing in conversion. Such believing is the outcome of "the working of God's *mighty* power." Not a single word of Holy Writ is superfluous, and there is good reason why the power of God is here called "mighty". Speaking after the manner of men, we may say that God *proportions* His power according to the work before Him, exercising more in one particular operation than another—as we put forth the utmost of our strength only when faced with a more than ordinary occasion. This is clearly borne out by the language of Scripture, wherein its Author is pleased to accommodate His terms to our feeble intelligence. Thus, where physical miracles were wrought it was by "the *finger* of God" (Exodus 8:19; Luke 11:20), but it was by strength of *hand*" He brought forth His people from Egypt (Exodus 13:3) and "upholdeth" His saints (Ps. 37:24). In other passages we read that God has a "mighty *arm*" (Ps. 89:13) and that "he hath shewed strength with his arm" (Luke 1:51).

Had such distinctions as the above, particularly their import and purport, been more closely attended to, it would have been much easier to bring to a decisive conclusion our age-long controversy between Arminians and Calvinists concerning the invincibility of God's power upon the unconverted. The great majority of Calvinists erred when they denied the contention of their opponents that there is a power of God which works in the hearts of men that can be and is *resisted,* as they failed to fairly interpret many of the verses advanced by Arminians. "Ye do always resist the Holy Ghost" (Acts 7:51) must not be explained away but honestly expounded in harmony with the Analogy of Faith. There are "differences of administrations" and "diversities of operations" of the Spirit (I Cor. 12:5-6) according to His several designs. The Spirit puts forth different proportions of power according to the various ends before Him. Those spoken of in Hebrews 6:4-5 and II Peter 2:20 were the subjects of His lesser operations but not of His regenerating power. Many are enlightened by the Spirit (as Balaam), their corruptions are restrained, their consciences pricked, yet without His making them new creatures in Christ Jesus.

A Vital Distinction

The writer has no hesitation in declaring he is convinced that thousands of people have been drawn by God to sit under a faithful preaching of His Word, been convicted by the Spirit of their sinful and lost condition, felt something in their souls of "the powers of the world to come" (Heb. 6:5), but were not brought from death to life. Yet while we believe many are the subjects of God's power working upon and within them, which power they resist and quench, yet we emphatically deny that a single soul ever did or will defeat or defy the "working of God's *mighty* power." That such a distinction is a necessary and valid one is surely indicated in the verse now before us, else why should the Holy Spirit here declare that God's work in bringing us to believe holds proportion with that stupendous wonder when He "raised him [Christ] from the dead, and set him at his own right hand in the heavenly places!" Such power He does not put forth in His lesser and lower works. This "working of His *mighty* power" is effectual, prevailing, invincible, and cannot be withstood.

The Working of God's Mighty Power

The force of the Greek is conveyed more vividly by the marginal rendering of the Authorized Version "according to the working of the might of his power." One word was not sufficient to express the power that works so mightily, so the apostle doubled it, as was the manner of the Hebrews: "holy of holies" signifies the most holy, and "the might of His power" His utmost strength. When Scripture would express the greatness of God's might and the certainty of bringing a thing to pass it adds one term to another or doubles the expression: God is "mighty in strength" (Job 9:4). "Lift up your eyes on high, and behold who hath created these things, that bringeth out their host by number: he calleth them all by names by the greatness of his might, for that he is strong in power; not one faileth" (Isa. 40:26). There can be no failure when He putteth forth the might of His strength. Despite what they are by nature, and notwithstanding the might of Satan and his determination to retain all his subjects, the mighty power of God works efficaciously and infallibly in all them that believe. The combined efforts of all creatures in the universe could not have prevented God from raising Christ from the dead. Neither can they hinder Him from working faith in His elect.

There has been much disputing among theologians concerning the power put forth by God in the converting of sinners, yet there is no real occasion for it. If you would know what power is put forth in any work, ask the worker himself. Here the Converter of souls is the Inditer of this very verse, and He tells us it is by "the working of the might of his power." In view of those words all argument on the subject should be at an end. And in view of those words every preacher of the gospel ought to be bowed before God, conscious of his own impotency, begging Him to graciously exercise His omnipotence among his spiritually dead hearers. It is true that in connection with the sudden conversion of a sinner beholders do not perceive that a miracle of divine power has been performed. When the woman was healed by a touch of the hem of Christ's garment, those that stood by discerned no such thing. But what did He say? "Virtue is gone out of me" (Luke 8:46). His life-giving power had effected the cure instantaneously. Nor was the subject of that miracle unaware of the grand change wrought, "knowing what was done in her" (Mark 5:33).

Why is the working of God's "mighty power" necessary in order for a soul to be converted? Because of the nature of the work performed. As in the case of one who is physically ill, the more desperate his case the more skill is required from the physician if he is to be healed. Only as we learn from Scripture and actual experience the hopeless condition of fallen man can we see the need of Omnipotence intervening if ever man is to be saved. The converting of a sinner is a greater miracle and calls for the putting forth of more power than the creating of man did. How so? Because creation is simply the bringing of a creature into existence, but conversion is the transforming of one who is opposed to it. In the one there is no impediment; in the other there is every possible resistance. Though there is nothing to help, yet in the creation there was nothing to oppose. But in connection with the new creation there is the carnal mind which "is enmity against God: for it is not subject to the law of God, *neither indeed can be*" (Rom. 8:7). Water is not more unlike fire than sin is unlike holiness, the natural man unlike God. Only Omnipotence can subdue that enmity and impart a love for His law.

"For the weapons of our [ministerial] warfare are not carnal, but mighty through God to the pulling down of strong holds: casting down . . . [reasonings], and every high thing that exalteth itself against . . . God, and bringing into captivity every thought to the obedience of Christ" (II Cor. 10:4). In those words the apostle intimates something of the difficulties which face the preachers of the gospel. He likens the reasonings of the carnal mind and the prejudices of the depraved heart, behind which the natural man seeks shelter against the demands of the gospel, to a company in a powerful fort who refuse to surrender. No matter how winsomely the invitations are given or how authoritatively the requirements of the gospel are pressed, the natural man has a score of objections which do not yield to these. Only as the truth is made *"mighty* through God" is the sinner's pride subdued and is he brought to yield to the claims of Christ's lordship. So wedded is man to his lusts, so in love with his idols, that unless the "mighty power" of God works within him, all the persuasions of the whole apostolate and the endeavors of all the angels could not induce him to forsake them.

"Who believe according to the working of his mighty power." Was not the truth of those words most strikingly and blessedly exemplified by the one who first penned them? See Saul of Tarsus consenting to the death of Stephen and making "havock of the church, entering into every house, and haling men and women committed them to prison" (Acts 8:1, 3). See him "yet breathing out threatenings and slaughter against the disciples of the Lord" (Acts 9:1) and going to the high priest and requesting letters of authority that if he found any such in the synagogues of Damascus, "whether . . . men or women, he might bring them bound unto Jerusalem." Why was it that less than a week later he preached Christ in the synagogues of Damascus? What had wrought such an amazing transformation? What was it that made this rebel cry, "Lord, what wilt thou have me to do?" What transformed the persecuting Saul into the evangelizing Paul? Nothing less than the mighty power of God, and he declared *his* was a "pattern" case (I Tim. 1:16). True, there was something extraordinary in the manner of it, but the *power* is the same in every instance.

In conclusion let us carefully observe that this working of God's mighty power is not restricted to the past: it is not "who believed," but "who believe according to." The reference is not to be limited to God's working faith in us at the first but takes in His *maintaining* it. The Christian can no more exercise faith of himself, still less increase it, than he could originate it. This is clear from another prayer of our apostle, in which he requested God to "fulfil all the good pleasure of his goodness, and the work of faith with power" (II Thess. 1:11). Faith could continue working only by the divine power. This point is jealously guarded: "This is the victory that overcometh the world, even our faith" is immediately preceded by "whatsoever is *born of God* overcometh the world" (I John 5:4). While faith is the instrument, God alone makes it effectual, and therefore we must exclaim, "Thanks be to God, which giveth us the victory" (I Cor. 15:57).

Chapter 14

PRAYER FOR APPRECIATION OF
CHRIST'S TRIUMPH

EPHESIANS 1:20

WE HAVE BEEN OCCUPIED with the power of God as it is exercised in connection with His people. First we have described the *excellency* of the same: "the exceeding greatness of his power," and then a brief declaration that it is "to us-ward," which comprehends in general terms *all* its operations upon, within, to the saints. Second, we sought to magnify its *efficiency*: "who believe according to the working of his mighty power." Briefly, that includes two things: the quickening of the soul and the communication of the principle of faith as a divine gift. One who is spiritually dead cannot spiritually believe. The natural man is able to believe the Scriptures in a natural or mental way (as he believes authenticated human history) but he cannot savingly believe the gospel until he is born again (John 1:12-13; 3:3, 5). We need to pray for a better apprehension of those things: "that we may *know* what is." And now, third, we are to consider how that mighty power of God operated in connection with our Saviour.

Four Important Questions

"Who believe, according to the working of his mighty power, which he wrought in Christ, when he raised him from the dead" (Eph. 1:19-20). In our examination and contemplation of these words, four questions will supply our focal points. First, what, in connection with the raising of Christ, called for the putting forth of the strength of God's might? Second, why is God's raising of Christ made the unit or standard of measurement of the power which He exerts in those who believe? Third, what is the precise nature of the power which God then exercised? Was it simply His omnipotence, or something in addition to it? Was it merely physical power? If not, what? Fourth, what are the principal points of analogy between God's raising Christ from the dead and His bringing us to believe? While quite distinct, these questions overlap at certain points, so, while attempting to supply answers to all of them, we shall not confine ourselves to a strict observance of their order.

Ephesians 1 is not the only passage which directly associates the divine power with the raising of Christ from the dead. In Romans 1:3-4 we are told that our Lord Jesus Christ was "made of the seed of David according to the flesh, and declared to be the Son of God with power, according to the spirit of holiness, by the resurrection from the dead." Of all the wondrous works which God did for Christ—in the miracle of His incarnation, in preserving Him as an infant from the malice of Herod, in anointing Him with the Holy Spirit—this bringing Him forth from the tomb is singled out for particular mention. Christ had presented Himself to Israel as their Messiah and had affirmed, "I and the Father are one." Had His claims been false, the grave would have retained Him; by raising Him from the dead by His power, God set His seal upon all Christ's teaching and demonstrated that He was indeed "the Son of God." "Though he was crucified through weakness"—for He made no effort to resist His enemies and deliver Himself out of their hands—"yet he liveth by the power of God" (II Cor. 13:4). Other passages state that Christ rose again by His *own* power, but that is not the side of the truth which is now before us.

The first question to consider: What was there particularly in connection with the raising of Christ from the dead which made God's mighty power far more manifest than the future raising of the whole human race will. Since the death which Christ died was no ordinary one, His resurrection must be an extraordinary one. Here we enter the realm of profoundest mystery, and only as our thoughts are formed by the clear teaching of Scripture can we, in any measure, enter into its meaning. God made Christ to be sin for His people when He laid upon Him the iniquities of them all. Consequently He was "made a curse" and was required to receive the awful wages of sin, which involved much more than the dissolution of soul and body. Christ not only died but was committed to the grave. "Christ being raised from the dead dieth no more; death hath no more *dominion over* him" (Rom. 6:9). This clearly implies that during those three days He was under death's power. He was death's prisoner, He was death's "lawful captive" (Isa. 49:24), held fast in its terrible grip.

"Whom God hath raised up, having loosed the pains of death: because it was not possible that he should be holden of it" (Acts 2:24). Here is New Testament proof that Christ was held by death and that God loosed Him from something in order for His resurrection. There is such a fullness to the words of Scripture that often no single definition can bring out their meaning. Such is the case here. The "pains of death" refer to what Christ endured upon the cross: not only, and not primarily, the bodily pains of natural death (acute and many though they were) but the soul anguish of spiritual death. John Calvin stated, "If Christ had merely died a corporal death, no end would have been accomplished by it: it was requisite also that He should feel the smart of the divine vengeance in order to appease the wrath of God and satisfy His justice. Hence it was necessary for Him to contend with the power of hell and the horror of eternal death." The pains of *that* "death" came upon Him when He exclaimed, "Now is my soul troubled" (John 12:27). Those pains increased in their intensity in Gethsemane, and were experienced in their fullness during the three hours of darkness, when God then "loosed" them, so that Christ experienced a resurrection of soul.

The Greek word for "pains" in Acts 2:24 is rendered "*travail* upon a woman with child" in I Thessalonians 5:3. Literally the term means "the birth throes of death." Light is cast on that almost paradoxical expression by Isaiah 53:11, where it was foreannounced that the Saviour should "see of the travail of his soul, and shall be satisfied." Before His Church could be vitally brought forth,

Christ had to endure in His soul the pangs of labor, and He *died* under the same pangs spiritually, when He was separated from God, though three hours later He was loosed from them. Those words "the pains of death" are a quotation of a Messianic utterance in Psalm 18:5: "the *cords* of hell compassed me about," which, under another metaphor, brings out a *different* aspect of Christ's death, namely, imprisonment and binding (cf. Matt. 5:25-26 for the same figure). As our Surety, Christ was arrested by divine justice and could not be discharged till He had paid our debt to the uttermost. His "It is finished" announced that full payment had been made, yet His body was not "loosed" from the grave till three days later (cf. "he was taken from *prison*," Isa. 53:8).

The *two* things are distinguished again in Christ's declaration "Thou wilt not leave my soul in hell [it was "loosed" and went to paradise]; neither wilt thou suffer thine Holy One to see corruption" of body (Ps. 16:10). Christ not only died but was "buried," and for three days remained in the *death state*. Hence God raised Him not merely from death but "from the dead," from the state of death: had He "revived" or quickened Him immediately after His expiring on the cross, that would have been raising Him from "death" but not "from the dead." Christ gained a victory not only over death but also over the grave. The two are distinguished in "O death, where is thy sting? O grave, where is thy victory?" (I Cor. 15:55). That explains "He raised him up from the dead [i.e., the death state], now no more to return to corruption" (Acts 13:34). Christ entered the state or place of corruption, namely, the grave but, according to Goodwin, "as His body was free from sickness while He lived, so it was free from corruption when He died."

Christ Not Merely Raised from Death but from the Dead

We believe, then, that there is a threefold *double* allusion in Acts 2:24. First, that the "death" from whose pains and cords God loosed Christ was the second death, which he "tasted" (Heb. 2:9), and physical dissolution. Second, that He was "loosed" from the pangs of the former at the close of the three hours of darkness (for His "Father, into thy hand I commend my spirit" evinces He was again in communion with Him); and that He was loosed from the latter when He came forth from the sepulcher. Third, that the Greek word in Acts 2:24 is rightly rendered "pains" or "travail throes," whereas the Hebrew word of Psalm 18:5 signifies "cords"—a clear hint of a *double* line of truth—bringing in the idea of one held in prison. It "was not possible that he should be holden" of death because the divine veracity was involved (God had announced His resurrection), because His covenant faithfulness was at stake, because the basic principle of His government ("Them that honour me I will honour") required Christ should be raised, and because the law demanded He should receive its award.

Now as it was God who delivered up Christ for our offenses (Acts 2:23; Rom. 4:24-25)—not only physical death but the whole of what is included in "the wages of sin"—so He alone could deliver Him from that death, and subsequently from the prison house of the grave. Personally we believe that God also then delivered Christ from *the powers of darkness*. On this point Scripture is not very explicit, yet we consider it is quite implicit. We know of no writer who has attempted to deal with this point—an admittedly mysterious one—and therefore we would be doubly cautious, and inform the reader that what we now advance is in no spirit of dogmatism. First, from the law of analogy does it not seem highly probable that Satan would make every possible effort to *prevent* the resurrection of Christ? Very shortly after Christ's birth the devil stirred up Herod to slay Him (Rev. 12:4), and should we not regard the second temptation (Matt. 4:5-6) as another desperate move in the same direction? We do know he put it into the heart of Judas to betray Him (John 13:2).

Second, when arrested in the Garden, Christ said to His enemies, "This is your hour, and the power of darkness" (Luke 22:53). For how long was that "hour" protracted? If Revelation 12:4 warrants the conclusion that the devil prompted Herod to slay Christ as a child, may we not fairly infer that he inspired the chief priests and Pharisees to say to Pilate, "Command therefore that the sepulchre be made sure" (Matt. 27:64) so that a heavy stone was placed over its mouth, the stone "sealed," and "a watch" of soldiers set to guard it? Third, does not "having spoiled principalities and powers, he made a show of them openly, triumphing over them in himself" (Col. 2:15) clearly imply a concerted effort on the part of the powers of evil to *oppose* His resurrection and ascension? How else did He "triumph over them"? Why was "the King of glory," on His entrance into heaven, greeted as "the LORD strong and mighty, the LORD mighty *in battle*" (Ps. 24:7-8)? Is not the likely reference to His victory over the infernal forces? Isaiah 58:18 seems to supply confirmation.

God's "Mighty Power"

Finally, does not *the analogy* drawn here with our conversion necessitate this conclusion? We are here said to "believe, *according to* the working of God's mighty power, which he wrought in Christ, when he raised him from the dead, and set him at his own right hand in the heavenly places." Now we know beyond any doubt that the mighty power of God in bringing us to savingly believe is concerned, in considerable part, in delivering us from the bondage of Satan (see Acts 26:18; Col. 1:13; Heb. 2:14-15). If then Satan sought to hold us forever but was foiled by divine omnipotence, and if there is an accurate and perfect parallel between that aspect of our conversion and what God wrought in Christ when He raised Him from the dead, then must we not conclude that Satan also sought to forever hold Christ in the grave, but that God defeated Him and triumphed over all his resistance? There is no doubt at all in our mind on the matter.

We turn now to consider why God's raising Christ from the dead is made the unit or standard of measurement of the power which He exercises in those "who believe." It is both the pattern and pledge of what God can and will do for His people. In the Old Testament the standard miracle was the deliverance of Israel from Egypt: again and again reference was made to the Red Sea as the supreme demonstration of God's power to help and to save. When the prophets sought to inspire courage and confidence they pointed back to that mighty deliverance (Isa. 43:16-18; 51:9-10). When God renewed His promise to Israel He took them back to the same spot and said, "According to the days of thy coming out of the land of Egypt will I show unto him marvellous things"

(Micah 7:15). But in the New Testament the Red Sea is superseded by the empty tomb, and the resurrection of Christ from the dead is pointed to as the grand triumph of Omnipotence and the standard of what God will do for us "who believe."

What comfort this should impart! What holy confidence it should inspire in the hearts of believers, that the mighty power of God is engaged to act for them! That the same power which wrought in Christ in raising Him from the dead operates both toward and in them. It is a power which is beyond resistance: "If God be for us, who can be against us?" It is a power which is superior to and triumphs over all our weakness: "Now unto him that is able to keep you." It is a power all-sufficient to supply our every need. When the Saviour taught us to pray for our daily sustenance, deliverance from evil, the forgiveness of our sins, what arguments did He bid us use? "For thine is the kingdom, and the power, and the glory." It is a power which will do for us exceeding abundantly above all that we ask or think (Eph. 3:20). How thankful we should be that this is so. How constantly we should look to and depend upon that power. How it should strengthen our faith to know that the One who brought again from the dead our Lord Jesus will yet make us "perfect in every good work to do his will" (Heb. 13:20-21).

Let us now endeavor to supply an answer to the question, What is the precise nature of the "power" which God exerted in raising Christ and in bringing us to savingly believe? Was it simply His omnipotence, or something in addition to it? Was it merely physical power? If not, what? By "physical power" we mean the might of God operating in the material realm, producing physical effects. Now if we keep in mind the nature of Christ's death as a satisfaction for sin, it should be quite obvious that more was involved in the raising of Him from the dead than there will be in the destruction of this earth and the creating of a new one. It may not be easy to find terms suited to express what we have in mind, still less to convey the ideas intelligently to our readers, yet we will make the attempt. When Christ cleansed the leper, opened the ears of the deaf, gave sight to the blind, there was an exercise of omnipotence. There was the same when God raised Christ from the dead, but there was something more.

The death of Christ was a legal transaction, therefore the *legal element* entered into His resurrection. His death was an enduring of the full penalty of the law, inflicted by the Judge of all. It was endured "the just for the unjust," the holy Surety receiving the awful wages due those He represented. And it was endured with fullest confidence as to the blessed issue. When Christ had "magnified the law" by serving and suffering, doing and dying, He "committed himself to him that judgeth righteously" (I Peter 2:23), declaring, "I know that I shall not be ashamed: he is near that justifieth me" (Isa. 50:7-8). And God's raising of Him from the dead was His *answer* to the dying appeal of the One who had been cast out by the world: it was God's response to the Saviour's trust in Himself. It was God acting as the divine Umpire in the controversy between His own Anointed and the world which had disowned Him—God reversing their erroneous verdict and exonerating the One who endured their malice to the extreme limit.

Christ Raised as Head of His People

Righteousness required that God should raise Christ from the dead. The law demanded that He who had so illustriously honored it should enter into its award. Holiness insisted that the sinless One should be released from the grave. By raising Him from the dead God openly declared that all Christ taught was true, set His seal upon the triumphant ending of His stupendous mission, and attested His acceptance of the satisfaction which He had made for His people. The original creation displayed the "eternal power and Godhead" of the Creator (Rom. 1:20), but what we are now considering did more than that: "Christ was raised . . . by the *glory* of the Father" (Rom. 6:4). Christ was raised not simply as a private person but as the Head of His people. The Church rose in and with Him (Eph. 2:5-6; Col. 3:1). To create was an act of power, but to bring forth a new creation out of the wrecked and ruined old creation was glorious power, a moral triumph. It was glorious power which transformed a curse into never ending blessing.

Christ was "made a curse for us" yet God has "made him most blessed for ever" (Ps. 21:6). Down to the grave itself the power which prevails over man (and which prevailed over the Son of man) is that of *death*. Thus the universal empire of sin has been attested: "Sin reigned in death" as the Greek of Romans 5:21 may be rendered. But resurrection makes manifest the more excellent power of *righteousness* by the triumphant reentering of the once-slain Just One into life. And with His liberty His people are freed. Hence, the verse which declares, "That as sin hath reigned unto [or 'in'] death" concludes by saying, "Even so might grace reign through righteousness unto eternal life by Jesus Christ our Lord." Thus our answer to the third question is not only the bare omnipotence of God but the power and glory of His righteousness, or His righteous power. That very expression is found substantially in His promise to the trembling saints: "Fear thou not; . . . I will uphold thee with *the right hand* of my *righteousness*" (Isa. 41:10).

What are the principal points of analogy between God's raising Christ from the dead and His operation in and for those who believe? Before answering that question let it be pointed out that the resurrection of Christ was not only the pattern of ours but also both the pledge and procuring cause thereof, for "he was raised again for *our* justification" (Rom. 4:25). The resurrection of Christ was necessary not only to evince God's acceptance of His satisfaction on our behalf but as a necessary step to secure the application of the merits of His sacrifice to us, to communicate "the sure mercies of David" (Acts 13:34) to us. "Because I live," said He, "ye shall live also" (John 14:19); otherwise He would be a Bridegroom without a bride, a Redeemer with no redeemed, the living Head of a lifeless body. God's raising of Christ from the dead was the pledge that He would quicken into newness of life all for whom He died. The Corn of wheat which died "bringeth forth much fruit" (John 12:24).

The margin of Isaiah 53:9 tells us that Christ was "with the wicked in his *deaths*," for in His soul He tasted of the second death and in His body He suffered natural death; thus He experienced both a spiritual and a natural resurrection. So too do His people: the former at their regeneration, the second at Christ's return. As Christ was delivered from penal death by the righteousness of God, so too are all who believe (Rom. 1:16-17). As Christ was delivered from the forces of Satan, so are we from "the power of darkness" (Col. 1:13). As Christ has been made "after the power of an endless life" (Heb. 7:16), so we shall "never perish but have everlasting life." As Christ was raised to honor and glory, so shall we be. Even now are we the sons of God, but it is not yet made manifest what we shall be: "but we know that, when he shall appear, we shall be *like him;* for we shall see him as he is" (I John 3:2). Hallelujah!

We have been occupied with the exceeding greatness of God's power in connection with His work of grace within His saints. Let us remind the reader that the passage we have been and are considering is not part of a formal statement of doctrine but rather of a *prayer*. In it the apostle made request that God's people might know, first, what is the sublime excellency of that power; second, that it is "to us-ward"—for us, acting on our behalf, our grand recourse; third, that it is effectual, for we "believe" according to its invincible might; fourth, that it operates to and within us "according to" what it wrought in Christ when God raised Him from the dead. A might no less than *that is* carrying forward the good work in our souls to a triumphant completion. Now it is of vast importance that Christians should more firmly and fully "know" and apprehend these things, otherwise we should not be taught (by Paul's example) to make earnest supplication for them. Before passing on, let us briefly point out the kind of "knowledge" which is here in view.

How to Obtain a Knowledge of Spiritual Things

There are three ways by which the believer may obtain a knowledge of spiritual things: by a diligent application of the mind to the teaching of Scripture, by the exercise of faith on what is revealed, by a personal experience of spiritual things in the soul and life. Obviously it is not a mere mental understanding of them that is here in view, for that may be obtained without having recourse to prayer. Nor do we think that this fourth petition had reference to an enlarged experience of the substance of it. Those who have followed *closely* our exposition of Ephesians 1:17-19 should neither be surprised nor stumbled at our conclusion. When Paul expressed the longing "That I may know him, and the power of his resurrection" (Phil. 3:10) he was undoubtedly referring to a closer acquaintance with Christ and an increased measure of the virtue of His resurrection *in the effects* of it—that he might experience more deliverance from that spiritual deadness which the workings of unbelief produce even in the renewed. But this is not the particular aspect of truth or of Christian experience which is before us in Ephesians 1:19-21.

In our comments on "in the knowledge of him" (close of v. 17) we sought to show that the reference there is to a more intimate and influential knowledge of God in Christ, an increasing experimental acquaintance with Him, resulting in our delighting ourselves in Him and enjoying closer fellowship, leading to an open acknowledgment of Him by lip and life. Then we pointed out that "ye may know what is the hope of his calling" means "ye might perceive the clear evidences of the same, the grounds on which rests your realization of having received an effectual call from God, and thereby be assured of your filial relation to Him. "And what the riches of the glory of his inheritance in the saints" we defined as "a better apprehension of the object of your hope, and realization of the glory to which you have been called." "And what is the exceeding greatness of his power" signifies that our hearts may be assured that, notwithstanding all hindrances and obstacles, God will complete His good work in us and bring us safely into the promised inheritance.

Observe, it is not "what is the exceeding greatness of God's power which has wrought or is working *in* us" but "which is to us-ward"—something objective for faith and not subjective in experience. We thus concur with Goodwin: "For a man to take in and understand that he may glorify God and believe what a great power it was that raised up Christ from death to life, and that no less power works in believers when it produces faith, *that* is the 'knowledge' the apostle meant here." Oh, that believers might realize from the effects produced in them by the presence and operations of a God-given faith, what a mighty power must have wrought in them, and will continue doing so. That they might not only have evidence of what God's power has wrought in them but also perceive more clearly *the character of* that power itself and be trustfully occupied with it. The power of God infinitely transcends all our feelings or experiences of it. Faith needs to be absorbed with the power itself and not merely with the effects of it.

The knowledge faith conveys to the soul is all too little realized. Saving faith enables its possessor to conceive of things which are incomprehensible to mere human reason, imparting a knowledge to which scientists and philosophers are strangers. "Through faith we *understand* that the worlds were framed by the word [or mere fiat] of God" (Heb. 11:3). Faith gives a subsistence in the mind to the things hoped for and makes real things unseen. Faith engages the heart with objects which lie far beyond the reach of any natural sense, for example, the future resurrection of our bodies. Faith knows what reason cannot grasp and that with which feelings have nothing to do. Man wants to know before he will believe, but faith has to be exercised before the things of God can be *known:* "which believe *and* know the truth" (I Tim. 4:3). It is not that we are assured and therefore believe, but "we believe and *are sure*" (John 6:69). If we would experience more of God's power, we must *know* more about it through the exercise of faith upon it. "If thou wouldest believe, thou shouldest see the glory of God" (John 11:40)—that is His unchanging order.

Working of God's Mighty Power

In the preceding chapter we dwelt on the fact that the power exercised by God in His work of grace within us is "according to the working of his mighty power, which he wrought in Christ, when he raised him from the dead." But that does not complete the inspired statement: "*and* set him at his own right hand in the heavenly places, far above all principality, and power" (vv. 20-21). That also exemplifies the power of God to us. Not only God's raising of Christ but His translation and exaltation of Him are also essential parts of the standard of His operations in and for His saints. *This* is what God would have us know, and this is what our faith needs to be engaged with and exercised upon: that what God wrought in the Head, He will work in His members; that Christ is here represented as the pattern or standard of His operations to Christians. The love which moved the Father to work so gloriously in His Son is the love which the Father has for His sons (John 17:23). The physical, legal, and moral power which the Father put forth for Christ is being exercised for us. The wondrous works that power performed on the Redeemer will be duplicated in the redeemed.

"And set him [caused Him to sit] at his own right hand in the heavenly places." This brings before us one of the grand articles of the Christian faith. The death, resurrection, and exaltation of Christ form the threefold foundation on which rest all our hopes. Each transcends the grasp of finite intelligence, yet they are "without contradiction" to those taught of God. The moment we begin to reason about them we create difficulties and confuse ourselves. Only as we receive in simplicity what is divinely revealed thereon will our faith "stand in the power of God." The exaltation of Christ is as profound a mystery to carnal wisdom as His death and resurrection, but the one is as clearly set forth as the other in the Word of truth. Is the question raised, How was it possible for God the Son to be exalted? It is sufficient reply to inquire, How was it possible for Him to be abased? It is not God the Son simply and absolutely that we are here contemplating, but God the Son as He had taken human nature into personal union with Himself. It was the God-man who died, who was raised again, who was exalted.

The question of how it was possible for a divine person to be exalted is best resolved by considering what that exaltation consisted of. So far as we can perceive, it included three things: the removing of that veil which had been thrown over the divine glory of the Son of God by His incarnation, the elevation of human nature into heaven, the divine reward bestowed upon the person of the Mediator for His blessed work. Thomas Manton stated, "His exaltation answered His humiliation: His death was answered by His resurrection, His going into the grave by His ascending into heaven, His lying in the tomb by His sitting at God's right hand." So much for a general statement. Now let us proceed to amplify it. None who accredit the declarations of Holy Writ will challenge the statement that in the Son's becoming incarnate his glory was *veiled;* and it had to be, for no man can see God and live (Exodus 33:20). "Who, being in the form of God, thought it not robbery to be equal with God: but made himself of no reputation, and took upon him the form of a servant, and was made in the likeness of men" (Phil. 2:6-7).

The earthly life of our Saviour was one of profound abasement. From the manger to the tomb His life was a course of shame, suffering, and sorrow. During those thirty-three years His divine glory was eclipsed, though some rays of it broke through occasionally, manifesting to the attentive and especially the spiritual observers something of His essential and official dignity. The angelic hosts announcing His birth, the holiness of His life, the miracles He performed, the testimony of the Father from heaven, His transfiguration on the mount, all proclaimed Him to be the Son of God, the promised Redeemer of Israel. Even the dark scene of His death was relieved by phenomena which signified He was no ordinary sufferer: the darkness at midday, the earthquake, the rending of the temple veil by an invisible hand. Nevertheless, sorrow and shame were

Christ's experience from infancy to death. He was, for the most part, despised and rejected of men and had not where to lay His head. It was not until His resurrection that the ignominy of His crucifixion was removed, the hope of His disciples renewed. It was then His prayer in John 17:15 began to receive answer.

Let it be clearly understood that at the incarnation there was no diminishing of the Son's essential glory, for that can neither decrease nor increase; but it was obscured in its manifestation before the eyes of both angels and men. The Puritans were wont to illustrate this by a total eclipse of the sun. During that eclipse the sun loses none of its native light and beauty but remains the same in itself; however, because of heavy clouds or the moon coming between it and the earth, the sun appears dark to us. Yet as soon as the clouds are dispersed or the sun is freed from the lunar interposition, its splendor is again revealed. So the divine majesty of the Son was obscured when "the Word became flesh," for "the mighty God" took upon Him "the form of a servant," entering the place of subservience and submission, and became obedient to death; yet it was "Immanuel"—none other than "the Lord of glory"—who was crucified.

The Exaltation of Christ

It was necessary that the divine glory of Christ should, in large measure, have been concealed during "the days of his flesh," for had it been manifested in its native brightness the sons of men would have been utterly overwhelmed. But it was not right that His divine majesty should be obscured after He had accomplished His great work: "Ought not Christ to have suffered these things, and to enter into his glory?" (Luke 24:26). That "ought" governs and applies equally to both clauses. The sufferings of Christ were necessary for the expiating of our sins, and His exaltation was equally necessary for applying to us the merits of His death. The resurrection of Christ was a requisite step to His elevation or entrance into glory, as the fetching of Joseph out of prison was, before he could be made next to Pharaoh: he could not be the governor of Egypt while he was a prisoner! Having accomplished the undertaking assigned Him by the Father and being brought forth from the tomb, there was no occasion for Christ to prolong His stay on earth.

After establishing the faith of His apostles, His "ambassadors," by "many infallible proofs" that He had triumphed over death and the grave, thereby vindicating His character from the aspersions of His enemies and demonstrating that He had "obtained eternal redemption" for His people, it was expedient that Christ should be taken to heaven so that He might exercise His priestly office within the veil and send the Holy Spirit to them to carry forward His works on earth (John 16:5-7). In ascending to heaven, Christ did not leave behind the veil of His flesh but went there as still clothed in humanity, having taken the same into eternal union with His divine person, and so He entered the Father's presence in our nature. Scripture is too plain for any mistake on this score. The risen Christ appeared to His disciples in a body of "flesh and bones" and ate food before them (Luke 24:39, 43). And after being seen of them forty days, "while they beheld, he was taken up; and a cloud received him out of their sight." Yet two angels assured them, "This same Jesus, which is taken up from you into heaven, shall so come in like manner as ye have seen him go into heaven" (Acts 1:9, 11).

The change of place was followed immediately by a change of state. Stephen Charnock declared, "As He descended to assume our nature, so He ascended to glorify our nature. By translating it to heaven, assurance was given that it should never be laid aside, but be forever preserved in that marriage knot with the Divine." The glorification of our Lord's humanity (a foreshadowing of which was vouchsafed upon the holy mount) is altogether beyond human comprehension, but several details are given to help us form some conception of it. At His baptism God anointed Him "with the Holy Spirit and with power" (Acts 10:38), but upon His ascension it is said of Him, "Thy God hath anointed thee with the oil of gladness [the Spirit] above thy fellows" (Heb. 1:9). We believe this was to capacitate His humanity for the offices which were henceforth to be performed in it. We quote Charnock again: "It was so enlarged and spiritualized as to be a convenient habitation for all the fulness of His Deity to reside in and perform all its proper operations: 'in him dwelleth all the fulness of the Godhead bodily' (Col. 2:9): not dwelling as if imprisoned, but to break forth in all its glories and graces; not 'formerly so dwelling' in it, but now 'dwelleth.' If the righteous are to 'shine forth as the sun in the kingdom of their Father' (Matt. 13:43) the Head of the righteous shines with a splendor above the sun, for He hath a glory upon His body, not only from the glory of His soul (as the saints shall have), but from the glory of His Divinity in conjunction with it. The glory of His Divinity redounds upon His humanity like a beam of the sun that conveys a dazzling brightness to a piece of crystal."

What that dazzling brightness appears like may be gathered from the blinding effect which a momentary appearance of it had on Saul of Tarsus: "There shone from heaven a great light round about" him, accompanied by the voice of "Jesus of Nazareth," and we are told that for a while he "could not see for the glory of that light" (Acts 22:6-11). How necessary it was for Christ to be taken to heaven: no mortal could have lived in the presence of the glorified Christ on earth. The man of sin will be destroyed by "the brightness of his coming" (II Thess. 2:8).

Third, the exaltation of Christ was the divine reward bestowed on the Mediator for His blessed work. It was fit that God should glorify Christ because of the glory which redounded to Him from His work. The Redeemer was but stating a fact when He said to the Father, "I have glorified thee on the earth: I have finished the work which thou gavest me to do" (John 17:4). God received more glory from the completed work of Christ than He did from all the works of His own hands. His law was magnified, His government vindicated, His archenemy overthrown, His image restored to His people, and therefore it was fitting that He should crown the Mediator with glory and honor. Because He had poured out His soul unto death, God said, "*therefore* will I divide him a portion with the great" (Isa. 53:12). Because He had loved righteousness and hated iniquity, therefore God anointed Him with the oil of gladness above His fellows (Ps. 45:7). Because He became obedient unto death, even the death of the cross, "God also hath highly exalted him, and given him a name which is above every name" (Phil. 2:9). That was a mediatory glory which was conferred upon Him.

The closing verses of Ephesians 1 go on to inform us what that reward consists of. It was the seating of Christ as the Mediator at God's own right hand. It was the elevating of Him above all the celestial hierarchies. It was the putting of all things under His feet, so that the very forces of evil are now beneath His immediate control. It was the giving Him to be Lord over all things as actual Governor of the universe. It was that He might exercise universal dominion for the good of His Church. It was that He might fill all things. Thus we see again the necessity for translating Christ from earth to heaven. Since all providence is administered from heaven, and since all power (Matt. 28:18) and all judgment (John 5:22) have been committed to Christ, it was right that He should sit upon a celestial throne. He who has been given the nations for His inheritance and the uttermost part of the earth for His possession could not suitably sway His scepter from some local corner of His empire. As Charnock points out, "It was not congruous that He who was made the Head of principalities and powers, the Governor of the angelic spirits, should have a meaner dwelling than the greatest of His subjects and as low as the vilest of His vassals." "Such an high priest became us, . . . holy, harmless, undefiled, separate from sinners, and made higher than the heavens" (Heb. 7:26).

The French Puritan Daille ably argued: "The wisdom of God hath disposed all causes in an order superior to those effects which depend upon them: the heavens are above the earth because the earth is influenced by them, and the sun above the earth because the earth is enlightened by it. It was no less necessary according to the order of God's wisdom, that He who was made by God His Viceroy both in heaven and in earth, and had the management of all things conferred upon Him, should be lodged in a place superior to all His subjects."

It was fit that as an earthly king should have an earthly palace, our great High Priest should dwell in a temple not made with hands. How could He fittingly bring the Church to a happy immortality unless He was first in possession of that heaven to which He was to conduct it? Since He is ordained the Judge of the whole world, must He not sit in the heavenly court and there in majesty execute that solemn charge!

The Mediator Exalted Above All

As Mediator, Christ was and is both God and man, or the God-man, and as such He has been exalted and rewarded. His divine glory is no longer eclipsed, for instead of acting in the form of a servant, He now reigns as King of kings and Lord of lords. His humanity has been elevated to heaven and glorified with a glory that outshines every other creature. Though He is still clothed with flesh, yet his divine glory is not now veiled as it once was. His humanity is now filled with all the divine perfections of which a created nature is possibly capable. It is not deified but glorified.

John Owen wrote regarding Christ's humanity, "It is not made omniscient, omnipresent, omnipotent, but is exalted in a fulness of all Divine perfections and infinitely above the glory of angels and men. For the *substance* of this glory of the human nature of Christ believers shall be made partakers of it, for when we shall see Him as He is 'we shall be like Him'; but as unto the degrees and *measure* of it, His glory is above all that we can be made partakers of."

Chapter 15

PRAYER OF ADORATION

EPHESIANS 1:20-23

THOSE CHRISTIANS are greatly the losers whose thoughts about Christ are almost confined to the manger of Bethlehem and the cross of Calvary. While we cannot be sufficiently thankful for Christ's death, for our salvation, and for everlasting bliss hinged thereon, we must bear in mind that His death at Golgotha was not the termination of His history. Important instructions and spiritual advantages are derived by directing our attention to His resurrection also, for that blessed event not only bore conclusive testimony to the divinity of His mission and supplied the most solid ground for our faith in Him; it is likewise the pledge and assurance that we too shall be raised from the dead. The Word of truth goes on to inform us that, after continuing on earth for forty days, the risen Saviour ascended to heaven, that He is now seated at the right hand of God, where He intercedes for His people. In the epistles our gaze is frequently directed to the glorified and exalted state of our Saviour, and it is the privilege and duty of faith to follow Him into the Father's presence, view Him within the veil, and eye Him as the King of kings.

The Supremacy of the God-Man Mediator

In the closing portion of the apostle's prayer in Ephesians 1 we are reminded that the risen Redeemer has been invested with all power, authority and dominion. That was part of His reward and triumph (Phil. 2:9). It was as the God-man Mediator that He was thus invested and given the scepter of the universe. Also, as the Head of the Church Christ passed within the veil "whither the forerunner is for us entered" (Heb. 6:20). How that ought to strengthen the faith and encourage the hearts of all who have put their trust in Him! No room is left for doubt or uncertainty of the value and acceptableness to God of Christ's obedience and death. The Father has given to the very One who bore the sins and curse of His people the supreme place of honor in heaven. How that intimates the place which the salvation of His saints occupies in God's counsels and government! The position to which the Saviour has been elevated demonstrates beyond any doubt the degree of importance which God Himself attaches to the redemption of His Church. The position which Christ now occupies and the power which has been given to Him are for the sake of His blood-bought ones.

"That ye may know . . . what is the exceeding greatness of his power to us-

144

ward . . . which he wrought in Christ, when he raised him from the dead, and set him at his own right hand in the heavenly places" (Eph. 1:18-20). The whole emphasis is here thrown upon the mighty and wondrous operations of the Father, and not upon the exercise of the Son's divine attributes as in John 10:18 and Ephesians 4:8. That power of God in the raising, exalting, and glorifying of Christ was not according to or directed by the ordinary course of nature; it was special, extraordinary, supernatural—contrary to nature and beyond the power of any creature to effect. So also are the regeneration and sanctification of all the members of Christ's mystical Body. Their faith is "of the operation of God, who hath raised him from the dead" (Col. 2:12). Therefore, the transitive "and set," or "caused to sit," is here used rather than the intransitive "to sit on his throne" as in Acts 2:30, because God is seen bestowing upon the Mediator His well-earned reward as well as expressing His love for the Son.

This expression of Christ's sitting at God's right is not to be carnalized, as though it were a literal form of speech depicting His present posture in heaven; rather is it to be understood as a metaphor or simile, and interpreted by its use elsewhere. That Christ is not actually and permanently seated is quite clear from such statements as "the Son of man standing on the right hand of God" (Acts 7:56) and the One "who walketh in the midst of the seven golden candlesticks" (Rev. 2:1), and "in the midst of the elders stood a Lamb" (Rev. 5:6). The passages just quoted also make it plain that Christ's being "seated" is far from importing that He is now in a state of inactivity; rather, He is constantly engaged on behalf of His Church, employing His power and honors in promoting its interests, until His work of mediation is carried forward to perfect consummation.

At least four things are connoted by Christ's being "seated." First, it is emblematic of *rest from a finished work*. We cannot contemplate aright the present state of our Lord without calling to mind the circumstances of His being there: "*When* he had by himself purged our sins [He] sat down on the right hand of the Majesty on high" (Heb. 1:3). His sacrificial service and sufferings are ended: His work of expiation is completed. "It is finished," He cried from the cross, and proof thereof is His being seated on high. "Every priest [of Judaism] *standeth*, daily ministering and offering oftentimes the same sacrifices, which cannot take away sins" (Heb. 10:11). Among the furniture of the tabernacle and temple there was no chair! "But this Man, after he had offered one sacrifice for sins, for ever *sat down* on the right hand of God" (v. 12). Israel's priests never accomplished the design of their office, but Christ's perfect oblation fully satisfied justice, and God bore testimony to the same by translating Him to heaven.

Second, it marks *the beginning of a new work*. This is taught us in Acts 2 where we are told that on the day of Pentecost "there appeared unto them [i.e., the apostles of 1:26, the "them" of 2:1-3; cf. 2:14] cloven tongues like as of fire, and it *sat* upon each of them. And they were filled with the Holy Ghost." For three years the apostles had companied with Christ and been trained by Him, but now their apprenticeship was over, and their real mission, as the ambassadors of the King, was about to commence. To equip them for their exalted task they were anointed by the Spirit. Thus it was with Christ: His work of expiation was completed, but His enthronement on high marked the beginning of His administration of His kingdom. The life, death, and resurrection of Christ simply laid the foundation upon which His royal conquests are now being achieved. His work as the King-Priest only began when He was invested with "all power." He is now "upholding all things by the word of his power." (Heb. 1:3), wielding His scepter to good effect.

Third, Christ's being "seated" is indicative of honor and dignity. When used officially, to sit denotes dignity and exaltation: a superior raised above his inferiors, as a king upon his throne, a judge on the bench. Thus that Old Testament expression to sit in the gate (Ruth 4:1-2; cf. Deut. 16:18) signified the holding of a judicial court. Job alluded to that when he said, "When I went out to the gate through the city, when I prepared my [magisterial] seat in the street, the young men saw me . . . and the aged men arose, and stood up" (29:7-8). When the Most High is pictured as holding session, the august scene is portrayed thus: "The Ancient of days did sit . . .: his throne was like the fiery flame . . .: thousand thousands ministered unto him, and ten thousand times ten thousand stood before him: the judgment was set, and the books were opened" (Dan. 7:9-10; for other examples of this third meaning, see Matt. 25:31; Rev. 20:11).

Fourth, Christ's seating signifies a state of continuance. Christ's humiliation was only temporary, but His exaltation and enthronement are permanent. Jacob, in speaking of Joseph's suffering and then his glory, said, "The archers have sorely grieved him, and shot at and hated him: but his bow abode in strength" (Gen. 49:23-24). The Hebrew verb is literally "sat" but fittingly rendered "abode," as in this verse: "Therefore shall ye abide [sit] at the door of the tabernacle" (Lev. 8:35). The position of highest honor belonging to Christ is a perpetual one. He is "seated" surely and durably. "In mercy shall the throne be established: and he shall sit upon it in truth in the tabernacle of David" (Isa. 16:5). To have Christ sit upon it and to have the throne established is all one. "His dominion is an everlasting dominion, . . . and his kingdom that which shall not be destroyed" (Dan. 7:14).

Christ at God's Right Hand

Being incorporeal, God has no physical members; when mention is made of them, they are to be understood metaphorically. His seating of Christ at "his own right hand" intimates His love for Him. The first occurrence in Scripture of that figurative expression is found in the marginal rendering of Genesis 35:18. When his beloved Rachel gave birth to her second son, Jacob called him "Benjamin" which signifies "the son of the right hand"—a name of endearment. Benjamin was the last of the aged patriarch's sons. Jacob, in styling Benjamin the son of his right hand, was expressing his deep affection for him as inheriting the tender place which his mother had formerly possessed in his heart. We believe this is the basic idea here. As God had "spared not his own Son" (Rom. 8:32) when He was propitiating His judicial wrath, so on the completion of that work He placed Him "at his own right hand." If the Father loved Christ because He laid down His life (John 10:17), would not His love be prompted to stronger manifestations after He had laid it down?

Christ's being at the right hand of God signifies His enjoyment of all blessedness. This is brought out in Psalm 16:11. It is to be carefully noted that its words are those of Messiah and spoken by Him expressly with a view to His exaltation. After saying, "Thou wilt not leave my soul in hell; neither wilt thou suffer thine Holy One to see corruption" He went on to declare, "Thou wilt show me the path of life: in thy presence is fulness of joy; at thy right hand there are pleasures for evermore." This denotes the intimacy of His fellowship with the Father in the full light of His countenance.

Christ's being "at God's right hand" tells of *His dignity, honor, and glory.* When kings expressed their respect for those whom they favored, they did so by setting them at their right hand. An illustration of that is found in I Kings 2:19, where Solomon bestowed this honor upon his mother; the same thought was in the mind of the wife of Zebedee when she made request that, in the day to come, her sons might sit one at Christ's right hand and the other at His left (Matt. 20:20-21). God's placing of Christ at His right hand signified the conferring of supreme honor upon Him—the place of eminence and glory. God translated Enoch and Elijah to heaven, but they are nowhere said to sit at His right hand. "To which of the angels said he at any time, Sit on my right hand?" (Heb. 1:13). That is a dignity peculiar to Christ Himself.

To be seated "at God's right hand" announces Christ's supreme power and dominion. "Hereafter shall ye see the Son of man sitting on the right hand of power" (Matt. 26:64). It signified the investing of Christ with supreme authority. He sits "on the right hand of the majesty on high" and is personally "upholding all things by the word of his power" (Heb. 1:3). "All power is given unto me *in heaven* and on earth" (Matt. 28:18) is His own ringing averment. The throne over the whole universe is "the throne of God *and* of the Lamb" (Rev. 22:3), "that all men should honour the Son even as they honour the Father" (John 5:23).

If on the one hand it was the Father who bestowed this blessedness, honor, and authority upon the God-man Mediator, on the other hand the Son had full right to them. Things are so carried out between the Father and the Son that each is distinctly magnified. Christ's exaltation is the Father's gift, and therein He is owned; likewise it is the Son's due, and so He is recognized. All power is given to Him, yet He said plainly to His apostles, "I appoint unto you a kingdom" (Luke 22:29). As the Father raises up the dead and quickens them, even so the Son quickens whom He will (John 5:21). There is perfect oneness of accord: Christ exercises sovereignty of will, for it is His right to do so, yet He does nothing but what pleases the Father. As the man Christ Jesus was united to the Son of God, He had *the right*—not simply as a reward for His work, but because of His Godhead—to all that has been bestowed on Him. As Jehovah's "fellow" nothing less befits Him.

We don't agree with those writers who say it was the humanity of Christ alone that was exalted. The Son of God Himself, though in our nature, was accorded the highest throne in heaven: "and set him [not 'it'] at his own right hand." It was a Person who was thus magnified. The whole Christ rose, and the whole Christ sits at God's right hand. We are not able to comprehend this mystery, yet faith gladly receives it. Faith has to do with what is written, not in reasoning, nor answering the objections of the carnal mind. If we abide by what is recorded in Holy Writ we cannot err, and Scripture declares, "The LORD said unto my Lord [not simply 'unto the Son of man'], Sit thou at my right hand" (Ps. 110:1). This verse is quoted more frequently in the New Testament than any other verse. Now the foundation of Christ's being David's "Lord" lay in His being the Son of God, and it was the second Person in the Trinity, who had taken human nature into union with Himself, that Jehovah the Father invited to sit at His own right hand. The throne belongs to Him both as God and as man (see Ps. 45:6; John 5:27).

The Glorified Humanity of Christ

The human nature of Christ, subsisting in His divine person, has been exalted above all creatures in dignity, glory, and authority. That evinces the infinite love of the Father for Him and His ineffable delight in Him. It should greatly delight our hearts and be constantly contemplated, not by fancy and imagination but by faith and in adoring worship. As we pointed out in the preceding chapter, Christ's change of place (from earth to heaven) was at once followed by a change of state, His human nature then being glorified and its capacity enlarged. We are strongly inclined to believe there is a reference to that in "God was manifest in the flesh, justified by the Spirit, *seen of angels,* preached unto the Gentiles" (I Tim. 3:16). The position of that clause intimates as much. Nor are we alone in that view. So cautious and conservative a commentator as Ellicott interpreted it thus: "The angels now for the first time saw, gazed upon, and rejoiced in the vision of the Godhead in the glorified humanity of the Son; and what the angels gained in the beatific vision, the nations of the world obtained through the preaching of the Gospel, namely, a knowledge of the endless love of God and the surpassing glory of Christ."

"We have such a high priest, who is set on the right hand of the throne of the Majesty in the heavens; a minister of the sanctuary" (Heb. 8:1-2). Here an additional aspect is emphasized, namely, that Christ is exalted as our great High Priest. His is a royal priesthood: He is endowed with regal as well as sacerdotal authority. Note well this verse comes immediately after Hebrews 7, where we have Christ set forth as the antitypical Melchizedek or Priest-King. As such He ministers in the heavenly tabernacle: a "priest upon his throne" (Zech. 6:13), that is, a Priest in kingly state, invested with royal dominion. Christ does not await a future millennium to enter upon His kingly office; He exercises it now. "Majesty" signifies the kingly power of God, and Christ is seated at the "right hand" of that very Majesty (Heb. 1:3). The One who when here had not where to lay His head is now crowned with glory and honor. The One whom men spat upon and smote is now the Lord Sovereign of heaven and earth. All heaven owns His scepter and renders homage to Him.

"And set him at his own right hand in the heavenly places, far above all principality, and power" (Eph. 1:20-21). Here is the place where Christ now dwells: in heaven itself. Acts 7:48-49 tells us that heaven is the court of the great God, where His throne is. It is there that God has appointed Jesus Christ to be honored. His advancement corresponds to His abasement: as He descended into unparalleled depths of shame and woe, so He has been elevated to surpassing heights of honor and bliss. As I Peter 3:22 tells us, He "is gone into heaven, and is on the right hand of God." There in "the ivory palaces" (Ps. 45:8) our Redeemer abides. Though by His Deity He is omnipresent—in the midst of every two or three who are gathered together in His name—yet in His theanthropic person He is localized—for His humanity is not ubiquitous (everywhere). Hence when He judges the wicked, because they cannot be suffered to enter heaven, He comes down to them—though bringing heaven with Him, for He "shall come in the glory of his Father with his angels" (Matt. 16:27).

"And set him at his own right hand in the heavenly places, far above all principality, and power." That tells of the eminence of His elevation. God has not only exalted but "highly exalted" Him (Phil. 2:9), not only "above" but "far above all principality, and power" or, as Hebrews 7:26 expresses it, "made higher than the heavens." That One who glorified the Father so superlatively on earth has been exalted to the highest conceivable honor and glory. Christ has been raised above the celestial hosts not only as their Head but of vastly superior rank and dignity. There are ranks or grades among the angels, though precisely what those differences are, we do not know. There is "principality and power, and might and dominion," but Christ is advanced high above them all, being set in authority over them all. This is dwelt on in Hebrews 1:4: "Being made so much better than the angels, as he hath by inheritance obtained a more excellent name than they." The glory He entered into upon His ascension was proportionate and consonant to the name which is His by essential right.

Ephesians 1:21 gives us a detailed account of our Lord's supremacy. He passed by the dignitaries of heaven when in love He descended to assume the form and name of a servant for our sakes. But when God exalted Him, He "glorified his Servant Jesus" (Acts 3:13, R. V.) as well as openly confirmed His Son (Heb. 1:4-5). That supremacy of Christ is not only eminent but universal: "angels and authorities and powers being made subject unto him" (I Peter 3:22). "And every name that is named, not only in this world, but also in that which is to come" (Eph. 1:21), i.e., both on earth and in heaven, here and hereafter. Christ has been advanced above every other excellence and honor. Not only has supremacy of position been conferred upon Him but also supremacy of name. His name is accorded the worship due God alone, not only by the Church below but by the angels above (Heb. 1:6). To His name every knee shall yet bow (Phil. 2:10). Then what is Christ due from us? Our hearts, our lives, our all.

That which is set before us in the closing verses of Ephesians 1 is purely a matter of divine revelation and therefore can be received and enjoyed only by a God-given faith. What is there made known to us by the Holy Spirit is wholly beyond the reach of physical observation and completely transcends the realm of Christian experience. That God has seated Christ at His own right hand is plainly affirmed in the Word of truth. Though it lies far above the present verification of our senses, nevertheless it is a glorious fact which faith unhesitatingly receives on divine authority. The same is equally true of the other facts here mentioned. Christ's exaltation over the celestial hosts, all things being put under His feet, the use He is now making of His mighty power, and the relations which the Church sustains to Him transcend the sphere of our senses. They are things which can neither be seen nor felt by us, yet they are real and glorious to faith. Unless *that* be firmly grasped by the expositor, he is bound to err in his interpretation of the details.

Christ Given Supreme Governmental Authority

The exaltation of Christ is exhibited to us under the double metaphor of God's *seating* Him at his own right hand, which signifies (in brief) the investing of the Mediator with that supreme governmental authority which hitherto had been exercised by God alone: the scepter of the universe is now wielded by the God-man, Christ Jesus. What follows is an account of the distinctive honors which have been conferred on Him. First, He has been advanced "far above all principality, and power, and might, and dominion, and every name that is named, not only in this world, but also in that which is to come" (v. 21). All intelligences being reduced to one common level is certainly not the law or principle which obtains in heaven! Nor is this true of those in the kingdom over which Satan now presides, as Ephesians 6:12 makes clear. The glory of a king lies not only in his having subjects but in his having a "court" or subjects of varying ranks: commoners, knights, nobles. Such is the glorious court of the King of kings.

Second, all creatures are *set in subjection* to Christ, for that is the meaning of "and hath put all things under his feet" (v. 22), an expression importing the highest sovereignty and power. Christ is not only elevated above all creatures but He has dominion over them. They are subordinated to Him and governed by Him. Jesus Christ has been made Lord (Acts 2:36), "he is Lord of all" (Acts 10:36), He is "Lord over all" (Rom. 10:12), He is "Lord both of the dead and living" (Rom. 14:9). The One who died at Calvary is now the Ruler of the universe. This very day He holds in His hand "the keys of hell and of death" (Rev. 1:18). Since the hour of His ascension He has been "upholding all things by the word of his power" (Heb. 1:3). At this moment He is *ruling* "in the midst of . . . [His] enemies" (Ps. 110:2). "And hath put all things under his feet" is an accomplished fact and not a future prospect, though He still awaits the final subjugation of His foes. Christ *is* Lord over all, little as the profane world realizes and owns it. It is a present reality, though the full results of it do not yet appear to our senses.

This investing of the Mediator with universal dominion was the subject of Old Testament prophecy. "And I saw in the night visions, and, behold, one like the Son of man came with [in] the clouds of heaven [i.e., in manifested majesty], . . . to [not from] the Ancient of days, and they [His celestial attendants] brought him near before him. And there was given him dominion, and glory, and a kingdom, that all people, nations, and languages, should serve him: his dominion is an everlasting dominion, which shall not pass away, and his kingdom that which shall not be destroyed" (Dan. 7:13-14). The words "one *like* the Son of man" (cf. Rev. 1:13; 14:14) need cause no difficulty. It is the selfsame Person who is so frequently designated "the Son of man" in the first three Gospels but in an altered state—then in abasement and humiliation, now exalted and glorified. "The Ancient of days" signifies the Father: from Him Christ came to this earth (John 16:28), to Him He returned (John 20:17), by Him He was then rewarded and enthroned. The verb "hath put" assures us that this prediction has been fulfilled.

"And hath put all things under his feet" is another metaphor, but its meaning is plain, namely, that God has exalted Christ to such dignity and dominion that everything is under His power, in subjection to Him. This is clear from the first passage in which the expression occurs: "Thou madest him to have dominion over the works of thy hands; thou hast put all things under his feet" (Ps. 8:6). The one clause defines the other. The scope of the "all things" is amplified in the words that follow: "all sheep and oxen, yea, and the beasts of the field; the fowl of the air, and the fish of the sea" (vv. 7-8). Hebrews 2:8 still further points out, "For in that he put [not 'will put' in some future era] all in subjection under him, he left nothing . . . not put under Him," nothing visible or invisible, in heaven or earth, friend or foe. "But now we see not [with our natural eyes] yet all things put under him," though we shall one day behold that too. Meanwhile, "we see Jesus [with the eyes of faith] . . . crowned with glory and honour" (Heb. 2:8-9) as exhibited in the closing verses of Ephesians 1.

"And hath put all things under his feet." As is so often the case, many of the commentators have unjustifiably restricted the scope of these words, limiting them to the subjugation of His enemies. Undoubtedly that is part of their meaning, yet their primary significance and extent is the subjection of all— friends and foes alike. "All the people that follow thee" (Pharaoh, Exodus 11:8) and "all the people that follow me" (Benhadad, I Kings 20:10) are rightly rendered in the margin "at thy feet" and "at my feet." Thus it is all one to say, "All the people that are 'thy subjects' or 'at thy feet.' " As we have seen, "Thou hast put all things under his feet" (Ps. 8:6) is interpreted in "Thou hast put all things *in subjection* under him"; "nothing" is excepted (Heb. 2:8). Bowing one's head to another indicates reverence, but falling down at his feet expresses the utmost subjection.

Christ the Head of All Principality and Power

There should be no difficulty in perceiving that this expression is applicable and appropriate to the holy angels: their subjection to Christ is voluntary and joyous. The same is true of the Church, for Christ is her Head, and each of her members is "made willing in the day of his power" to submit to His rule. That is exactly what is meant by "Take my yoke upon you": "Yield to My Lordship, give Me the throne of your hearts, surrender your will to My governance." When the Church is spoken of as the Body of Christ, that sets forth her dignity. Yet when Christ is spoken of as the "head of the Church" (Eph. 5:23), that expresses His superior dignity. The king's consort sustains a double relation to him: she is a subject of the monarch, but she is a queen as his wife. Hence, while Psalm 45:9-11 states of Christ, "Upon thy right hand did stand the queen," adding, "So shall the king greatly desire thy beauty," yet she is at once told, "He is thy Lord; and worship [be subject to and adore] thou him."

But the expression also refers to Christ's triumph over His enemies. After Joshua had gained that remarkable victory over the combined armies of the Canaanites, he said, "Open the mouth of the cave, and bring out those five kings unto me out of the cave." And they did so. And he said to his captains, "Come near, put your feet upon the necks of these kings." And they did so. And Joshua said to them, "Fear not, nor be dismayed, be strong and of good courage: for thus shall the LORD do to all your enemies" (Joshua 10:22-25; cf. Isa. 51:22-23). Psalm 110:1 alludes to such passages: "until I make thine enemies thy footstool," i.e., crushed and destroyed. The Church is under Christ's feet by way of subjection, but she is not His footstool by way of subjugation and degradation.

Providence Directed by the Mediator

Yet we believe that "hath put all things under his feet" includes even more: not only all friends by ways of voluntary submission and all foes by forced subjugation, but all events by way of His immediate operation. It is not simply "all creatures" but "all things." Providence itself is now directed by the Mediator: all history is shaped by His imperial hand. Every movement, every occurrence, both in heaven and in earth is ordered by the King of kings and Lord of lords. He is clothed with all authority and invested with universal dominion, and He is now actually engaged in exercising the same. But let it not be overlooked that the exaltation and sovereignty of Christ are revealed in Scripture as something more than a historical reality: the very fact this truth is here brought in at the close of the apostle's prayer intimates it is a grand verity which ought to affect our hearts and lives. Do we conduct ourselves as those in complete subjection to Him? As we view those who oppose us, do we realize the force of His "Fear not, little flock"? As we contemplate the troubled waters of this world, do we recognize that our mighty Captain is at the helm?

"And gave him to be the head over all things to the church" (v. 22). That means far more than that Christ is the Church's Head. In those words and the ones which follow, the Holy Spirit reveals some of the distinctive blessings which accrue to the redeemed as the result of the exaltation of the Redeemer. Not only for the sake of His Son did God place Him upon the throne but also for the benefit of the Church. "Thou hast given him power over all flesh, that he should give eternal life to as many as thou hast given him" (John 17:2) is a parallel statement—though not quite as broad in its terms. Christ has been given universal and absolute rule over the whole of creation, that He might bestow eternal life on the elect. The fact that all power is given to Christ in heaven and in earth gives force to "Go ye therefore, and teach all nations" (Matt. 28:18-19). No weapon formed against His servants shall or can prosper.

Absolute lordship has been conferred upon the Mediator with the particular design of advantage for His blood-bought people. Christ's universal headship and power are being employed in the service of His beloved. "Him hath God exalted with his right hand to be a Prince and a Saviour." With what design? "For to give repentance to Israel, and forgiveness of sins" (Acts 5:31). Christ has been elevated so high that He may disburse the gifts of salvation to those who belong to the spiritual Israel—"the Israel of God" (Gal. 6:16). He has not only gone into heaven to "prepare a place" for His own (John 14:2); He is also active on their behalf while they are on earth. Upon His ascension we are told that "they [His ambassadors] went forth, and preached everywhere, the Lord working with them, and confirming the word with signs following" (Mark 16:20). He is completely ordering all the affairs of providence on behalf of His saints; their enemies are beneath His control; Paul said, "All things are for your sakes" (II Cor. 4:15).

The Church and the Mediator

It is important that we should consider and apprehend God's object in subjecting all things to the Redeemer: not only as illustrating the principles of His moral government ("He who humbleth himself shall be exalted"; "Them that honour me I will honour") and the good which results to us from them, but also the bearing which it should have upon our character and conduct. The salvation of the Church was the direct design of the whole of Christ's mediation. For her He voluntarily suffered humiliation and death; for the promotion of her interests God exalted Christ and now employs for her benefit the powers which have been bestowed on Him. Though raised so high, He has neither lost His love for His sheep nor relinquished His purpose concerning them. All hearts are now in His hand: by Him kings reign, and princes decree justice (Prov. 8:15), yet He is exercising His dominion in subservience to His purpose of grace, disposing all the affairs of the universe for the good of His Church. To the accomplishment of *that* the whole series of events which form the history of individuals and nations is directed and subordinated.

Yet how faintly that is realized by any of us: that Christ is over men and angels, demons and Satan himself. This world is under the control of the One whose hands were nailed to the cross. Christ rules and overrules for the good of His Church the deliberations of the senate, the conflict of armies, the history of the nations. The Neros, the Charlemagnes, the Napoleons, the Hitlers, who for a brief season proudly strut upon the stage of this world's drama, are but puppets in the hand of the enthroned Christ and are made to accomplish His purpose and serve the highest and ultimate interests of His people. Even when the nations are convulsed like the angry sea and things appear to be quite out of control, "the LORD hath his way in the whirlwind and in the storm" (Nahum 1:3). Then there is nothing for us to be alarmed at. The ark of the covenant is in no danger!

"And gave him to be the head over all things to the church." To the angels, Christ is a "head" by virtue of sovereignty and power (Col. 2:10), but He is the Church's "head" by mystical union as well. The angels are but His servants; the Church is His Spouse. He is the Church's "head" first by way of *distinction*, as her King and Lord, for in all things He must have the preeminence (Col. 1:18). Second, by way of authority: "the church is subject unto Christ" (Eph. 5:24), so that in all spiritual matters she refuses domination or direction by either state or people. Third, in a way of *influence*: the Church receives her life, strength, and grace from Him "from which all the body . . . [has] nourishment ministered" (Col. 2:19; cf. Eph. 4:16). All her springs are in Him: from

His fullness she receives. Christ is not only a commanding but a compassionate Head, therefore is touched with the feeling of her infirmities.

"The church, which is his body." Christ has a natural body, by virtue of His incarnation. He has a sacramental body, which is seen in the Lord's Supper. He has a ministerial body, the local church or assembly (I Cor. 12:27), where His ordinances are administered and His truth proclaimed. He has also a mystical Body, so designated because the mysterious union of its members with one another and with their Head is altogether beyond the purview of our physical senses. It is this Body, we believe, which is here meant, as in Ephesians 4:12-13 (which has never been realized by any church on earth), the Church for which Christ gave Himself (Eph. 5:25). The term cannot be restricted to any local assembly. It includes "the general assembly and church of the first-born, which are written in heaven" (Heb. 12:23)—the sum total of all God's elect. That mystical Body has been in process of formation since the days of Abel and will not be completed until the end of human history.

View this controversial expression in the light of what precedes. Christ's being seated at God's right hand is perceptible to faith alone. All things being put under His feet is not comprehensible by our senses: "Now we see not yet all things put under him" (Heb. 2:8), neither do we yet see "the church, which is his body." Contemplate it in the light of what follows: the Church is not only the Body of Christ but also "the fulness of him that filleth all in all" (v. 23), which could never be said of any local assembly, nor even of any denomination. The Church is the mediatorial "fulness" of Christ: there cannot be a Redeemer without redeemed, a Shepherd without sheep, a Bridegroom without a Bride, a living Head without a living Body. He is *her* "fulness" (John 1:16) as the Lord of life and grace; she is *His* fulness since by means of the glory He has put upon her He will hereafter be magnified (II Thess. 1:10).

We conclude as we began. The relation of the Church to Christ is entirely a matter of divine revelation. Verses 21-23 bring before us that which pertains wholly to *faith*—not fiction or fancy, nor reason or sense. But though each of these objects is as yet unseen by the outward eye, they are nonetheless real, and shall yet be beheld by a wondering universe. The indwelling of the Holy Spirit makes the Church Christ's mystical Body, for only those He indwells are members of it. The Church is Christ's "fulness" as it completes His mystical person: the Head and the Body form the *mystical* "Christ" of I Corinthians 12:12, Ephesians 4:13, and perhaps Galatians 3:16. Christ did not place this inestimable honor on angels: they are neither His "body" nor His "fulness." He loved His mystical Body above His natural body, for He gave the one for the other.

Chapter 16

PRAYER FOR INNER STRENGTH

EPHESIANS 3:14-16

NOTE THE CONTENTS of our present portion. Consider the radical and immense difference between that prayer and those we are accustomed to hear in public—and our own in private. Must there not be a reason, some very definite cause, why the petitions of most Christians today are so very different from those of the apostle? Must it not be because many of God's people are now living upon a much lower plane of spiritual experience? Surely that cannot be gainsaid. And why do they dwell so much in the valleys and so little on the mountains? Is it not because they have failed to apprehend the wonderful portion which is theirs in Christ, because they do not grasp and enjoy the inestimable privileges which are already theirs, because they do not possess their possessions, because they are regulated so much by their moods and feelings instead of living by faith in the One who loved and gave Himself for them? This is true, in varying degrees, of all of us.

It has been pointed out that the fervor and subject of our prayers are in accordance with our knowledge and apprehension of God and our practical relation to Him. If our concept of God is virtually restricted to Maker, Lawgiver, and Judge, and we rarely view Him or address Him in any other character than "the Most High," though our hearts may be awed and our souls humbled before Him, yet there is likely to be very little freedom of approach or joy of heart in our communion with Him, and our requests will be regulated accordingly. Or, if we regard Him as having given us only the *hope* of obtaining salvation by Jesus Christ, then naturally and necessarily our constant desire before Him will be for the strengthening and brightening of that hope, for we shall feel that is the one thing most needed for the comfort of our hearts and the peace of our minds. We can feel but little interest in any further revelation which God may have given regarding the purpose of His grace to His people.

So long as we entertain a doubt of our being personally concerned and having a portion in the riches of divine grace, they can have no power on our hearts. On the other hand, if the Christian realizes that the first Person in the blessed Trinity sustains to him precisely the same relation as He did and does to Christ, namely, covenant God and personal Father, and if in faith he takes his stand on the sure foundation laid for every believing sinner in the incarnation, death, resurrection, and exaltation of God's dear Son, then his desires will naturally be for a fuller knowledge of the purpose of God in connection with the manifestation of the glory of Him "in whom we have obtained an inheritance."

And thus it is in the prayer we are about to ponder. Request is made to the Father that, by the strengthening operation of the Spirit and the indwelling of Christ, the saints may know the "mystery," learn by deeper experience the unsearchable love of Christ, and be filled with all the fullness of God. Oh, that our souls may be so quickened that the petitions we are considering will become our own breathings.

It will help us to an understanding both of the scope of this prayer and the meaning of its petitions if we observe the place it occupies in this epistle, namely, at the close of the doctrinal section and introductory to the practical portion, for it turns the contents of the former into supplication and prepares the heart for obedience to the precepts of the latter. When doctrine is rightly apprehended, it exerts a powerful effect upon the heart and influences our devotional life. Likewise, when the affections and the conscience are stirred by God's exhortations to His people, they are brought to their knees before Him seeking grace. These two features—doctrine and exhortation—throw light on our present passage.

An analysis of the prayer indicates the following general divisions. First, the *occasion* of it, indicated by "for this cause I bow my knees" (v. 14). Second, its *Object,* namely, "the Father of our Lord Jesus Christ, of whom the whole family in heaven and earth is named" (vv. 14-15). Third, its *appeal,* "that he would grant you, according to the riches of his glory" (v. 16). Fourth, its *petitions,* which are four in number (vv. 16-19). Fifth, its *doxology* (vv. 20-21).

Occasion of This Prayer

"For this cause I bow my knees." In those words the apostle tells us what moved him to so address the throne of grace on this occasion, for the obvious meaning of them is "On this account, for this reason, I now approach the mercy seat." For what cause? This requires us to examine the context and note the contents of the preceding verses. The attentive reader will observe that the same clause is also found at the beginning of the chapter: "For this cause I Paul, the prisoner of Jesus Christ for you Gentiles." Scholars have pointed out that there is no verb there of which "I Paul" is the nominative, and hence there has been considerable diversity of opinion as to the probable construction of the passage. The most natural conclusion seems to be that the sentence begun in verse 1 is recommenced and completed in verse 14. That is the view taken by numerous commentators. Thus, what the apostle intended to say at the beginning of the chapter was interrupted by the flowing of other thoughts into his mind.

"For this cause I Paul" (in view of the wondrous and blessed truth which had engaged his pen throughout chapter 2) "bow my knees unto the Father." But he was interrupted from immediately doing so, for as soon as he added, "I Paul, the prisoner of Jesus Christ for you Gentiles," the realization of his "bonds" awakened a fresh train of ideas which he expanded to the end of verse 13. Consequently the "for this cause" of verse 14 has a double reference: immediately to the divine revelation made in verses 2-13 which chiefly concerns an unfolding of "the mystery of Christ," that is, of the mystical Christ, the spiritual Body of which He is the Head—that Body in which the elect of God from the Hebrews and from the Gentiles have been made fellow members, fellow heirs and fellow partakers of God's promise in Christ by the gospel. More remotely, the "for this cause" of verse 14 looks back to verse 1 and makes known the breathings of Paul's soul as evoked by what had occupied his mind throughout chapter 2, where he had expounded the grand doctrine of regeneration and reconciliation— the reconciliation of Jew and Gentile, and of both to God.

"For this cause." Combining the double reference in verse 1 and again in verse 14 and what each looks back to, we understand Paul to be saying, "Since the saints have been divinely quickened, reconciled to God, made members of the mystical Body of Christ, I long to see them living and acting as becomes those so highly favored of God and made partakers of such inestimable privileges. Therefore I supplicate God on their behalf to that end."

It is both interesting and instructive to closely compare this prayer with that found at the close of chapter 1. The principal difference between them is not accounted for so much by the different aspects of truth presented in Ephesians 1 and 2 as it is by the different effects which the apostle desired might be wrought in those to whom he wrote. There are indeed different branches of doctrine unfolded in those two chapters, and undoubtedly that difference determined the keynote of each of the prayers, yet that is neither the sole nor main reason for their varied tones. The variations in the petitions of those respective prayers expressed the particular quickenings the believers needed in order to respond suitably to the glorious revelations he had set before them.

God's Sovereign Grace to His Elect

In Ephesians 1 we have a wonderful opening up of the eternal purpose of God's sovereign grace concerning His elect, an unveiling of those spiritual blessings with which He has blessed them in the heavenlies in Christ, having chosen them, accepted them, and given them an inheritance in the Beloved. So transcendent and amazing are those riches of the divine grace, so entirely different from anything which man had conceived, that the apostle requests the Father would vouchsafe "the Spirit of wisdom and revelation in the knowledge of him" so that, the eyes of our understanding being enlightened, we might *know*. It is important that the saint should apprehend that it is the sovereign grace of God which has brought him into the place of unchanging blessing in Christ, for he had been made " the righteousness of God in him." This is the first thing that the converted soul needs to learn, that he has been reconciled to God by the blood of the Cross and thereby established in peace in Him forevermore: that he has been justified once and for all by the obedience of Christ, that he has been perfected forever and made fit for the inheritance of the saints in light. There can be no lasting peace within, no growth in grace, no loving and grateful obedience, until that is laid hold of by intelligent faith.

But essential as it is for the believer to recognize the perfect standing which is his in Christ before the throne of God, it is no less necessary for the glory of God, the honor of Christ, and his own good, that he should be exercised in his soul: that his affections should be set upon Christ, that he should be more and more conformed to His image both experimentally and practically, that he should "grow up unto him in all things." Accordingly, while in Ephesians 1 the apostle had unfolded what God had purposed for us and prayed that we might know the same, in Ephesians 2 he treated more of what God has wrought in the saints, and asked Him to fully accomplish the same in them. While we are to hold fast in our minds the perfect and unchanging *standing* which is ours in Christ, we also need to be deeply concerned about our *state*: about health being maintained in our souls, about Christ having His proper place in our hearts, about the whole household of faith being cherished in our affections, about being filled with all the fullness of God.

Thus the prayer of Ephesians 3 is supplementary or, rather, complementary to the prayer at the close of chapter 1. As might be expected, the two together present a perfect balance between the principal aspects of the Christian's life— the objective and the subjective—faith being occupied with the riches of God's grace outside himself, love being concerned with what is going on within himself. That wondrous portion which he has in Christ does not change, for it is perfect and entire; but that which has been wrought within him needs perfecting until the day of redemption. His justification can never be more complete than it was the moment he first believed, but he may and should obtain a better understanding of it. Hence in Ephesians 3 the apostle prays not merely that the saints should know what divine grace had wrought for and given to them but what God would now work by His Spirit in them. The first petition is that they might be "strengthened with might by his Spirit in the inner man," that is, renewed by Him day by day. And what would be the evidence of that? This, Christ dwelling in our hearts by faith, our hearts fixed on Him as their Object, their supreme Attraction.

Its Object

The One whom Paul addressed is here named "the Father of our Lord Jesus Christ, of whom the whole family in heaven and earth is named" (vv. 14-15). God is our Father, first, as the Author of our beings, and in this sense we are His "offspring" (Acts 17:28); He is our Father, second, as we are formed after His natural image: God is spirit (John 4:24) and therefore "the Father of spirits" (Heb. 12:9). In both these senses God is the Father of angels, and therefore they are designated "the sons of God" (Job 1:6; 38:7). God is our Father, third, in a higher sense, spiritually, having by regeneration made us partakers of His nature, or moral likeness (James 1:18; II Peter 1:4). He is "the Father of our Lord Jesus Christ" as the God-man Mediator, by covenant relation, and was owned by Him as such all through His life (Luke 2:49; John 5:17; 20:17). Because God is the Father of our Lord Jesus Christ He is our Father in the spiritual and highest sense of the term, as John 20:17 intimates. All mercies flow to us through Christ from the Father, and all our petitions ascend through Christ to the Father. Because God is the Father of the Redeemer He is the Father of the redeemed, and therefore we have access to Him by faith in prayer. This relation, which God sustains to the Lord Jesus as His Father, is made the ground of the apostle's appeal. Blessed truth for us to lay hold of.

The attentive reader will note the change of address of this prayer of the apostle. In chapter 1 he approached Him as "the God of our Lord Jesus Christ"

(v. 17), which still more distinctly views Him in the covenant relationship in which He stands both to Christ and to us. That is the foundation of His being "the Father of our Lord Jesus Christ" and "our Father" (note the order in John 20:17), as it is the ground on which we have access to Him. Charles Hodge said, "We can approach Him in no other character than as the God who sent the Lord Jesus to be our propitiation and Mediator. It is therefore by faith, as reconciled, that we address Him as the Father of our Lord Jesus Christ." Thus we see again how the doctrinal contents of those chapters give tone to the details of their respective prayers. Not in Ephesians 1 but in Ephesians 2 is the fact of God's reconciliation to us brought out, and therefore in the prayer which follows that doctrinal revelation He is addressed as "the Father of our Lord Jesus Christ." Just as the wonders of God's handiwork in creation are made more apparent under the microscope, so the more closely we examine the Word its perfections are revealed in every detail. That Word which He has magnified above all His name will bear the most minute examination. Only as we so examine it shall we perceive its excellence on every jot and tittle.

The Titles of Deity

Our appreciation of the titles by which God is addressed (and described) will be determined by the measure of our apprehension of the doctrinal expositions which occasioned those prayers. In chapter 1 the apostle had desired both light and knowledge for the saints, that as the conscious objects of Almighty grace and power they might understand the nature, reality, and blessedness of their calling. But now he requests for them an enlarged ability to taste, with a fuller and more sensible perception of its blessedness, the communion of that love which had been so unreservedly lavished upon them in making them participants of the unsearchable riches of Christ. God, in the majesty of His government, is fully glorified to the eye of faith as the just Awarder of all honor in the exaltation of Christ. His will, wisdom, and power all have their own exemplification in giving the Lord Jesus the seat of preeminence. But the One who thus magnified the Mediator is also the Father of His beloved Son, and in Him, too, Father of those whom Christ is not ashamed to own as "brethren" (Heb. 2:11). That is what regulated the apostle in his choice of this particular address.

It was with particular regard for the foregoing doctrine in chapter 2 that Paul now addressed God as "Father." Note carefully how our special relation to Him who begat us is brought out. We are spoken of as "his workmanship, created in Christ Jesus" by Himself (2:10). We are viewed as "reconciled" to Him (2:16). It is declared that "we have access by one Spirit unto the Father" (v. 18). We are spoken of as "the household of God" (v. 19), yes, as a "habitation of God through the Spirit" (v. 22). The same blessed fact also gave color to the particular requests which the apostle made here. That which occupies the central place in the petitionary part of this prayer is the saints' apprehension of the surpassing love of Christ. This request for increased enjoyment of divine *love* is most suitably made to the *Father*, as that is the believer's privilege by virtue of his filial relationship—even as the hope of glory is his righteous expectation as a justified heir of salvation (Rom. 5:1-2).

"Of whom the whole family in heaven and earth is named." Concerning the precise meaning of that clause there is perhaps room for difference of opinion as to the exact meaning of its terms. First, as to whether the antecedent of the "of whom" is "the Father" or "our Lord Jesus Christ." Grammatically the antecedent is a double one, but we prefer to take the *nearest* and understand it of the latter. Second, as to what is the "whole family in heaven and earth." Most commentators restrict it to the household of faith, those who have finished their earthly pilgrimage and those who are still left in this scene. But in view of Ephesians 1:10, Colossians 1:20, and Hebrews 12:22-23, we would not limit its scope thus. We understand "the whole family" to be the entire company of the redeemed plus the holy angels. Third, the word "named" does not mean that all are *called by* the same name, that the designation "Christian" is given to angels, but, as one writer says, "The expression is taken from the custom in a family, where all bear the same name as the head of the family." All God's elect among angels and men are gathered together under one Head and constitute one community.

According to Hebrew custom, a group or class of families all claimed descent from one father, for instance, the twelve tribes of Israel. Joseph was "of the house and lineage [family; Greek *patria*] of David" (Luke 2:4). The word occurs only in Luke 2:4, Acts 3:25, and Ephesians 3:15, and indicates a clan of persons descended from the same root. Thus the word was well suited to express the community which is headed up in Christ.

"For this cause I bow my knees" (Eph. 3:14). In effect Paul was saying, "Because God has dealt so wondrously and bestowed upon you such favors [as those described in 2:1—3:12], I seek from Him further blessings on your behalf; yea, in view of those marvelous exercises of divine grace and power, my heart is drawn out to ask for the highest possible benefits." "Unto the Father of our [not the] Lord Jesus Christ." That is to say, "I supplicate *our* gracious Father, and He is such as the covenant God of our Head." "Of whom the whole family in heaven and earth is named." Since all things have been gathered together in one in Christ, "both which are in heaven, and which are on earth; even in him" (Eph. 1:10), the entire family receives its name from Him. Since Christ has been made the Head of all—of the celestial hierarchies as well as of the Church (Eph. 1:21-23; Col. 2:10)—He has a proprietary right in the whole community: they all own Him, and He owns them all. Such is our understanding of verse 15.

Its Appeal

"That he would grant you, according to the riches of his glory, to be" (v. 16). That states the rule by which the Lord is entreated to confer His favors: on the one hand, not according to the faith or faithfulness of His people; on the other, not according to their spiritual indigence and need; but rather and better, according to His own glorious riches. Indirectly it is indeed an admission of our poverty and unworthiness, but directly it is faith eyeing the fullness and sufficiency of the Lord of glory. Everything in God renders Him glorious. He is the proper Object of adoration. The apostle prayed for God to deal with His people according to the plenitude of His grace and power, which constitutes His glory and makes Him the source of all good. But "the riches of his glory" includes more than His grace and power; it comprehends everything in God which makes Him glorious. The apostle's prayer was an appeal to God's goodness, His munificence, His infinite resources, and the plenitude of His perfections.

"That he would grant you according to the riches of his glory." To aid our feeble understanding, the Spirit here, as so frequently, speaks after the manner of men. The things which they count of highest value are termed their "riches." Now elevate that concept to a vastly superior plane. The Lord too has his "riches." As our thoughts can rise no higher than that which is supereminent or glorious, these riches are styled "the riches of his glory." They are not only the riches of glory, or glorious riches, but "riches in glory" too (Phil 4:19), that is, celestial riches, His riches on high—an earnest or foretaste of which the saints are granted even in this life. The reference is to Christ's abundant fullness, as He is "the heir of all things" (Heb. 1:2). As such He is possessed of inexhaustible resources for the supplying of our every need. There are in Him amplitude and plenitude of glory. And "according to" the same we should ask Him to minister to us.

Glory

Glory is something more than excellence. It is excellence made manifest and brought into high esteem. It is the perfection of the divine character displayed and made real and ineffable to our hearts. The wondrous and blessed fact is that God has joined His glory with the good of His people. The two things are inseparably connected together: they glorying in Him, He being glorified in them. It is therefore our happy privilege to present our requests with this fact before us and ask Him to bestow His favors on us accordingly. The apostle was about to rise to the very pinnacle of petitionary prayer, seeking for Christians the most glorious things they could be granted. He stated as his *plea,* "Will it not be to Thy glory to grant such requests and vouchsafe such blessings!" If we are straitened, it is not in the Lord but in ourselves, and the fault is entirely our own. We should eye by faith the fullness of the divine perfections, for the riches of the God-man Mediator are as unlimited as the illimitable glory of the divine nature itself.

Its Petitions

Before turning to the petitions in detail, let us proffer a few general remarks. The requests which the apostle was about to make are prefaced by the explanatory words "for this cause." He was on the point of asking that they should be strengthened with might by the Spirit in the inner man and that Christ might dwell in their hearts by faith, from which petitions it might be inferred that their condition was critical, or at any rate that they were in a weak and low state. Yet there is nothing whatever in the whole of the context which lends color to that idea. Rather, because of the wonderful things God had already done for them, Paul was encouraged to ask Him that these saints might be granted enlarged apprehensions and enjoyment of His favors. Far from settling on our leas when the Lord has bestowed signal blessings on us, we should be stimulated to desire and seek further gifts from His hand.

But that is not all there is for us in the particular detail to which we have just directed attention. There is something else in it which we need to take to heart, namely, that those who have received the highest favors from God are in real need of prayer, of coming to the mercy seat. Why? That they may be enabled to make good use of what has been conferred on them and walk worthy of the same. "For unto whomsoever much is given, of him shall be much required" (Luke 12:48). Only fresh supplies of divine grace can enable us to meet that requirement; and such supplies must be earnestly and daily sought by us. Privileges entail obligations, and spiritual obligations cannot be discharged in our own strength. God had richly blessed the Ephesians, and for that cause or reason the apostle prayed for them to be strengthened with might by Christ's Spirit in the inner man, that they might truly appreciate those blessings and express their gratitude in lives which would redound to the glory of the Giver of them.

We should also ponder these petitions in the light of how God is here addressed and the plea made to Him. No doubt the reader, like the writer, has heard prayers in which the body bore little or no relation to the opening language: prayers that began by addressing the Deity in high-sounding names but which had no connection with or appropriateness to the petitions that followed. The prayers of Scripture are very different. There we find the introductory ascriptions are most suited to what follows; the particular character in which God is addressed bears an intimate respect to the requests made to Him. For example, when Jacob was in deadly fear of Esau he prayed, "O God of my father Abraham, and God of my father Isaac, the LORD which saidst unto me, Return unto *thy country*, . . . deliver me, I pray thee, from the hand of my brother" (Gen. 32:9-11). It was to his fathers (and their seed) that God had promised to give Canaan! Also when the souls under the altar begged God to avenge their blood, they addressed Him as "O Lord, holy and true" (Rev. 6:10).

In the prayer before us, the address is made to "the Father of our Lord Jesus Christ," and what follows is an appeal to His fatherly affection and solicitude. He has told us that "like as a father pitieth his children, so the LORD pitieth them that fear him" (Ps. 103:13). What freedom of heart the realization of that blessed fact should give us when we approach the throne of grace! The Redeemer has assured us, "If ye then, being evil, know how to give good gifts unto your children, how much more shall your Father which is in heaven give good things to them that ask Him?" (Matt. 7:11). The saint approaches not an unwilling Bestower, whose reluctance to communicate has to be overcome by entreaties, but a loving Father who is more ready to give than we are to ask. How that ought to melt and encourage us! Because He is the Father of our Lord Jesus Christ, He is our Father too, and as such more ready to impart good things to us than the tenderest earthly parent can be to his little ones. The apostle here viewed Him thus, and he framed his requests accordingly.

Nor should we overlook the clause that immediately follows: "of whom the whole family in heaven and earth is named." It seems to us that the apostle turned that into a plea also. It was as though he said, "Blessed Lord, many of Thy dear children are now in Thine immediate presence on high, but there are some of Thy beloved ones still in the place of need here below. Those with Thee above are enjoying the beatific vision. Let not all blessedness be confined to them, but grant at least a portion of the same to those who are yet in this howling wilderness."

So should we make practical use of every doctrinal statement of the epistles, turning each into a supplicatory *plea*. "That he would grant you, according to the riches of his glory." Paul's gaze was directed upward to a sphere of ineffable purity and felicity, to the One who occupied the central place in it. It was that which moved him to seek for no ordinary favors but for blessings which were according to and commensurate with the infinite riches of His glory.

The blessings Paul here sought for the saints stand out in glaring contrast from the mean and meager petitions which many believers are wont to make today. The great majority of professing Christians seem to regard the substance and sum of salvation as consisting in deliverance from the penalty of their sins and the assurance that they will spend eternity in heaven. They appear to have little or no concept of the glorious privileges that are theirs in this present interval: their being mightily energized by the indwelling Holy Spirit, their access to and enjoyment of Christ within the veil, their growing up unto Him in all things, their being filled with all the fullness of God. Those petitions of Paul present possibilities in the Christian life that few contemplate, and fewer still strive after. A knowledge of sins forgiven is indeed an inestimable boon, yet that stands at the very onset of Christian experience and is but an earnest of far greater and grander blessings which the Father will bestow on us if we follow on to know Him, and seek to lay hold of that for which we were laid hold of by Christ Jesus, reaching for those things which are before (Phil. 3:12-14).

"Open Thy Mouth Wide"

We say again, if we are straitened it is in ourselves and not in the Lord; the fault is entirely ours. He has set before us a rich feast in the gospel: "a feast of fat things, a feast of wines on the lees, of fat things full of marrow, of wines on the lees well refined" (Isa. 25:6). Our God is no niggardly Host, nor would He have us partake sparingly of His bounties: "Eat O friends; drink, yea, drink *abundantly*, O beloved" (Song of Sol. 5:1) is the call of His largess to us. "Open thy mouth *wide*" is His invitation; "and I will fill it" is His promise (Ps. 81:10). How deeply ashamed of ourselves we should be if we have occasion to cry, "My leanness, my leanness, woe unto me!" (Isa. 24:16). Such "leanness" brings no honor to Him. Such leanness reveals how far below our privileges we are living. Such leanness is the consequence of failing to avail ourselves of the rich provisions God has made for us, and such failure is traced back to the defectiveness of our prayer lives: "Ye have not, because ye ask not" (James 4:2).

Observe that the apostle did not preface his petitions by saying, "O God, if it can be possible, bestow these glorious spiritual riches on Thy people." No indeed, he would not insult the One who has told us, "He that spared not his own Son, but delivered him up for us all, how shall he not with him also freely give us *all* things?" (Rom. 8:32). "Freely," not grudgingly. Not once in their prayers for the saints do we find any of the apostles qualifying their petitions with "*if* it be thy will." It is true that the Redeemer prayed in Gethsemane, "O my Father, if it be possible, let this cup pass from me: nevertheless, not as

I will but as thou wilt"; but He was there in a situation which we can never occupy, and never once did He teach His disciples to pray thus. Compare Matthew 7:7; John 14:13-14; 15:16; 16:23; compare too His own "Father, I will" of John 17:24! True, our wills must be subordinated to the divine, yet it is both our privilege and duty to be "understanding what the will of the Lord is" (Eph. 5:17).

His Revealed Will

"This is the confidence that we have in him, that, if we ask anything according to his will, he heareth us" (I John 5:14). That does not refer to His eternal decree, or secret will, which concerns no part of our responsibility, but to His revealed will as made known to us in the Word. In the Word, God has plainly declared that He is ready to bestow, in response to the prayer of faith, whatever will be for His glory and for our good. Nor has He left undefined what is for His glory and our good: the recorded prayers of the apostles plainly reveal the same to us. We need therefore have no hesitation whatever in praying that we may be strengthened with might by His Spirit in the inner man, that Christ may dwell in our hearts by faith, that we may be filled with all the fullness of God; for it is God's revealed will that we should ask for those very things, and it is nothing but a false or mistaken humility for us to add to His words "if it be thy will." It *is* God's will or the apostle would not have been moved by the Holy Spirit to make such requests and then place them on record for our guidance.

In view of such passages as Psalm 81:10, Song of Solomon 5:1, and Romans 8:32, it is truly pitiful to hear so many professing Christians praying as though God were either a hard master or one whose riches were limited. He has expressly bidden them to "covet earnestly the best gifts (I Cor. 12:31), yet how few of them do so. They have so little holy ambition to enter into God's best for them, to grow in grace, to be fruitful branches of the Vine, to show forth His praises. How little of His truth, His holiness, His grace seems to satisfy them! They exist rather than live, paddle in the ocean of His love rather than swim in it. Their desires are weak, their expectations small, their aspirations almost nil. To "covet earnestly the best gifts" is to long intensely for them with the implication of a corresponding zealous effort to obtain those divine bestowments which will make for increased piety and usefulness; not only for ourselves but for our fellow saints too. That is exactly what the apostle was doing here: coveting earnestly the best gifts for the Ephesians.

Better Things

"That he would grant you, according to the riches of his glory, to be strengthened with might by his Spirit in the inner man" (Eph. 3:16). That was the first thing which Paul requested of the Father on their behalf. Let each Christian ponder it thoughtfully and hopefully. Let him seek to realize now, if he has never done so before, that the pardon God bestowed upon him at the hour of conversion was but the beginning of the fulfillment of His purposes of grace toward him, that He has far better things awaiting him in *this* life. God's forgiveness of his sins was but a means to an end, with a design of something further and richer. Let the Christian reader recognize that he has not yet begun to conceive of the rich heritage unto which God has begotten him unless he perceives that it is his privilege, his duty, his rightful portion, to be strong with the strength of the divine Spirit. The devil seeks to persuade us that God would have His children remain frail and feeble in this life, but that is one of his many lies. God's revealed will for us is the very reverse, namely, "Be strong in the Lord, and in the power of his might" (Eph. 6:10). Reader, do not allow Satan to deceive you any further, but seek right now to possess what Christ has purchased for you.

Seek Expectantly

Because it is God's revealed will that we should be spiritually hale and hearty, we are to seek strength from Him, and seek it expectantly. Had He not shown us His good pleasure in this matter, we might have been in some doubt how to act; but since He has made known His mind on it, our course is quite clear. Let the reader turn to Ezekiel 36:25-36 and observe the blessed promises which God has there made to His people, closing with the declaration "I the LORD have spoken it, and I will do it." Then let the reader attentively observe that in the very next verse (v. 37) we are told, "Thus saith the Lord GOD; I will yet for this *be enquired of* by the [spiritual] house of Israel, *to do it* for them." Divine favor does not release us from our duty of realizing and acknowledging our dependence on Him. Divine promises are given for faith to lay hold of and plead before the throne of grace. It is God's revealed will that Christians should be strengthened with might by His Spirit in the inner man, but it is also His will that they should earnestly covet the same and believingly seek it by fervent supplication.

Our Responsibility

The Apostle Paul had declared, "Though our outward man perish, yet the inward man is renewed day by day" (II Cor. 4:16). Nevertheless, the knowledge of that fact did not render it meaningless or needless to pray for that very thing! God does not treat us as though we were irrational creatures, but as moral agents, and therefore He requires our concurrence and cooperation—not to assist Him, but for the discharge of our responsibility, and especially for the calling into exercise of those spiritual graces which He has imparted to His children.

We must ask if we would receive. And we must ask expectantly, for according to our faith will it be unto us. It is much for which to be thankful if we have been made conscious of our deep need, yet that will avail us nothing unless we have also learned how to obtain daily supplies of grace. In answer to importunate prayer God gives of His best to us. David was in sore straits, but he knew where to turn for relief: "In the day when I cried thou answerest me, and strengthenedst me with strength in my soul" (Ps. 138:3).

The Christian is as entirely dependent on the continued operations of the Spirit as he was for His initial workings, for of himself he can no more sustain his spiritual life or maintain his faith than he would originate them. If the Spirit were to suspend His operations, we should be helpless, for He it is who works in us both to will and to do of God's good pleasure. The flesh is not weakened by regeneration, and it never ceases its exertions. So it is from without: Satan is ever seeking an advantage against us. Moreover the soul is strangely deluded by the treachery of our senses and the result of our passions when temptations assail us; so unless opportune relief is granted we are soon overcome. Without the Spirit's help we can neither mortify our lusts (Rom. 8:13), pray aright (Rom. 8:26), nor bear fruit (Eph. 5:9). Yet there must be our concurrence: we may, we can, concur or we should not appear different from the unregenerate. God works all works for and in us, yet also by us.

"That he would grant you, according to the riches of his glory, to be strengthened with might by his Spirit in the inner man; that Christ may dwell in your hearts by faith; that ye, being rooted and grounded in love, may be able to comprehend with all saints what is the breadth, and length, and depth, and height; and to know the love of Christ, which passeth knowledge, that ye might be filled with all the fulness of God." What a prayer is this! As it was an apostle, one who in some respects was the most highly favored of the apostles, who made those petitions, so it requires one with deep spiritual experience to open to us the sublime contents of the petitions. Far more than strength of intellect or even exegetical skill is required in opening up such a portion of the Scriptures as this. Spirituality of mind, elevation of heart, and close communion with God are also required. In proportion as an expositor realizes that, he will be conscious of his own unfitness for such a task.

"That he would grant you . . . to be strengthened with might by his Spirit in the inner man." That is our first great need, and it is good for us to be truly aware of it. As none but the Spirit of God could impart spiritual life to our souls, so He alone can maintain that life. It is true that, for the most part, the Spirit works by our concurrence, blessing the means of grace to us as we make proper use of them. It is also true that the Spirit first works in us the desire and the diligence in using those means, and only by His gracious operations in subduing our native pride are we preserved from being complacent with our diligence. We are entirely dependent upon Him to strengthen that gracious principle which He communicated to us at the new birth, for the exercise and employment of it. If it is true, naturally, that "in him we live, and move, and have our being," it is nonetheless so spiritually even as Christians.

The "Inner Man"

Expositors differ as to exactly what we are to understand by "the inner man": whether the reference is only to the new nature, or principle, of grace and holiness, or whether it includes the soul with all its faculties. We define it as the soul so far as it is renewed by divine grace. The body, considered separately, is not the subject of moral good or evil: the soul is the seat of all moral qualities. It is true that in many passages indwelling sin or the principle of evil in fallen man is denominated "the flesh," yet it must be borne in mind that the Scripture speaks of the *mind of* the flesh (Rom. 8:7), and among its "works" or products mentions hatred, variance, envyings (Gal. 5:19-21), which are more than physical passions. When the apostle said, "I delight in the law of God after the inward man" he undoubtedly referred to the new nature within him. And when he added, "But I see [perceive] another law [or principle of operation] in my members [the faculties of his soul], warring against the law of my mind" (Rom. 7:22-23), he had in mind his native depravity.

Thus the "inner man" signifies the soul so far as it is renewed, for the principle of evil remains unchanged. That renewing consists of a supernatural enlightenment of the understanding, so that things are now viewed in God's light; the spiritualizing of the affections, so that they are now drawn out to new objects, and the heart is engaged with God; the freeing of the will from the dominion of sin, and the inclining of it to holiness. In addition to that renewing and sublimating of the original faculties of the soul, there is communicated a new "spirit," or principle of grace—a new life. Let us recognize that what takes place at regeneration is but the *beginning* of God's good work in the soul, and that the same work is "performed" or continued throughout the Christian life (Phil. 1:6). We "are renewed" (Col. 3:10), but there is also "the renewing of the Holy Spirit" (Titus 3:5), for "though our outward man perish, yet the inward man is renewed day by day" (II Cor. 4:16). The divine promise is "I will water it every moment: lest any hurt it, I will keep it night and day" (Isa. 27:3).

The Necessity of Being Constantly Renewed

Continual renewing is necessitated by the incessant opposition made by the indwelling flesh ever seeking to possess and direct the faculties of our soul, because the new nature received at the new birth is but a creature—entirely dependent upon its Author. It is therefore both the duty and the privilege of the believer to turn to that Author for daily quickening and energizing, begging Him to strengthen him with might by His Spirit in the inner man, pleading His promise: "They that wait upon the LORD shall renew their strength" (Isa. 40:31), until he is enabled to say, "But truly I am full of power by the Spirit of the LORD" (Micah 3:8). This renewing is the vitalizing of the soul as the dwelling place and organ of the Holy Spirit: the soul in its entirety, including all its faculties—intellectual, emotional, moral. It is also the invigorating of the graces of the new man: holy faith, reverential fear, love, gratitude, hatred of sin, hope, and patience.

"In the day when I cried thou answeredst me, and strengthenedst [*rahab*] with strength [might, *oz*] in my soul" (Ps. 138:3). That verse is the Old Testament parallel of the petition of Ephesians 3:16, and as the "strengthened [Greek *krataioo*] with might [*dunamis*]" exactly corresponds with the two Hebrew words, so "the inner man" is defined as "my soul." David was in sore straits—walking "in the midst of trouble," encountering the wrath of his enemies (v. 7). Conscious of his own insufficiency, he cried to the Lord, "Revive me; stretch forth thine hand." God at once responded and afforded him relief by strengthening the faculties of his soul and animating the grace of his spirit. The effect of that strengthening would be courage, fortitude, spiritual heroism. The Spirit can make the feeble mighty, the trembling brave, and the weary cheerful. "He giveth power to the faint; and to them that have no might he increaseth strength" (Isa. 40:29).

But we must now consider more closely the relation of this first petition to what immediately follows. The apostle yearned for an increased measure of grace to be granted the saints and for their spiritual abilities to be enlarged—not with a view to the performance of the outward acts of obedience and duty, but that the believing soul might be empowered to enjoy its spiritual portion and privileges. He longed that Christians might be more in the habit of living by faith in Christ, so that He might be in them not by transient visits but abiding constantly in their thoughts and affections, and that thereby they would be established in joy and abounding fruitfulness. He longed that they might not only have love but be "rooted and grounded" in it, so that their communion with Christ might be a steady experience rather than an occasional luxury. But such is our native weakness in contemplating heavenly objects that without continued grace preparing us, they would be altogether beyond our reach. We need the wind of heaven to blow our barks forward.

Dependence on the Holy Spirit

"That ye may be strengthened with might by his Spirit in the inner man" is a request for the communication of energizing enablement that we may be fully absorbed with Christ. As the Christian owes his new life, or nature, to the Spirit, so by His power alone can it be vigorous and flourishing. Only by His strengthening of the heart are we delivered from being engrossed in the things around us, and our earthbound affections are drawn to things above. He it is who creates the desire for Christ, who shows us the things of Christ, who causes us to make Him the grand subject of our spiritual meditations. Only by the supernatural quickening of the Spirit can we be girded for that extraordinary effort of mind if we are to be "able to comprehend . . . and to know the love of Christ which passeth knowledge." And beyond any doubt, only by the operations and influences of the gracious Spirit may we be "filled with all the fulness of God." We are to daily seek from Him that quickening, enablement, and girding.

Chapter 17

PRAYER FOR CHRIST-CENTEREDNESS

EPHESIANS 3:17

"THAT CHRIST may dwell in your hearts by faith" is the second petition. We readily grant that we are considering a realm that is beyond the compass of any created mind, yet that does not warrant our denying God's Word. We freely admit that the God-man Mediator does not indwell the saints, for His humanity is localized in heaven. But Christ is, essentially, a divine person, coequal with the Father and the Spirit, and in becoming flesh the Word lost none of His divine attributes. Omnipresence pertains as much to Him now as it did before He became incarnate, and as a divine person He indwells His people as really as do the other Persons of the Godhead. God the Father dwells in His children: if I John 4:12-15 is read attentively, it will be seen that in that passage "God" clearly has reference to the Father. The Holy Spirit dwells in the saint individually and in the Church corporeally (Rom. 8:8, 11; I Cor. 3:16; 6:19); and God the Son dwells in believers. "God is in you of a truth" (I Cor. 14:25) is to be understood as the triune God.

Yet it is not only in the sense that He is omnipresent that Christ indwells His people. "Do not I fill heaven and earth? saith the LORD" (Jer. 23:24) refers alike to the omnipresence of each Person in the Godhead. But when we are told that the infinite God dwells "in the heavens" (Ps. 123:1), "among the children of Israel" (Num. 35:34), "in Zion" (Ps. 9:11), "with him also that is of a contrite and humble spirit" (Isa. 57:15), a particular appropriation is signified, where He is specially manifested.

Let us consider more closely the meaning of our petition. That Christ personally and immediately inhabits His people is a blessed fact, and therefore there is no need to make request for the same. But over and above that, the apostle here prayed "that Christ may dwell in your hearts by faith," by which we understand him to mean that by spiritual meditations upon and loving contemplations of His complex person, His glorious titles, His mediatorial offices, His precious promises, His wise precepts, He may have a constant place, the supreme place, in our thoughts and in our affections. The apostle prayed that the saints might have a spiritual sight of Christ, a spiritual knowledge of Him, a spiritual enjoyment of Him, so that He would be *present* and precious to the soul; and that can only be by the exercise of faith in Him as He is revealed in the Scriptures. The apostle prayed for their hearts to be occupied with the excellency of His person, with His love and grace, with His blood and righteousness.

Our text refers to an objective dwelling of Christ in the heart—as the subjects which engage our thoughts obtain a dwelling place in our minds, and as the objects of our love secure a place in our affections. As the eye beholds an object, an image of it is introduced and impressed upon the mind; and as the eye of the spirit—faith—is engaged with Christ, an image of Him is formed on the heart. The sun is stationed in the heavens, yet when we gaze upon it steadily an image of it is formed upon the retina of the eye. As by opening the door or the window the sun shines directly into our rooms, so by the exercise of faith upon Christ, He obtains a more real and abiding presence in our hearts. Christ is the grand Object of faith, and faith is the faculty whereby we, through the light of the Word and the power of the Spirit, receive and take into our renewed minds the knowledge of His person and perfections. Thereby He is admitted into our hearts and we have real communion with Him.

As the fancy—that faculty of the mind by which it records and represents past images or impressions, forming a picture of them in the mind—is an aid to our natural knowledge in the understanding of natural things, so does faith much more help our spiritual knowledge of divine things—giving real substance to them in the soul. The beholding of Christ is not by way of fancy, but by faith giving a subsistence to Him, so that the heart finds a reality of what it believes. Yes, it has so great an influence and leaves such an impression that it changes the heart into the same image (II Cor. 3:18). Faith, by the Spirit, makes Christ a living actuality. Moreover faith produces love, and then works by it, so that the object of faith is sealed upon the heart. As Christ was received by faith at first, so by the same principle of faith we continue to receive of His fullness, feed upon Him, and commune with Him. And as the mind is exercised with believing meditations on Christ we give Him entertainment in our hearts.

"That he would grant you . . . to be strengthened with might by his Spirit in the inner man, that Christ may dwell in your hearts by faith." Cannot the reader now perceive more clearly the relation between those two petitions? There is no exercise of faith in Christ apart from and except by the operations of the gracious Spirit within the believer's soul. Said the Lord Jesus, "No man can come to me, except the Father which hath sent me draw him" (John 6:44). To "come" to Christ is the same as to "believe" on Him as verse 35 of the same chapter shows, and none can come or believe unless his heart is drawn to Christ by the Father, and that "drawing" He does both personally and by the operations of His Spirit. True, John 6:44 has reference to our initial coming to or believing on Christ, yet we are equally dependent upon the Spirit for every subsequent exercise of faith. Thus we read of "faith of the operation of God" (Col. 2:12), and of Paul praying that God would "fulfil all the good pleasure of his goodness, and the work of faith with power"—i.e., His power (II Thess. 1:11). Thus the principal effect of our being strengthened by the Spirit is that our hearts are drawn out to Christ and our faith is exercised upon Him.

As the Spirit is from Christ (John 15:26; Acts 2:33), so the great mission of the Spirit is to direct souls to Christ (John 16:14-15). If He first convicts of sin, it is simply to convince us of our need of a Saviour. If He communicates to us a new nature, it is so that new nature may be absorbed with Christ. If He strengthens us, it is in order that faith may act upon Christ. The Holy Spirit never acts except in and through Christ with respect to His people; furthermore, Christ is never received except by and with the influences of the Spirit. A man cannot truly believe in Christ except by the power of the Holy Spirit, nor can he have the Spirit if he does not truly believe in Christ. There is mutual action in the two divine offices. The Spirit is the Water of life from the Fountain of life, Christ. The Spirit waters the soul to fit it to believe on Christ.

The majority of Christians do not realize that they are as wholly dependent upon the gracious operations of the Spirit within them as they are upon the meritorious righteousness of Christ without them. Therefore they need to seek God and count on the enablings of the former as definitely and as constantly as they trust in and rely on the finished work of the latter. As they are completely devoid of anything to commend themselves to the notice of the Lord, so they are equally without any power of their own to serve and glorify Him now that He has deigned to look on and recover them from their lost estate. Because of their helplessness He has bestowed the Holy Spirit on them: to maintain life in their souls and to draw forth that life to suitable exercise and action. It is our privilege and duty to recognize our dependency on the Spirit in order to avoid those things which grieve Him, and to seek His daily renewings. "I know that this shall turn to my salvation through your prayer, and the supply of the Spirit of Jesus Christ" (Phil. 1:19). A fresh supply of the Spirit comes to us in response to prayer!

Daily Spiritual Renewing

Until the Christian has learned his dependence upon the Spirit's workings within him, until he personally realizes his urgent need of a fresh "supply of the Spirit," being daily renewed by Him, he will not and cannot make any true spiritual progress. Faith upon Christ will not be operative, love for Him will not be warm and regular, communion with Him will not be enjoyed. That is why this request for the saints to be strengthened with might by the Spirit in the inner man precedes the other petitions. Christ has an objective and influential dwelling in our hearts only as faith is kept in exercise upon Him and as our affections are set upon Him. As Christ was received by faith at first, so it is by the same faith we delight ourselves in Him, feed upon Him, have fellowship with Him, and draw from His fullness. But our faith is exercised only in proportion as we are first strengthened within by the Spirit. Faith is indeed an act of ours, yet it does not act by or from anything of ours, but only as it is stirred into action by the Spirit.

"That Christ may dwell in your hearts by faith." When one dwells in the heart of another, that one is the object of the intense affection of the other. For Christ to dwell in the heart is for Him to have the chief place in our thoughts and affections. Alas, how many other objects plead our notice, claim our attention, and absorb us. How spasmodically is faith occupied with its grand Object! This shows our urgent need for praying that we may be strengthened with might by the Spirit in the inner man, for the believer cannot put forth a single act of spiritual life except by His agency. The Christian is as wholly dependent upon the Spirit's operations within him as he is upon Christ's work without him. He has no more power of his own separate from the Spirit than he has righteousness of his own apart from Christ. As he looks outside of himself for the latter, so he must for the former. The Spirit alone gives us strength to act grace, grow in grace, and bring forth the fruits of grace. "Thou also hast wrought all our works in us" (Isa. 26:12).

The Spirit Renews the Soul

As the Spirit graciously renews the soul of the saint, his heart is drawn out afresh to Christ and he exercises faith upon Him; and as his thoughts are occupied with Him, Christ obtains an *objective* entrance into his heart. He is received by us as our Lord and Saviour, welcomed as the Sovereign of all our affections and actions, the Source of all our holiness and joy. If we have been sorely wounded by sin, we welcome Him as our Physician to heal, for if faith is exercised, instead of listening to Satan's lies, we shall turn to Him who has the balm of Gilead. On the other hand, when the smile of God is enjoyed and His peace possesses our souls, if faith is exercised, instead of looking within and being occupied with our graces and comforts, we shall look to Him who is the Author and Finisher of faith, seeking a closer communion with and delighting ourselves in Him (Ps. 37:4). Thus He will "dwell" in us as a Guest to be entertained by us. "A single eye is needed to discern Him, and a single heart to hold Him fast."

As faith is engaged with Christ He receives not only an objective but also an *influential* entrance into our hearts—as the admitting of the sun's rays into a room brings light, warmth, and comfort. The more Christ becomes the supreme and constant Object of our hearts, the more we shall experience His gracious influences and sanctifying consolations. And they, in turn, will issue in more devotedness to His service; for as Matthew Henry pointed out, "Faith both admits and submits to Him." Christ is in us as the vine is in its branches—the vitalizing and fructifying life or energy. "Abide in me, and I in you" (John 15:4). The "abiding" there is identical with the "dwelling" here in Ephesians 3:17. To abide in Christ is to cleave to and commune with Him in the exercise of faith, the consequence of which is His influential abiding in us—vivifying, assuring. As Christ indwells us we become more conformed to His image and we are transformed by the renewing of our minds. As Christ indwells us we show forth His virtues (I Peter 2:9).

As faith is engaged with Christ, as we cultivate frequent and devout meditations on His surpassing glories, the benefit gained by the soul will be immeasurable. The more the mind is thus preoccupied and filled with Him, the stronger will be its resistance to the insidious advances and entangling encroachments of the world. Carnal enjoyments will lose their attractions. A spiritual sight of Immanuel will abase self; sorrows will weigh down less; afflictions will press upon us less hard. The more our spiritual minds are exercised on the eternal Lover of our souls, the more fervent and constant will be our love to Him, which brings us to examine the next clause of this wonderful prayer. The words "that ye" in the middle of verse 17 in our English Bibles are, in the judgment of many competent expositors, out of their proper place, and should rather be attached to the petition which follows—i.e., they should begin verse 18. We quite agree, for that is certainly the order of the Greek: "for to dwell the Christ, through faith in your hearts, in love being rooted and founded; that ye may be fully able to apprehend with all saints what [is] the breadth . . ." (Bagster's Interlinear N.T.).

"That Christ may dwell in your hearts by faith: being rooted and grounded in love." One of the principal effects of faith is to establish our souls in love: Christ's love to us, or ours to Him? Both, though here principally the latter. Our consciousness of Christ's love for His people produces an answering love in our hearts for Him. There should be no difficulty raised by our defining this clause as the Christian's love. The more I recognize and feed upon Christ's love to me, the more there will be a response to His love. "Rooted" and "grounded": each of those words has its own peculiar force and beauty. A double metaphor is there used: that of a tree and that of a building. The idea of the former is of its striking deeper and spreading wider into the soil; the idea of the latter is of the firm and solid basis on which the building rests. Just so far as faith daily acts upon Christ and He occupies the central place in my affections, will love for Him be the soil in which my Christian life is rooted and grounded.

Love to Christ

"The life which I now live in the flesh I live by the faith of the Son of God, who loved me, and gave himself for me" (Gal. 2:20). Here we have three things: the present life of the Christian in the body, the life sustained and energized by acting faith upon the divine Redeemer, the heart engrossed with His love as expressed in His great sacrifice. Love to Christ is the motive of all genuine obedience and the ground of all spiritual fruitfulness. When he is rooted in love, the progress of the believer's life will not be the result of self-effort but the spontaneous effect of an inherent power drawn from its nourishing soil. That is blessedness indeed: that is a real foretaste of heaven—love the spring of worship. When Christ dwells in the heart, love will be the foundation on which the Christian life is erected, steadfast and sure. The blessed consciousness of His love and the joyful answer of our hearts to it—this becomes the base on which the soul rests, this produces stability, security, serenity. Consciously founded upon Him, I shall be strong and "unmoveable" (I Cor. 15:58).

"Being rooted and grounded in love." Since that expression is in nowise qualified, it should be taken in its widest latitude, and understood as including the whole scope of that love which flows from faith, of which not only God in Christ but His people also are the objects. Faith and love enlarge the heart until it embraces the whole family of God: "Everyone that loveth him that begat loveth him also that is begotten of him" (I John 5:1). As Christ dwells in our hearts by faith, our affections are widened as well as deepened, so that we become sharers of His affections, which embrace the entire Church, yes, all mankind; and thereby we obtain sure evidence that we have "passed from death unto life" (I John 3:14).

"That ye . . . may be able [Greek "fully able" or "have full power"] to comprehend with all saints what is the breadth, and length, and depth, and height;

and to know the love of Christ, which passeth knowledge" (vv. 17-19). We have sought to show the relation which the last clause of verse 17 has to the petition preceding it. Let us now consider the bearing which those words "rooted and grounded in love" have upon this third petition. First, Christ Himself must be laid hold of by faith, for a doubting spirit is incapable of comprehending anything but the fact of its own wretchedness. As another has pointed out, "A purged conscience is the first lesson that the Spirit of grace imparts to our souls as the Revealer of Jesus. *Then,* and not earlier, are we enabled [by the power of the same Spirit] to enter, with all saints, on the study of that which is the children's portion," or, as we would prefer to express it, "enter upon the joyful contemplation of the children's portion," namely, the infinite and amazing love of Christ. By Christ's indwelling the heart, its capacity to comprehend is enlarged and expanded.

But since the second petition was "that Christ may dwell in your hearts by faith," which signifies His being steadfastly enshrined in our affections, it may seem that this third request is almost a repetition of the former. It would be if the "rooted and grounded in love" meant our apprehension of His love to us, and this is the chief reason why we feel obliged to understand it of ours to Him. If the tree is not well rooted or the building securely based, the higher it rises, the greater will be its danger of falling. What, then, is the preventative and preservative? This: a knowledge of the character of Christ and His love. A man would be greatly pleased with a stranger who, at fearful cost to himself, saved his life. Perhaps he would be happy to take him permanently into his home. But as he came to know him better, he might regret his action and find it impossible for them to dwell happily together. He would esteem him as a deliverer, but dislike him as a close companion. But in the case of the believer, the more he knows of Christ and His love, the more he longs for Him to constantly abide in his heart: thus he is rooted and grounded in love to Him.

We Must Exercise Love to Christ

If on the one hand it is true that we must have an experimental knowledge of Christ and His love to us, it is equally true that we must exercise love to Christ in order to better know Him and His love. There is a knowledge of Christ and His love which evokes no answering love in the heart of its possessor. There are many in Christendom today who have as clear an intellectual understanding of the person, work, and love of Christ for sinners as has the saint who enjoys the most intimate fellowship with Him; yet it does not kindle a single spark of love within them for Him. Nor can anyone feelingly realize the difference between an intellectual knowledge of Christ and His love and a personal acquaintance with the same unless he has actually experienced it. Experience is the only teacher of feelings and emotions, as it is in the lower sphere of taste and sense. A man knows nothing of the real pangs of hunger until he is at the point of starving. One must actually sample wormwood or honey before he can know from taste the bitterness or the sweetness of each. One cannot know sorrow except by feeling its ache, and one must love before he can know what love is.

A deaf man can read a treatise on acoustics, but that will convey to him no notion of what it is to hear the harmonies and melodies of real music. We must *have* love to Christ before we can know what love to Christ *is*, and we must consciously experience the love *of* Christ before we can know what the love of Christ is. We must have a warm and steady love for Christ in order to have a deep and living possession of the love of Christ, though reciprocally it is also true that we must have the love of Christ known and felt in our hearts if we are to love Him back again.

As our being "rooted and grounded in love" is the *consequence* of Christ's dwelling in our hearts by faith, so also is it the necessary *preparation* for our being able to "comprehend" and to "know" the surpassing love of Christ. Do we not see that blessedly illustrated and exemplified in the case of the one who has appropriately been designated "the apostle of love," the one who was chief of the three nearest to the Lord, who was privileged to lean on His breast? Of all the disciples none was so loving as he, and therefore he—rather than James or Peter or Jude—was the one selected (because so well qualified experimentally) to write so largely upon the love of God and of Jesus our Lord. Yes, the more intensely and steadily we love Christ, the more capacitated we are to comprehend His love to us. Even in the natural, only the loving heart really knows and appreciates love. As faith is the medium of understanding, so love is the avenue for receiving love. We may speak of God's love and think we have deep insight into the teaching of the Word, but if Christ's name is not dearer to us than life, all our speaking will mean little or nothing.

Meaning of "to Comprehend"

"That ye may be able to comprehend." The Greek word *katalambano* is rendered "comprehend" in John 1:5 and here; "apprehend" in Philippians 3:12-13; "take" (in the sense of "grasp") in Mark 9:18; John 8:3-4; "attain" in Romans 9:30; "obtain" in I Corinthians 9:24; and "overtake" ("come upon") in I Thessalonians 5:4. Young's concordance defines the word as "to receive fully." Perhaps John 1:5 helps us most to perceive its force: "the light shineth in darkness; and the darkness comprehended it not." The reference there is to the Lord of glory as He tabernacled among men. The unregenerate are designated "the darkness" (cf. Eph. 5:8), which tells of the fearful effects of the Fall. The natural man is "alienated from the life of God" (Eph. 4:18), and therefore from His love and light. So far from desiring the Light, the darkness repelled and repulsed it. Men despised and rejected the Light, hating Him without a cause. Here in our text is the direct antithesis. Since the regenerate both believe in and love the One who is the Light, they are "able to comprehend" His love.

Also carefully note that this "comprehend" is distinguished from the "know" at the beginning of verse 19, and that it precedes rather than follows it—as we had probably thought. The difference between the two is that the former is more a matter of effort, the latter of intuition; the one pertains more distinctly to the mind, the other to the heart. Yet the former is something far more than a mere intellectual or speculative thing, namely, that which is obtained by the renewed understanding. Nor is the one to be so sharply distinguished from the other as though there was no definite relation between them. The "and" at the beginning of verse 19 clearly shows the contrary. No, rather is there a most intimate connection between the two: in all spiritual exercises the mind is largely influenced by the heart, and in turn, the affections are regulated by the understanding. The action of the spiritual understanding is always in sympathy with the affections of the heart. If in one sense we must comprehend before we truly love, yet love thus awakened becomes in turn the fountain of desires which nothing can satisfy but *perfect* knowledge—hence the force of "I shall be satisfied, when I awake [on the resurrection morn], with thy likeness" (Ps. 17:15).

Light and love, understanding and affection, are mutual handmaids. The mind has its part to play in leading the heart to love, as is indicated in the passage before us—the "able to comprehend" coming before the "to know"! The heart must first be informed about its Object before our affections are fixed on Him. First, faith's apprehension of Christ as He is made known to us in the Word of truth, then the clear perception of His excellency and the heart's enrapturement with His perfections. First, the understanding's comprehension of the dimensions (manifestations) of His love, then the affection's experience of its blessedness. "O taste *and see* that the LORD is good" (Ps. 34:8) expresses what we are striving to convey. First the personal appropriation of the Lord and the soul feeding upon Him, and then the fuller discernment of His loveliness. "Taste and see [perceive, realize, know] that the LORD is good." It is thus we obtain an experimental knowledge of Him. By means of this faculty of spiritual comprehension the believer is enabled to explore the dimensions of Christ's love (as also the whole boundless field of divine revelation); but by means of his affections he obtains an experimental realization and appreciation of the same.

Samuel E. Pierce said, "In this prayer of Paul's he prayed like an apostle indeed, for he begged here for the greatest blessings which believers can, in this life, enjoy, or God Himself can bestow upon them. It may be said of this prayer that it is the greatest prayer which is to be found in the New Testament, that of our Lord in the seventeenth chapter of John only excepted." And Alexander Maclaren pointed out, "In no part of Paul's letters does he rise to a higher level than in his prayers, and none of his prayers are fuller of fervor than this wonderful series of petitions. They open out one into the other like some magnificent suite of apartments in a great palace-temple, each leading into a loftier and more spacious hall, each drawing nearer the presence chamber, until at last we stand there."

A Most Sublime Prayer

We are entirely in accord with the above opinions. Oh, that we had the capacity to humanly and relatively at least do this prayer justice as we attempt to "open" its sublime contents. That the apostle was here making requests for no ordinary blessings is at once apparent by its opening sentence, for he asked the Father of our Lord Jesus Christ to grant His people according to the riches not only of His grace but of His *glory*. That is, he besought the Father to bestow in accord with that rule or standard of measurement, asking for the most valuable and glorious things that the renewed mind can conceive. Four particular favors he requested, and the order in which he preferred them is a strictly logical and necessary one, which cannot be changed without doing violence to it. That order is both doctrinal and practical, experimental and climacteric. They are distinguished from each other by the recurring "that ye," and the force of "that" ("in order that") is causative and preparative.

There is a most intimate relation between the several petitions, each of them rising above and being a consequence of the preceding, the second being suggested by and leading out from the first, and the second in turn being both the condition and occasion of the third, and so with the subsequent one. They are like four steps of an ascent, each of which has to be trodden before the next can be reached. At the summit or top of the ascent is the petition that the saints might be "filled with all the fulness of God," for there can be nothing above or beyond that. *There* is the climax of all prayer, of all spiritual experience, of all soul bliss. We boldly say that no uninspired mind could ever conceive of such a favor or experience. Yet that very experience is what writer and reader should earnestly covet, and that very favor is what *we* are fully warranted in asking! But bear carefully in mind that the prayer does not begin there: that is the summit, and an ascent has to be made in order to reach it.

The first step, the initial favor sought, is to "be strengthened with might by his Spirit in the inner man." That is not only an indispensable requirement if we are to take the second step but equally necessary as a preparation for the third and fourth. Only by the energizing enablement of the blessed Spirit are we capacitated to move forward and upward. The next step toward the summit, the second favor sought, is "that Christ may dwell in your hearts by faith." The consequence of our being believingly occupied with His perfections is our "being rooted and grounded in love"—i.e., our life of devotedness and obedience to Christ thus growing out of and being based upon our love for Him—the reflex of His love to us. The third step of spiritual ascent and blessing sought is to "be able to comprehend . . . and to know the love of Christ, which passeth knowledge." Love begets love. Love is reciprocal. First, faith centering upon the person and work of Christ stimulates love to Him, and that in turn fits the heart to enter more deeply into an understanding and enjoyment of His love. This is how we personally understand the ground covered to this point.

Chapter 18

PRAYER FOR COMPREHENSION
OF GOD'S LOVE

EPHESIANS 3:18-21

"THAT YE ... may be able to comprehend with all saints what is the breadth, and length, and depth, and height, and to know the love of Christ, which passeth knowledge" (vv. 18-19) was Paul's third petition. It is of prime importance for the nourishment, health, and fruitfulness of the believer's spiritual life that he should be constantly occupied with the love of Christ, which is a bottomless, shoreless sea. Samuel Pierce designated Christ's love thus: "A subject altogether wonderful, mysterious, and Divine, so great and so immense that the more real saints think of it, the more the Holy Spirit is pleased at any time to give them spiritual conceptions of it, the more they are swallowed up in admiring and adoring thoughts of it, and crying out, 'O the depth!'" There is nothing in nature which illustrates Christ's love, nothing in human history or experience which exemplifies it. Only in the divine relations can we find any analogy. There one is given us which, though it fills the heart with joy and satisfaction, is nevertheless far above the grasp of our finite minds. Said the Lover of our souls, "As the Father hath loved me, so have I loved you" (John 15:9). Such a love we can neither express nor conceive, yet it should be the one subject on which our hearts are continuously set and from which we daily drink.

Christ's Love for His Church

"As the Father hath loved me, so have I loved you." As the Father loved Christ from everlasting, so Christ loved them: with delight, with special affection, with an unchanging, abiding, eternal love. Christ has loved His Church with all His soul from everlasting. His heart was fixed upon His Bride before all time. He loved her as the gift of the Father's love to Him. He loved her as presented to Him by the Father in all her beauty, glory, and excellence, in which she was forever to shine forth as His Wife in the kingdom of glory. He loved her as His mystical Body, in whom all His glory was to be displayed and admired. He loved her as His "peculiar treasure," as His very own. He was to be her life, her light, her holiness, her righteousness, her perfection and glory; for she was to receive all from Him as her eternal Head and Husband. The origin—the spring—of Christ's love to His beloved is high and incomprehensible.

178

His love originated in the Father's everlasting love to Him as God-man and to believers as the Spouse which He had chosen, loved, beautified, and bestowed on His dear Son.

The love of Christ for His people and His feeling toward them transcends all conception. His divine person stamps eternal perfection on His love, as well as everlasting worth, virtue, and efficacy on all His mediatorial acts. He who is the Son of the living God as considered in His distinctive person in the Trinity, who is the God-man in His theanthropic person, is the One in whom the Church was loved, chosen, and accepted before the foundation of the world. His people were divinely appointed to partake with Him in all His communicable grace and glory, to share in all His honors, titles, and dignities, so far as they are shareable. Nothing would satisfy the heart of Christ but that His redeemed should live with Him in heaven, to behold Him in His glory, and to be perfected in happiness by seeing Him as He is. The wonders contained in Christ's love can never be fully explored. All that is contained in His love will never be comprehended by the saints this side of glory. That which has been manifested of it in His incarnation and in His obedience and suffering is altogether beyond what saints can ever sufficiently appreciate and bless Him for. It is cause for deepest gratitude that we have been brought to know it, to believe it, and to enjoy it.

But since the love of Christ is so transcendent and mysterious, so infinite and incomprehensible, how can it be comprehended and known by us? Completely and perfectly it cannot, yet truly and satisfyingly it may be. Christ's love to us is discovered in the Word of truth, and as the Holy Spirit enlightens our understanding we are capacitated to apprehend something of its wonders and blessedness. As the Holy Spirit strengthens us within and calls our faith into exercise, we are enabled to take in some spiritual views of Christ's love. Faith is to the soul what the eye is to the body—the organ or faculty by which light is admitted and by which objects are seen and known. "Through faith we understand" (Heb. 11:3) that which is beyond the comprehension of mere reason. Though we cannot fathom the love of Christ, we may drink deeply of it. We can know how wonderful, how free, how transcendent, how selfless, how long-suffering, how constant, how infinite is His love. And this knowledge will have a sanctifying influence on our lives. Though we shall never be able to exhaust its unsearchable fullness, it is our privilege to know very much more of this love and have a fuller enjoyment of it than any of us have yet obtained.

The chief spiritual employment of the Christian should be to live in consideration and admiration of the wonderful love of Christ, to dwell on it in his thoughts until his heart is warmed, until his soul overflows with praise, until his whole life is constrained or influenced. He should meditate daily on its characteristics: its freeness, its pureness, its unstintedness, its immutability. Christ loves us more than we love ourselves. He loved us even while we hated Him, and nothing can change His love for us. We should ponder the manifestations of His love: first, in His acceptance of the Father's proposals in the everlasting covenant, whereby He freely consented to become the Sponsor of His fallen people and serve as their Surety; and then in His actual carrying out of that engagement. View Him leaving the holy tranquillity and ineffable bliss of heaven, where He was so worshiped and adored by all the celestial hosts, and coming down to this scene of sin, strife, and suffering! What love that was!

Consider Jehovah's condescending to take upon Him a nature that was inferior to the angelic, so that when the Word became flesh His divine glory was almost completely eclipsed. Contemplate the unspeakable humiliation into which the Son of God descended, a humiliation which can only be gauged as we measure the distance between the throne of heaven and the manger of Bethlehem. Bear in mind that even as the incarnate One He made Himself of no reputation, that instead of appearing in pomp and splendor, He "took upon him the form of a servant." That He came not to be ministered to but to minister, not deeming the most ignominious acts as beneath Him. Remember that He knew from the beginning the kind of treatment He would receive from those He befriended. He knew that instead of being welcomed, appreciated, loved, and worshiped, He would be despised and rejected of men. He knew that though He went about doing good, healing the sick, relieving the needy, preaching the gospel to the poor, He would be opposed and persecuted by the religious leaders, hated without a cause, and misunderstood and ultimately deserted even by His own disciples. What love that was—love indeed which passes knowledge, love which should ceaselessly occupy our hearts and shape our lives.

The Unparalleled Sufferings of Christ for Us

Reverently contemplate the unparalleled and immeasurable sufferings which the eternal Lover of your soul endured. Remove the shoes of carnal curiosity from your feet and enter the dark shades of Gethsemane, and behold your Saviour in agony of soul so intense that He shed great drops of blood. Then observe Him led as a lamb to the slaughter and treated as the vilest of criminals. Ponder afresh the horrible insults which were heaped upon the Holy One as wicked hands smote Him, spit in His face, plucked out His hair, and scourged Him. Behold the blasphemy of that mock coronation when they put a purple robe upon Him, placed a reed in His hand and a crown of thorns on His head, and cried, "Hail, King of the Jews." View Him suspended upon the cross between two malefactors; mocked with vinegar and gall when He said, "I thirst"; derided by the spectators. But more: contemplate Him there made sin for His people, made a curse for them, and accordingly smitten by the sword of divine justice, so that He exclaimed, "My God, my God, why hast thou forsaken me?" In view of this must we not say, "Christ . . . hath loved us, and hath given himself for us an offering and a sacrifice to God for a sweetsmelling savour" (Eph. 5:2).

But the love of Christ for His people did not cease at His death, nor did the manifestations and evidences of it. His love was as fresh, as intense, and as active when He ascended on high as it was when He was here below. He ascended with the interests of His people before Him, entering heaven in their name: "whither the forerunner is *for us* entered" (Heb. 6:20). Having purged our sins with His own precious blood, Christ sat down upon the mediatorial throne and, having been given a name which is above every name, was crowned with glory and honor *as* the Head of the Church, as the triumphant Conqueror over Satan and the grave. There, in His exalted state, He now shines forth within the veil before the saints, His heart filled as ever with the same love toward His people. As Aaron wore a breastplate on which were inscribed all the tribes of Israel, so our great High Priest bears all the names of His people on His heart as He appears before God on their behalf. The exercise of His love to them is seen in that "he ever liveth to make intercession for them" (Heb. 7:25). So tender is His heart for His own that, even in the glory, He is still "touched with the feeling of our infirmities" (Heb. 4:15).

Manifestations of the infinite and unchanging love of Christ are made to His people while they are left in this wilderness of sin: by His supplying their every need, by His making all things work together for their good, by His personal communings with them. The gift of the Holy Spirit was an outstanding evidence of His love to them (John 16:7; Acts 2:33). Nor was that all. "He gave some, apostles; and some, prophets; and some, evangelists; and some, pastors and teachers; for the perfecting of the saints, for the work of the ministry, for the edifying of the body of Christ" (Eph. 4:11-12). Are you favored to sit under the ministry of a faithful pastor who breaks to you the Bread of life, feeds you with knowledge and understanding, and stimulates you to run with patience the race that is set before you? Then you should look upon that pastor as the love gift of your ascended Saviour. Do you find a book written by a servant of God, or even a monthly magazine, edifying to your soul, made a blessing to your heart, supplying motives for a godly walk and affording comfort and encouragement amid the difficulties of the way? Then you should look upon the same as a gracious provision made for you by the love of Christ.

The Dimensions of Christ's Love

Note that the apostle did not pray that the saints might comprehend absolutely the love of Christ itself but rather the dimensions of it. First, "what is the breadth." This writer has long been impressed with the fact that the breadth comes first, for is it not *there* our thoughts are most faulty? Are not many of us so wrapped up in the consideration of Christ's wondrous love to *us,* that we fail to appreciate its wider scope and blessed extent? Is it not to correct this selfish tendency that the Holy Spirit mentions the breadth of Christ's love first? And is it not also to counteract that sectarian spirit which cramps the affections of so many of God's people? It is also opposed to the error of those who would restrict the riches of Christ's love to New Testament believers. No doubt the placing of this phrase was immediately intended for the instruction of the Jewish saints, who were so slow to realize the love of Christ reached also to sinners among the Gentiles. Christ's love extends to all the elect, in every age, in every place, in every state and case. It is a love which embraces the *whole* family of God, from the least to the greatest.

"And length." Is not the order of these measures quite different from the manner in which an uninspired writer would have arranged them? Is it not different from the natural and logical order? Would we not have gone from "breadth" to "depth"? But the Holy Spirit places first what we are apt to put last. If we are slow to grasp (in an experimental way) the compass of Christ's love, many are most tardy in apprehending (in a doctrinal way) the eternity of it. How many suppose that Christ began to love them only when they set their own affection upon Him; but "we love him, because he first loved us" (I John 4:19); and as His love knows no end, so it has no beginning, being from everlasting to everlasting. The Lord says to each of His people, "Yea, I have loved thee with an everlasting love, therefore with lovingkindness have I drawn thee" (Jer. 31:3). His drawing us to Himself is the effect of His love. Nor can our infirmities or even our iniquities quench it. "Having loved his own which were in the world, he loved them unto the end" (John 13:1). Nothing can separate us from His love (Rom. 8:35-39).

"And depth." That can indeed be best comprehended by considering the amazing love of Christ to me personally, for if I have been made the subject of an inward work of grace, then I realize to some extent, actually and experimentally, the horrible pit in which I lay and the awful moral distance to which my sins had separated me from the Holy One. I can better apprehend my own sad case than I can the plight of others, and therefore I can better comprehend the amazing love of Christ in stooping so low to lift me out of the miry clay than I can in the cases of others. The depth of Christ's love is to be contemplated in the light of the abject wretchedness into which the fall plunged the Church, for its members "are by nature the children of wrath, even as others" (Eph. 2:3). This love is to be contemplated in the light of our individual history, when as unregenerate we departed farther and farther from God. It is to be contemplated in the light of the unparalleled depth of abasement and suffering into which the Lord of glory descended to effect the deliverance and salvation of His people.

"And height." If the breadth of Christ's love is boundless, its length endless, its depth fathomless, then assuredly its height is measureless. The "height" to which the love of Christ has elevated His redeemed is to be viewed in the light of two things: their present privileges and their future happiness, both of which are best set forth in the language of Holy Writ itself. "He raiseth up the poor out of the dust, and lifteth up the beggar from the dunghill, to set them among princes, and to make them inherit the throne of glory" (I Sam. 2:8). "Even unto them will I give in mine house and within my walls a place and a name better than of sons and of daughters: I will give them an everlasting name, that shall not be cut off" (Isa. 56:5). "The Spirit itself beareth witness with our spirit, that we are the children of God: and if children, then heirs; heirs of God, and joint-heirs with Christ" (Rom. 8:16-17). "They shall see his face; and his name shall be in their foreheads. And there shall be no night there; and they need no candle, neither light of the sun; for the Lord God giveth them light: and they shall reign for ever and ever" (Rev. 22:4-5).

"That ye . . . may be able to comprehend with all saints what is the breadth, and length, and depth, and height, and to know the love of Christ, which passeth knowledge." Is not the reader at once struck with the difference between this request and those he is accustomed to hearing in public prayers— very likely in his own prayers? Many of God's people are wont to ask for an increase of *their* love to Christ. We generally ask for more *enjoyment* of Christ's love for us. But even that is not what Paul directly made supplication for. His request was that we might have a fuller comprehension and a deeper knowledge of *Christ's* love. We may be sure that he prayed aright; therefore it is wise to follow his example. Man ever reverses God's order, and of course he is the loser by doing so. Our poor love is increased by faith's occupation with the infinite love of Christ and meditations upon its characteristics and manifestations.

The Apostle's Request for the Saints

The apostle here made request that God's people might have a more spiritual and enlarged view of the immeasurable love of Christ, that their understanding might be swallowed up in it, that their renewed minds might be more and more filled with the wonders of it, that they should enter into a deeper experimental acquaintance with the same. All the discoveries of the love of Christ which the Holy Spirit makes unto us are in the Word and by the Word, and we are brought to spiritual discernment of that love by the exercise of faith. Christ's love is apprehended only as it is evidenced in its manifestations, and we obtain a spiritual knowledge thereof only as we personally imbibe it. Even the renewed understanding is not able of itself to grasp the surpassing love of Christ, but the understanding led by the heart can lay hold of it and find in it fuller satisfaction. Though necessarily imperfect and incomplete, the Christian's knowledge of Christ's love is real and ravishing, and it should be constantly deepening and enlarging. It "passeth knowledge" not only because it is infinite and therefore incomprehensible to the finite mind but also because our personal experience and enjoyment of it can never exhaust it—we but touch its edges and skim its surface.

We have intimated somewhat in the last paragraph what we regard as the difference between "comprehending" and "knowing." Perhaps it was no part of the Spirit's design that we should draw any broad line between them, but so far as we can perceive, it seems to us that the "comprehending" is via the understanding, the "knowing" via the heart; the former being more the result of mental effort, the other of intuition. Thus "knowing" in addition to "comprehending" is feeling a sense of the love of Christ or having an experimental acquaintance with it. Though it transcends the grasp of our intellect, yet it is a subject of inward consciousness. Though it can be only faintly recognized, it may be adoringly appreciated. As the Spirit graciously takes of the things of Christ and shows them to us, as He opens to us more and more the love of Christ by His own effectual teaching, and as He opens our minds in a gradual and imperceptible way to understand, to exercise our thoughts upon it, we enjoy the same in our hearts. That knowledge being formed within becomes a spiritual part of us, so that what we read in the Word concerning the love of Christ we *know* to be truth, for we have the reality of it within our own souls.

Knowledge of the Love of Christ

"To know the love of Christ, which passeth knowledge." We do not agree with those who say that phrase is a paradox: rather it is a plain statement of fact. We may, we can, we do, know the love of Christ in the sense explained above. We believe it, we experience it, we enjoy it as a blessed and glorious reality. Yet our knowledge is inadequate and imperfect, for the infinite love of Christ can never be entirely compassed, explored, or exhausted by us. As Pierce pointed out, "All that is known of the love of Christ in and by all the saints on earth: all that is known and enjoyed of the love of Christ by all the saints in heaven, is far below what is contained in the person and love of Christ, as considered in His own heart towards us. I have under this view of the subject often said we shall never know anything of the love wherewith Christ hath loved us, either in time or eternity, but by its *fruits and effects*. . . . The love of Christ surpasseth the whole of His sufferings, as much as they surpass all our guilt and sin. His love was the cause, and His sufferings the effect of it." As the cause excels the effect, as the tree is greater than its fruit, so the fountain of Christ's love exceeds all the streams which flow from it to us.

The angels never can enter fully into the love of Christ for His Church and people. Also, the finite-minded saints can never fully understand the fullness of Christ's love. Nevertheless it is important that the saint should make it his paramount concern to be more and more absorbed with the love of Christ, exercising his mind thereon, feeding his soul therefrom, delighting his heart therein, praying earnestly that he may more fully understand the love of God. He should attentively consider the revelation given of it in the Word of truth, meditating on its ineffable characteristics, contemplating its wondrous manifestations, and realizing that Christ's love to His own is eternal, infinite, and unalterable—not only without cessation but without the least diminution. Such a subject is worthy of the saint's best attention and constant pursuit. It will amply repay his best efforts and greatly enrich his spiritual life. Nothing will so much excite gratitude in his heart as a contemplation of the love of Christ to such an unlovely creature as he. Nothing will prompt so effectually to a life of self-denial. Nothing will make so pleasant and easy a walk of obedience to God. Nothing will so deaden the saint to the world. Nothing else can so fill him with peace, yes, and with joy, in a season of affliction or bereavement.

Saints to Be Filled with All the Fullness of God

"That ye might be filled with all the fulness of God" (v. 19). This is the closing and climactic request. It is one which has met with ridicule from skeptical and cold critics, for regarding its language in a carnal manner, they suppose it teaches the absurdity of the finite compassing the Infinite, or of man being deified. They imagine the apostle's enthusiasm ran away with him, that in his devotional ecstasy he forgot the limits that separate the creature from the Creator. But of those who would, by grace, promptly reject such horrible impieties, some are probably inclined to ask, How is it possible for such creatures as we are, compassed with infirmity, harassed and handicapped by indwelling sin, to expect such a favored and exalted experience to ever be realized by us in this life? It appears to us that such a doubting and doleful question ought to be met with the retort, How was it possible that such a prayer should ever have issued from inspired lips, unless the blessings requested *are* attainable? Surely no real Christian is prepared to affirm that the beloved apostle was wasting his breath in so supplicating God.

Instead of questioning this petition, we ought to be rebuked and humbled for being surprised at Paul's asking that saints might be "filled with all the fulness of God." Such a petition should shame us for the paucity and pettiness of our requests, indicative as they are of comparative contentedness with a sadly low level of spirituality—failing to act according to our privileges, as those who are "heirs of God, and joint-heirs with Christ." Instead of counting upon the divine munificence, instead of availing ourselves of the fullness which there is in Him, we limit the Holy One and think of Him almost as though He were as poor as ourselves. Alas, how often our expectations are measured by our meager attainments, instead of our expectations being formed by the revealed character of the One who is "the God of all grace." View this petition then as the spiritual corrective to our faithless doubtings and groveling hopes. View it as intimating what the Christian, every Christian, may legitimately aspire to and what he ought daily to pray for. View it as a revelation of the Father's heart, making known to His children the high privilege and favored portion which it is His will for them to enjoy. Yet remember that this is not the first but the final petition!

We have sought to show how that our being "rooted and grounded in love" was both a consequence of Christ's dwelling in our hearts by faith and also the necessary condition of our being able to comprehend and know His surpassing love. It is equally true that having our hearts and minds constantly occupied with the love of Christ is an essential preparation for our becoming "filled with all the fulness of God." For it is by the increasing apprehension and experience of the former that we are fitted for and led on to the latter. The more we revel in the wonderful love of God in Christ, the more our minds are exercised upon the same, and the more largely we drink of that divine nectar, the more are our capacities enlarged and the greater and higher become our expectations for the reception of other blessings. Then we too begin reasoning with the apostle: "He that spared not his own Son, but delivered him up for us all, how shall he not *with him* also freely give us *all things?*" (Rom. 8:32). As we become more and more occupied with the love of God in Christ, both our desires and our expectations are raised, so that we look to God and count on His giving us all things necessary for our holiness, happiness, and satisfaction.

The Fullness of the Divine Character Displayed in Christ

Is there not a glorious fitness in God's imparting His fullness to us through our knowledge of the love of Christ? In the first place, it is in, by, and through Christ, and particularly in His dying love, that the fullness of the divine character is displayed. Not a little is seen of Him in His other works, but only in Christ are His perfections fully revealed. "No man hath seen God [adequately and clearly; cf. Matt. 5:8] at any time; the only begotten Son, which is in the bosom of the Father, he hath declared him" (John 1:18). Some of God's attributes were exhibited in creation and in God's providence, but in the work of redemption—and in that alone—His full excellence appears. Great as were some of the displays of His glory under former dispensations—as at the Flood and His appearing at Sinai—they contained only a partial manifestation of Him. "God, who at sundry times and in divers manners spake in time past unto the fathers by the prophets"—whose communications were at most but occasional and fragmentary—"hath in these last days spoken unto us by his Son" (Heb. 1:1-2). Christ is the perfect, final, climactic revelation of God. He said, "He that hath seen me hath seen the Father" (John 14:9).

In the second place, through the dying love of Christ a way has been opened for the communication of divine blessing for guilty creatures. The fullness of God, especially His philanthropy and munificence, may be likened to a mighty stream, and sin to an extensive and high mountain, which stands in the way of God's fullness, and so prevents our being filled by it. Had He so pleased, God could, by the simple fiat of His invincible will, have removed that mountain. But then how would His justice and holiness have been displayed? Nor could man by his own efforts—not even the combined efforts of the entire human race —obliterate that abominable thing which kept him at a guilty distance from God and cut him off from His favor. God deemed it most for His glory, best suited to His moral perfections, to ordain that the mediatorial work of His incarnate Son should take away the sins of His people and open a way through which His infinite blessings should flow forth to them. Accordingly, by the sacrifice of Christ the mountain of our sins was removed and cast into the depths of the sea. Then the way was all clear for the fullness of God's heart to believing sinners to flow forth to them without the least dishonor attaching to His character as having connived at sin. Through Christ the bounties of God come to His people.

In the third place, as we come to partially know the love of Christ, we imbibe, drink of, become recipients of, the divine fullness. To be filled with the fullness of God it is not only necessary that that fullness be exhibited to us, and a way opened for its being consistently (or morally) communicated to us, but also that the soul be emptied of those impediments which obstruct its entrance. The unrenewed mind is incapable of being filled with the fullness of God: there is no room in it for the same, for it is already preoccupied with other things. All its thoughts, desires, and affections are centered upon the trash of this world. Even though it assumes a religious pose, it is still so bloated with self-sufficiency and self-righteousness that there is no place for a free salvation, for divine grace. But where the love of Christ is personally and experimentally known, as revealed in the gospel and realized in the soul by the supernatural operations of the Holy Spirit, all other things are counted loss, and the fullness of God finds ready access. Occupation of the heart with Christ and His love both capacitates us for and causes us to imbibe the divine fullness. So much then for the connection of the fourth to the third petition.

"That ye might be filled with all the fullness of God." What a petition is this! It is cumulative in its force. That ye might be filled: filled with God; filled with the fullness of God; filled with all the fullness of God. Who can comprehend all it contains? What human pen is capable of opening its significance? We can only do our poor best according to our limited measure and the light which God has granted us. It should be obvious to any anointed eye that such language cannot signify that the finite shall ever contain the Infinite, or that we should cease to be human creatures and become as God Himself. No, that can never be. But the Christian may be filled with all the fullness of God according to his measure as a new creature in Christ, and in such a proportion as he is capable of in this life. Not that he is ever to be satisfied with any present measure of attainment in divine things, but constantly seeking after and reaching forth to an enlarged degree of the same. Only those who "hunger and thirst" are assured of being "filled" (Matt. 5:6).

How to Understand the Fullness of God

The expression "the fullness of God" is capable of being grammatically construed in two ways, according as we regard "God" as the genitive of the subject (i.e., the "fulness" of which God Himself *is full*), or the genitive of the object, namely, the fullness which flows from Him or that plenitude which He *communicates* in His gifts to us. The commentators differ as to which is to be preferred. Personally we take both, declining to place any limitation on the expression, and shall discuss it accordingly. It may also be pointed out that the Greek word "filled *with* all the fullness of God" is rendered in the Revised Version "filled *unto* all the fulness of God," which suggests the idea of a continuous process, a progressive and enlarging experience, for the ultimate aim of all genuine spiritual desire is to know God so intimately as to be filled to satiety by Him. This too we include in our understanding of the expression. Thus, a vessel may be filled up to its very brim. But suppose the size of that vessel should be enlarged, and continue to be enlarged, then its capacity to receive is ever increasing! Such is indeed the case, and ever will be throughout the unending ages of eternity, with the heart of the regenerate. The more the soul finds its satisfaction in God Himself, the larger its desires become and the more it takes in of Him.

How many of our difficulties are self-created! How the exercise of our natural minds upon such a statement as "filled with all the fullness of God" serves to prevent us from grasping anything of its true import. We need to be much on our guard lest our mental approach to those words *filled* and *fullness* is altogether too gross and carnal: not that we are to evacuate them of all meaning, but rather that we should endeavor to contemplate them spiritually and not materially. Do we not cause ourselves unnecessary perplexity when we ask how the finite can contain the Infinite? Are we to think of God, principally and chiefly, as the eternal, infinite and immutable One? Surely not, for those are His incommunicable attributes, which bear no relation to us, and about which we know next to nothing. But there are other attributes of His nature and being which come closer to us, for they are communicated to His people. The final words concerning Him are "God is light," "God is love" (I John 1:5; 4:8), and surely we should be most occupied with them, for they best enable us to comprehend Him. Cannot the light which is in God pour itself into my darkness? Cannot His love be shed abroad in my heart? Filled with all the fullness of God as "light" and as "love"!

This prayer asks that by viewing God objectively, believers may, through a contemplation of His manifold perfections, take into their renewed minds a full-orbed concept of His excellency. It includes such a contemplation of the Deity that can fill the mind with a satisfying view of all three Persons—like the sun, shining through clear windows, fills a room with light. The prayer requests that God will abundantly communicate His grace and comforts to us, that we may be filled with His light and love—like a vessel filled to overflowing. It also requests that we shall be constrained to yield ourselves wholly to God, that He may fill and possess our entire being—like a king occupying the whole of the royal suite in his palace.

Paul's Longing for the Saints

"That ye might be filled with all the fulness of God." Regard the expression relatively and comparatively. Paul longed that the saints might not rest content with a contracted and inadequate concept and apprehension of the divine character, but aspire after a well-balanced, full, and symmetrical view and experience of God. Many believers are satisfied with a most limited idea of the divine perfections. Some almost restrict their thoughts to His majesty and sovereignty, some to His power and holiness, some to His love and grace; while others also take in His goodness, His faithfulness, His immutability, His righteousness, His longsuffering. We should not dwell on one or two of His glorious attributes only, to the exclusion of others, but should pray for and strive after spiritual knowledge and experimental acquaintance with each alike, that our minds and hearts may be filled with *all* His excellences. We should pant after such views of His manifold glory that would produce peace in the conscience, love in the heart, and satisfaction in the soul. We should be occupied with the riches of His grace, the wonders of His wisdom, the miracles of His might, with *all* His blessed attributes as engaged for His people and pledged to them in the everlasting covenant.

"That ye might be filled with all the fulness of God" is not to be restricted to the perfections of Deity abstractly considered, but is to be regarded as pertaining to all three Persons of the adorable Trinity. So we also understand it as signifying "filled with all the fullness of the triune God," and not of one Person only to the exclusion of the others. There are some denominations which make most of the Father, some which make most of the Son, some which make most of the Spirit. Each is equally glorious, each is equally interested in us: our salvation is due to Their joint operations and combined counsels, and therefore They should have an *equal* place in our thoughts and affections. Do not confine your minds to the grace of the Father in choosing and in so loving His people as to give His only begotten Son for them; for we are required to "honour the Son, even as . . . [we] honour the Father" (John 5:23). Do not confine your meditations to the amazing condescension and inconceivable sufferings of the Son on behalf of His saints, but contemplate also "the love of the Spirit" (Rom. 15:30) as He quickened you when dead in sins, as He indwells you, as He takes of the things of Christ and shows them unto you. Seek to be filled with the triune God.

How may we be filled with all the fullness of God? First, by our contemplation of Him *objectively:* the affections of the new man drawing out the heart after its Author, faith enabling us to take in such satisfying views of Him as lead to intimate fellowship with Him, fill the soul with a real and absorbing knowledge of Him, and cause us to make Him our all-sufficient Portion. Second, by our receiving *subjectively* from Him, God communicating to us out of the plenitude of His own being. To be filled with Him thus is to have Him imparting all that He can bestow upon us and all that we are capable of receiving, showering down upon us His richest blessings, that we have no further sense of want, no aching emptiness. We, whose hearts were by nature empty of any good, who drank from the streams of this world only to thirst again, who experienced the insufficiency and vanity of all earthly things, may be filled to all satiety with what He bestows from Himself. We may experience the amplest measure of His grace and consolation; we may be filled with such peace and joy that no rival will have any power to attract us.

Let us now consider more directly the phrase "that ye might be filled." Was not the apostle here praying that God might more fully possess us in a personal way, that we might be brought to yield ourselves more completely to Him? Think of the Christian being filled by and with God, not only as a dwelling may be filled with sunlight or a vessel with liquid, but also as a many-roomed house may be completely occupied with guests. The saint desires that Christ should dwell in his heart by faith, but is there any restriction on that desire? Is there any portion of his being marked "private"—reserved solely for himself? In other words, is there any part of his complex being not fully given up to God in Christ, not yet consciously, definitely, voluntarily, and gladly surrendered to His occupancy and sway? That is a searching question which each of us needs to honestly face. If there is any department of my outward life or any compartment of my inner man which is not fully surrendered to God, then I am *not* filled with Him. Am I really yielding my entire self to Him, so that I am sanctified in my "whole spirit and soul and body" (I Thess. 5:23)?

The Place This Prayer Occupies

Earlier we pointed out that it will help us to an understanding both of the scope of this prayer and the meaning of its petitions if we observe the place it occupies in this epistle: at the close of the doctrinal section and as introductory to the practical portion. The prayer turns into supplication the contents of the former and prepares the heart for obeying the precepts of the latter. Among those precepts is this: "Be not drunk with wine, wherein is excess; but be filled with the Spirit" (Eph. 5:18), that He should occupy us unreservedly, pervading the innermost depths of our beings, energizing and using all our faculties. Have we not reason then to pray earnestly and daily that in this sense too we might be filled? Not that God may possess us in part, but wholly; that our obedience may be such as to receive the fulfillment of Christ's promise: "My Father will love him, and we will come unto him, and make our abode with him" (John 14:23). May the surrender of myself be so complete that I may say, "Bless the Lord, O my soul: and *all* that is within me, bless his holy name" (Ps. 103:1). I cannot do so unless all is freely dedicated to Him.

How full and many-sided is this fourth petition! In addition to those meanings and applications of it given above, we point out still another, which for want of a better term we will call its practical bearing, namely, that the Christian ought to be filled with a knowledge of God's will. The believer should indeed have His mind on all things, for to walk in darkness is one of the marks of the wicked. But observe that we have placed this signification of the request last, for we shall not have light upon our path nor divine wisdom for our problems unless we are first fully yielded to God. Let us also call attention again to the relation of this prayer to the section which follows it. Among the exhortations found in that portion is "Wherefore be ye not unwise, but understanding what the will of the Lord is" (Eph. 5:17), for all the details of our daily lives, for the various decisions we have to make constantly. Hence in another of the prayers of this apostle we find him asking for the saints that they "might be filled with the knowledge of his will" (Col. 1:9). Being ignorant of God's will is not merely an innocent infirmity but a sin which should humble us. If the Word dwells in us richly, if we are filled with the Spirit, then we shall have clear discernment, good judgment, a knowledge in all circumstances of that which will be pleasing to Him.

While we think the apostle primarily desired that God's people should receive a fulfillment of this prayer in *this* life, it is by no means to be restricted to this life only. Coming as it does at the close of the petitions, and in view of the language used in the next verses, it seems clear that Paul's anointed eye was also looking forward to the endless ages of eternity—as ours should too. This view of the petition is also confirmed by the fact that the Greek may be legitimately rendered "that ye might be filled *unto* all the fullness of God," which, as previously pointed out, suggests the idea of a continuous process, a progressive and enlarging experience. The ultimate aim of all genuine spiritual desire is to know God so intimately as to be filled with all the glory of God, filled to satiety by Him—wh'ch will only be when heaven is reached. Here human language fails us, for our minds are incapable of conceiving such ineffable heights of bliss. All we can say is that this request expresses an approximation to the supreme perfection which is begun in this life and shall be forever growing in the holiness and bliss of the future state, though an infinite distance will always remain between the Creator and the creature.

Chapter 19

PRAYER OF DOXOLOGY

EPHESIANS 3:20-21

HAVING CONSIDERED the particular occasion or cause of this prayer, the character in which God is addressed, the rule or measure by which He is entreated to confer His favors, and the several petitions of it, we turn now to contemplate the doxology that concludes it. "Now unto him that is able to do exceeding abundantly above all that we ask or think, according to the power that worketh in us, unto him be glory in the church by Christ Jesus throughout all ages, world without end. Amen" (vv. 20-21). This doxology may be considered from two viewpoints. First, as an adoring outburst of the apostle's own heart; and second—from the fact of its having been placed on record—as containing needful and valuable instruction for us. Anyone with spiritual discernment will at once perceive that, from either of these viewpoints, the doxology forms a most fitting climax and sequel to the prayer itself, constituting as it does a natural termination of it—a reverberation of praise to the One supplicated. A "doxology" is an expression of adoration which rises above the level of ordinary speech, being more the language of ecstasy. It is a fervent utterance of praise: yet it is not so much the *act* of praise as it is the realization of the praise which is due to God and the consciousness that He is due infinitely more than we are capable of rendering to Him. We are lost in Him, overwhelmed with a sense of His ineffable glory.

There are three things in this doxology which especially claim our attention: first, the particular character in which God is here contemplated—"He is able"; second, the standard to which faith should appeal in prayer—"the power that worketh in us"; third, the ascription of glory, concerning which we have: its medium—"the church"; its Agent—"Christ Jesus"; its perpetuity—"world without end." Let us consider how blessedly appropriate it is to view God thus in this particular connection.

As experienced Christians well know, the certain effect of growing in spiritual knowledge of God and of the love of Christ is a deepening sense of our own weakness and unworthiness. Thus we are here reminded that we have to do with One who is infinitely sufficient to supply our every need and satisfy our every longing. How can such as we expect to obtain such wonderful privileges and enter into the enjoyment of such transcendent blessings as those expressed in the preceding verses? "He is able to do exceeding abundantly above all that we ask or think." Perhaps some reader has lost heart and hope in the efficacy of prayer and has become almost stoically content with a state of comparative emptiness. Ephesians 3:20 reveals the remedy.

To be strengthened with might by the Spirit in the inner man, to know Christ's constant presence in our hearts by faith so that we are rooted and founded in love, to be able to comprehend the dimensions and to know the love of Christ which passes knowledge, and to be filled with all the fullness of God—such experiences may seem visionary and impossible. They should not, they will not, if faith really views God as the apostle here did. Such experiences may indeed exceed anything we have yet attained, they may transcend what we have even seriously thought of and prayed for, yet they *are* possible and realizable even in this life, "according to the power that worketh in us." It is the express design of the Spirit in recording this doxology to encourage us, to afford confidence in our approaches to God, to enlarge our petitions. The Spirit's purpose here is the same as was Christ's in the closing section of that prayer which He gave to His disciples. The children are to ask of their Father in heaven, remembering "for thine is the kingdom, and the power, and the glory, for ever." This is a confirmation of faith taken from the excellency of God— His ability, His sufficiency, His glory. However great our need, His resources are illimitable; however powerful our foes, His power to deliver is infinite; however high our desires, He can fully satisfy them.

God Is Able

It will be a great tonic for faith if we take to heart how frequently God is set before us in this most blessed character. "God is able to make all grace abound toward you" (II Cor. 9:8). "He is able to succour them that are tempted" (Heb. 2:18). "He is able also to save them to the uttermost that come unto God by him" (Heb. 7:25). "He is able even to subdue all things unto himself" (Phil. 3:21). "He is able to keep that which I have committed unto him against that day" (II Tim. 1:12). He "is able to keep you from falling, and to present you faultless before the presence of his glory with exceeding joy" (Jude 24). Yes, *He is able* to save, to succor, to subdue, to sanctify, to supply, to secure, to satisfy; and therefore "he is able to do [for us] exceeding abundantly above all that we ask or think." In this character God is viewed not only as the omnipotent One but also as the munificent One, as being not only all-powerful but abundantly generous. God not only gives, but He "giveth to all liberally" (James 1:5). Very often His liberality exceeds not only our deserts but even our desires, bestowing upon us more than we have either wisdom or confidence to ask. Many illustrations of that fact are recorded in the Scriptures, and many are met with in the experience of God's children today.

Every Christian already has abundant proof that God can give him and do more for him than he can ask or think, for He has already done so! It was not in answer to my prayers that God elected me and inscribed my name in the book of life, for He chose me in Christ before the foundation of the world. It was not in response to any petition of mine that an all-sufficient Redeemer was provided for my hell-deserving soul, for God sent forth His Son into this world to save His people from their sins nearly two thousand years before I had any historical existence. It was not in return for any eloquent request of mine that the Holy Spirit quickened me into newness of life when I was dead in trespasses and sins, for to pray for life is not a faculty of the unregenerate. Rather the new birth itself capacitates us for living desire and spiritual longing. The new birth imparts life which causes the soul to long for more life. No, God's people are spiritually dead and far from Him when He regenerates them and thereby fulfills to all of them that word "I am found of them that sought me not" (Isa. 65:1). God's gracious dealings with us are above even our faith and requests!

In connection with the apostle's doxology, let the Christian reader honestly face the Lord's own question "Believe ye that I am able to do this?" (Matt. 9:28). Perhaps you believe He is able to do so, but you fear He may not be willing to. If you really think God is able to bring you into a closer walk and a more constant fellowship with Himself, that He is able to make all grace abound toward you and fill you with Himself, but doubt His willingness to do so, then your heart is deceiving you and causing you to think more highly of yourself than you have any right to do. The fact is, dear friend, you do not believe He is able. If you did, you would not doubt His willingness.

The Heart Is Deceitful

Your heart is more deceitful than you realize; your case is far worse than you will admit. You have too good an opinion of yourself. You are trying to hide your unbelief under the fair cover of humility. You persuade yourself that it would be presumptuous to entertain the assurance that God is willing to work miracles on your behalf, and congratulate yourself for your humble-mindedness. How you delude yourself! You may indeed believe intellectually in the ability and all-sufficency of God, but your heart has not laid hold of the same: if it had, you would not call into question His willingness. The fact is that you entertain a horribly distorted view of God. In reality, you fondly imagine that you are more anxious to receive spiritual blessings than He is desirous of bestowing them; that you are more willing, more concerned about your spiritual prosperity, than He is. Call things by their proper names. Confess to God your excuseless unbelief and cease posing as a very humble person. God does not mock His people by declaring to them that He is able while at the same time He is unwilling. Reexamine the passages quoted previously: "He is able also to save them to the uttermost that come unto God by him" (Heb. 7:25). Does not that include His willingness? Of course it does. "He is able to succour them that are tempted" (Heb. 2:18). Yes, and willing too, or such a word would have no comfort in it. "He is able to keep that which I have committed unto him" (II Tim. 1:12). What assurance could that give me if He were unwilling to keep? When the Lord rebuked the skeptical laughter of Sarah, was it because she questioned His willingness or because she doubted His power? The latter, as is clear from His challenge: "Is any thing too hard for the LORD?" (Gen. 18:13-14). When He rebuked Moses for his unbelief, was it because he distrusted God's willingness or because he doubted His might? Clearly the latter: "Is the LORD's hand waxed short?" (Num. 11:22-23). And if you really believed in God's omnipotence you would promptly avail yourself of it!

God Both Able and Willing

"He is able" briefly but comprehensively affirms God's goodness, willingness, sufficiency, and munificence. Because God is good, He withholds no good thing from them that walk uprightly, and makes all things work together for good to them that love Him. Because God is good, He is willing and ready to supply all our need according to His riches in glory by Christ Jesus. Because He is God, He is self-sufficient: no creature can thwart Him, no situation dismay Him, no emergency arise which is beyond His resources. Because God is munificent, He is the Rewarder of them that diligently seek Him. Because God is the almighty and all-sufficient One, "he is able to do exceeding abundantly above all that we ask or think." What a God is ours! How different from the creature! Have we not in some hour of need appealed to one of our fellows who had the wherewithal to succor, but refused? And have we not witnessed a fond mother anxious to relieve her suffering child, but unable to do so! But the One with whom the Christian has to do, his Father in heaven, has both the willingness and the power.

How different many of our prayers would be if we always viewed God thus when approaching His mercy seat! If faith regarded Him in this character, our petitions would be framed accordingly, and our confidence would be greater and more honoring to Him. Each word in that wonderful doxology should be duly weighed and its cumulative and climacteric force grasped by us. God is able to do not only what we "ask" but also what we "think." Some of our thoughts are beyond expression. He is able to do all that we ask or think, not merely some or even most, but even our loftiest conceptions. Furthermore, He is able to do *above all* that we ask or think, exceeding our highest aspirations and largest requests. Better still, He is able to do abundantly above all that we ask or think. Oh, that the Holy Spirit would enable us to understand that and strengthen our faith to obtain a better grip upon it. Best of all, He is able to do "*exceeding* abundantly above *all* that we ask or think." Human language is utterly incapable of expressing the infinite sufficiency and illimitable bounty of the One to whom prayer is addressed. He has declared, "As the heavens are higher than the earth, so are my ways higher than your ways, and my thoughts than your thoughts" (Isa. 55:9).

For the further encouraging of our hearts and strengthening of our faith, let us consider some recorded examples of God's answers far exceeding the requests of His people. "Abram said, Lord GOD, what wilt thou give me, seeing I go childless?" What was the response of the bountiful Giver? "He brought him forth abroad, and said, Look now toward heaven, and tell the stars, if thou be able to number them: and he said unto him, So shall thy seed be" (Gen. 15:2-5)! Jacob's thought rose no higher than "bread to eat, and raiment to put on" (Gen. 28:20), but the divine munificence bestowed upon him "oxen, and asses, flocks, and menservants, and womenservants" (Gen. 32:5). The Hebrews would have been quite content to remain in Egypt if deliverance from bondage had been granted them (Exodus 2:23), but God brought them into a land flowing with milk and honey! David asked life of God, and He not only gave him "the request of his lips" but bestowed upon him a throne as well (Ps. 21:1-4).

Solomon sought "an understanding heart" and God not only supplied it but said, "I have also given thee that which thou hast not asked, both riches, and honour" (I Kings 3:13).

And has it not been thus with each of us? Has not the bountiful One given above our expectations? Go back, my brother, my sister, to the dawn of your Christian life. Recall the season when you were under conviction of sin and a weighty sense of the wrath of God oppressed you. Did your desires at that time ascend any higher than to be delivered from the everlasting burnings and be granted an assurance of pardon? Bring your mind back to that time when you were painfully aware of being in the far country, where you sought in vain to find satisfaction in the husks that the swine feed on, and when you cried, "I perish with hunger!" At that time did your aspirations go beyond that of the prodigal? Would you not have been quite content if the Father had made you one of His "hired servants"? Ah, how truly did He then do exceeding abundantly above all that you asked or thought! He gave you a welcome such as you never dreamed of. He greeted you with manifestations of love that completely melted your heart. He decked you out with clothing befitting His favored child. He spread a feast before you and filled your heart with merriment. And my friend, He has not changed! He is still the all-bountiful One!

Christ the All-Sufficient One

Because He has not changed, He presents Himself before you here in Ephesians 3:20 as the all-sufficient One. When you approach the throne of grace, He would have you view Him as the One whose resources are illimitable, whose ability to use them is infinite, and whose willingness so to do is demonstrated once for all in giving His only begotten Son for you and to you. Shadrach, Meshach, and Abednego showed such confidence and assurance when Nebuchadnezzar appointed that they should suffer a horrible death if they refused to worship the golden image which he had set up. Hear their intrepid reply: "We are not careful to answer thee in this matter. If it be so [that you really mean to carry out your threat], our God whom we serve is *able* to deliver us from the burning fiery furnace, and *he will* deliver us out of thine hand, O king" (Dan. 3:17). With faith steadfastly fixed on God's power, they had no doubt whatever about His willingness! And that, together with the glorious sequel, is recorded for our instruction as well as our encouragement. God has not changed. He is still the omnipotent One.

Ponder carefully the following passage concerning Abraham. "Who against hope believed in hope, that he might be the father of many nations; according to that which was spoken, So shall thy seed be. And being not weak in faith, he considered not his own body now dead, when he was about an hundred years old, neither yet the deadness of Sarah's womb: He staggered not at the promise of God through unbelief; but was strong in faith, giving glory to God; and being fully persuaded that, what he had promised, *he was able* also to perform" (Rom. 4:18-21). To carnal reason it seemed an impossibility that the aged Sarah should bear the patriarch a son in his old age; but Abraham refused to be dismayed by the insuperable obstacles presented to sight. From the standpoint of experience also the situation appeared hopeless. But even that did not daunt

him. Why was he strong in faith? Because he had a tight grip on God's promise. How did he remain "fully persuaded"? His heart relied upon the infinite
sufficiency and almighty power of the Promiser. That was what sustained, yes,
rejoiced, him while awaiting the fulfillment of God's promise. God did not disappoint him! This too is recorded for our learning. God has not changed. He
is still El Shaddai, the all-sufficient One.

"Now unto him that is able to do exceeding abundantly above all that we
ask or think, according to" what? According to His sovereign pleasure? According to His eternal decree? According to His secret will? "According to the
power that worketh in us." Say what we may, plead as plausibly as we please
of our uncertainty about God's willingness to show Himself strong on our behalf,
at the bottom it is our wicked unbelief, our doubting of His *power*, our secret
questioning of His ability to extricate us from such and such a predicament or
furnish a table for us in the wilderness. At that point the faith of Zechariah
failed—doubting the power of God to make good the word He had given through
the angel (Luke 1:18-20). Peter's questioning of Christ's power caused Him
to chide Peter with "O thou of little faith, wherefore didst thou doubt?" (Matt.
14:31). Because the apostles lacked confidence in Christ's omnipotence, none
of them expected Him to rise again on the third day. It was not His willingness but His power which they doubted. So it is with us.

As we approach the mercy seat, we should view God as the One "able to do
exceeding abundantly above all that we ask or think." "According to the power
that worketh in us" is the standard to which faith should ever appeal in prayer.
It is that wonderful power of which we already have personal experience. It is
a *mighty* power, for it brought us from death to life and called us out of darkness into His marvelous light. "For God, who [in the beginning] commanded
the light to shine out of darkness, hath shined in our hearts" (II Cor. 4:6).
It is an *invincible* power, for it subdued our inveterate enmity to God, overcame
our stubborn obstinacy, and made us willing to receive Christ as our Lord and
King, to take His yoke upon us and submit to His scepter.

It is a *holy* power, for it caused us to repudiate all our righteousnesses as
filthy rags and made us nothing in our own sight. It is a *gracious* power, for it
wrought within us not only when we had no merits of our own but when we had
no desire to be subjects of God. It is a *"glorious* power" (Col. 1:11), for by it all
our godly affections are sustained and all our acceptable works wrought.

It is an *infinite* power: "whereby he is able even to subdue *all* things unto
himself" (Phil. 3:21). Sinful corruptions cannot thwart that power, Satan and
his hosts cannot hinder it, death and the grave cannot defy it. That power can
make a clean thing out of an unclean, can cause the blind to see and the dumb
to sing. That power can restore the years that the locusts have eaten (Joel
2:25), and give "beauty for ashes, the oil of joy for mourning, the garment of
praise for the spirit of heaviness" (Isa. 61:3). However urgent our situation
may be, that power can relieve it; however great our need, that power can supply it; however potent our temptations, that power can deliver us; however sore
may be our trials, that power can support us in them; however distressing our
circumstances, that power can keep our hearts in perfect peace. It is an *eternal*
power. It is not exhausted by expenditure. It never wearies or diminishes; there-

fore, since it has begun a good work within us, it will most certainly complete the same. That power will yet make us perfect in every good work to do God's will, working in us that which is well pleasing in His sight.

Our Response to This Doxology

1. The language of this doxology ought to deeply *humble* us. Its lofty terms rebuke our groveling petitions and expectations. Look at it again—we cannot ponder it too frequently: "Unto him that is able to do exceeding abundantly above all that we ask or think, according to the power that worketh in us." Should not that make us thoroughly ashamed of our petty requests, our feeble anticipations, our low spiritual attainments? We need to realize that there is such a thing as a modesty in our asking which *dishonors* God, that we come far short of seeking from Him that which accords with His benevolence and bounty. We are coming to a King and should therefore "large petitions with us bring." "Is there any thing too hard for me?" (Jer. 32:27) is His own challenge. No matter how sore our strait or how staggering our difficulty, it will be as nothing to Him. Alas, we are like Joash who, when bidden by the prophet to strike the ground, struck it three times and "stayed," when he should have struck "five or six times" and thereby obtained a far greater victory (II Kings 13:18-19).

2. This doxology should greatly *encourage* us. Was not one of the patent purposes of the Spirit in recording this doxology to raise the expectations of God's people? Another purpose was to show them how faith should view God. It is most important that the saints should at all times contemplate God as the infinitely sufficient One, but it is peculiarly necessary that they do so as they are about to approach Him in prayer. Nothing is more calculated to enlarge our desires, warm our hearts, deepen our confidence, than to regard Him as here set forth. We ought not to be straitened either in our thoughts of Him or in our expectations from Him. "Open thy mouth wide, and I will fill it" (Ps. 81:10) is His own gracious invitation and assurance. Men may talk of receiving "sips" of His goodness and "bites" of His bounties, but that is something to be ashamed of rather than to proclaim with satisfaction. "Eat, O friends; drink, yea, drink abundantly, O beloved" (Song of Sol. 5:1) opens His heart concern for us. As the Puritan Thomas Manton well expressed it, "God's bounty is not only ever flowing, but overflowing." The fault is wholly ours if we have only "sips" from it.

3. This doxology should serve as a *challenge* to us. In its language God is saying to us in another way, "Prove Me now. Bring your hard problems to Me. Spread your deep needs before Me. Make known your largest spiritual desires to Me, and count on My sufficiency and bounty." As Carey counseled, "Ask great things of God; expect great things from God." Do not question His willingness, for that is reflecting on His goodness and doubting His benevolence. Do not allow Satan to deceive you any longer with a feigned humility, under the pretense of deterring you from spiritual arrogance and forwardness. Recall the case of those who brought to Christ the one sick of the palsy and, when they could not reach Him because of the press, broke through the roof and let down the bed on which the sufferer lay! Was the Lord displeased at their impudence? No indeed, He honored the faith of those who so counted upon His compassion

and grace. When the centurion besought Him on behalf of his sick servant, did Christ rebuke him for his presumption? No, He "marvelled at his faith." He delights to be trusted.

4. This doxology should *instruct* us. Having presented the petitions recorded in verses 16-19, the apostle closed with this adoring doxology: "Now unto him that is able. . . . , unto him be glory in the church by Christ Jesus throughout all ages, world without end. Amen." We often beg the Lord to teach us to pray. He has already furnished us with the necessary instructions, both in His own prayers and in those given us through His apostles. In them He has plainly revealed that we should be deeply concerned with *the glory* of God, that it should actuate and regulate us in all our supplications. In that prayer which He taught His disciples—and after which ours should always be patterned— He bade us conclude our addresses to the Father with "For thine is the kingdom, and the power, and the glory, for ever. Amen." Not only should those words be on our lips but the substance and sentiment of them should ever affect our hearts. We should make the glory of God our one supreme and constant aim, we should ask only for those things which will promote His honor, and we should make that our prevailing plea in making all our requests. "Help us, O God of our salvation, for the glory of thy name: and deliver us, and purge away our sins, for thy name's sake" (Ps. 79:9).

At this very point we may clearly perceive one of the great differences which exist between the spiritual believer and the carnal professor. The formalist and the hypocrite never seek God (except when, Pharisee-like, they would parade themselves before men) except under the pressure of their *own* needs, and not from any concern for God's honor. But the upright seek God because they delight in Him and desire communion with Him, and their love to Him makes them deeply concerned for His glory. When their God is dishonored, they grieve deeply: "Rivers of waters run down mine eyes, because they keep not thy law" (Ps. 119:136; cf. Ezek. 9:4). The regenerate prefer God's interests to their own and set *His* glory high above *their* comforts and concerns. In *that* they follow the example which Christ has left them: "Father, save me from this hour." That was the innocent inclination of His humanity. "But for this cause came I unto this hour. Father, glorify *thy* name" (John 12:27-28). He subordinated everything to that.

It is fitting then that we should conclude our prayers thus. As Matthew Henry said, "When we come to ask grace from God, we ought to give glory to God." To give glory to God is to ascribe all excellency to Him. "Unto him be glory": that was the adoring language of one whose heart was filled with love to God. It was an expression of fervent praise to Him because He is the all-sufficient and bounteous One. If God is spiritually viewed as the Fountain of all blessings, whose fullness is inexhaustible, whose resources are illimitable, whose benignity is infinite, then the soul cannot help but burst forth in the acclamation "Unto him be glory." It was also an avowal of expectation. The apostle was assured that the Father of our Lord Jesus Christ would grant the petitions which he had just presented, and he gave thanks for the same. This is the ground of the saint's confidence: that God has joined together His glory and our good. His honor is bound up in promoting the interests of His people, "that *we* should be to the praise of *his* glory" (Eph. 1:12). The possession which Christ purchased is "unto the praise of his glory" (Eph. 1:14). He is "glorified in his saints" (II Thess. 1:10).

Unto Him Be Glory

"Unto him be glory" was the homage of the apostle's own heart. Then it was as though he felt his own personal worship was altogether inadequate, and added, "in the church," as though he were saying, "Let all the redeemed unite with me in exalting Him." The Church is indeed the grand seat of His glory: "the branch of my planting, the work of my hands, that I may be glorified" (Isa. 60:21). He calls her "Israel my glory" (Isa. 46:13). None do, none can, truly honor and acknowledge Him except the Church. But the apostle knew that even the Church, ordained though she is as the subject and instrument of the divine glory, is yet not equal to the task, and so he added, "By Christ Jesus." As Spurgeon so beautifully put it, "Thou, Lord Jesus, Thou art He alone among men eloquent enough to express the glory of God. Grace is poured into Thy lips, and Thou canst declare our praises." But even then the apostle was not satisfied. He continued: "Throughout all ages, world without end," that a revenue of praise should be paid Him during all generations and that eternity itself should never cease to resound with the glory of God! And what more suitable response can we make to such sentiments than by adding our *"Amen"*!

Chapter 20

PRAYER FOR DISCERNING LOVE

PHILIPPIANS 1:8-10

THE PRAYERS OF HOLY MEN are usually the choicest expressions of their souls—the pourings forth of their deepest desires as directed by the Spirit in them. It must be so for where a man's treasure is, there will his heart be also. The more spiritual a man becomes, the more his soul is engaged with and enraptured by spiritual things, and the more experimental and practical holiness will be his supreme quest. "Out of the abundance of the heart the mouth speaketh" (Matt. 12:34). When a spiritually minded person has liberty in prayer he will necessarily seek both for himself and his fellow saints an increased measure of grace, that his and their eyes may perceive more clearly the inestimable value of divine things and have their hearts set upon them more constantly, in order that the fruits of righteousness may abound in their lives. Such were the utterances of the apostle on this occasion.

Many Types of Christians

Variety marks all the works of God. Men's intellectual endowments are as dissimilar as their countenances. There are many different types of Christians, though broadly speaking they may be grouped under two classes—the intelligent or well instructed, and the affectionate.

The Corinthians were "enriched by him, in all utterance, and in all knowledge" (I Cor. 1:5), yet their love was weak and low. This is implied by the contrast pointed between knowledge and love in 8:1-3, and is still more plainly intimated where the apostle tells them, "Yet shew I unto you a more excellent way" (12:31)—which he proceeded to do in the next chapter, where he set forth at length the nature, excellency, and preeminence of spiritual love. The fearful imprecation of 16:22—found nowhere else in the New Testament—also illustrates the weakness of the Corinthians' love.

In sharp contrast with the Corinthians, the Philippian saints were a more plain and less gifted order of Christians. They were warmly devoted to Christ and His people, but they had an inadequate understanding of His mind. Their affection exceeded their knowledge—as is the case with some simple but sincere and ardent Christians today. Generally—and markedly so in Christendom now—those with more light in their heads than love in their hearts have greatly outnumbered the others. Now Paul was far from despising or disparaging the case of the Philippian saints, but he longed for a better balance in their char-

200

acters. Therefore he prayed (not as most of *us* need to—that our love may increase in proportion to our light, but) that their intelligence might be commensurate with their affections; that their love might "abound yet more and more in knowledge and in all judgment"; that both knowledge and love might grow and develop together, so they might be well-proportioned Christians. By this means they would more fully conform unto God, who is both "light" (I John 1:5) and "love" (I John 4:8).

An Analysis of the Apostle's Prayer

Let us analyze this prayer. First, its *spring:* "How greatly I long after you all in the bowels of Jesus Christ" (v. 8). The apostle's fervent affection for these brethren prompted his supplication on their behalf. The measure of our love for others can largely be determined by the frequency and earnestness of our prayers for them. Second, its *petition,* namely, that their love might "abound yet more and more in knowledge and in all judgment" (v. 9). That was the "one thing" (Ps. 27:4) he "desired" on their behalf, the comprehensive blessing which he requested for them. What follows in verses 10 and 11 we do not regard as additional petitions, but rather as the effects which would result from the granting of his single petition. Thus, we view the contents of verses 10 and 11 as third, its *reasons:* "That ye may approve things that are excellent; that ye may be sincere and without offence till the day of Christ; being filled with the fruits of righteousness, which are by Jesus Christ, unto the glory and praise of God."

First, its spring. "For God is my record, how greatly I long after you all in the bowels of Jesus Christ" (v. 8). This was a solemn avowal to the Searcher of hearts of the reality and intensity of Paul's love for the Philippians. Whether or not *they* knew or realized it, *God* did. Having them in his heart, Paul longed for their spiritual welfare. He not only longed after them but did so "greatly"— and not only after a few special favorites among them but "after you all," and that with intense affection and goodwill, and "in the bowels [or 'compassions'] of Jesus Christ." The Hebrews regarded the "bowels" as the seat of affections and sympathy, as we regard the "heart." This expression, "the compassion of Jesus Christ," is susceptible of a twofold meaning. First, it refers to the personal love which the Redeemer Himself bears for the redeemed. Second, it has reference to that tender compassion for His saints which Christ had infused in the heart of His servant. Paul regarded the Philippians with something of the tenderness which the Lord Jesus had for them. This was the warmest and strongest expression which he could find to denote the ardor of his attachment.

If then Christ had infused such love in the heart of His servant for these saints, what must that love be in its fullness for them in the heart of Christ! If such be the stream, what must the Fountain be like! What a marvelous change had been produced in the apostle! Probably the Holy Spirit here moved him to emphasize this love in order to contrast the transformation which grace had produced in him as against what he was in former days. As Saul of Tarsus, how ferocious and cruel he had been to the followers of Christ! What havoc he had wrought among them by his threatenings and persecutions! What had changed the lion to the lamb? Who had made him so tender and considerate, so solicitous of the welfare of the Philippians? Who had given him such affection for them? The Lord Jesus. "Through the tender mercy of our God" (Luke 1:78) is literally "the bowels of the mercy of our God." And cannot each Christian reader, to some extent at least, join with the apostle in calling God as witness of the blessed change which His grace has wrought in him, so that from being self-centered and ice-cold to God's people, his heart is now compassionate and warm to them, yearning to promote their welfare!

Second, *its petition*. "And this I pray, that your love may abound yet more and more in knowledge and in all judgment" or "sense." Paul not only prayed for these saints, but he acquainted them with the particular things he requested for them, so that they might know what they should ask for and earnestly strive after. In like manner, his prayer is placed on permanent record in the Word that saints in all generations might be similarly instructed. If we would ascertain our special spiritual needs, if we would be better informed of the specific things we most need to ask for, then we should pay more than ordinary attention to these prayers of the apostle. We should fix them in our minds, meditating frequently on them, begging God to open to us their spiritual meaning, and to effectually impress our hearts with the same. There is nothing provincial or evanescent about these prayers, for they are suited to and designed for Christians of all ages, places, and cases. There is a wealth of heavenly treasure in them which no expositor can exhaust, and which the Holy Spirit will reveal to humble, earnest, seeking souls.

Those Philippian saints already loved God and His Christ, His cause, and His people, yet the apostle prayed that their love might "abound yet more and more," which illustrates what we pointed out in a previous chapter. The more we discern the grace of God at work in an individual Christian or church, the greater encouragement we have to make request that a still larger measure of it may be communicated to him or them. Goodwin pointed out that the Greek word here used for "abound" is a metaphor taken from the bubbling up and flowing of a spring of water, and showed the force and appropriateness of it. A spring flows naturally and spontaneously, and not by the mechanical efforts of men. Such is divine love in the soul: it operates freely and not by constraint, it works readily, and requires no urging from without. Where Christ is known to the soul, the heart cannot help being drawn out unto Him and delighting in Him. "But as touching brotherly love ye need not that I write unto you: for ye yourselves *are taught* of God to love one another" (I Thess. 4:9). No one can be made to love one another, but where there is love it will act freely and readily.

As you take from a fountain, still more comes. As a spring does not keep its water to itself, so love keeps nothing to itself, but it flows out for the use and benefit of others. Love is selfless: its very nature is to give, seeking to promote the glory of God and the good of men. As fountains have their rise in hills, so love is first in God's heart in heaven. "We love him, because he first loved us" (I John 4:19). To the phrase "that your love may yet abound," or spring up and flow forth, the apostle added "yet more and more." God can never have enough of our love, nor us of His grace. If we would receive an enlargement of love we must be more and more engaged with its Object.

"That your love may abound yet more and more *in knowledge.*" As the understanding needs to be enlightened and the conscience informed, so love requires *instructing.* Love is necessarily connected with knowledge for its inception, continuance, and development. A person must be known by us before we can love him. Christ must become a living reality before the heart is drawn out unto Him. There must be a personal and spiritual acquaintance with divine things before they can be delighted in. Where God is truly known, He is necessarily adored. And as has been pointed out in the last paragraph, if our love for Him is to increase, we must be more occupied and absorbed with His perfections. But love not only needs to be fed and nourished; it also needs to be taught, if it is to act intelligently. Spiritual love should not act by blind impulse, but be scripturally regulated. The Jews had "a zeal of God, but not according to knowledge" (Rom. 10:2). They sincerely believed they were serving God when they excluded Christians from their synagogues, and later killed them because they supposed those Christians were heretics (John 16:2), yet they erred grievously, and their case has been recorded as a solemn warning for us.

Love to Be Informed and Controlled by the Truth

It is painful to witness sincere and affectionate believers making mistakes and falling into wrong courses through lack of light, yet there are many such cases. A wrongly instructed and injudicious Christian causes trouble among his fellow Christians, and often increases the reproaches of the world. Paul here prayed for an intelligent affection in the saints, for a warmheartedness based upon and flowing from an enlarged perception of divine things, that they might have a clear apprehension of the just claims of God and of their brothers and sisters in Christ. The world says that love is blind, but the love of the Christian should be enlightened, well instructed, and directed in all its exercises, effects, and manifestations by the Scriptures. Unless love is regulated by an enlarged and exact knowledge of the Word, and by that good judgment which is the result of matured discernment and experience, it soon degenerates into fanaticism and unwise exertions. An affectionate regard for our brethren is to be far more than a mere sentiment, namely, "love in the truth" (II John 1), love informed and controlled by the truth.

Some Christians have a good understanding of the truth yet are considerably carnal in their walk (I Cor. 3:1-3). Others, though defective in knowledge and unsettled in the faith, are yet warmhearted, having much zeal toward God and His cause, and a considerable command over their passions. God's people should labor for *both.* It was love and zeal for Christ which prompted the apostles to say, "Lord, wilt thou that we command fire to come down from heaven, and consume them, even as Elias [Elijah] did?" when they saw how their Master was slighted. Yet it was misdirected love and zeal, as His "Ye know not what manner of spirit ye are of" (Luke 9:54-55) showed. Love must be *instructed* if it is to be placed on legitimate objects and restrained from nonpermissible ones, if it is to be rightly exercised on all occasions. And the needed instruction can be obtained only from God's Word. Only as love is regulated by light, and light is accompanied by and infused with love, are we well balanced.

"That your love may abound yet more and more in knowledge and in all *judgment.*" Something more than bare knowledge, even though it is a knowledge of the Word, is needed if love is to be duly regulated and exercised. That something is here termed "judgment," or in the margin, "sense." That word occurs in the singular number nowhere else in the New Testament, and only once (Heb. 5:14) in its plural form, where it is rendered "senses." In *Young's Analytical Concordance to the Bible* it is defined as "perfection, sense, intelligence." Not only do we need to be thoroughly familiar with the Scriptures. If we are to make proper use of such knowledge, then *good judgment* is required in the governing of our affections and the ordering of our affairs.

Our Love to Abound in Knowledge

Many are wise in the general principles and in the letter of the Word, but err grievously in the applying of those principles in detail. There is a vast variety of circumstances in our lives. These call for much prudence in dealing with them aright. If our hearts are to be properly governed and our ways suitably ordered, much instruction and considerable experience are required. Besides a knowledge of God's will, the spirit of discretion is needed. There are times when all lawful things are not expedient, and wisdom is indispensable to determine when those times and where those places are, as well as by which persons they may be used or performed. Indiscretion and folly remain in the best of us. The chief work of our judgment is to perceive what is proper for the time, the place, the company where we are, that we may order our behavior aright (Ps. 50:23); that we may know how to conduct ourselves in all relations civil and sacred, in work or in recreation; that we may conduct ourselves wisely as husbands, fathers, wives, or children; as employers or employees. Love needs to be directed by good judgment in all its exercises and expressions.

How different are the prayers of Scripture from those which we are accustomed to hear in religious gatherings! Who ever heard this petition offered in public: "This I pray, that your love may abound yet more and more in knowledge and in all judgment"! How many would understand its purport if they should hear it? True spirituality, vital godliness, personal piety, has almost become an unknown quantity in Christendom today. How very different is this bold and comprehensive request "may abound yet more and more" from the halting and halfhearted "if it can please Thee to favor us with a sip" of those who seem utterly afraid to ask for anything worthy of such a God as ours! How little can such souls be acquainted with "the God of all grace." Seriously ponder the petitions of Paul and observe that *he* was not straitened, and therefore he asked for no half measures or scanty portions. Above all, realize that these prayers are recorded for our instruction, for our encouragement, for our emulation.

The Substance of the Apostle's Prayer

As pointed out, the substance of this petition was that there might be a better balance in these saints, that their love and knowledge might keep pace with each other, that their affections should be intelligently exercised. Paul longed that their warmheartedness should be accompanied and directed by a well-instructed understanding, that they might have spiritual judgment which would cause them to weigh things and enable them to discriminate between the true and the false, that they might perceive what to love and what to hate, what to seek and what to shun. He desired that they should be able at all times to distinguish between duty and sin, and know what *was* their duty, no matter how dark the times or how difficult their circumstances. The apostle requested, first, that they be granted a better and fuller knowledge—that they be more thoroughly instructed from the Word. Second, he urged that their love be regulated by judgment, or spiritual instinct—and by enlightened perception of the fitness of things. Third, Paul was concerned that they might possess something more than a mere theoretical knowledge obtained by and through "sense." The soul has faculties which correspond to the five senses of the body. "Sense" here has the force of *faith*, for it is through faith we perceive, know, and understand spiritual things.

"Sense" also means *experience*—something distinct from and following faith. In Romans 5, after declaring that we are justified by faith and have peace with God through our Lord Jesus Christ, the apostle went on to show how faith is educated and added to through God's dealings with us: "Tribulation worketh patience; and patience, experience." By means of the trials which faith encounters and the disciplines of daily life, we are taught humble submission to God and, notwithstanding obstacles and failures, to persevere in the path of duty. As we do so, God graciously supports the soul and communicates His consolations, and faith is strengthened to meet the next trial. We obtain a personal experience of God's goodness and faithfulness, as well as of our frailty and sinfulness. We acquire a first hand acquaintance with the reality of the snares against which His Word warns us and of the veracity of His promises by which He cheers us. This experience breeds hope (Rom. 5:1-4), a steady confidence and growing expectation that God will not allow us to abandon our profession and make shipwreck of the faith, but will continue ministering to us, delivering us from our foes, and finally bringing us safely through to glory.

The Faithfulness of Our God

This experience is an acquired knowledge in spiritual matters, founded on sense. It is a personal realization of the mercy, power, longsuffering, and grace of God. The Christian starts out with bare faith in the veracity of God, in the certainty of His promises. He does not doubt that in due course God will make them good to him. But later, as God performs one promise after another, there is a sense of experience added to his faith, which deepens his assurance and enables him to face the future with still greater confidence in God. "By this I know that thou favourest me, because mine enemy doth not triumph over me" (Ps. 41:11). The young Christian, believing that his Father is a prayer-hearing God from the declarations of His Word, has no doubt about it. But in process of time he has occasion to say, "I love the LORD, because he hath heard my voice and my supplication" (Ps. 116:1), for he now has sensible proof, visible demonstration of the fact.

The things of God are first cognized and apprehended by faith, and then by experience—by personal contact and more intimate acquaintance with them.

By God's effectual working in them that believe (I Thess. 2:13), the saints find that what the Word affirms of them is true. This experimental knowledge of the Lord is spoken of as a "tasting" of Him. (I Peter 2:3)—which is something even more convincing and satisfying than sight. To taste His goodness, to feel His power, to experience His tender compassion, is to have real proof within ourselves. The human side of this is presented in Hebrews 5:14: "those who by reason of use have their senses exercised to discern both good and evil." As we discover what foods agree or disagree with us by eating and drinking, so we learn what things and persons are helpful or harmful to us by the exercise of our graces. As we become proficient scholars by our studies at school, so we become proficient believers by experimental knowledge—gained by exercising the faculties of our souls.

"Sense" also signifies deep and glorious impressions on the soul, over and above the light of faith or knowledge by ordinary experiences. And such impressions are truly more sense than knowledge, as all find that enjoy them. They are therefore said to pass knowledge (Eph. 3:19). Have you received fulfillment of this promise: "They shall be abundantly satisfied with the fatness of thy house; and thou shalt make them drink of the river of thy pleasures" (Ps. 36:8)?

Paul longed to see the affections of these Philippian saints intelligently directed in order that they might "approve things that are excellent"; that they might "be sincere"; that they should be "without offence till the day of Christ"; and that they should be "filled with the fruits of righteousness, which are by Jesus Christ, unto the glory and praise of God." Those were the reasons *why* he asked for them that particular blessing. How they serve to emphasize the great importance and value of love being enlightened! How much depends upon having our affections educated by spiritual knowledge and controlled by spiritual sensibility! How the walk of a well balanced Christian will honor his Lord! What blessed consequences follow when heavenly wisdom and mature experience guide the actions of a heart that is warm toward Christ and His redeemed! Then let us strive diligently after such.

"That ye may approve things that are excellent." Here again there is a fullness in the Greek terms which is difficult to translate adequately by any single equivalent in English, the margin giving us the alternative "that ye may try things that differ." However, in this instance the two renderings come to much the same thing. Following our usual custom, we will put the reader in possession of the main facts, so that he can check our exposition and draw his own conclusions. The Greek word here, rendered "try" in the margin, denotes that kind of trial to which metals are subjected when their nature and genuineness are being tested. Thus, when the apostle says, "That the trial of your faith, being much more precious than of gold that perisheth, though it be tried with fire, might be found unto praise and honour and glory at the appearing of Jesus Christ" (I Peter 1:7), the resemblance is that of the goldsmith submitting the ore to a process of proof in his crucible. All is not gold that glistens! The uninstructed eye is not able to distinguish the genuine from the counterfeit: the metal must be properly examined and tested to ascertain beyond doubt whether it is precious or worthless.

The Necessity of Proving Our Profession

Elsewhere the Apostle Paul frequently made use of this same metaphor. "To *prove* the sincerity of your love" (II Cor. 8:8) denotes to give opportunity to attest the genuineness of your love. "Examine yourselves, whether ye be in the faith; *prove* your own selves" (II Cor. 13:5). Take nothing for granted, but honestly and diligently examine your hearts and lives, and ascertain whether your profession is a valid one. "*Prove* all things; hold fast that which is good" (I Thess. 5:21). In the preceding verse he had said "despise not prophesyings," which, though they proceeded from gifted men, were not infallible, and therefore needed to be carefully pondered and weighed. In each passage (as also Gal. 6:4; I Tim. 3:10, etc.) the same Greek word (*dokimazo*) is used as the one rendered "try" and "approve" in our text. The reader needs to realize that before he is capable of attesting the genuineness of his love, verifying the validity of his profession, or proving the worth or worthlessness of the preaching he hears or reads—whether that teaching relates to doctrine or practice—his love must be warm and enlightened by knowledge and directed by good judgment, otherwise he is likely to be deceived by what is erroneous.

But the Greek word also signifies "an *approving* or judgment of what is good, a savoring, a relishing, closing with and cleaving to the goodness of it *as* good and best." A love which is directed by an enlightened mind and a holy heart not only has the capacity to detect counterfeits but sweetly realizes the excellence of divine things and delights in them. Thus in Romans 12:2, "And be not conformed to this world: but be ye transformed by the renewing of your mind, that ye may *prove* what is that good, and acceptable, and perfect, will of God," the Greek word for "prove" is the same as that rendered "approve" in our text. In the preceding verse, Christian duty as a whole is viewed in reference to God Himself; but in verse 2 it is contemplated in connection with that system of things seen and temporal, amid which we live our lives day by day. Both of the inoperatives are in the present tense, denoting a process. There is to be an ever widening gulf between the character and conduct of the world and that of the saint, and an ever growing conformity to Christ, not only outwardly but inwardly. The saint's thoughts and affections are to be more and more set upon things above—the "mind" here being the equivalent of the whole soul.

Regeneration, or the communication of spiritual life, is a divine act, once for all, in which we are wholly passive. But "renewing," as the tense denotes, is continuous. This too is a divine work, as Titus 3:5 and II Corinthians 4:16 inform us; yet it is also one in which *we* are called upon to be active, in which we are required to cooperate, as Romans 12:2 and Ephesians 4:23 clearly show. "Be ye transformed by the renewing of your mind" is the human responsibility correlative of "that your love may abound yet more and more in knowledge and in all judgment." "Be ye transformed by the renewing of your mind" is accompanied by our responding to or making use of the light which God has given us— which is the necessary condition of our obtaining further light from Him. That light has to a considerable extent already dispelled from our understandings and hearts the mists of self-love, and has revealed to us infinitely worthier objects and pursuits, and if those objects have the supreme place in our affections and those pursuits become the dominant quest of our energies, those mists will be still further cleared away and we shall perceive yet more clearly the excellence and desirability of divine and spiritual things, and we shall become more absorbed in and satisfied with them.

As "be ye transformed by the renewing of your mind" is the counterpart of "that your love may abound yet more and more in knowledge and in all judgment," so "that ye may *prove* what is that good, and acceptable, and perfect, will of God" is parallel with "that ye may *approve* things that are excellent." Just in proportion as we disdain and reject the principles, policies, and practices of the world (which may be summed up in self-love and self-pleasing) and earnestly endeavor to be governed by the precepts and promises of God, seeking to please and glorify Him, delighting ourselves in Him and being more assimilated to His holy image, do we acquire the capacity to *prove* for ourselves the excellence of His will. As by a spiritual touchstone, we perceive and realize the immeasurable superiority of the divine will to self-will, and joyfully surrender ourselves to it. In other words, as our spiritual love to God and to His people is regulated by the knowledge of His Word and is confirmed by our spiritual sensibilities, we discover for ourselves that Wisdom's "ways *are* ways of pleasantness, and all her paths are peace" (Prov. 3:1-7). We learn by experience what peace and joy there are in being conformed to God's will.

God's Commandments "Not Grievous"

There is a vast difference between a theoretical conviction that God's will is "good, and acceptable, and perfect" and actually proving it to be so for ourselves, yet that is what we *do,* just so far as we heed the injunction "Be not conformed to this world, but be ye transformed by the renewing of your minds." Just so far as we render a willing and more constant obedience to this exhortation, we not only prove for ourselves that God's commandments "are not grievous" (I John 5:3) but we discover that "in keeping of them there is great reward" (Ps. 19:11), that is, in this life. Then it is that we "sing in the ways of the LORD" (Ps. 138:5). Then it is that we obtain a personal acquaintance, an experimental realization of the goodness, the acceptableness, and perfection of the divine will. We determine for ourselves both by inward relish and outward practice the excellence of His will. We both prove and approve that it is designed for *our* "good," for our being acceptable, or pleasing, to God, for our being "perfect." We prove that God's will contains everything necessary to make us spiritually complete and to be all that we ought to be. How much we lose when we allow ourselves to follow the dictates of self-will and be in any degree conformed to this evil world—the ways of the ungodly!

How far, to what extent, have you and I proved for ourselves, by actual experience, by rendering obedience to God, the goodness, acceptableness, and perfection of His will? That is the question which each one of us should seriously put to himself. How far have we perceived the will of God in all the latitude and excellence of it, and how far have our heart and actions approved the same? A great variety and a vast number of sins are forbidden. Many duties are commanded. To what extent have we discerned the *spiritual part* of them, to what degree do we really relish them? Do we cherish His precepts? Do we hold fast to them amid a perverse generation, which universally despises and flouts them?

Are all of our ways ordered by them? Can we truly say with the Psalmist, "Therefore I love thy commandments above gold; yea, above fine gold. Therefore I esteem all thy precepts concerning all things to be right; and I hate every false way" (Ps. 119:127-128)? For it is in God's commandments and precepts that His will is made known. Only so are we really "approving things that are excellent" as Paul requested in this prayer.

The connection between the clause we have been considering and the one preceding it is therefore clear and simple. Where there is an increasing love which is directed by spiritual knowledge and holy sensibility, there is an enlarged capacity in the understanding to judge and discriminate: both to discern and detest what is injurious and to recognize and cherish what is beneficial. Or, to invert the order of thought: the apostle longed that these saints should "approve things that are excellent"—that they choose them, cleave to them, delight in them, and be regulated by them. But in order to do so, their love must both abound and be educated, so that they might have a true judgment and sense of the real worth of the different objects which competed for their hearts, and be suitably affected by the same. And that could only be obtained by trying these things. Love is not to be exercised indiscriminately. Objects must be esteemed only according to their nature and worth, and that worth is experimentally ascertained by an actual acquaintance with them. As the sweetness of honey is best known by the eating of it, so the preciousness of divine and spiritual things is realized in proportion as the soul is actually and actively engaged with them.

Note the twofold meaning of "try things that differ" and "approve things that are excellent." The attentive reader will observe how this twofoldness of thought meets us at every turn. First, the apostle had prayed that the love of these saints "might abound yet more and more in [1] knowledge and [2] judgment." Next we saw that the Greek word rendered "judgment" also carries in it the meaning of "sense," and as it is "*all* sense," therefore the meaning is "senses" as in Hebrews 5:14. Then we pointed out that the effect of that petition being answered would be their being enabled to "try" and "approve" things. That twofold significance of *dokimazo* corresponds to and is in perfect apposition with the two things prayed for in the previous verse—"knowledge" being needed in order to test and try, and spiritual "senses" to prove and approve. And now we find that the objects of those actions may be translated "things that differ" and/or "things that are excellent"—the former linking with the verb "try" and the latter fitting better with "approve." *Diaphero* is rendered "one star *differeth from* another star in glory" in I Corinthians 15:41 and "ye are of *more value* than many sparrows" in Matthew 10:31.

The Apostle's Burden

The apostle longed that their love might be so informed and their understanding so guided by spiritual judgment and sense that on all occasions they would be able to distinguish between truth and error in doctrine. He prayed that on controverted points (where there is often aptness to mislead and deceive by means of resemblance or likeness) when each side of the case had been presented, they might weigh both and be able to know which was the truth, and to approve of it. Paul was burdened that, in all matters of practice, in cases of conscience or where courses of duty were concerned, amid all the vicissitudes and perplexities of life, they might be able to rightly discern and judge, and that they might know this clearly so as not to be mistaken or deluded, but be able to act in comfort and confidence, assured that they were doing the will of God. Thus it was predicted of Christ: "The spirit of the LORD shall rest upon him: the spirit of wisdom and understanding." And this should "make him of quick understanding ["scent," margin] in the fear of the LORD" (Isa. 11:2-3), that is, quick-sighted and keen-sensed to discern the difference of things. And in his measure, each Christian is endued with "the Spirit of Christ" (Rom. 8:9).

Paul also desired that their judgment would be so equipped that their hearts would approve or taste the goodness and relish the excellence of things spiritual according to the several degrees of their worth as was best for them. It was important that they would value Christ and all His perfections high above all worldly things and persons, so as to count them but dung in comparison with the excellence of the knowledge of Christ, as the apostle himself did (Phil. 3:8).

The children of disobedience despise and reject Christ, seeing in Him no beauty that they should desire Him; but to those who believe, He is precious (I Peter 2:7), and should become increasingly so. So too the "saints"—rather than the famous, wealthy, and mighty—should be esteemed as "the excellent" of the earth, as they were by David (Ps. 16:3) and Christ. Likewise, the things of God's law are excellent, and should be prized by us above silver and gold. Relatively, we should distinguish and approve among things spiritual those that are *most* excellent, as "meat" surpasses "milk" (Heb. 5:12-14). Thus we should not only be able to distinguish between one Christian and another who is more spiritual and Christlike, and seek his fellowship, but between one company of professing Christians and another, cleaving to those who keep nearest to the Word and walk closest to God.

The Meaning of Sincerity

We turn now to examine the second reason why the apostle prayed that the love of the saints should abound yet more and more in knowledge and all judgment, or sense, namely, "that ye may be *sincere*." The Greek word used here occurs nowhere else in the New Testament except in II Peter 3:1, where it is rendered "I stir up your *pure* minds by way of remembrance." The noun form is found in I Corinthians 5:8, II Corinthians 1:12 and 2:17, where in each instance it is rendered "sincerity." Sincerity is the opposite of counterfeit and dishonesty, of pretense and imposture. To be sincere is to be genuine, to be in reality what we are in appearance—frank, true, unfeigned, conscientious. It is one of the characteristic marks which distinguish the regenerate from empty professors. The latter, though they may have much light in their heads, make no conscience of the integrity of their hearts and are little exercised about the uprightness of their daily walk. The Christian needs to be constantly on his guard against dissembling; he must judge unsparingly everything in and of himself which savors of unreality. Christ warned His disciples (and us), "When thou prayest, thou shalt not be *as* the hypocrites," whose religion is a pose to obtain the high regard of men.

The Greek word for sincerity in our text properly means "that which is judged in the sunshine, that which is clear and manifest." As a rule we attach little importance to the derivation of Hebrew and Greek words (many of which are most uncertain), preferring to ascertain their significance from the manner and connections in which they are used in Holy Writ. But in this instance the etymology of *eilikrines* is borne out by its force in II Corinthians 1:12, "For our rejoicing is this, the testimony of our conscience, that in simplicity and godly sincerity, not with fleshly wisdom, but by the grace of God, we have had our conversation in the world." "Godly sincerity" is really "the sincerity of God." The "sincerity of God" means the sincerity of which He is not only the Giver and Author but also the Witness, which may be brought to Him and held up before Him for His scrutiny. The idea expressed is that of John 3:21: "He that doeth truth cometh to the light, that his deeds may be made manifest, that they are wrought in God."

Our English word *sincere* is derived from the Latin *sine cera*, which means "without wax," and the origin of that Latin expression approximates very closely the etymology of the Greek word. The ancient Romans had a very delicate and valuable porcelain, exceedingly fragile, and only with much trouble could it be fired without being cracked. Dishonest dealers were in the habit of filling in the cracks that appeared with a special white wax, but when their ware was held up to the light the wax was evident, being darker in color than the porcelain. Thus it came about that honest dealers marked their ware *sine cera*, "without wax," having sun-tested it. Hence this grace of spiritual sincerity is the opposite of not only false pretense but unholy mixture. As the apostle said of himself and his companion ministers, "We are not as many, which corrupt the word of God: but as of sincerity, but as of God, in the sight of God speak we in Christ" (II Cor. 2:17), where the words "which corrupt" literally mean "which huckster" (which deceitfully mingle false and worthless articles among the genuine).

Sincerity is opposed to mixture: of truth and error, of godliness and worldliness, of loveliness and sin. A sincere person has not assumed Christianity as a mask, but his motives are disinterested and pure, his conduct is free from double-dealing and cunning, his words express the real sentiments of his heart. He is one who can bear to have the light turned upon him, the springs of his actions scrutinized by God Himself. He is of one piece through and through, and not a hypocrite who vainly attempts to serve two masters and make the best of both worlds. He is not afraid to be tested by the Word, for he is without guile or sham and is straightforward and honest in all his dealings. As we have seen, in II Corinthians 1:12, "sincerity" is joined with "simplicity," which is expressed by "if . . . thine eye be *single*" (Matt. 6:22), where the same word is used. The one with a "single" eye refuses to mix fleshly craftiness with spirituality: he aims *solely* at pleasing and glorifying God. Hence, a sincere heart is a true heart (Heb. 10:22), a heart genuinely holy, true to God, faithful in all things. A sincere heart is a pure heart (II Tim. 2:22).

The Origin of Sincerity

Now the springs from which sincerity flows are the three things mentioned by Paul in his petition. First, it arises from love to God—which consists not only of the understanding and the affections adoring His perfections but also of the will's esteeming *His will* as it is made known in His commandments. Therefore the apostle prayed that their love might abound yet more and more. Second, sincerity proceeds from knowledge, for the more the understanding is divinely enlightened and the heart awed by an apprehension of God's ineffable majesty, the more careful we are to approach Him with a true heart and the more fearful we are of acting hypocritically before Him. It is spiritual ignorance of the true and living God which causes the unregenerate to suppose they can impose upon Him with mere external performances and bodily postures, while their hearts are alienated from Him; hence the apostle prayed that love might abound "in knowledge." Third, sincerity issues from that sense of taste which the believer has of the blessedness of walking with God and communing with Him, and from proving for himself the excellence and sweetness of His Word, so that he declares, "O how love I thy law." Thus the apostle prayed that their love might abound in knowledge and in "all judgment."

As II Corinthians 1:12 intimates, sincerity has special reference to the eyes of the heart being fixed upon God in all that we do. David referred to such sincerity or soundness of spirit when he said, "Judge me, O LORD; for I have walked in mine *integrity*" (Ps. 26:1). The Lord referred to the same when He said to Solomon, "If thou wilt walk before me, as David thy father walked, in integrity of heart, and in uprightness, to do according to all that I have commanded thee, and wilt keep my statutes and my judgments: then I will establish the throne of thy kingdom" (I Kings 9:4-5). David had declared, "I have inclined my heart to perform thy statutes alway, even unto the end" (Ps. 119:112). In just such an inclining of the heart, constant to the divine precepts, sincerity lies. Job claimed sincerity of heart (Job 27:5-6). That patriarch was not referring, as has been so commonly misunderstood, to his acceptance *with* God on the ground of his works but to the purity of his motives and the sincerity of his heart *before* God. He knew he was no hypocrite, and could appeal to the Searcher of hearts in proof.

Such sincerity as has been described above constitutes one of the radical differences between the truly regenerate and the pretender, for, as John Newton well pointed out in his piece on simplicity and sincerity, "It is an essential part of the Christian character." The religionist may be very diligent and regular in performing his devotions and very careful in making clean "the outside of the cup and of the platter," but he takes no stock of what passes *within* himself. A slave may do just as much for his master as the child of that master does for his dear father; in fact, because of his superior strength and skill, the former may do much more than the latter; yet there is a vast difference as to the *affection* with which and the *end* for which those two work—but they are inward and invisible! So is the service rendered by an unregenerate employee and another possessing godly sincerity: the latter will heed that injunction "Servants, be obedient to them that are your masters according to the flesh, with fear and trembling, in singleness of your heart, as unto Christ [serving *Him* in it]; not with eyeservice, as men-pleasers; but as the servants of Christ, doing the will of God from the heart" (Eph. 6:5-6)—as appointed by Him and performed conscientiously unto Him.

Things Wherein Vital Godliness Consists

Sincerity is found principally in the will: in respect to sin, in refusing evil: in respect to holiness, in choosing the good. Where the will is savingly sanctified, it gives God the preeminence, making ease, credit, pleasures, profits, honors, relations, aspirations, all stoop to Him. It is much, very much, when we can solemnly claim this grace before God Himself. That is what Hezekiah did when (in those little-understood words of his) he said, "I beseech thee, O LORD, remember now how I have walked before thee in truth [reality, knowing Thine eye was ever upon me] and with a perfect [upright, or sincere] heart" (II Kings 20:3). When we are not afraid to come to the light and have our innermost desires and designs examined by the holy One, we may know that we have responded to His just call and claim. Peter, despite his terrible fall, after his sincere repentance could unhesitatingly say to the Searcher of hearts, "Lord, thou knowest all things; thou knowest that I love thee" (John 21:17). That was not a presumptuous boast but a plain statement of fact.

Sincerity eyes the *omniscience* of God and, knowing that He cannot be imposed upon, acts accordingly. It is exercised and manifested in various ways. The sincere soul shuns *sinful thoughts* and imaginations, which, though hidden from the sight of our fellows, are "naked and opened unto the eyes of him with whom we have to do" (Heb. 4:13). Therefore a sincere or upright soul prays and strives against them, mourns over and confesses the same. If the reader is a stranger to such experiences, then his religion is worthless and his profession empty. The sincere soul will not allow himself *secret sins*. Although the thickest curtains of night and darkness may be drawn about him, he dare not, for he knows that "the eyes of the LORD are in every place, beholding the evil and the good" (Prov. 15:3). And when his lusts gain a temporary mastery, far from excusing himself, he abhors himself, and with a broken heart acknowledges his faults before God. The sincere soul will guard against performing holy duties *coldly* and mechanically, afraid to mock the omniscient One with empty words and with the feigned reverence of outward postures.

It is in just such things as we have mentioned above that vital godliness chiefly consists: in the things of the *heart*. Alas that the great majority of God's own people receive no instruction on such matters today, from either the pulpit or the religious magazines. Alas that there is now so little to search out and expose an empty profession. Instead, nominal Christians are bolstered up with the idea that so long as they are orthodox in their beliefs, attend to their church duties, and lead respectable lives, all is well with them, no matter what may be the state of their hearts in the sight of God. A sincere soul is not occupied with how much time he spends in prayer, but *how real* and genuine his prayer is. He is concerned about the *spirituality* of his worship. Thus Paul said, "God is my witness, whom I serve with my spirit" (Rom. 1:9)—not in mere external rites. To the hypocrites Christ said, "This people draweth nigh unto me with their mouth, and honoureth me with their lips; *but their heart* is far from me";

and therefore He added, "In vain they do worship *me*" (Matt. 15:8-9). For He looks on the heart. Sincerity is conscientious about the *inward* part of worship and service. Sincerity is the salt which alone savors any sacrifices: where that is lacking, they are an offense to God, because of our play-acting.

To Walk "Without Offence"

We must pass on now to the third reason by which the apostle supported his request: "That ye may be sincere, and *without offence* till the day of Christ." The Greek word here rendered "offence" means to walk without stumbling. Thus, as "sincerity" has reference to the integrity of the heart, "offence" looks principally to the external conduct. Goodwin defines the term as signifying "the errings, mistreadings, stumblings, and bruisings of the feet in walking." How may we walk without offense? First, to walk without offense is to carefully avoid those ways and works before believers that might induce them to sin, or such which we know would prove an occasion of stumbling to others, or that would strengthen and confirm the wicked in their corruption. The same word is used in this manner in I Corinthians 10:32, "Give none offense, neither to the Jews, nor to the Gentiles, nor to the church of God." That which occasioned scandal must be sedulously avoided. We must never by our example invite others to follow us in evil.

Second, to walk without offense is to abstain from every action which would be contrary to the light which the Christian has received from God and the principles which he professes before others. A case of failure in this particular respect is found in Peter's withdrawing and separating himself from the Gentile saints, "fearing them which were of the circumcision" (Gal. 2:12). Such conduct was reprehensible, and Paul "withstood him to the face," for "they walked not *uprightly*" (v. 14). Literally, the Greek means "They walked not with a right foot": their walk did not square with the rule God had given, and therefore was "not uprightly according to the truth of the gospel." Peter had been the first to receive a divine revelation, by means of a vision from heaven (Acts 10), that he must not regard the Gentile saints as unclean, and refuse to eat with them. But the fear of man brought a snare and caused him to walk contrary to the light God had vouchsafed him. Thereby he stumbled the Gentile believers—the very reverse of being without offense. Peter's failure here is recorded as a case for us to solemnly take to heart.

Third, to walk without offense goes even further than the maintaining of a blameless conversation or conduct before men, including as it does a blameless conscience before God. This is clear from Acts 24:16 where the apostle again used the same term: "Herein do I exercise myself, to have a conscience void of offense toward God, and men." He resolved that there should be nothing in his behavior which could occasion accusation of conscience before God. Paul's conscience had received more light than any man's then living in the world, and therefore he had the hardest task to walk up to that light, and needed to give more thought and diligence in managing every action and the circumstances of it. He endeavored to so conduct himself that there might not be a single dark spot on his conscience, that there might be no act of spirit converse to that light which had shined in his soul, nothing that would cast any shadow upon it. That he succeeded therein is clear from II Corinthians 1:12, and that he prayed for the same experience in the saints is evident from our text. Therefore we should be satisfied with nothing short of that.

To live without offense does not mean to be sinless—for that would contradict James 3:2 and I John 1:8; but it means to refrain from everything which causes others to sin, to do no action contrary to the light we have received from God, and to avoid everything which would issue in a guilty conscience before Him. That is indeed a high standard of conduct, yet we must aim at nothing short of it. It is the highest realization in this life, approximating to perfection outwardly. That it is, by the grace of God, attainable, appears from the case of the parents of John the Baptist: "They were both righteous before God, walking in all the commandments and ordinances of the Lord *blameless*"—though not sinless (Luke 1:6). The Apostle Paul declared, "I have lived in all good conscience before God until this day" (Acts 23:1). As Goodwin says, "If a holy man is often kept from such sins a week, a month, a year, then it is also possible, in this state of frailty, to be kept all his lifetime."

Chapter 21

PRAYER FOR FRUITS OF RIGHTEOUSNESS

PHILIPPIANS 1:11

"THAT YE MAY BE SINCERE and without offence till the day of Christ, being filled with the fruits of righteousness." By the "day of Christ" we understand the time when He shall be revealed before an assembled universe as King of kings and Lord of lords, when He shall judge the world in righteousness (Acts 17:31), "taking vengeance on them that know not God, and that obey not the gospel," and being "glorified in his saints" (II Thess. 1:7-10). For the redeemed it will be a day of examination and adjudication (Rom. 14:12; II Cor. 5:10), not for the purpose of ascertaining their justification, but to attest their sanctification, to exhibit what grace had wrought in them, that the radical difference between the regenerate and the unregenerate, the blessed and the cursed, may be fully displayed, that Christ might be owned and magnified as the Author of all their godliness, and that they may be rewarded for their good works. It will then appear that the outstanding characteristic which distinguishes the children of God from the children of disobedience is that of personal holiness, holiness both of character and conduct, and since holiness has both a negative and positive side to it, the apostle has here designedly linked together "without offence" and "being filled with the fruits of righteousness."

This phrase "till the day of Christ" coming in between "without offence" and "being filled with the fruits of righteousness" belongs to each of them, both in grammatical sense and doctrinal purport. From its insertion there, we may gather at least three things. First, it is required that this negative and positive holiness be maintained without interruption until that day: or, in other words it enforces the necessity of the saints' perseverance to the end of their course. Second, it intimates the special relation which holiness has to that "day" when "every man's work shall be made manifest" (I Cor. 3:13) and the Lord "both will bring to light the hidden things of darkness, and will make manifest the counsels of the hearts" (I Cor. 4:5). Third, it sets before us a powerful incentive to live hourly with the judgment seat of Christ before us, that "we may have confidence, and not be ashamed before him at his coming" (I John 2:28). Christ warned His disciples against carnality, lest "that day come upon you unawares" (Luke 21:34), and His apostle exhorted believers in view of that day to "cast off the works of darkness, and . . . put on the armour of light" (Rom. 13:12).

216

Practical Righteousness

"Being filled with the fruits of righteousness." Of *what* righteousness? No doubt quite a number of our readers would answer, "The imputed righteousness of Christ." Yet they would be mistaken. It is important to recognize the three-fold distinction the New Testament makes. There is a righteousness God communicates to His people in regeneration, there is a righteousness reckoned to their account at justification, and there is a righteousness wrought out by them in their sanctification. Those who confound those three things confuse themselves and imbibe error. "The effectual fervent prayer of a *righteous* man availeth much" (James 5:16) signifies more than one to whom the obedience of Christ has been imputed, namely, one whose *heart* is right and whose *ways* are pleasing to God. One who has been justified may be in a backslidden state; while that is the case, his prayers will avail nothing (Isa. 59:2; James 4:3)! If we would ask and receive of God, then we must "keep his commandments" (I John 3:22). Righteousness is right doing, walking according to the divine rule, namely, the law of the Lord; and keeping His commandments is termed practical righteousness—righteousness wrought out in our practice. But since by nature "there is none righteous, no, not one" (Rom. 3:10), a miracle of grace must first take place within us.

As the Lord Jesus declared, "Make the tree good, and his fruit good" (Matt. 12:33), for grapes are not borne by thorns nor figs by thistles. The heart must first be made right, before our conduct will become so. Only a righteous man will produce the fruits of righteousness: he must have a righteous root within from whence they come. At regeneration a principle of righteousness is imparted to the soul. In that miracle of grace the heart is made right with God. At the new birth a nature is received "which after God is created in righteousness and true holiness" (Eph. 4:24). When the saints are there exhorted to "put on [as a uniform] the new man," they are enjoined to live and walk *as* new creatures in Christ. That principle of righteousness received from God at regeneration, that new and holy nature, is expressly said to be "his workmanship, created in Christ Jesus *unto* good works" (Eph. 2:10). That is the end for which He regenerates us, that our lives may glorify Him. The tree is made good that it may bear good fruit. "Created in Christ Jesus" means that at the new birth we are made vitally one with Him, and as faith in Christ (a cleaving to Him) is the first act of the spiritual babe, His righteousness is then imputed to him, so that he is legally as well as experimentally righteous before God.

"If ye know that he is righteous, ye know that every one that doeth righteousness is born of him" (I John 2:29). That tells us one of the ways by which we may recognize the regenerate, and distinguish them from unregenerate professors, namely, by their conduct, for trees are known by their fruit. In sharp contrast with "the children of disobedience," the regenerate children of God walk in obedience to Him, treading "the paths of righteousness for his name's sake" (Ps. 23:3), heeding His precepts and keeping His statutes. Like begets like: God is righteous and He makes His children so. Like father like children: if the reader will carefully ponder John 8:38-44, he will see how that truth is argued and proved—the Son being like the Father, the wicked bearing the features and performing the will of their father, the devil. The regenerate, then, are "trees of righteousness, the planting of the LORD, that he might be glorified" (Isa. 61:3); and He is glorified by their bearing the fruits of righteousness. Only the *doer* of righteousness is really born of God; therefore one whose character and conduct are unrighteous cannot be a righteous person, and should not be regarded so by the saints.

"Filled with the Fruits of Righteousness"

Now the "fruits of righteousness" brought forth by a righteous person are those acts which are agreeable to the law of God and which have the Word of God for their rule. Righteousness is right doing, and only that can be right which accords with the revealed will of God. Unless He has appointed a certain line of conduct for us to engage in, our actions would either be men-pleasing or self-seeking. A succinct summary of God's will is made known to us in the Ten Commandments, the moral law being the rule for us to walk by. The gospel precepts or exhortations found in the Epistles are but so many explications of those commandments, applied to the varied relations and details of our lives. As "sin is the transgression of the law" so righteousness is conformity to it (I John 3:4-7). The fruits of righteousness, therefore, are those works which the Christian performs according to that which the Word of God warrants and requires: in other words, they are acts of obedience to the Lord. "Neither yield ye your members as instruments of unrighteousness unto sin: but yield yourselves unto God, as those that are alive from the dead, and your members as instruments of righteousness unto God" (Rom. 6:13).

"Being *filled* with the fruits of righteousness": this was the God-honoring standard of excellence which the apostle longed that the saints should attain to. Here again we are struck with the vast difference between *his* large-heartedness and the parsimony of those whose supplications are so cramped in spirit and limited in scope. It is false humility which restricts our requests within narrow bounds. It is nothing but unbelief which limits the bounty of God to the bestowing of trifling favors. Nor is the plea of our unworthiness any valid reason to justify the poverty of our asking. No saint has ever presumed to approach God and seek blessings from Him on the basis of his own worthiness. The most spiritual and pious Christian who ever lived was heavily in debt to God, and therefore could only supplicate for mercy on the ground of His infinite grace. Paul, then, was not content to see these Philippians bearing *some* fruit, but prayed that they might be *"filled* with the fruits of righteousness." He did not base that request on anything which they had to their credit, but he eyed the munificence of God and asked accordingly. Let none of us ever be satisfied with a small measure of grace.

The Believer to Bear "Much Fruit"

Bringing forth the fruits of righteousness abundantly should be the deep and daily concern of every child of God, for His honor is never more promoted than when we are so engaged. Said the Lord Jesus, "Herein is my Father glorified, that ye bear much fruit; *so* shall ye be my disciples" (John 15:8). In this manner the truly regenerate can make evident the real and radical difference between themselves and hypocrites. The Father is not glorified by our lip service, but by the tenor and texture of our daily lives, by having all our steps and actions ordered by His Word. "Let your light so shine before men, that they may see your good works, and glorify your Father which is in heaven" (Matt. 5:16). Those "good works" are the same as these "fruits of righteousness," and we should be wholly taken up with performing them. We believe that in His "*so* shine" Christ gave warning of a danger: we need to beware of aiming at our *own* glory in such fruit-bearing. God has not given us His spirit for the purpose of serving and magnifying ourselves. He who aims to gain a reputation for eminent piety before his fellows, has yielded to the spirit of Pharisaism. Divine grace is not bestowed on the Christian to advance his honor but to glorify its Giver.

"Being filled with the fruits of righteousness" has a threefold force. First, the Christian's whole life should bear these fruits. As the heart of man is the bulk and body of this tree, so every power of the soul, each member of the body, is a branch. Before conversion were not all our inward faculties and external organs used in the service of unrighteousness? If not designedly so, yet actually, for they were not employed in serving God. What were our affections set upon? What chiefly engaged our minds? How were our eyes and ears, lips and hands, occupied? As we formerly yielded our members to iniquity, now we are to yield our members as servants to righteousness—*all* of them—so that we may be filled with such fruits. The godly man is likened to a flourishing tree in Psalm 1, and one of the fruits there mentioned is the budding of holy thoughts: "In God's law doth he meditate day and night." He stores his mind with its precepts and promises, he studies how best he can please God.

Second, a Christian is filled with fruit when good works of all sorts are produced in his life. "Being fruitful in every good work, and increasing in the knowledge of God" (Col. 1:10). If the believer is to be "filled with the fruits of righteousness," every grace must be active. "Giving all diligence, add to your faith virtue; and to virtue knowledge; and to knowledge temperance; and to temperance patience; and to patience godliness; and to godliness brotherly kindness; and to brotherly kindness love" (II Peter 1:5-7). The Christian differs from all other trees, for though a natural tree may be heavily laden, it bears only one kind of fruit. But "the fruit of the Spirit is in *all* goodness and righteousness and truth" (Eph. 5:9). Said the apostle, "Therefore as ye abound in every thing, in faith, and utterance, and knowledge, and in all diligence, and in your love to us, see that ye abound in *this* grace also" (II Cor: 8:7), i.e., contributing to the needs of the poor of the flock. He wanted them to be lacking in nothing. If we are to be filled with fruits, then we must have respect to *all* the divine commandments (Ps. 119:6), being remiss in no duty and failing in no practice of godliness, withholding nothing that is due the Lord.

Third, to be filled with the fruits of righteousness is to be filled with them at all times. All our time is to be filled with some good work or other: our vocation, recreation, holy duties. A man brings forth fruit in recreation as well as in holy duties, if his purpose is to have greater vigor, health, and enthusiasm in order to perform holy duties. But if a man wisely and conscientiously proportions his time, according to his conditions, and with holy purpose, he will be filled with the fruits of righteousness.

All Is of God

"Being filled with the fruits of righteousness which are by [or 'through'] Jesus Christ." How jealous was the apostle for the glory of his Master, giving honor to whom honor was due! Though these fruits are borne by the saints (and without them they would not be saints), yet they do not originate from them, and therefore they have no ground for boasting. "From me is thy fruit found" (Hosea 14:8). He is the vitalizing Vine of which we are the branches. Yet our verse is far from teaching that Christians are entirely passive in their fruit-bearing, or that they may excuse comparative fruitlessness by attributing the same to the sovereignty of the Lord—rationalizing that it was not His good pleasure that they should be more productive. Such an idea is a wicked perversion of a blessed truth. Christ Himself declared, "Herein is my Father glorified, that ye bear *much* fruit" (John 15:8). If we are not consistently bearing fruit, the blame rests wholly upon ourselves, and it is a horrible and satanic slander to attribute it to anything in God. The teaching of the Puritans was very different from such Antinomianism.

These fruits "are by Jesus Christ." They are created in Christ Jesus (Eph. 2:10). They issue from our being made vitally one with Him at regeneration. These fruits arise from the Spirit of Jesus Christ dwelling in the heart. Christ is the root; the new nature is the branch springing forth from Him; the Holy Spirit is the energizer and fructifier. Fruits of righteousness result from a man's laying hold of the righteousness of the Lord Jesus Christ for his righteousness. These fruits develop by motives drawn from Christ. When the love of Christ constrains us to obedience, when His grace teaches us to deny all ungodliness and worldly lusts, and to live soberly, righteously, and godly in this present world, when we realize He redeemed us to be a peculiar people zealous of good works, our resultant holy actions are the fruits of righteousness.

The fruits of righteousness flow from our growth in Christ. The apostle speaks of our growing up into Christ in all things (Eph. 4:15). As a man grows up in Christ, in nearer union and communion with Him, he grows more holy. The example of Christ moves me to bear the fruits of righteousness. "He that saith he abideth in him ought himself also so to walk, even as he walked" (I John 2:6). He is to be our Model and Pattern in all things. We are to be conformed to His holy image, and just so far as we follow His steps (I Peter 2:21) do we bear the fruits of righteousness which are by Him. Our actions are fruits of righteousness when we look for all the acceptance of our fruits in Jesus Christ, or when we expect that they shall all be accepted of God in and through Jesus Christ, and not as they come from us. Thus our services are "sacrifices acceptable to God by Jesus Christ" (I Peter 2:5). Our best performances are faulty, and are only pleasing to God as they are presented in the name of Christ and perfumed with His merits.

Fruits of righteousness are by Jesus Christ as we wear His yoke. The key passage on fruit-bearing is John 15, and there, as all through Scripture, is a perfect blending of the divine and human sides. If on the one hand we learn that Christ is the true Vine and His Father the Husbandman, who purges every branch that it may bring forth more fruit, on the other hand Christ there exhorts us, "abide in me, and I in you" (which enforces our responsibility), and

eral testimony of antiquity favors the view that Epaphras sent by Paul from Ephesus was the one who carried the gospel to that city and organized its church. But the point is not one of any practical importance.

Though Paul was not the planter of this church, he was far from being indifferent to its welfare, nor did he make any difference between it and those he had personally founded. Those who had been converted under others were as dear to him as his own converts. Oh, for more of his largeheartedness. His deep solicitude for the Colossians is evidenced by the trouble he took in writing this epistle to them. A careful reading of its contents makes it evident that it was penned in view of certain errors which extensively prevailed among the churches in that part of Asia Minor. Some knowledge—a general understanding at least— of those errors is necessary in order to correctly interpret some of the details of this epistle. Those errors consisted of a mixture of Grecian philosophy (2:4-8) and Jewish ceremonialism (2:16)—a type of Gnosticism which was really a Grecianized form of Oriental mysticism. The chief design of the apostle in this epistle was to assert the superior claims of Christianity over all philosophies, and its independence of the peculiar rites and customs of Judaism.

Thomas Scott's Summary of This Prayer

The best summary we have met with of this prayer is that furnished by Thomas Scott: "He especially requested that they might be 'filled' or 'completely endowed with' the knowledge of the will of God: both in respect of His method of saving sinners and their duties to Him and to all men as His redeemed servants; that they might understand the import and spiritual extent of His commandments, and how to obey them in the several relationships, situations and offices which they sustained in the church and in the community, and for the improvement of their different talents. That they might know how to apply general rules to their own particular cases, and so do the work of Christ assigned to each of them in the best manner, from the purest motives and with the happiest effect. Thus they would proceed 'in all wisdom and spiritual understanding,' with sagacity and prudent discernment of seasons and opportunities, distinguishing between real excellency and all deceitful appearances; wisely attending to their duties in the most inoffensive and engaging manner without affording their enemies any advantage, or losing opportunities of usefulness out of timidity, or failing of success through want of caution and discretion.

"He was desirous of this especially, that they might habitually behave in a manner worthy of that glorious and holy Lord, whose servants and worshippers they were: not dishonoring Him or His cause by any inconsistency or impropriety of conduct, but acting as become persons so highly favored and Divinely instructed: and that their conduct might be in all respects well-pleasing to Him, while fruitfulness in every kind of good work was connected with a still further increase in the knowledge of God, and of the glory and harmony of His perfections, and a happy experience of His consolations. The apostle and his helpers prayed also that the Colossians might be most abundantly strengthened in all the graces of the new nature with an energy suited to their utmost need, according to the glorious power of God by which He converted, upheld and comforted believers; that so they might be enabled to bear all their tribulations and persecutions with patient submission, persevering constancy, meekness of long-suffering, and joy in the Lord. While, amidst all trials, they gave thanks to the Father of our Lord Jesus, whose special grace had made them meet to partake of the inheritance provided for the saints in the world of perfect light, knowledge, holiness and happiness: at a distance from all ignorance, error, sin, temptation and sorrow."

An Analysis of the Apostle's Prayer

Before considering it in detail, let us first give a brief analysis of this prayer. (1) Its *address:* The majority of writers appear to regard this prayer as being one without an address, but this we consider a mistake. It is true that none is found at the beginning of verse 9, but that was not necessary since in verse 3 the apostle had said, "We give thanks to God and the Father of our Lord Jesus Christ, praying always for you." (2) Its *supplicators:* In contrast with the "I" of Ephesians 1:15 and Philippians 1:9-10, this proceeded from a "we"—Paul himself, Timothy (v. 1), Epaphras (v. 7) who was with him (Philemon 23), and possibly others. (3) Its *occasion,* or spring: "For this cause." Probably the saints at Colossae had sent their minister Epaphras to learn the apostle's mind on certain matters, a summary of which is intimated in this prayer. Moreover, the knowledge of their "love in the Spirit" for them (v. 8) had drawn out their affections, which were now expressed in fervent supplication for them. (4) Its *petitions:* Request was made that they might be intelligent Christians— pious, strong, and thankful ones.

The Breadth of Paul's Request for the Saints

Once more we see the breadth or comprehensiveness of the requests which Paul was wont to make for the saints. The "large petitions" which he spread before God were a marked feature of all his approaches to the throne of grace on behalf of God's people, and it is one which we need to take to heart and emulate. For the saints at Rome he had prayed that God would fill them "with *all* joy and peace in believing," that they might *"abound* in hope" (15:13). For the Ephesians that they might be "filled with all the fulness of God" (3:19). For the Philippians that "their love might abound more and more" and that they might "be filled with the fruits of righteousness" (1:9, 11). So Paul prayed here: that they might not merely have a knowledge of God's will in wisdom but "be *filled* with the knowledge of his will in *all wisdom.*" This was not a bare and general request that their conduct should adorn the gospel, but rather that they "might walk worthy of the Lord unto *all* pleasing, being fruitful in every *good* work." How different is this largeheartedness of the apostle from that cramped spirit which is evident in much of our praying!

The Order of These Petitions

Once more we would press upon the reader the great importance of paying heed to the order of these petitions if he would rightly apprehend and duly appreciate them. Usually this is best accomplished by considering them in their inverse *order.* We are in no fit condition to be "giving thanks unto the Father" for "the inheritance of the saints in light." In fact, we lack an essential part of the evidence that *we* have been "made meet" to be partakers of it if we are not exercising "all patience and longsuffering with joyfulness" despite the difficulties and trials of the way. Nor will such graces as those be active unless we first are "strengthened with all might, according to his glorious power." But that, in turn, is dependent upon our "increasing in the knowledge of God." Yet that will not be our happy experience except we "walk worthy of the Lord unto all pleasing, being fruitful in every good work." And how can we possibly do that unless we are first filled with the knowledge of His will in all wisdom and spiritual understanding?

"For this cause [the declaration of their love] we also, since the day we heard it, do not cease to pray for you [which is the most effective way of reciprocating Christian affection], and to desire ["make request for you," R.V.] that ye might be filled with the knowledge of His will in all wisdom and spiritual understanding" (v. 9). As intimated above, in order to discern and appreciate the force of this opening petition it is necessary to observe the relation it bears to those that follow: as cause to effect. As our being granted "the spirit of wisdom and revelation in the knowedge of him" (Eph. 1:17) is required in order for the eyes of our understanding to be enlightened, that we may know what is "the hope of his calling"; as our being "strengthened with might by his Spirit in the inner man" (Eph. 3:16) must precede Christ's dwelling in our hearts by faith, our being rooted and grounded in love, and our being filled with the fullness of God; and as our love must "abound yet more and more in knowledge and in all judgment" (Phil. 1:10) if we are to approve things that are excellent; so must we be "sincere and without offence" to be "filled with the knowledge of his will in all wisdom and spiritual understanding" so that we may "walk worthy of the Lord unto all pleasing, being fruitful in every good work."

Paul's Prayer for the Colossian Saints

"That ye might be filled with the knowledge of his will in all wisdom and spiritual understanding." To be without such knowledge is to be like the captain of a ship starting out on a long voyage without a chart, or for builders to erect a house or factory with no architectural plan to guide them. With rare exceptions, when we read in the Epistles of "the will of God," the reference is to His revealed will and not His secret will, His authoritative will rather than His providential will—His will made known to us in the Scriptures. Neither his understanding, conscience, nor "new nature" is sufficient to serve the Christian as the director of his ways. Only in His *Word* is God's authoritative will discovered to us. There alone do we have an all-sufficient and infallible guide— a lamp to our feet, a light to our path. To be filled with the knowledge of the divine will should not only be the main burden of our daily prayers but the principal quest of our lives: to obtain a better, fuller, closer knowledge of what God requires of us. Without that we can neither please nor glorify Him, nor shall we escape the innumerable pitfalls in our path.

This Is a Gradual Process

At least three things are implied by the wording of this opening petition. First, by nature we are devoid of such knowledge: before regeneration we are actuated only by self-will and satanic suggestions—"we have turned every one to *his own way*" (Isa. 53:6). Second, to become filled with the knowledge of God's will is a gradual process, for the filling of a vessel is accomplished by degrees, by steady increase. And thus it is with the Christian: "precept upon precept, line upon line, here a little, there a little." Third, it is our duty to attain to this state, yet constant recourse must be had to the throne of grace for divine assistance. Ignorance is deplorable and inexcusable, yet wisdom comes from above and must be diligently sought. To be "filled with the knowledge of his will" includes a comprehensive and abundant knowledge as well as a well-proportioned one. The apostle here made request for something intensely *practical:* not speculations about the divine nature, prying into the divine decrees, nor inquisitive explorations of unfulfilled prophecy, but the knowledge of God's will as it respects the ordering of our daily walk in this world. As one has said: "The knowledge of our duty is the best knowledge." "That the soul be without knowledge . . . is not good" (Prov. 19:2).

The Daily Renewal of Our Consecration

It is a most serious mistake to suppose that at regeneration the understanding is enlightened once for all, that it is so completely illumined as to be in no further need of divine assistance afterward. It is as grave an error to imagine that the surrender of the will to God at conversion was so entire that it is unnecessary for the saint to daily renew his consecration to Him. Such errors are manifestly refuted by a prayer of David's: "With my whole heart have I sought thee: O let me not wander from thy commandments" (Ps. 119:10). Though David had fully yielded himself to the Lord and had made more than ordinary progress in godliness, yet he felt himself to be in deep need of perpetual quickening, directing, and upholding, lest he lose the knowledge he already possessed and backslide from that course upon which he had entered. The truth is that the more experience we have of God's ways, the more sensible we become of our deplorable proneness to wander from Him. On the other hand, the more we truly seek God with the whole heart, the more our spiritual light will be increased, for by a closer walking with Him we obtain a clearer and fuller apprehension of His holiness; and that in turn makes us more conscious of our defects, for it is in His light that we see light.

Every healthy saint experiences such a longing after a knowledge of God's will as this prayer breathes. The more knowledge he obtains of God's will the more he becomes aware of his ignorance. And why is this the case? Because he has acquired a larger concept of his duty. At first Christian consciousness of duty consists more in the general than in its details, more of the outward walk and the external acts of worship, more of quantity than of quality. But before long he discovers that God requires him to regulate the inner man and subdue his soul to Him. In fact, he learns that this is the *principal task* assigned him. As the believer more and more realizes the breadth of God's commandment (Ps. 119:96) and the exceeding spirituality of His law (Rom. 7:14), he becomes painfully conscious of how far, far short he falls of discharging his responsibilities, and how sadly he has failed in this and that respect. Nevertheless, such a humbling discovery is evidence that his sense of duty has been enlarged, and that his own inability to perform it is all the more apparent to him.

Walking with God Begets an Enlarged Sense of Duty

As a closer walking with God begets an enlarged sense of duty, it also produces an increased realization of the difficulties attending the performance of it. As the natural man in his youth is full of vigor and hope, and in his inexperience and impetuosity rushes into engagements for which he is unqualified and is forward to rashly embark upon ventures which later he regrets, so the young Christian, on fire with affection and zeal, attempts tasks for which he is not fitted and then smarts for acting presumptuously. But in the school of experience he discovers something of his ignorance, his weakness, the inconstancy of his heart, and learns to distinguish between the natural energy of the flesh and true spirituality. God has made him to know something of wisdom "in the hidden part" (Ps. 51:6), which works in him self-diffidence and holy fear. He becomes more dependent upon God, more diligent in mortifying his lusts, more humble in his approach to the throne of grace, more frequent in crying, "Give me understanding, and I shall keep thy law" (Ps. 119:34).

Thus the babe in Christ will not advance very far along the Christian path before he realizes how perfectly suited to his case is the opening petition of this prayer. To be filled with the knowledge of God's will becomes his ever deepening desire, and that "in all wisdom and spiritual understanding." Those added words intimate, first, the sort of knowledge for which the Christian is to pray and strive: not merely a theoretical but an experimental knowledge, not simply in the letter but in the power of it, an inward, affectionate, operative knowledge wrought in the soul by God. As we saw when examining Philippians 1:9, light is needed to direct our activities; instruction is needed that we may act judiciously. Heavenly wisdom is required that love may have a proper sense of the relative worth of objects, and suitable guidance in every instance of its exercise. Holy affections are no more all heat without light than are the rays of the sun, but are induced by spiritual instruction received into the mind. The child of God is graciously affected when he perceives and understands something more than he did formerly of the character of God, the sufficiency of Christ, the glorious things exhibited in the gospel. Such knowledge of those objects produces in him wisdom and spiritual understanding.

Paul's opening petition was for something more than a bare acquaintance with the divine will; rather it was a request that the saints should be brought to a fuller and more acceptable *obedience*. The "knowledge" of God's perceptive and authoritative will is a practical and operative one, evidenced in a worthy walk. The babe in Christ has the principle of obedience in his heart (divinely communicated grace and holiness), but it needs feeding, strengthening, quickening, illuminating, directing, so that the believer may act aright and perform those things which God has appointed, not those which human tradition has invented, or which natural sentiment or personal inclination may dictate. We saw that this came first in the prayer of Ephesians 1: "That God . . . may give unto you the spirit of wisdom and revelation in the knowledge [and "acknowledgment," margin] of him" (v. 17). It also was made the opening petition for the Philippian saints: "That your love may abound yet more and more in knowledge and all judgment" (1:9). Thus we see the prime importance of this blessing.

The Soul Influenced by the Beauty of Divine Things

This petition has respect to an affectionate and operative knowledge, which is increased as the child of God is favored with a better understanding of divine objects. The clearer and fuller are his views of them, the more is his heart drawn out to them. The more we perceive the ineffable beauty of divine things, the more the soul is sensibly influenced by them. Those things on which the Christian's love is to be placed, particularly the divine precepts, must be discerned in their true nature and excellence before there can be spiritual delight in them. When there is no spiritual understanding of spiritual things, there can be no spiritual pleasure in them. We are deceived if we suppose our love for God's commandments is increasing unless there is a growing realization of their worth. There can be no growth of spiritual love without an increase of spiritual knowledge. The more a Christian knows the importance and value of God's rule, the more he will be occupied with it. The defect of much modern religion is that it either attempts to stir the emotions by sentimental appeals, or exhorts the exercise of love without presenting those things which feed love and spontaneously draw it forth.

Faith is fed by knowledge and works by love. Therefore, the fuller and deeper is the soul's experimental acquaintance with God and the more his affections are drawn out to and centered on Him, the more will faith and love produce that obedience which is honoring to Him. As spiritual knowledge of the Lord, as He is revealed to the heart, causes us to put our trust in Him (Ps. 9:10), as believing sight in Him as our suffering Surety opens the floodgates of evangelical repentance (Zech. 12:10), so a sense of our deep indebtedness to Him, a spirit of gratitude, issues in acceptable obedience. The more we apprehend God's infinite worthiness, the more we shall strive to walk worthily before Him. The more we behold His excellence, the more our hearts will be warmed toward Him. The more intimate and constant is our communion with Him, the more shall we delight ourselves in Him, and the more tender shall we be of those things which grieve Him. So too the more we perceive of the high sovereignty and majesty of God, the more we shall be awed by and be amenable to His authority, and the more diligent we shall be in cleaving to the only path in which fellowship with Him can be enjoyed—the path of obedience to His blessed will.

What Fellowship with God Consists of

Many today have a most inadequate and defective idea of what fellowship with God consists of. They regard it as a special luxury which is only enjoyed occasionally, whereas it should be experienced regularly. They imagine it is known only when their souls are ecstatically elevated by some uncommonly powerful sermon, during some season of unusual liberty in prayer, or when meditating on some precious portion of the Word. But *that* is more a time when the saint is aware of the Lord's having drawn near to and lifted up the light of His countenance upon him, favoring him with a special love token.

But we now have something else in mind. Intimate fellowship with God can be enjoyed not only by one in the cloister but by the housewife while engaged in her domestic tasks and by her husband as he works for his daily bread. God graciously communes with each of His people while they are about their secular duties as they are discharged in obedience to Him.

Only One Way for a Closer Walk with God

What we particularly have in mind are these words: "He will teach us of his ways, and we will walk in his paths" (Isa. 2:3). God holds communion with us only in His ways, "the paths of righteousness." We cannot walk with God in a way of self-will and self-pleasing, nor in the broad road trodden by the world. Every step we take in the right way—the way of God's revealed will—must be one of obedience. But the moment we forsake the path of duty and wander into what Bunyan styles "By-path meadow," we turn away from God, and leave the only place where fellowship with Him may be had.

Wisdom from God Required for Life's Path

"In all wisdom and spiritual understanding." Those added words intimate not only the sort of knowledge for which the Christian is to pray but also what is necessary in order for him to employ such knowledge to advantage. In this superficial age, knowledge and wisdom are often confounded, yet they are far from being synonymous. There are many learned fools in the world. Frequently the almost illiterate exercise more natural intelligence than does the average university graduate. "Wisdom" is the capacity to make right and good use of knowledge. Even when we have considerable knowledge of God's will, much wisdom and spiritual understanding are required in order to go in the path of His commandments. Sometimes it is the Christian's duty to admonish an erring brother, yet he is likely to do him more harm than good unless he speaks discreetly. There is a time and a season for everything, but good judgment and spiritual discernment are requisite in order to recognize them. Much prudence is called for to rightly distinguish between relative duties: to deliberately neglect secular duties in order to feast upon spiritual things, to deprive my family of things which they urgently need in order to give more liberally to the Lord's cause, to forsake my wife in the evenings to engage in religious activities, betrays an absence of spiritual understanding.

"Cause Me to Know the Way Wherein I Should Walk"

How the believer needs to pray, "Make me to understand the way of thy precepts" (Ps. 119:27). He needs to be taught how to walk in each duty and every detail of conduct! It is not sufficient to have a general, superficial knowledge of the Word: it must be translated into practice, and spiritual insight is required for that, so that we may perceive when and where and how to perform each action. Some are wise in general details but err sadly in particular details. Only that wisdom which comes from above will enable us to order our lives in every relation and situation according to the revealed will of God. "Give me understanding, and I shall keep thy law" (Ps. 119:34, 73, 144, 169). See how often David repeated that petition! Many times God's children are placed in a dilemma when they have to choose between duty and duty—duty to God, to their family, to their neighbors. And wisdom and spiritual understanding are required to show them when the one is to be dispensed with and the other performed, when the inferior is to yield to the superior. Circumstances have to be observed as well as actions that we may know when to "stand still" and when to "go forward." We are not to act on impulse but be regulated by principle.

"That ye might walk worthy of the Lord unto all pleasing, being fruitful in every good work, and increasing in the knowledge of God." This is the second thing Paul requested for the saints and there is an inseparable connection between them, for this cannot be realized except the first be actualized. The walks and works of a person are determined, both in quality and quantity, by His ignorance or knowledge of God's will and by the measure of his wisdom and spiritual understanding. Or to state it another way: Here we are shown the use to which such knowledge is to be put. As another said in a different connection, our aim in getting an understanding of God's Word is not that we may argue about questions but order our conversation. The Word was not given us to test the sharpness of our wits in disputing. It was given to test the readiness of our obedience in performing. That knowledge of God's will for which the Christian should pray and labor does not consist of prying into God's decrees; speculating about the personal relations between the three Persons in the Trinity, or the eternal destiny of those who are cut off in infancy; nor theorizing about the future history of this world under the guise of studying prophecy. Rather that knowledge consists in learning what God requires from us and how we may be enabled to meet those requirements.

The Believer's Walk

"That ye might walk worthy of the Lord." That is, of Christ the Lord (Luke 2:11, as is always the case except in two or three passages like Acts 4:29; Rev. 11:15). "Walking" is applied in Scripture to the conduct or behavior of persons. It points to the active rather than the passive side of the Christian's life. It expresses not only motion but voluntary motion in contrast to being carried or dragged. It imports progressive motion, going forward, advancing in holiness. It signifies fixing and holding a steady course in our journey heavenward. "Walking" is in contrast with sitting and lying down, also with aimless meandering. It is keeping to the way which God has marked out for us. But what is meant by "walking *worthily*," as it should be rendered? Certainly not meritoriously, for it is impossible for the creature to do anything to make God his debtor or entitle him to reward as a matter of justice: "When ye have done all those things which are commanded you, say, We are unprofitable servants: we have done that which was our duty to do" (Luke 17:10). But no Christian ever did all that he was commanded, and even if he had, his efforts would have been imperfect and unacceptable to God were it not for the mediation of the Redeemer.

"Worthy Is the Lamb"

But we are told, "Worthy is the Lamb" (Rev. 5:12). Is not that the same term? Yes, except that it is in its adjectival form. The Lamb is indeed worthy, infinitely worthy, but no mere creature is so, not even the holy angels, as this very same passage expressly declares. When the question was asked, "Who is worthy to open the book to loose the seals thereof?" we are informed, "And no man in heaven or in earth, neither under the earth, was able to open the book, neither to look thereon. And I wept much because no one was found worthy to open and read the book." But there is a worthiness of fitness as well as a worthiness of deservingness, and it is the former which is here in view. To walk worthily of the Lord signifies to conduct ourselves as saints should, to act in accordance with the character of the One whose name we bear and whose followers we profess to be. To walk worthily of the Lord means to conduct ourselves suitably and agreeably to our relation and indebtedness to Him, to carry ourselves as those who are not their own. The same Greek word is rendered "as becometh" in Romans 16:2 and Philippians 1:27.

"As obedient children, not fashioning yourselves according to your former lusts in your ignorance: but as he which hath called you is holy, so be ye holy in all manner of conversation [or 'conduct']" (I Peter 1:14-15). Let your daily lives make manifest your change of masters. Formerly you served your lusts, but that was in the days of your ignorance when you were strangers to God. Now that you have enlisted under the banner of the Lord Jesus and have "the knowledge of God's will," evince it in a practical way: walk becomingly of the Lord. How? "Let this mind be in you, which was also in Christ Jesus" (Phil. 2:5). And what was that? The mind of self-abnegation—veiling His glory and taking upon Him the form of a servant. The mind of self-abasement—making Himself of "no reputation." The mind of voluntary subjection and unreserved surrender—"He became obedient unto death, even the death of the cross." How may we do all this? By the life of Christ being reproduced in us so far as our measure and capacity admit, that we may "grow up into him in all things" (Eph. 4:15). How? By making Him our Exemplar. "Because Christ also suffered for us, leaving us an example that ye should follow his steps" (I Peter 2:21). Only in proportion as we do, shall we "walk worthy of the Lord."

The Christian's Constant Employment

To "walk worthy of the Lord" is the great task which is assigned the Christian, and it is to be attempted with the utmost seriousness as his principal care, and attended to with unwearied diligence as a matter of the utmost importance. To honor that blessed One whose we are and whom we serve, to so conduct myself that fellow saints glorify God in me (Gal. 1:24), to "adorn the doctrine of God our Saviour in all things" (Titus 2:10), should be my supreme quest and business, never to be forgotten or laid aside. The Christian ought to be even more earnest in endeavoring to approve himself to God than they who contend so zealously for the honors of this world and those who devote all their energies to acquiring its riches. We should make it our constant concern to bring no reproach upon the name of Him who loved us and gave Himself for us. Otherwise we cannot magnify Him nor His cause here upon earth. It is not our talk but our walk that most furthers His interests. People soon forget what we say but they long remember Christlike conduct. Actions speak louder than words. The Lord has called us out of darkness into His marvelous light that we should *"shew forth* his praises" or "virtues."

If we are not walking worthily of the Lord, we lack evidence of our title to heaven. Of Enoch it was said that "before his translation [to heaven] he had this testimony, that he pleased God" (Heb. 11:5). That looks back to Genesis 5:24 where we are told that "Enoch walked with God." Therein he "pleased" Him, and that testimony bore witness to his eternal inheritance. Only as holiness is our aim do we have a token and an earnest that heaven is our portion, for without holiness "no man shall see the Lord" (Heb. 12:14). The merits of Christ alone give anyone title to the inheritance, yet personal holiness confirms that title for us. There is no good hope toward Christ where there is no sincere effort to honor Him: "Hereby we do know that we know him, if we keep his commandments" (I John 2:3). Only those are fit to live with Him hereafter who are conscientious about walking with Him here. At death we change our place but not our company. "They shall walk with me in white: for they are worthy" (Rev. 3:4)—fitly disposed and prepared to do so. On the other hand, "Know ye not that the unrighteous shall not inherit the kingdom of God? Be not deceived" (I Cor. 6:9-10). Those who gratify the flesh are necessarily excluded.

"As ye have therefore received Christ Jesus the Lord, so walk ye in him" (Col. 2:6). Unless we give the utmost attention to our daily walk and order it by the revealed will of God, we break that covenant which we solemnly entered into with Him at our conversion. It was then that we renounced all other lords, forsook our idols, surrendered ourselves to the righteous claims of the Lord, and promised that thenceforth we would love Him with all our hearts and serve Him with all our strength. We voluntarily and deliberately entered on a course of obedience to Him, where we "choose the things that please" God, and thereby "take hold of his covenant" (Isa. 56:4). Consequently, to return to the pleasing of self, or to seek the favor of men or the applause of the world, is a denial of the covenant and a throwing off of the yoke of Christ which formerly we took upon us. It is a practical denial that we are not our own but bought with a price. Such deplorable backsliding will issue in having a conscience that no longer is "void of offence" but rather accuses and condemns us. The joy of salvation is then lost, the light of God's countenance is then hid from us, that peace which passes all understanding is no longer our portion. Instead, darkness and doubts possess the heart, the rod of divine chastisement falls heavily upon us, our prayers remain unanswered, relish for the Word is gone.

We cannot enjoy conscious communion with Him unless we walk worthily of the Lord. We cannot have the comfort of His presence in every company or in all conditions. If we consort with the ungodly, the Lord is grieved and will evince His displeasure. If we turn to the pleasures of this world for satisfaction, His smile will be withheld from us. If we indulge the lusts of the flesh, He will say to us as He said to His people of old, "Your iniquities have separated between you and your God" (Isa. 59:2). The one who has Christ's commandments and keeps them proves his love to Him. To this one He says,

"I will love him, and manifest myself to him." And again, "If a man love me, he will keep my words: and my Father will love him, and we will come unto him, and make our abode with him" (John 14:21, 23).

The Christian has been called to the fellowship of God's Son, Jesus Christ our Lord (I Cor. 1:9). What an inestimable favor is that! How highly it should be valued, how tenderly cherished! The root idea of fellowship is partnership—one having something in common with another. In wondrous love and amazing condescension the Lord Jesus deigned to make the interests of His people His own. That was unspeakable grace on His part, and what does it call for from us? Surely that deepest gratitude should now make His interest ours. We should exercise the utmost circumspection in avoiding everything that would injure His interests; we should now exert ourselves to the utmost in promoting the honor of His name on earth. "Love so amazing, so divine, *demands* my love, my life, my all!" What shall I render to the Lord for all His benefits but to earnestly endeavor to walk worthily of Him.

"Unto All Pleasing"

"That ye might walk worthy of the Lord unto all pleasing, being fruitful in every good work" (v. 10). Having already pointed out the relation of this petition and its dependence upon the former one, and having explained what we conceive to be the meaning of "walk worthy of the Lord," we turn now to the next clause. Those added words "unto all pleasing" serve both to define and amplify the previous sentence, informing us *how* we are to walk worthily and the *entirety* of that duty and privilege. We are to pray and strive to walk worthily of the Lord unto *all* pleasing, not merely on the Sabbath but every day. We must not simply conduct ourselves reverently in the house of prayer but act becomingly in the outside world. Our aim and endeavor must be to approve ourselves to Christ, and please Him not only in those things which are esteemed by common consent, nor in those which are agreeable to us, but also in those things which cross our wills and pinch the flesh. Nothing short of universal and uniform obedience is required of us. Christ died to deliver His people from the curse of the law, but not from the duty of practicing its precepts. He died not to free His people from the service of God but rather that they might be enabled to serve Him acceptably and with peace of conscience and joy of heart.

Two Classes of People in the World

There are but two classes of people in the world, namely, those who are offensive to God, and those who are esteemed by Him. The ones are self-pleasers, the others self-deniers. Therein lies the essential difference between sincere souls and hypocrites: the former honestly endeavor to please Christ, and are regarded by Him as the excellent of the earth (Ps. 16:3); the latter seek the approbation of men and live to gratify self, and therefore are they to God as "a vessel wherein is no pleasure" (Hosea 8:8). There is no other alternative possible but either living to please self or living to please the Lord. No matter what may be their pretensions—what name they go under, what is their creed, how highly they are regarded by their fellows—if self is their "God," they are hateful to the Holy One. Those in whom God delights are the ones who are regulated by His will, who live for His glory, whose daily walk honors Him, who are fruitful in good works. How that simple but discriminating classification serves to expose the empty profession all around us! Tens of thousands call themselves by the name of Christ, but they do not wear His yoke, do not take up their cross (the principle of self-abasement and sacrifice), do not follow His example.

Unless we have fully given ourselves up to God and are genuinely seeking to please Him in all that we do, our supposed conversion was merely a delusion. If the gratifying of our natural desires is our chief pleasure, we are yet in our sins. If we are sowing to the flesh, we shall of the flesh reap corruption. Make no mistake, dear reader, whoever you are. The Omniscient One cannot be imposed upon, neither will He accept a divided heart. No man can serve two masters. If you think you can placate God by acting piously on the Sabbath, while being thoroughly worldly through the week, you are woefully mistaken. God will not be served with any reserve or limitation, but requires us to love Him with all our heart, soul, and strength. In order to please Him we have to shun whatever He hates: mortify the flesh, live separate from the world, resist the devil. The Lord will not be served with that which costs us nothing (II Sam. 24:24).

Can a Fallen, Sinful Creature Please a Holy God?

But is it possible that a mere creature of the earth—a fallen and sinful one at that—can please the great and holy God? Certainly it is. Of Enoch it is recorded that "he pleased God" (Heb. 11:5). That must not be carnalized as though God were subject to emotions; neither must it be emptied of all meaning. The Lord is so infinitely above us that no analogy can be found in human relations. But to aid our feeble perceptions, let us imagine a tutor who has gone to particular pains in instructing one of his scholars. Is he not gratified when he sees him at the top of his class? When parents see their children putting into practice those precepts which they have so lovingly and earnestly instilled into them, do they not rejoice? So, when we act as it becomes His people, we are approved in God's sight. Said David, "He delivered me [from enemies], because he delighted in me" (II Sam. 22:20). Those who are upright in the way are His delight (Prov. 15:8). In reality, it is God approving His own handiwork, esteeming that which His Spirit has wrought in us. Nevertheless, we are not passive, but determine and perform as He works in us both to will and to do of His good pleasure.

As there are degrees of wickedness and obnoxiousness to God, so there are degrees of bringing delight to Him. That for which Christians are here taught to pray—and therefore to diligently and constantly strive after—is to so "walk worthy of the Lord unto *all* pleasing," which includes not walking "in the counsel of the ungodly" (Ps. 1:1) but walking "in the law of the LORD" (Ps. 119:1). We should be concerned to "walk in newness of life" (Rom. 6:4), to "walk by faith, not by sight" (II Cor. 5:7), to "walk in the Spirit" (Gal. 5:16), to "walk in love" (Eph. 5:2), to "walk circumspectly" (Eph. 5:15).

Approved of God

As an aid in doing this, observe the following rules. First, be always on your guard in avoiding everything that is grievous to God, and in order to do that, cultivate a sense of His presence. If you are on your best behavior when in the company of cherished friends, how much more should you be in the presence of your heavenly Friend! If the knowledge of human onlookers restrains you from acts of sin, how much more should a respect for the Holy One! That was what governed Joseph in Egypt: "How then can I do this great wickedness, and sin against God?" (Gen. 39:9).

Second, be diligent in choosing those things which God esteems. When Solomon sought wisdom that he might rule Israel righteously, we are told it "pleased the Lord, that Solomon had asked that thing" (I Kings 3:10). The more our hearts are set upon things above, the more we aim at God's glory, the greater pleasure will He have in us. Third, be wholehearted in your devotedness to the Lord. There must be no picking and choosing among His precepts: no in with one duty and out with another. The whole scope of the Christian life should be a studying to show oneself approved to God: the understanding perceiving what is due to Him, the conscience swayed by His authority, the affections drawn out in adoring homage, the will surrendered to Him. Caleb was one who greatly pleased the Lord, and of him it is recorded that "he wholly followed the LORD God" (Joshua 14:14). Fourth, meditate in God's law day and night (Ps. 1:2). Make it your constant concern how to serve and honor Him, remembering that He is more pleased with obedience than with your sacrifices and free-will offerings (I Sam. 15:22). Fifth, maintain a steady dependence upon the Lord, for you have no strength of your own: He must be looked to daily for the needed wisdom and power. Frequent the throne of grace that there you may "find grace to help in time of need" (Heb. 4:16).

Further, if we are to be approved by God, it is by no means sufficient that "we make clean the outside of the cup and platter," although many suppose that is all that matters. "Cleanse first that which is within" (Matt. 23:26) is our Lord's command. Unfortunately, in this degenerate day such a task is not merely relegated to second place but it is given none at all. The devil seeks to persuade people that they are not responsible for the state of their hearts, that they can no more change them than they can alter the stars in their courses. Such a lie is very agreeable to those who think they are to be carried to heaven on downy beds of ease—and there are few left to disillusion them. But no regenerate soul with God's Word before him will credit such a falsehood. The divine command is plain: "Keep thy heart with all diligence, for out of it are the issues of life" (Prov. 4:23). That is the principal task set us, for God ever looks at the heart, and there can be no pleasing Him while it is unattended to. Yes, woe be to those who disregard it. He who makes no honest endeavor to cast out sinful thoughts and evil imaginations, who does not mourn over their presence, is a moral leper. He who has no pangs over the workings of unbelief, the cooling of his affections, the surgings of pride, is a stranger to any work of grace in his soul.

"Keep Thy Heart with All Diligence"

Not only does God bid you to keep your heart; He requires you to do it "with all diligence," that is, to make it your main concern and constant care. The Hebrew word for "keep" meant "to guard." Watch over your heart (the soul, or inward man) as a precious treasure, of which thieves are ever ready to rob you. Guard it as a garrison into which enemies will enter if you are not on the alert. Attend to it as a garden in which the Lord would refresh Himself (Song of Sol. 6:2), removing all weeds and keeping its flowers and spices fragrant. That is, be diligent in mortifying your lusts and in cultivating your graces. The devotions of your lips and the labors of your hands are unacceptable to the Lord if your heart is not right in His sight. What husband would appreciate the domestic attentions of his wife if he had good reasons to believe her affections were alienated from him? God takes note not only of the matter of our actions but the springs from which they proceed, the motives actuating them, as also the manner in which they are done and their motive. If we become slack and careless in any of these respects, it shows that our love has cooled and that we have become weary of God.

God Weighs Our Spirits

The One with whom we have to do "is a God of knowledge, and by him actions are weighed" (I Sam. 2:3) in the balances of righteousness and truth; whatever is "found wanting" (Dan. 5:27) or is deficient is rejected by Him. "All the ways of a man are clean in his own eyes; but the *Lord* weigheth the spirits" (Prov. 16:2), i.e., that which lies behind the actions, which colors as well as prompts them. Self-love may blind our judgment and make us partial in our own cause, but we cannot deceive the omniscient One. God brings to the test and standard of holiness not only our actions but the attitudes of our spirits which inspired them. "The righteous God trieth the hearts and reins" (Ps. 7:9), that is, the inward principles from which our conduct proceeds. He scrutinizes our affections and motives, whether we are sincere or not. The Lord God is "he that pondereth the heart" (Prov. 24:12), observing all its motives: its most secret intentions are open to Him. He perceives whether your contributions to His cause are made cheerfully or grudgingly. He knows whether your gifts to the poor are made in order to be seen of men and admired by them, or whether they issue from disinterested benevolence. He knows whether your expressions of goodwill and love toward your brethren are feigned or genuine.

Since the Lord looks on and ponders the heart, should not we do so too? Since from the heart proceed the issues of life, should we not make it our chief concern and care? Out of man's heart proceed all evils mentioned by our Lord in Mark 7:21-22. But it is equally true that out of the heart proceed the fruit described in Galatians 5:22-23. "A good man out of the good treasure of the heart bringeth forth good things" (Matt. 12:35), but the good man will not do so unless he diligently resists his inward corruptions and tends and nourishes his graces.

If we are to walk worthily of the Lord "unto all pleasing," we must frequently "search and try our ways" (Lam. 3:40), take our spiritual pulse, and ascertain whether all is well within. We must heed that injunction "Stand in awe, and sin not: commune with your own heart upon your bed, and be still" (Ps. 4:4) that we may ascertain our spiritual condition. We must daily attend to that precept "Little children, keep yourselves from idols" (I John 5:21) lest anything is allowed that place in our affections which belongs alone to Christ. We must constantly examine our motives and challenge our aims and intentions, for *they* count most with God. We must "cleanse ourselves from all filthiness of the flesh and spirit" (II Cor. 7:1).

A Great Lack

Alas, how sadly has the standard been relaxed! How little is now heard, even in centers of orthodoxy, of "walking worthy of the Lord unto all pleasing"! How very few today are being informed that God requires them to keep their *hearts* with all diligence, and to work out their own salvation with fear and trembling. Will not the Lord yet say to many an unfaithful occupant of the modern pulpit, "Ye have not spoken of me the thing that is right" (Job 42:7)? No wonder the churches are in such a low state of spirituality. But the failure of those in the pulpit does not excuse those in the pew. The individual still has access to God's Word, and even if there were none others left on earth who respect it, *he* is responsible to be regulated by its elevated and exacting teachings.

Christian reader, whatever others do or do not, see to it that you turn Colossians 1:10 into daily prayer, and strive to translate it into practice, for the glory of God and your own good. If you are careless about your walk, and indifferent as to whether the state of your heart is pleasing or displeasing to the Lord, His ear will be closed to your prayers! The Scriptures are explicit on that fact: "Whatsoever we ask, we receive of him, *because* we keep his commandments, and do those things which are pleasing in his sight" (I John 3:22). That cannot be labeled "legalistic," for those are the words of the Holy Spirit. It is not because our obedience is in any way meritorious but because this is the *order* of things which divine holiness has established. God has appointed an inseparable connection between the acceptableness of our conduct and that of our petitions. If we would have His ear then we must attend to His voice. We cannot expect God to grant our requests while we ignore what He requires of us. Not that our obedience ingratiates us into God's favor; but it is a necessary adjunct to our receiving favors at His hand. We must delight ourselves in the Lord if we would have Him grant us the desires of our heart (Ps. 37:4).

Keeping His Commandments

As prohibitions always imply the performance of their opposites—as "Thou shalt not kill" (Exodus 20:13) signifies that man shall use all lawful means to preserve life, and "Thou shalt not commit adultery" (Exodus 20:14) obligates man to live chastely—so each positive precept argues its negative. I John 3:22 also implies that we shall not receive from God those things we ask of Him if we do not keep His commandments and do not do those things which are pleasing in His sight. If any uncertainty remains on this point, Proverbs 28:9 at once removes it: "He that turneth away his ear from hearing the law, even his prayer shall be an abomination." God has appointed an inseparable connection between the performance of duty and the enjoyment of privilege. Psalm 66:18 is even more searching, showing again what God requires within as well as without: "If I regard iniquity in my *heart,* the Lord will not hear me." If I countenance and secretly foster any sin, even though I do not practice it, if I view it favorably or even palliate or excuse it, His ear is closed against me. Unsorrowed and unconfessed sins prevent many a prayer from being answered. The Holy One will not wink at sin. Spurgeon said, "For God to accept our devotions while we are delighting in sin, would make Him the God of hypocrites."

The Cultivation of Faith

If we are to "walk worthy of the Lord unto all pleasing," we must be most attentive to the cultivation of *faith,* for "without faith it is impossible to please him" (Heb. 11:6). The more fully and constantly we trust Him, the more we walk by faith, the more will the Lord delight in us. God is pleased when we cling to Him in the darkness, look to Him for the fulfilling of His promises, count upon His loving kindness. But He is displeased when we doubt His Word or suspect His love. Faith in God, in His precepts, in His promises, is the grand and distinguishing principle which is to actuate all our conduct.

"By him therefore let us offer the sacrifice of praise to God continually . . . giving thanks to his name. But to do good and communicate forget not: for with such sacrifices God is well pleased" (Heb. 13:15-16). Then let us not be backward in offering them. God loves to hear the songs of His children. The "sweet psalmist of Israel" is how He designated David (II Sam. 23:1). "Whoso offereth praise glorifieth me" (Ps. 50:23). Praise is an exalting of God's name, a proclaiming of His excellence, a publishing of His renown, an adoring of His goodness, a breaking open of the box of our ointment; therefore it is a "sweet savour" to Him, ". . . magnify him with thanksgiving. This also shall please the Lord better than an ox" (Ps. 69:30-31). How comforting that was for the one who was unable to bring Him a costly offering! Let us be frequently engaged in this delightful exercise of praise, and act like spiritual larks.

Our Conduct and Dealings with Others

But it is not only in the devotional side of our lives that we may give delight to God. Different by far is the teaching of His Word. The Lord takes notice not only of our attitude toward and actions to Himself but also of our conduct and dealings with our fellowmen. We may please Him—and it should be our diligent aim to do so—in the shop, home, factory, office. "A false balance is an abomination to the LORD: but a just weight is his delight" (Prov. 11:1). Under that word *balance* we are to include all weights and measures, descriptions of articles, and profits from them. Such a verse as that should be carefully pondered and kept constantly in mind by all who are engaged in any form of business, whether they are employers or employees, weighing all their words and deeds. To misrepresent a piece of merchandise, to overcharge, or to deliberately shortchange a customer, is a grievous sin. Though it may escape the notice of men, it is recorded against us by the Holy One, and we shall be made to pay dearly for the same. Contrariwise, to be fair and honest in our trading is pleasing to God: "Such as are upright in their way are his delight" (Prov. 11:20).

God Refuses the Homage of the Unjust

Not only does God take notice of and record the sins of those who are guilty of unjust and fraudulent practices but He refuses their hypocritical homage. There is no bribing of the divine Judge, nor can He be imposed upon by a pious demeanor in those who wrong their fellows. They who grind the faces of the poor through the week and, equally, those who fail to supply a fair day's work for a fair day's pay only mock the Lord when they sing His praises and make an offering to His cause on the Sabbath day. "The sacrifice of the wicked is an abomination to the LORD: but the prayer of the upright is his delight" (Prov. 15:8). The external acts of worship of those whose business dealings are corrupt are an offense to the Most High, and it is the sacred duty of pastors to announce it. "He that turneth away his ear from hearing the law [which enjoins loving our neighbor as ourself], even his prayer shall be abomination" (Prov. 28:9). We do but deceive ourselves if we imagine God hearkens to our petitions while our everyday lives betray our devotions. On the other hand, "the righteous LORD loveth righteousness; his countenance doth [favorably] behold the upright" (Ps. 11:7). Everything we do either pleases or displeases God.

To walk worthily means to conduct ourselves becomingly, to act agreeably to the Name we bear, to live as those who are not their own. To walk "worthy of the Lord unto all pleasing" is to be uniformly and universally obedient, taking no step without the warrant of God's Word, seeking His approbation and honor in every department and aspect of our lives. "Being fruitful in every good work" is a further extension of the same thought, evincing again how high and holy is the standard at which we should aim continually. Grace is no enemy to good works; it is the promoter and enabler of them. It is utterly vain for us to speak and sing of the wonders of divine grace if we are not plainly exhibiting its lovely fruits. Grace is a principle of operation, a spiritual energizer which causes its possessor to be active in good works and makes him a fruitful branch of the Vine. It is the empty professor who is viewed as a barren tree, a cumberer of the ground. By the miracle of regeneration God makes His people "good trees" and they bear "good fruit." It is their privilege and duty to be "fruitful in every good work," and in order to do so they must constantly endeavor to "walk worthy of the Lord unto all pleasing."

Saints of God to Be Fruitful in Good Works

Saints are "trees of righteousness" (Isa. 61:3), the planting of the Lord, and their graces and good works are their fruit. There is a tendency in the minds of some to ascribe all glory to the heavenly Husbandman and virtually reduce the Christian to an automaton. We must distinguish between the fruit-Producer and the fruit-bearer. We are first made trees of the Lord, and then we receive grace from Him, and then by grace we ourselves really do bring forth fruit. We must indeed thankfully own the truth of our Lord's words "From me is thy fruit found" (Hosea 14:8). But while freely acknowledging that all is of His ordination and gracious enablement, we must not overlook the fact that even here God Himself terms it *"thy* fruit." Because it is of His origination, that does not alter the fact that it is also of our cooperation. While there may be many who make far too much of man, there are others who make too little of him—less than Scripture does—repudiating his moral agency. We must be careful lest we press too far the figure of the "branch": the branch of the tree has neither rationality, spirituality, nor responsibility; the Christian has all three. God does not produce the fruit independently of us. We are more than pipes through which His energy flows.

The very fact that Paul here prays that the saints *might* be "fruitful" clearly implies two things: they could not be fruitful without God's enabling; it was their privilege and duty to be so. We mock God unless we ourselves diligently strive after those spiritual enlargements for which we supplicate Him. We dishonor Him if we suppose we can attain to them in our own strength. When God has renewed a person, He does not henceforth treat him as though he were merely a mechanical entity; rather He communicates to him a gracious willingness to act and stirs him into action; then *the saint* actually performs the good works. In fruit-bearing we are not passive but active. It is not fruit tied onto us but fruit growing out of us which manifests that we have been grafted into Christ. If the believer's personal and practical holiness were not the outflowing of his renewed heart, then it would be no evidence (as it *is*) that spiritual life has been imparted to his soul. Perhaps an evidence that, in one sense, the fruits and good works which I bear are mine, is that I am dissatisfied with and grieve over them. I regret that my love is fickle, my zeal unstable, my best performances defective; if they were God's fruits and works, independent of me, they would be perfect.

Saints to Walk in Newness of Life

When God in His sovereign benignity communicates grace to a person it is for the purpose of equipping him for the better discharge of his responsibilities. That is to say, grace is given to animate and actuate all the faculties of his soul. And what He works in, we are to work out (Phil. 2:12-13). Having imparted life to His people, He requires them to walk in newness of life. Having bestowed faith on them, He expects that faith to be active in producing good works. Or, following the order of this prayer, if we have been "filled with the knowledge of his will in all wisdom and spiritual understanding" it is in order that we "might walk worthy of the Lord unto all pleasing, being fruitful in every good work." Those last words express both variety and abundance. It is not fruitfulness of one kind only, but of every sort. Said the Lord Jesus, "Herein is my Father glorified, that ye bear *much fruit*" (John 15:8). Alas, that any of His children should be content if they can just be persuaded that they bear a little fruit and thereby be convinced they belong to His family— setting more store on their own peace than upon their glorifying Him. Little wonder their assurance is so feeble.

Good Fruit Includes and Involves Holy Affections

That word of Christ's "Herein is my Father glorified, that ye bear much fruit" supplies further confirmation of what we have pointed out above. In a very real sense it is the saints' fruit: "ye bear." Though the fruit indeed comes by divine energizing, notwithstanding it is by their own activity. But observe too and admire the strict accuracy of Scripture. It does not state "that ye *produce* much fruit," for God is both the original and efficient Cause of the fruit. Mark the beautiful harmony of the two verses: "Walk worthy of the Lord unto all *pleasing,* being fruitful in every good work"; "Herein is my Father *glorified,* that ye bear much fruit." By doing so you exhibit the power and reality of His transforming grace, display the lineaments of His image, reflect the beauty of His holiness. "Much fruit" involves and includes the exercise of all holy affections: not merely some acts of holiness, but the putting forth of every grace in all the variety of their actings, not only inwardly but outwardly as well, laboring to abound in them, and this not spasmodically and only for a season, but steadfastly. As long as we are left on earth, we are to "bring forth fruit with patience" (Luke 8:15), persevering in it.

"Being fruitful in every good work, and increasing in the knowledge of God" (Col. 1:10). Observe that those two things are not separated by a semicolon but are linked together by an "and," the latter being closely connected with and dependent upon the former. "Increasing in the knowledge of God" is the *reward* of "walking worthy of the Lord unto all pleasing, being fruitful in every good work." Or, if some of our readers prefer the expression, it is the *effect* of it, though they should not object to the former when Scripture itself declares that "in keeping of them [the divine statutes] there is great reward" (Ps. 19:11)— a considerable part of which consists in a growing acquaintance with and a deeper delight in the Lord. Our Saviour said, "I am the light of the world: he that followeth me shall not walk in darkness, but shall have the light of life" (John 8:12). What does it mean to *follow* Christ but to yield to His authority, practice His precepts, and keep His example before us? The one who does so will not be the loser but the gainer. He will be delivered from the power and misery of sin, and made the recipient of spiritual wisdom, discernment, holiness, and happiness: in a word, he shall enjoy the light of God's countenance. So the consequence of a sincere endeavor to please the Lord and glorify Him by bearing much fruit will be an increase in our experimental knowledge of God.

An Increase in the Knowledge of God

It is not simply an increase in "knowledge" which is here spoken of but "increasing in the knowledge *of God,*" which is a vastly different thing. This is a kind of knowledge for which the wise of this world have no relish; it is one to which those with empty profession are total strangers. There are many who are keen "Bible students" and eager readers of a certain class of expository and theological works—works which explain types, prophecies, and doctrines, but contain little or nothing that searches the heart and removes carnality—and they become quite learned in the letter of Scripture and in the intellectual apprehension of its contents, yet have no personal, saving, or transforming knowledge of God. A merely theoretical knowledge of God has no effectual influence upon the soul, nor does it exert any beneficial power on one's daily walk. Nothing but a vital knowledge of God will produce the former, and only a practical knowledge of Him secures the latter. A vital and saving knowledge of God is His personal revelation of Himself to a soul in quickening power, whereby He becomes an awe-inspiring but blessed reality. All uncertainty as to *whether* He is or as to *what* He is, is now at an end. That revelation of God creates in the soul a panting after Him, a longing to know more of Him, a yearning to be more fully conformed to Him.

It is not so much increasing in the vital or even the devotional knowledge of God of which our text speaks but rather what that issues in, which, for want of a better term, we designate the practical knowledge of God. The passage before us in Colossians 1:10 is very similar to that word of Christ's "If any man will do his will, he shall know of the doctrine" (John 7:17). As the Christian is in earnest about walking becomingly of the Lord, and as he is diligent in performing good works, he discovers by practical experience the wisdom and kindness of God in framing such a rule for him to walk by. He obtains personal proof of "that good, and acceptable, and perfect, will of God" (Rom. 12:2) and is brought into a closer and more steady communion with Him, and procures a deeper appreciation of His excellence. "Then shall we know, if we follow on to know the LORD" (Hosea 6:3). This is both the appointed way and means for such attainment. If we perform the prescribed duty, we shall receive the promised blessing; if we tread the path of obedience, we shall be rewarded by an increasing and soul-satisfying knowledge of the excellence of our Master.

The School of Christ

This knowledge cannot be acquired by art or taught us by men, no, not even by the ablest "Bible teachers." It can be learned nowhere but in the school of Christ, by practicing His precepts and being fruitful in every good work. Yet this increase in the knowledge of God does not follow automatically upon our performing good works, but only as God Himself is sought—a matter of first moment although frequently overlooked. As there were those who followed Christ during the days of His flesh for the loaves and fishes or because they were eager to witness His miracles, and not because their hearts were set upon Him, so there are some in the religious world today who are active in various forms of good works, yet they do not perform them out of love for or gratitude to Christ. The good works of the Christian must not only be wrought by faith which works by love, but his aim in doing them must be the glory of God. That should be our chief design and end in all duties and ordinances—in reading the Word or in hearing it preached, in prayer, and in every act of obedience: not to rest in the good works, but to learn more of God in them, through them, and from them.

The greatest need and the genuine longing of every regenerate soul is to increase in the knowledge of God. Yet most are slow in discovering the way in which their longing may be realized. Too many turn from the simple and practical to bewilder themselves by that which is mystical and mysterious. It should be obvious to even the babe in Christ that if he forsakes the paths of righteousness he is forsaking God Himself. To know God better we must cleave more to Him, walk closer with Him. Communion with God can only be had in the highway of holiness. The previous clauses of Colossians 1:10 reveal what is required from us in order to gain an increasing knowledge of God. If we are diligent and earnest in seeking to walk worthily of the Lord and to please Him in all things, being fruitful in every good work, the outcome will be a more intimate fellowship with Him, a better acquaintance with His character, an experimental realization that His commandments "are not grievous," daily proofs of His tender patience with our infirmities, and fuller discoveries of Himself to us. "He that hath my commandments, and keepeth them, he is it that loveth me . . . and I will love him, and will *manifest* myself to him" (John 14:21). God manifests His delight toward those who delight in Him.

This increasing in the practical knowledge of God is more an intensive thing than an extensive one: that is to say, it is not adding to our store of information about Him but becoming more experimentally acquainted and being powerfully affected with what is already known of Him. It consists not in further discoveries of God's perfections, as in a livelier appreciation of them. As the Christian earnestly seeks to walk with Him in His ways, he obtains a growing acquaintance with God's grace in inspiring him, His power in supporting, His faithfulness in renewing, His mercy in restoring, His wisdom in devising, and His love in appointing a course wherein such pleasure is found and whose paths are all peace. This is indeed practical and profitable knowledge. The more we know of God in *this* way, the more we shall love Him, trust in Him, pray to Him, depend upon Him. But such knowledge is not acquired in a day, nor fully attained in a few short years. We grow into it gradually, little by little, as we make use of both the divine precepts and promises, and from a desire to please and glorify Him, and with the design of having communion with Him.

Chapter 23

PRAYER FOR LONG-SUFFERING

COLOSSIANS 1:11-12

"STRENGTHENED WITH ALL MIGHT, according to his glorious power, unto all patience and longsuffering with joyfulness" (v. 11). This is the third petition of the prayer, and we will begin our remarks upon it by pointing out its *relation* to those preceding it, particularly verse 10. First, it seems to us that whereas verse 10 treats more of the *active* side of the Christian life, verse 11 has more definitely in view its *passive* side. Or, to express it in another way, whereas the former intimates the use we should make of communicated grace in a way of *doing*, this teaches us how to improve that grace in a way of *suffering*. And is not this usually the order in which divine providence affords the saint occasion to discharge each of those responsibilities? When the Christian is young and vigorous, those graces which are expressed in the performing of good works are afforded their fullest opportunity. But as natural strength and youthful zeal abate, as trials and infirmities increase, there is a call for another set of graces to be exercised, namely, patience and long-suffering. Even in old age, or even while lying upon a bed of sickness and helplessness, the Christian walks worthily of the Lord unto all pleasing if he meekly bears his appointed lot and does not murmur. And certainly he is bearing fruit to the glory of God if he endures his trials cheerfully and is "longsuffering with joyfulness."

The Consequence of "Walking Worthy of the Lord"

But we may trace a yet closer relation between the two verses. If by grace the child of God is enabled to walk worthy of the Lord, pleasing Him well, being fruitful in every good work, what is certain to be the consequence? He will not only increase in the practical knowledge of God but also incur the hatred of his fellowmen. The closer he cleaves to the standard set before him, the more conscientious he is about wholly following the Lord, the more he will stir up the enmity of the flesh, the world, and the devil. The more he endeavors to deny self and be out and out for Christ, the more opposition he will encounter, especially from those who profess but do not possess, who detest none so much as those whose uncompromising strictness exposes and condemns their vain pretensions. Yes, young Christian, you must be fully prepared for this and expect nothing else. The closer you walk with Christ the more you will be persecuted.

And what does such opposition, such hatred, such persecution and affliction call for from us? What will enable us to stand our ground and keep us from lowering the banner? What but being "strengthened with all might, according to his glorious power, unto all patience and longsuffering with joyfulness"?

Knowledge of God Through Obedience to His Precepts

Finally, a still closer connection may be seen in linking the closing clause of verse 10 with what follows in verse 11: "increasing in the knowledge of God; strengthened with all might, according to his glorious power, unto all patience and longsuffering with joyfulness." This will be the more apparent as we bear in mind the particular kind of "knowledge of God" which is spoken of here: not one that is obtained by theological study and reasoning, nor even by meditative devotions, but rather one which is acquired *through obedience* to His precepts. The order of the Greek—"increasing in the knowledge of God: with all might being strengthened"—makes this still clearer: the latter follows upon the former. Those who have schooled themselves to heed God's commandments will find it far easier than others do to submit themselves to His providential will. Those who have lived to please God rather than themselves are the ones least likely to be stumbled by afflictions, and are the last to sink in despair under them. Those who are zealous of good works will possess their souls with patience in adversity and cheerfully endure when the enemy rages against them.

We are the losers if we do not pay the closest attention to the *order* of the petitions in the prayers of the apostle and the *relation* of one petition to the other; for we not only fail to perceive their real import but miss valuable lessons for our spiritual lives. Those who cursorily scan them instead of giving them prolonged meditation rob their own souls. Many Christians bemoan their lack of "patience" under affliction. These must be startled if not staggered by weighing this expression, "longsuffering with joyfulness." Yet how few of them are aware of the reason why they are strangers to such an experience. That cause is here plainly revealed: it is due to the fact that they have been so little "strengthened with all might according to his glorious power." And that, in turn, is because they have "increased" so little "in the knowledge of God," i.e., that personal *proving* of the goodness, the acceptableness, and the perfection of the will of God (Rom. 12:1), which is obtained through obediently walking with Him, making a point of pleasing Him in all things, and "being fruitful in every good work." Failure in the *practical* side of our Christian lives explains why our "experience" is so unsatisfactory.

"Strengthened with all might, according to his glorious power, unto all patience and longsuffering with joyfulness" (v. 11). It will appear to some of our readers that we are drawing out this series to a wearisome length, but others will be thankful to find in them something more profitable than the brief and superficial generalizations which characterize most of the religious literature of this day. Our aim in them is to not only furnish bare expositions of the passages before us but to foster a spirit of devotion and provide that which will be of practical use in the daily life of the Christian. Take this present verse as an example. It is indeed important that the reader should obtain a correct idea of the terms used in it, yet he needs much more than that. To supply a full and lucid definition of what "patience" is, and then to exhort one who is in acutely trying circumstances to exercise that grace, will be of little real help. To tell him to pray for an increase of it is saying nothing more than he already knows. But to point out *how* patience is worked and increased in us, *what* are the means for the development of it and the things which hinder—in short, what God requires from us in order to increase its growth—will surely be more to the point.

What the Apostle Prays For

First, the apostle prays that the saints might be "strengthened with all might, according to his glorious power." Such language implies that it was not ordinary strength for which he here asked, but rather unusual "glorious power" for the particular task in view. His language argues that he had in mind an exercise of grace more difficult than any other, one from which our constitutions are so naturally remote that more than ordinary diligence and earnestness must be put forth by us at the mercy seat in obtaining this urgently needed supply. Every act of grace by us must have an act of divine power going before it to draw it forth into exercise. As the "work of faith" is "with power" (II Thess. 1:11), so the work of faith to bear afflictions requires divine strengthening of the soul; and to acquit ourselves with "*all* patience and longsuffering with joyfulness" necessitates our being "strengthened with all might, according to his glorious power."

To be "strengthened with all might" signifies to be mightily strengthened, to be given a supply of grace amply sufficient for the end in view. It means spiritual energy proportioned to whatever is needed, with all the believer may have occasion for, to enable him to discharge his duty and carry himself in a manner pleasing and honoring to God. "According to his glorious power" implies both the excellence and sufficiency of it. The glory of God's power is most seen when it appears as *overcoming* power, when victory attends it, as when we read that "Christ was raised up from the dead by the *glory* of the Father" (Rom. 6:4). Thus the apostle sets over against our utter weakness the "all might" of divine grace, and "his glorious power" against our sinful corruption. The special use to which this strength was to be put is "unto all patience," that is, sufficient for the enduring of all trials; and "longsuffering" would be patience drawn out to its greatest length; "with joyfulness" signifies not only submitting to trials without repining, but doing so gladly, rejoicing in the Lord always. This third petition, then, was for a supply of grace that would enable the saints to bear all trials with meek subjection, persevering constancy, and cheerfulness of spirit.

Help Available as Needed

Again we see what an exalted standard of conduct is set before us, yet at the same time what blessed supplies of help are available. Do not say such a standard is utterly unattainable when the Lord declares, "My grace is sufficient for thee"—sufficient not only to enable you to endure "a thorn in the flesh, the messenger of Satan to buffet" but also to make you resolve, "Most gladly therefore will I rather glory in my infirmities, that the power of Christ may rest upon me" (II Cor. 12:7, 9). Do not look in unbelief on either the number or might of your enemies or on your own weakness, but in the confidence of humble but expectant faith say, "I can do all things through Christ which strengtheneth me" (Phil. 4:13). Is not this "glorious strength" indeed, which enables its recipients to persevere in the path of duty notwithstanding much opposition, to bear up manfully under trials, yes, to rejoice in tribulations? What a glorious power is this which is proportioned to all we are called upon to do and suffer, enabling us to resist the corruptions of the flesh, the allurements of the world, and the temptations of the devil; which keeps us from sinking into abject despair or making shipwreck of the faith; which causes us to hold our course to the end.

How is "all might" secured? Some would say it is by no endeavor of ours; we in our helplessness can do no more in obtaining grace for the soul than the parched ground can do in causing refreshing showers to descend from heaven; we must submit to God's sovereign determination and hope for the best. But that is a denial of the Christian's responsibility. God indeed asks nothing from the ground, for it is an inanimate and irrational creature. But it is far different with moral agents—the more so when He has regenerated them. "For unto whomsoever much is given, of him shall much be required" (Luke 12:48). And much *has* been given to the one born of God: Christ is his in the forgiveness of sins, the Holy Ghost indwells him, life has been communicated to his soul, faith imparted to his heart; and therefore much may justly be required of him. Grace is not some mysterious influence which fortuitously descends and enters into the Christian's heart irrespective of how he acts. The opening word of our verse intimates the opposite, for "strengthening" implies God's blessing on our use of suitable means—whether it is the strengthening of the body, the mind, or the spiritual life. Observe, the first (though not the only) means is an earnest and importunate crying to God.

The Believer's Privilege and Duty

It is both our privilege and our duty to "come boldly [or freely] unto the throne of grace, that we may obtain mercy [for past failures], and find grace to help in time of need" (Heb. 4:16). Often we have not because we ask not, or because we ask amiss. Grace must be sought believingly, fervently, perseveringly. Moreover, there has to be a daily feeding on "the word of his grace" (Acts 20:32) if the soul is to be "nourished up in the words of faith" (I Tim. 4:6). If we neglect our daily bread, fail to meditate on and appropriate a regular supply of manna, we soon become feeble and faint. Further, exercise is essential: we must *use* the grace already given us if we would obtain more (Luke 8:18). Spiritual strength is not given to release us from the fight of faith, but to furnish and fit us for the same. Grace is not bestowed on the Christian in order that heaven may be won without engaging in a fierce conflict, as many seem to think, but in order that the believer may be "strong in the Lord, and in the power of his might." Therefore he is urged to put on the whole armor of God and thus be able to stand against "the wiles of the devil" (Eph. 6:10-11). We are strengthened with all might "unto [for this end] all patience."

The Particular Kind of Patience in View

We must now inquire into the nature of patience, or, more specifically, the particular kind of patience which is here in view. It is a steady persisting in duty which keeps one from being deterred by opposition or fainting under suffering. Actively, it finds expression in perseverance, or refusing to quit the race because of the difficulties or length of the course. Passively, it appears in a meek and quiet spirit, which endures afflictions without complaining. Primarily, though perhaps not exclusively, it is the latter that is spoken of here, namely, that frame of heart which bears submissively whatever trials and tribulations the Lord calls one to pass through. It is very much more than a placidity of temper which is not unduly provoked by the common irritations of life, for often that is more a matter of healthy nerves than a virtuous exercise of the mind and will. Grace is more potent than nature: it can make the timid courageous, cool the most hotheaded, quiet the impetuous. Grace works submissiveness in the most impulsive. It makes our hearts calm when outward circumstances are tempestuous, and though God lets loose His winds upon us, He can keep us from being discomposed by them and lay the same command upon our passions as upon the angry waves: "Peace, be still" (Mark 4:39).

The Grace of Patience

Patience is not stoical apathy toward the divine dispensations. It is no narcotic virtue to stupefy us and take away the sense and feeling of afflictions. If it had any such opiate quality, there would be nothing commendable or praiseworthy in it. That is not suffering which is not felt; and if patience deprived us of the feeling of sorrow, it would cease to be patience. We have witnessed the mass of our fellowmen stupefied and insensible under the hand of God, taking no notice of Him when His judgments fell heavily upon them, enduring them with stolidity, or rather moral stupidity; but the senseless boast "We can take it" was no more patience than is the non-writhing of a block of wood when it is sawed and planed. Patience quickens the sufferings of the saint, for he refers the sufferings to his deserts. Consciousness of his sins in provoking God pierces his conscience and brings pain to his inner man also. But the wicked look only upon *what* they suffer, and make no reflection upon their deserts.

Nor does the grace of patience stifle all modest complaints and moderate sorrow. A patient Christian is permitted this vent through which his grief may find relief. Grace does not destroy but regulates and corrects nature. God allows His children to shed tears so long as the course of them does not stir up the mud of their sinful passions and violent affections. It is not wrong to complain about what we suffer so long as we do not complain against God from whom we suffer. We may lawfully, and without any breach of patience, express our grief in all outward and natural signs of it so long as that agitation does not exceed its due bounds and measures. Job, who is commended to us as the great example of patience, when he received the sad news of the loss of his estate and his children, "rent his mantle and fell down upon the ground" (Job 1:20). And that we might not regard this as a display of impatience, the Spirit

1as added, "In all this Job sinned not, nor charged God foolishly" (Job 1:22).
The disciples made "great lamentation" over Stephen (Acts 8:2), though by
1is martyrdom he had greatly glorified God. It is not grief but the excess of
t which is disallowed.

Patience in Affliction

Nor does patience oblige us to continue in afflictions when we may warrant-
ably free ourselves from them. The eminent Puritan, Ezekiel Hopkins, rightly
pointed out that when God sends heavy afflictions our way, we ought to, for
principles of self-preservation, try to free ourselves from them; otherwise we
sin against nature and God. Generally, whatever calamity we experience, it is
1ot patience but obstinacy to refuse deliverance when we can obtain it without
violating our duty or dishonoring God.

Positively, patience consists of a willing submission to the dispensations of
divine providence. When Job said, "Shall we receive good at the hand of God,
and shall we not receive evil?" (Job 2:10), that was the language of patience.
"The cup which my Father hath given me, shall I not drink it?" (John 18:11)
was the supreme example of this grace. It is the ready acquiescence of the soul
to whatever God sees fit to lay upon it. It is the calm enduring of provocation
and persecution, especially trial which comes unexpectedly. It is a steady and
thankful bearing of all troubles, however grievous and long protracted, mortifying the opposite passions of fear, anger, anxiety, inordinate grief; refusing to be
overwhelmed by those troubles, persevering in the discharge of duty to the end;
relieving oneself by faith in what is to be had in God by communion with
Him: resting in His love, leaning on His arms, and encouraging oneself by
expectation of that eternal and blessed glory which awaits us after our appointed
race is run.

What Patience Does

Patience consists of tranquilizing or composing our minds, which issues in
the quieting of our unruly passions. Very impatient persons who fret and fume
within may express little emotion outwardly. That impatience which finds no
external vent is the most injurious and dangerous to character, just as latent
fevers, which lurk within and prey upon the body, may do much harm although
they are not outwardly evident. Patience calms those storms and tempests
which are apt to rise in the heart when a person is under any sore and heavy
affliction. The emotions will be stirred, but this grace takes away the violence
of them. All those turbulences and uproars of passions, all those willful and
wild emotions which distract reason and rend the soul, making us unfit for
the service of God or the employment of our business—these patience ought to
quell, and in measure suppress. He who can rule his body better than his soul,
his actions than his passions, lacks the principal part of patience.

All this must be done upon *right grounds*. This requires us to distinguish
sharply between natural and Christian patience. There is a natural patience
sometimes found in those devoid of true grace: such strength of character,
fortitude of mind, tranquillity of spirit, which often puts the people of God to
shame. Yet that is only a moral virtue, proceeding only from natural and moral

principles. How is the Christian who naturally is impulsive, fiery, fickle, to ascertain whether his patience is of a superior order? By the principles from which it proceeds, the motives actuating it, and the ends for which it is put forth. Moral virtue proceeds only from the principles of reason, is actuated by such arguments as human prudence furnishes, and is exercised to promote self-esteem or the respect of our fellowmen. Many an unregenerate person, by a process of self-discipline, has hardened himself to bear the evils which befall him by persuading himself it is folly to rebel against fate and torment himself over the inevitable, telling himself that what cannot be cured must be endured, that to give way to peevishness is childish and will effect no good, and that to yield to a spirit of fury will only lower him in the eyes of others.

But spiritual patience proceeds from a principle of grace, is actuated by higher motives, and is induced by greatly superior considerations than those which regulate the most refined and self-controlled unregenerate person. Spiritual patience springs from faith (James 1:3) and from hope (Rom. 8:25). Patience eyes the sovereignty of God, to which it is our duty to submit. It eyes His benevolence and is assured that the most painful affliction is among the "all things" He is making work together for our good. It looks off from the absolute nature of the affliction, considered in itself, to the relative nature of it, as it is dispensed to us by God, and therefore concludes that though the cup is bitter, in our Father's hand it is salutary. Though the chastisement itself is grievous, patience realizes it will make us partakers of God's holiness here and of His glory hereafter. Patience eyes the example Christ left us and seeks grace to be conformed to it. The Christian strives to exercise patience not out of self-esteem, because he is mortified when his passions get the better of him, but from a desire to please God and glorify Him.

The careful reader will find in the last three paragraphs several hints on those *means* which are best suited to promote and strengthen patience, such as faith, hope, love. But we will mention one or two others among which we place high the complete resigning of ourselves to God. Since most outbursts of impatience are occasioned by the crossing of our wills, it behooves each Christian to daily ascertain how fully his will is surrendered to God, and to be diligent in cultivating a spirit of submission to Him. While complete yieldedness to God does not include reducing of ourselves as serfs to our fellowmen, still less the condoning of the wrongs they have done, yet it does require us to be not unduly occupied with the instruments of our afflictions, but rather to look beyond them to Him who has some good reason for using them to stir up our nests.

God's Infinite Patience and Faithfulness

Meditate frequently upon the patience of God. What infinite patience He exercises toward us! He bears far more from us than we can possibly bear from Him. He bears with our sins whereas we bear only His chastisement, and sin is infinitely more opposite to His nature than suffering is to ours. If He is so long-suffering with our innumerable offenses, how inexcusable it is for us to fret and murmur at the least correction from His hand! Meditating on the faithfulness of God helps us to bear trials with more fortitude. There is no condition which needs more promises and there is none which has so many promises attending it as suffering and persecution. God has promised support under it (Ps. 55:22), His presence in it (Isa. 43:2), deliverance from it (I Cor. 10:13). He is faithful to His Word. Ponder His wisdom and goodness and you will find sufficient reason to acquiesce to His providences. If afflictions came by blind chance, we might indeed bemoan our hard fate; but since they are appointed by our omniscient and loving Father, they must be for our gain.

The more we set our hearts and hopes on creature enjoyments, the more bitter is our disappointment when they fail us or are taken away. Jonah was "exceeding glad" for the gourd which the Lord prepared to shade and shelter him (Jonah 4:6), but he was "angry, even unto death" (Jonah 4:9) when it withered away. This is recorded for our warning! If you immoderately value any earthly comfort, you will immoderately chafe at its removal. Pride is another enemy to patience. So is effeminate softness.

We will return to the subject of patience when we reach II Thessalonians 3:5. As for "longsuffering," the term defines itself, signifying a prolongation of patience to the end of the trial. Yet in view of the connections in which those terms are found, we may distinguish between them thus: "patience" looks more to the attitude of the heart Godward while we are being tried; "longsuffering" respects our attitude toward the instruments which He makes use of in the trial. Thus, "longsuffering" includes the ideas of being slow to anger with those who persecute or afflict us, meekly bearing for Christ's sake those injuries which His enemies inflict on us, refusing to retaliate when we are oppressed, following the example of our Master "who, when he was reviled, reviled not again" (I Peter 2:23).

Chapter 24

PRAYER FOR JOY AND THANKFULNESS

COLOSSIANS 1:11-12

"PATIENCE AND LONGSUFFERING WITH JOYFULNESS" now calls for consideration. "My brethren, count it all joy when ye fall into divers temptations [or 'trials']" (James 1:2). Someone will say that is asking an impossibility, that we cannot conjure up joy by any effort of will; only the Lord can produce rapture in a heart. But joy is not a thing apart, unrelated to the faculties of the soul, unconnected with the state of the mind. I cannot command the sun to appear, but when it *is* shining, I can retire into the shade and there sulk in my chilliness. So too the heart may turn away from the Sun of righteousness and, instead of dwelling upon His love and loveliness, occupy the mind with gloomy objects and subjects. The Christian is just as responsible to be joyous in adversity as in prosperity, when the devil rages against him as when he leaves him in peace for a season; and he will do so if his mind is properly employed and his heart delights itself in the Lord.

None of the empty pleasures of this world afford any solid happiness. As the natural man passes from childhood to old age, he changes his toys, only to discover that no gratification of his senses yields any real satisfaction. Neither sorrow nor joy is caused by environment or circumstance; nor is joy to be found in any creature. "Although the fig tree shall not blossom, neither shall fruit be in the vines, . . . the fields shall yield no meat; the flock shall be cut off from the fold, and there shall be no herd in the stalls"—what then? Will I deplore the situation and make myself wretched by contemplating a death of starvation? No indeed! "Yet I will *rejoice* in the LORD, I will joy in the God of my salvation" (Hab. 3:17-18). Note well that "I will" of personal resolution. As the king may be miserable in his palace (I Kings 21:5-6; Eccl. 2:1-11), so the manacled and bleeding occupants of the dungeon may sing praises (Acts 16:25). While sorrowing over things around us, we may continually rejoice (II Cor. 6:10).

James 1:2 does not exhort us to rejoice in the trials as such, but by an act of spiritual judgment to regard them as joyous. James here gives three reasons why Christians should do so. "Knowing this [being fully persuaded of it] that the trying of your faith worketh patience." Some facts there included should mightily further our joy. First, all our sufferings and afflictions are for the trial of faith, and that is a great privilege. If we were possessed of more spiritual discernment, we should readily perceive that as the *communication* of saving

252

grace to a soul is the greatest blessing which can be bestowed in this world, so the testing of that grace, exercised and drawn forth to the glory of God, is the next greatest mercy. For that grace to approve itself to God in a manner well pleasing to Him, is a matter of vast moment. So the genuineness of my faith being made manifest by overcoming the world in esteeming the reproach of Christ greater riches than the "treasures of Egypt"; by valuing the smile of God more than fearing the frowns of men; by firmly enduring persecution when others fall away (Matt. 13:21), should bring much comfort to my soul.

Trials Needed for Proving of Faith

Second, this trying of faith "worketh patience." Trials are not only designed for the approving of faith but for faith's fruitage, i.e., that it may yield its peaceable fruits. The more faith enables us to truly rest in the Lord and stand our ground in afflictions, the more we become inured to and patient under them. As faith draws out the heart to God and stays the mind upon Him, the soul is brought into a more sober attitude and more cordially acquiesces to the divine will. Faith brings home to the heart the dominion which God has over a man's person and life, and this quiets evil uprisings against Him. Faith assures the heart of the love of God and its investment in Him, and that strengthens the believer in the greatest distresses. When Ziklag was burned, David's goods plundered, and his wives carried away by the Philistines, he "encouraged himself in the LORD *his* God" (I Sam. 30:6). The more a Christian bears meekly but perseveringly, the more he is enabled to *bear*. The muscles of his graces become stronger by use. If trials produce such fruits, ought we not to rejoice in them!

Third, "Blessed [or 'happy'] is the man that endureth temptation." Why? "For when he is tried, he shall receive the crown of life" (James 1:12). That is the reward given to the victor in the day to come. In that happy expectation the soul may count it all joy that he is now being afflicted and persecuted. The object of his rejoicing is not his sufferings, for they, considered in themselves, are grievous, but rather the result of them. Paul reminded the Hebrews, "Ye . . . took joyfully the spoiling of your goods, knowing in yourselves that ye have in heaven a better and an enduring substance" (Heb. 10:34). Thus it was with the Saviour Himself: "Who for *the joy* that was set before him endured the cross" (Heb. 12:2). And thus He assured His followers, "Blessed are ye, when men shall revile you, and persecute you, and shall say all manner of evil against you falsely, for my sake: *rejoice*, and be exceeding glad: for great is your reward in heaven" (Matt. 5:11-12). When we "glory in tribulations" (Rom. 5:3)—because we realize the advantages which will accrue both here and hereafter—we are "more than conquerors" (Rom. 8:37).

Petition and Praise to Be United

"Giving thanks unto the Father, which hath made us meet to be partakers of the inheritance of the saints in light" (v. 12). This is the closing section of our prayer. Notice that in it the apostle exemplifies his exhortation: "Be anxious for nothing; but in everything by prayer and supplication *with thanksgiving* let your requests be made known unto God" (Phil. 4:6). When we come to the throne of grace, petition and praise should always accompany each other. There should be the thanksgiving of grateful love for mercies already received: of confident faith in God's promises, that He will certainly bestow the things for which we now ask, so far as to do so will be for His glory and our highest good; of joyous expectation of the things which He has prepared for us on high. The general relation of this verse to those preceding is apparent. The being "filled with the knowledge of his will in all wisdom and spiritual understanding" (v. 9) is to find expression in a worthy walk (v. 10), in the exercise of patient endurance (v. 11), and in grateful thanksgiving (v. 12).

The *order* of those things is not only according to the Analogy of Faith but it is verified in the experience of the saints in the several stages of their growth in grace. A knowledge of God's will (as made known in the Word) most engages the attention of the babe in Christ who is conscious of his ignorance. As the Spirit graciously opens the Scriptures to his understanding and applies them to his heart, he becomes more concerned with honoring the Lord in his daily walk and being fruitful in every good work. As he grows still older and meets with more trials and tribulations, he has an increasing realization of his need for being divinely strengthened so that he may not faint beneath the burdens of life and the difficulties of the way; that he may not become weary in well doing but run the race set before him, and meekly submit to all the dispensations of God's providence. Finally, as he approaches the end of his journey he is more and more occupied with the glorious inheritance awaiting him wherein he will be done forever with sin and suffering. The more joyful he is (v. 11) the more he will be filled with the spirit of thanksgiving.

The order of these things here also inculcates, in a most searching manner, an important practical lesson. This giving of thanks to the Father does not occur at the beginning of the prayer but at its close. Thereby it is intimated that none of us is warranted in concluding that he is among the number whom He has made "meet to be partakers of the inheritance of the saints" unless the things previously mentioned are in some measure really found in him. It would be highly presumptuous for me to complacently assume that I am fit for heaven *unless* I am sincerely endeavoring to walk worthy of the Lord, pleasing Him in all things, being fruitful in every good work, and unless I possess my soul with patience and long-suffering, and rejoice when I am persecuted for Christ's sake. Not that these things are qualifications for heaven, but rather the evidences that divine grace has suitably fashioned my soul for it. Not that these things are the procuring cause for which I shall enter the glory. They are but the marks that God has already wrought in me for the glory.

God Has "Made Us Meet"

It is equally necessary that we note carefully the tense of the verb here. It is not a promise that God *will* make us meet for the inheritance, nor is the reference to a present process that He is now *making* us meet. Some pastors in their presentation of what is termed "progressive sanctification" have handled it in a very legal manner and brought many of God's people into cruel bondage thereby. This confusion appears in such expressions as being "meetened for glory," "ripened for heaven." Few indeed make use of this prayer in giving thanks to the Father because He *has already* made them "meet" for the inheritance.

Believers Are "Complete in Him"

Our present verse brings before us a subject of vital moment and practical importance, although one of which most of God's children today are sadly ignorant. Many of them who ought to be rejoicing in the liberty of the gospel are enthralled in some form of legal bondage. Comparatively few of them are exulting in the self-abasing and soul-satisfying consciousness that they are *"complete* in him" who is their Head (Col. 2:10). If the only consequences of this were the disturbing of their peace and the overcasting of their joy, such evils would call for an earnest effort to correct them. In addition, the absence of such assurance (which is their legitimate portion) dishonors the Lord, cramps their energies, obscures their graces, and renders their spiritual state uncertain both to themselves and to others.

One form of this evil is found even in many who have a clear knowledge of the ground on which God justifies the ungodly. They claim that after a person has tasted of the blessedness of "the man whose transgression is forgiven, whose sin is covered" (Ps. 32:1), there remains much to be done before the soul is ready to enter his eternal rest. They hold that after his justification the believer must undergo a process of sanctification, and for this reason he is left for a time amid the trials and conflicts of a hostile world. The prevalence of this notion appears in much preaching, many hymns, and especially in prayers; for while many Christians may be frequently heard pleading to be made fit, rarely indeed do we hear one giving thanks to the Father because He *has* made us fit for the inheritance of the saints. Those laboring under such an impression can never know when the process is completed, nor can they say with any confidence to a dying man, "Believe on the Lord Jesus Christ, and thou shalt be saved" (Acts 16:31) here and now, for it would flatly contradict their own ideas.

One would suppose that those toiling under this view must be staggered by their own experience and observation. They see those whom they confidently regard as Christians cut off in apparently very different stages of this process, and if the contemplation of it is what is styled "perfect sanctification," then in how few cases, so far as we can perceive, is any such preparation for glory actually attained! On their deathbeds the most eminent saints confess themselves thoroughly dissatisfied with their attainments! Yet many who deem themselves the most orthodox insist that while justification is an act completed at once, "sanctification is a progressive work." If by that expression they mean growth in grace and the manifestation of it in this life, there can be no objection; but if it means a preparation for heaven, and that such preparation is to be the grand object of the believer's life, the expression should be rejected as a God-dishonoring and soul-enslaving error—a flat contradiction of the text before us.

Three Indispensable Qualifications for Heaven

These three things (none others or any more) are indispensable to qualify any sinner for heaven. First, he must be predestinated by the Father, which was effected "on the vessels of mercy, which he had afore [by His eternal decree] prepared unto glory" (Rom. 9:23). Second, he must have a valid legal right and title to the inheritance. The believing sinner has this in the merits of Christ, who by His one offering "hath perfected for ever them that are sanctified" (Heb. 10:14). Third, he must be experimentally fitted for the kingdom of God by the regenerating act of the Holy Spirit. As the natural babe is born complete in parts (though not in development), so that no new member or faculty can be added—though the members are capable of expansion, with a fuller expression and clearer manifestation—so it is with the spiritual babe in Christ. "He that hath wrought us for the selfsame thing [i.e., the glory to come (see context)] is God who hath also given us the earnest [or 'proof'] of the Spirit" (II Cor. 5:5).

The work of God the Spirit in regeneration is eternally complete. It needs no increase or decrease. It is the same in all believers. There will not be the least addition to it in heaven: not one grace, holy affection, or disposition which is not in it *now*. The whole of the Spirit's work, from the moment of regeneration to our glorification, is to draw out those graces into actual exercise which He has worked in us. And though one believer may abound in the fruits of righteousness more than another, not one of them is more regenerate than another. This work of the Spirit, in which our worthiness for the eternal fruition of God consists, is alike in every one that is born of the Spirit. The dying babe in Christ is as capable of high communion with God as Paul in the state of glory.

Our worthiness for heaven is evidenced by the very terms here used. First, it is called an "inheritance," and that is not something we purchase by good works, nor procure by self-denial and mortification. Rather it is that to which we lawfully succeed by our relationship to another. Primarily, it is that to which a child succeeds because of his relation to his father, as the crown which the son of an earthly king inherits. In this case the inheritance is ours by virtue of our being the *sons* of God, which we become actually at the new birth. "If children, then heirs; heirs of God, and joint-heirs with Christ" (Rom. 8:16-17). The next verse (Col. 1:13) tells us what this "inheritance" is: "the kingdom of his [God's] dear Son" into which we are already translated. Joint heirs with Christ must share His kingdom. He has *now* "made us kings and priests unto God" (Rev. 1:6).

Second, it is the "inheritance of the saints." Christians are saints from the first moment they savingly believe in Christ, for they are then sanctified or sainted by the very blood which procured their forgiveness (Heb. 13:12). Every Christian was sanctified essentially when he was anointed by the Spirit, whether we regard it as separation from those dead in sin, consecration to God, or sanctification by renewal in His image. Third, it is "the inheritance of the saints *in light*." We were "made meet" for it when by the new birth we became "the children of light" (I Thess. 5:5). At that time we were "delivered from the power of darkness" and called "into his [God's] marvellous light" (I Peter 2:9). By nature we were totally unfit for the inheritance, but by the gracious operation of the Spirit we are now fit for it, for He has made us sons, heirs.

The True Believer Fit for Heaven

It is indeed a monstrous absurdity to deny their fitness for the heavenly inheritance of whom God declares, "But ye are washed, but *ye are sanctified*, but ye are justified in the name of the Lord Jesus, and by the Spirit of our God" (I Cor. 6:11); whom "now hath he reconciled" (Col. 1:21), "made nigh by the blood of Christ" (Eph. 2:13), indwelt by His Spirit, delighted in as His sons; and to whom He says, "All things are your's" (I Cor. 3:21). Spurgeon rightly affirmed, "The true believer is fit for heaven now, at this very moment. That does not mean he is sinless, but that he has been accepted in the Beloved, adopted into the Family, and fitted by Divine approbation to dwell with the saints in light." No refining process of discipline, no preparation on our part, no progressive sanctification or growth in grace is necessary in order to fit a babe in Christ for Paradise. This truth is conclusively shown by the case of the dying thief, who in the *first day* of his saving faith was immediately translated from the convict's gibbet to the inheritance of the saints in light.

Why does God leave the Christian in this world for a season if he is already fit for heaven? For His own glory. As a monument of His mercy, an example of His distinguishing love, a witness of His sufficient grace, a proof of His faithfulness in bearing with his infirmities and supplying all his need. To give him an opportunity to honor Him in the place where he had so dishonored Him. To serve as salt in a corrupt community.

Let every Christian reader fervently thank the Father for *having* fitted him for eternal glory. The sloughing off of "the flesh" at death is not a qualification for heaven but the removal of a disqualification.

Chapter 25

PRAYER FOR BROTHERLY LOVE

I Thessalonians 3:11-13

"Now GOD HIMSELF and [even] our Father, and our Lord Jesus Christ, direct our way unto you. And the Lord make you to increase and abound in love one toward another, and toward all . . . [saints], even as we do toward you: to the end he may stablish your hearts unblameable in holiness before God, even our Father, at the coming of our Lord Jesus Christ with all his saints." There are five things which call for our consideration in connection with this prayer. First, its *setting:* it is necessary to ponder what is said in the foregoing verses in order to appreciate the request in verse 11. Second, its *intensity,* intimated in the phrase "night and day praying exceedingly that we might see your face" (v. 10). Third, its *objects:* God the Father and His Son in His mediatorial character (v. 11). Fourth, its *petitions,* which are two in number (vv. 11-12). Fifth, its *design:* that their hearts might be established "unblameable in holiness before God" (v. 13). May the Holy Spirit act as our Guide while we endeavor to fill in that outline.

At an early date in his ministerial labors Paul, accompanied by Silas and the youthful Timothy, visited Thessalonica (now called Salonika). Originally he had purposed to preach the gospel in Asia, but had been forbidden by the Spirit; then he sought to enter Bithynia, but again the Spirit of God checked him (Acts 16:6). Arriving at Troas the divine will was made known to the apostle by means of a vision in the night, wherein there appeared to him "a man from Macedonia" who besought him, "Come over into Macedonia and help us" (Acts 16:9). First, Paul and his companion made a very brief stay at Philippi where they were made a blessing to Lydia and her household. The enemy stirred up fierce opposition, which resulted in the beating of Paul and Silas and their being cast into prison; only for God to intervene by a miracle of grace, which eventuated in their release. From Philippi they came to Thessalonica where there was a synagogue of the Jews, which Paul entered and for three Sabbath days reasoned with them out of the Scriptures. Yet from a comparison of I Thessalonians 1:9 with Acts 17:1-10 it seems clear that the majority of those saved during this short sojourn in that city were Gentiles.

The Opposition of the Enemy

The enmity of the serpent was manifested at Thessalonica almost as bitterly as at Philippi, so that after a short stay there the brethren "sent away Paul

258

and Silas by night" (Acts 17:10). Nevertheless, brief as had been their visit, the Seed had been sown, the blessing of God had rested upon the preached Word, and an effectual testimony had been raised up to the glory of His great name. So much so that His servant declared to that infant church, "Ye were ensamples to all that believe in Macedonia and Achaia. From you sounded out the word of the Lord not only in Macedonia and Achaia, but also in every place your faith to God-ward is spread abroad" (I Thess. 1:7-8). What a grief it must have been to leave these young and unestablished converts, and how deeply Paul yearned to be with them again, appears in his statement "But we, brethren, being taken from you for a short time in presence, not in heart, endeavoured the more abundantly to see your face with great desire. Wherefore we would have come unto you, even I Paul, once and again; but Satan hindered us" (2:17-18).

Paul was no stoical fatalist who might reason that there was not any need for him to be concerned about the spiritual welfare of those babes in Christ, that since God had begun a good work in them He would assuredly carry it forward to completion. No, far from it. He was fearful that they might be stumbled at the opposition and be dismayed by the flight of His ambassador. Paul was uncertain whether their young faith could withstand such rude shocks. Therefore he sent one of his companions to inquire of their condition and to help them. "For this cause, when I could no longer forbear, I sent to know your faith, lest by some means the tempter have tempted you, and our labour be in vain" (3:5). Let our readers carefully ponder these words of the apostle and honestly ask themselves the meaning of this statement.

It is blessed to behold how God sets a balance to the trials and comforts of His people. The apostle was sorely exercised over the situation of those young believers, when God graciously afforded his heart relief. "But now when Timotheus came from you unto us, and brought us good tidings of your faith and charity, and that ye have good remembrance of us always, desiring greatly to see us, as we also to see you; therefore, brethren, we were comforted over you in all our affliction and distress by your faith" (vv. 6-7). How graciously God times His mercies! The good news brought by Timothy was just the cordial which the burdened soul of Paul now needed. But note the order in which he mentions the two things in verse 6. He does not place first their kindly remembrance of himself and their longing to see him again. No, rather he gives precedence to the favorable report supplied of their "faith and love"—*that* was for him the grand and principal item in the "glad tidings" of his messenger! How characteristic of this self-effacing herald of Christ! Those words, "your faith and love," were a brief but comprehensive expression of their spiritual case: if those graces were in healthy exercise, Paul knew there could be nothing seriously wrong with them.

Paul's Tender Affection for the Thessalonian Saints

"For now we live, if ye stand fast in the Lord. For what thanks can we render to God again for you, for all the joy wherewith we joy for your sakes before our God?" (vv. 8-9). How those words reveal again the spirit of the apostle! No mother's heart beats with more tender affection for her offspring than does that of the genuine evangelist or pastor for his own children in the faith. His delight lies in their spiritual progress: "my brethren dearly beloved and longed for, my joy and crown" (Phil. 4:1). Paul regarded his converts thus. Said another of the apostles, "I have no greater joy than to hear that my children walk in truth" (III John 4). Contrariwise, no mother suffers severer pangs of grief over the illness of her children or their waywardness when they have grown up than does a true servant of God as he witnesses the backsliding or apostasy of those who made a credible profession of faith under his ministry. So much then for the *setting* of our present passage, or the occasion of this prayer.

"Night and day praying exceedingly that we might see your face, and might perfect that which is lacking in your faith" (v. 10). The young Thessalonian Christians "desiring greatly to see" Paul and his party (v. 6) found an answering response in the hearts of Paul and his companions. The language which Paul here used indicates the *intensity* of his desire and the earnestness of his supplication. His praying was not cold and mechanical but earnest and persistent. The word here rendered "praying" means "beseeching," being the one employed in connection with the leper who, in his dire need and deep longing, "besought" the Lord to heal him (Luke 5:12). It is not the perfunctory nor the flowery petition which brings down answers from above but "the effectual *fervent* prayer of a righteous man" which "availeth much." Some are more occupied with their eloquence and the correctness of their grammar than they are with the frame of their spirit and the state of their heart—at which God ever looks. When the soul truly longs for a certain favor from God, the sincerity and intensity of that longing will be evinced not only by earnest crying unto Him but by importunity—asking, seeking, knocking "night and day" until the request is granted.

Real Prayer a Striving with God

Why are so much exertion and pains called for, seeing that God is fully acquainted with all our need and has promised to supply the same? First and foremost, for the exercise of our graces. God is pleased to try our faith and patience, for nothing more honors and pleases Him than to behold His people continuing to supplicate for that which He appears to deny them, as in the case of the Syrophenician woman (Matt. 15:28). Real praying is no child's play. Ponder that exhortation of the apostle's to the Roman saints: "Strive together with me in your prayers" (Rom. 15:30). This word is taken from the gymnastic contests, in which the combatants put forth their utmost strength. If we are to prevail with God, then we have to put forth all that is within us: we must stir up ourselves (Isa. 64:7) to lay hold of God. Again, this is recorded of Epaphras on behalf of the Colossians: "Always labouring fervently for you in prayers, that ye may stand perfect and complete in all the will of God" (4:12). Such praying cost Epaphras something! Yes, and such praying resulted in something!

Our Praying Sadly Defective

Is it not at this very point that our praying is so sadly defective? It is too mechanical and formal. Spiritual ardor, soul-exertion, reality are absent. Does someone reply, but it is not *my* prerogative to exercise faith or to supplicate acceptably and effectually when I will! I have no spiritual power of my own. We sometimes wonder what is meant by such language, and fear that in most cases it proceeds from a serious error, or else it is an idle excuse behind which dilatory souls seek to shelter. It is quite wrong for the Christian to suppose that he has less *spiritual* ability and strength than he has natural. The fact is that man, be he regenerate or unregenerate, is a dependent creature, wholly dependent upon his Maker for every breath he draws, every thought he thinks, every act he performs, spiritual or natural, for "in him we live, and move, and have our being" (Acts 17:28). Man may pride himself in his self-sufficiency, boast of his free-will, and imagine he is lord of himself, but he only deceives himself and denies his creaturehood in so doing.

When Pilate vaunted himself to Christ, asking, "Knowest thou not that I have power to crucify thee, and have power to release thee?" He answered, "Thou couldest have no power at all against me, except it were given thee from above" (John 19:10-11). Roman official though he was, and invested with Caesar's authority, yet Pilate was utterly impotent, with no more inherent and self-sufficient power to perform a natural act than a lump of inanimate clay *until* God should vouchsafe it unto him. The clear teaching of Holy Writ is that man has not a particle more of natural power in and of himself than he has spiritual power. "But thou shalt remember the Lord thy God [thy relation to Him, and thy complete dependency upon Him]: for it is he that *giveth thee power* to get wealth" (Deut. 8:18), i.e., who supplies thee with health, strength, and wisdom to perform natural acts, and who alone determines the measure of thy success therein. "For she did not know [nevertheless it was a fact!] that *I gave her* corn, and wine, and oil, and multiplied her silver and gold, . . . [yes, even when] they prepared [the same] for Baal" (Hosea 2:8).

What effect does such a belief have upon you? What fruit does it produce in your daily life? Does it merely result in Muhammadan apathy and fatalistic inertia, or does it cast you back upon God so that you seek His enabling for everything? Scripture not only reveals the dependency of the creature upon its Maker, his inherent helplessness, but it also teaches that man is a responsible creature, a rational and moral agent, accountable to God for all his thoughts, words, and deeds. Do you "believe" that too? If not, your creed is sadly defective. You are responsible to glorify your Maker, to be subject to His authority, to do those things which are pleasing in His sight. But, you reply, I am unable to do so. True, and you are equally unable to dig your garden unless God grants you strength, or to attend to your financial matters unless He gives you wisdom. Do you therefore lie in bed and do nothing? The only difference between our power and powerlessness to perform natural and spiritual acts is this, that our hearts are *averse* to the latter. The natural man hates God, and the things of the Spirit are foolishness to him. He loves material things, and therefore he pursues them eagerly.

"Ye Have Not Because Ye Ask Not"

Let us bring this matter down to a very simple and practical level. Here is a housewife who desires to make a cake. Suppose, for the sake of our illustration, that God has in His grace enabled her to purchase all the necessary ingredients. In such a case if she does not use the wisdom God has given her to perform her task successfully, if she does not concentrate her mind on what she is engaged in, if she becomes careless in following the recipe and the cake is a failure, whose fault is it? God has endowed you with reason, given you His Spirit, and His Word to instruct you, and bidden you to call upon Him for the supply of every temporal and spiritual need. Who is to blame if you do not appropriate and wisely use these mercies? Without Christ we can do nothing (John 15:5), yet strengthened by Him we "can do all things" (Phil. 4:13). It is therefore an idle excuse, a piece of wicked hypocrisy, if we plead our helplessness as an extenuation of our coldness and formality in prayer, and are not earnest and fervent in supplicating the throne of grace.

Having enlarged upon the intensity of the apostle's prayer rather more than we intended, let us return to the desire which prompted it, namely, that he "might perfect that which is lacking in your faith" (v. 10). First, those words reveal the exalted standard which this servant of the Lord kept before him and the high ministerial level at which he aimed. Notwithstanding the fact that Timothy had just brought Paul "good tidings" of their "faith and charity" (v. 6), still that did not content him, for he knew "there remaineth yet very much land to be possessed" (Joshua 13:1). Let the pastor be thankful when he sees his sheep in a healthy condition, but let him also labor for their further growth. Second, in these words we perceive the faithfulness of Paul. He did not feed their vanity by complimenting them upon their attainments, but gave them to understand that, far from having cause to be complacent, there was still room for much improvement, and that they needed to continue pressing forward to those things which are still before. Let the minister give credit to whom credit is due, but diligently avoid overdone praise, knowing that "a flattering mouth worketh ruin" (Prov. 26:28).

Things Lacking in Our Faith

"That . . . we might perfect that which is lacking ['the things lacking, plural in the Greek] in your faith" (v. 10). How many professing Christians would resent such a statement as that! Yes, some of God's own people are in such a sickly condition and so hypersensitive that their poor feelings would be hurt if such an imputation were made against them. Yet it is a fact that the most spiritual and mature Christian has various things lacking in his faith. First, in its scope: how many portions of the Word he has not yet apprehended, how many of its precepts and promises are still unappropriated. Second, in its operation: there is not the fruit from it which there should be in our daily lives. Third, take "faith" here as a *grace* also, and how much darkness and doubting mar the best of us. So it was with these Thessalonians. Just as Paul longed to visit the saints at Rome so that he might "impart unto . . . [them] some spiritual gift" (1:11), in like manner he desired to again see these young Thessalonian converts of his that he might be of further help to them.

"That we . . . might perfect . . . [the things which are] lacking in your faith." Egotism lies behind that touchiness which resents an insinuation of our ignorance. Oh, when shall we learn that pride—even more than unbelief—is the chief adversary to our making progress in the things of God? The more truly wise any man is, the more conscious he is of his ignorance, of the paucity of his knowledge. Only the conceited novice, the one who has a mere smattering of his subject, vainly imagines he is master of it and refuses to receive further instruction from his fellows. "If any man think that he knoweth any thing, he knoweth nothing yet as he ought to know" (I Cor. 8:2). As we have said so often, the grand secret of success in the Christian life is to continue as we began. And, among other things, that means to be emptied of our self-sufficiency, to maintain before God the attitude of a little child, to preserve a teachable spirit, and that to the end of our lives. If we persist in doing all these, we shall daily be aware of how much is still lacking in our faith, and we shall welcome every available help, no matter how weak the instrument.

Paul's Prayer for Them

Since Paul was providentially detained from immediately carrying out his desire, he prayed for and wrote to the new converts: "Now God himself . . . [even] our Father, and our Lord Jesus Christ, direct our way unto you" (v. 11). Thus this prayer, like the "grace be to you, and peace, from God our Father, and from the Lord Jesus Christ" found at the beginning of most of Paul's epistles, was addressed conjointly to the Father and to the Son in His mediatorial character. Therein we behold the Saviour's absolute deity, for it was an act of worship which was here being rendered to Him, and His divine law is explicit: "Thou shalt worship the Lord thy God, and *him only* shalt thou serve" (Matt. 4:10). We are expressly forbidden to accord divine homage to any creature. When the awestruck John fell down to worship an angel, he promptly said, "See thou do it not" (Rev. 22:10). Instead of the angels being fit objects of worship, as Rome blasphemously teaches, the divine edict is "Let all the angels of God worship him" (Heb. 1:6) who, as the context shows, is the incarnate Son. Being coessential and coeternal with the Father, all are commanded to "honour the Son, even as they honour the Father. He that honoureth not the Son honoureth not the Father which hath sent him" (John 5:23).

Prayer to Be Directed to the Son

Prayer is not only to be offered to God in the name of Christ but also directly *to Christ* as our Lord and Saviour. When a successor to Judas was to be chosen for the apostolate, prayer was made to the Lord (Acts 1:2-4). Apart from the fact that "the Lord" always has reference to Christ (unless there is something in the passage which clearly distinguishes the Father from Him), John 6:70 and 15:16 oblige us to regard that allusion as being to the Son. The dying Stephen specifically addressed his petitions to the Lord Jesus (Acts 7:59-60). From Acts 9:14 and 21 it is clear that it was customary for the early Christians to "call upon his name," i.e., supplicate Him. Upon the conversion of Saul of Tarsus, he was bidden to call on the name of the Lord (Acts 22:16). So prominent a feature was this in the lives of the primitive saints, that they received their characteristic designation from the same: "all that in every place call upon the name of Jesus Christ our Lord" (I Cor. 1:2). Timothy was instructed to "call on the Lord out of a pure heart" (II Tim. 2:22).

We turn now to consider the two *petitions* of this prayer: the one more immediately concerning Paul himself, the other the Thessalonian saints. The former is recorded in verse 11: "Now God himself . . . our Father, and our Lord Jesus Christ, direct our way unto you." First, that request concerned taking a journey. Second, it concerned a ministerial journey. Third, the one who desired to take it was exercised over it and wanted his steps to be ordered of the Lord. The terms of expression (and they are a legitimate and simple analysis of the petition), make it at once apparent that there is something here of interest and moment to each of us; that this petition has been placed on permanent record for our benefit—for our instruction and guidance. We should ponder each verse of Scripture, seeking to ascertain what in it will provide help for the details of our lives. God's Word is given us as a lamp to our feet and a light to our path—for us to walk by—an unerring guide to direct our way through the maze of this world. To put it another way, the apostle has here left us an example which is wise to follow.

We Are Dependent upon God's Will and Enablement

The strongest-willed and most resolute person on this earth cannot take a journey of so much as a hundred yards unless God wills and enables him. "Go to now [a word of rebuke], ye that say, to day or to morrow we will go into such a city, . . . whereas ye know not what shall be on the morrow. . . . For that ye ought to say, If the Lord will, we shall live, and do this, or that" (James 4:13-15). Even though God may grant us permission to carry out our plan, that is very far from saying that He will prosper the same. How that serves to illustrate what we have said about the entire dependency of man upon his Maker! In the verse now before us we are shown what *effect* that fact, that truth, should have upon us. It should counteract our spirit of self-sufficiency. It should cast us upon the Lord, seeking His enablement for all things. That was exactly what the apostle was here doing: acknowledging his dependency upon God and supplicating Him concerning his journey to Thessalonica.

"O LORD, I know that the way of man is not in himself: it is not in man that walketh to direct his steps" (Jer. 10:23). How very few professing Christians believe that! Nevertheless, that is the truth, and therefore we are bidden, "Trust in the LORD with all thine heart; and lean not unto thine own understanding. In all thy ways acknowledge him, and he shall direct thy paths" (Prov. 3:5-6), yet not without our concurrence. God treats us as rational creatures, as moral agents, and therefore we are required to trust Him fully, to repudiate the competency of our own reason, and to own Him in all our conduct. "The steps of a good man are ordered by the LORD" (Ps. 37:23)—not those of a wicked man, though *his* steps are "ordained" or appointed. Sometimes God lets us have our own way, as He did Israel of old, and then we miss His best and He sends leanness into our souls (Ps. 106:15).

When planning a journey, for instance, the first question to determine is simply this: "Is it your plain duty (as required by your calling or your obligations to others) to take this journey? If there be any uncertainty, then spread the matter before God and seek wisdom from Him. Observe how frequently it is recorded of David, the man after God's own heart (i.e., who in his official life was so completely subject to the divine will), that when contemplating a journey he "enquired of the LORD" (I Sam. 23:2, 4; 30:8; II Sam. 2:1; 5:19, 23), seeking His guidance each time and waiting upon Him. When your path *is* plain, then definitely pray God to give you good speed (Gen. 24:12), and grant you journeying mercies. Act on Psalm 37:5, and count upon the fulfillment of its promise. While on your journey, so far as conditions permit, endeavor to redeem the time by profitable reading (Acts 8:28).

Ministerial Journeys

Considering ministerial journeys, first we would observe that in Paul's case God's will respecting them was not made known to him uniformly, nor did he have any unmistakable leading as some today boast of. He and his companions had "assayed to go into Bithynia," but we are told that "the Spirit suffered them not" (Acts 16:7). Was he then acting in the energy of the flesh? Certainly not, no more than David was when he purposed to build the temple. Paul's trip to Macedonia was the result of a vision, but that was exceptional. Often persecution forced him to flee elsewhere. Sometimes Paul's movements were regulated by direct command from God, other times by providential circumstances, yet other times by his own spiritual instinct and desires. When he bade farewell to those at Ephesus he said, "I will return again unto you, if God will" (Acts 18:21)—if God permits and enables. Our "times" are in His hand (Ps. 31:15), and though we propose this or that, it is God who disposes (Prov. 19:21). Later, Paul did return to Ephesus (Acts 19:1).

"I will come to you shortly, if the Lord will" (I Cor. 4:19). Speaking generally, the apostles knew no more about the common events of life than did other men, nor were they usually directed by a supernatural impulse for their journeys. "Making request, if by any means now at length I might have a prosperous journey by the will of God to come unto you" (Rom. 1:10). Those words should teach us that, while the will of God concerning any event is not yet ascertained, we have the right and liberty to desire and pray for what we want, providing that our desires be conformed to God's holiness and our requests subject to His will. Our desires must at once be renounced as soon as it is clear that they are not agreeable to the divine will. Rightly did Moule point out "the indifference of mystic pietism, which at least discouraged articulate contingent petitions, is unknown to the apostles." And again Moule stated, "His inward harmony with the divine will never excluded the formation and expression of such requests, with the reverence of submissive reserve." Only One has ever had the right or necessary qualification to say, "Father, *I will.*"

"For which cause also I have been much hindered from coming to you. But now having no more place in these parts, and having a great desire these many years to come unto you; whensoever I take my journey into Spain, I will come to you: for I trust to see you in my journey" (Rom. 15:22-24). The opening "for which cause" is explained in the preceding verses: the pressure of continuous evangelistic labors had been the principal factor causing Paul to defer his visit, from which we learn that the call of *duty* deterred him from carrying out his earlier inclination. Matthew Henry well said, "God's dearest servants are not always gratified in everything they have a mind to. Yet all who delight in

God have 'the desire of their heart' fulfilled (Ps. 37:4), though *all* the desires in their heart may not be humoured." Note that Paul said, "I trust to see you," not "I *shall* see you," for he knew not what a day might bring forth. We ought to be very slow in making any promise, and those we do make should ever be qualified with "if God permit."

Guidance by the Holy Spirit

"For I will not see you now by the way; but I trust to tarry a while with you, if the Lord permit" (I Cor. 16:7). Here again we see the beloved apostle making personal acknowledgment of both the providential and spiritual government of Christ and his subservience thereto. Two things must concur; his purpose and conviction of duty as formed by the Spirit indwelling him, and the ordering of his external circumstances, confirming and making possible the execution of his purpose. Paul was crossed several times in his intentions. Sometimes he was forbidden by the Spirit (Acts 16:7), sometimes hindered by Satan (I Thess. 2:18), at other times prevented or long delayed by the pressure of work. Some doubt that he ever took his journey into Spain (Rom. 15:24).* Matthew Henry said, "The grace of God often with favor accepts the sincere intention, when the providence of God in wisdom prohibits the execution. Do we not serve a good Master, then! (II Cor. 8:12)."

A Special Word to Ministers

It is our desire and aim to furnish something in these pages suited to the needs of all classes of readers. We feel that a word or two should be offered for the particular benefit of those who are engaged in the ministry. One of the matters which, at some time or other in his career, deeply exercises the conscientious servant of God is that of his particular field of labor, especially when he is justified in leaving one field for another. Great care and caution need to be used and prayer is needed for patience as well as wisdom. Ours is an age of discontent and restlessness, and not only are most of God's people more or less infected by its evil spirit, but many of His servants are influenced by the same and suffer from wanderlust. Some who make a change of pastorate every two or three years suppose they find a warrant in doing so from the experience of the Apostle Paul: but that is a mistake. *He* was never settled in a pastorate, but was instead engaged in missionary or evangelistic activities, and therefore he furnishes no example to be followed by those who have the care of local churches.

When contemplating a change, spare no pains in endeavoring to make sure that the particular portion of the Lord's vineyard is the one where He would have you labor. If it is a church where you would be required to employ worldly and carnal methods in order to "attract the young people" or to "maintain its finances," it is no place for a servant of Christ. Take time and trouble to find out what the local conditions are, and you will probably be spared from entering a position where the *Holy* Spirit would not use you. Far better minister to a small company of saints than to a large one of unregenerate church members.

*[The Muratorian Fragment mentions Paul's departure from Rome en route to Spain. And several of the early church fathers refer to the spread of Christianity throughout Spain.— EDITOR]

No plan should be formed without reference to God's will. His glory and the good of His people must ever be your aim. If you are assured that God led you into your present field, be very slow in entertaining any thought of removal. An invitation to a more "attractive" field is far more likely to be a divine testing of your heart than an intimation that God would have you make a move. Consider not your own inclinations but the welfare of those to whom you are ministering. Seek grace to "endure hardness, as a good soldier of Jesus Christ" (II Tim. 2:3), and let faithfulness rather than "success" be your earnest endeavor.

"Now God himself . . . [even] our Father, and our Lord Jesus Christ, direct our way unto you." This prayer demonstrates that Paul was no fatalist, arguing that, since God had predestinated everything that would come to pass, there was no need for him to be uneasy about his plans for the near future. No, he was deeply exercised that his steps might be ordered of God, and therefore did he trustfully commit his way to Him (Ps. 37:5). In spite of his intense desire to visit these saints (vv. 6, 10), he refused to rush matters and act in the energy of the flesh. Nor did he assume that *their* yearning to see him again was a clear intimation of God's will in the matter: he waited to be definitely guided from on high. It is not for any minister of the Gospel to effect his own design without divine leave: rather it must be by God's permission and providence, by His directing and ordering, that each change is to be made. Until His will is clear, remain where you are (Rom. 16:23). If you are at a crossroads, entreat the Lord to block the way He would not have you take. Never force matters nor act hastily.

The "God himself" is emphatic, literally "But Himself, God even the Father, and our Lord Jesus Christ, may direct our way unto you." The "himself" is in contrast with "We would have come unto you, even I Paul, once and again; but Satan hindered us" (2:18). If God Himself directs us, then none can hinder! Scripture does not inform us what way Satan had "hindered," therefore it is useless and impious for us to speculate about it. Not that Satan had in any way hindered the execution of *God's* purpose, only the fulfilling of the apostle's "desire." God blessedly overruled and outwitted Satan, for in consequence of Paul's being hindered in the first century, *we* in this twentieth century now have the benefit of this epistle. In the all-too-brief comments of Ellicott's commentary a valuable point is here brought out: "The verb 'direct' is in the singular (which of course the English cannot [as explicitly] express), showing the *unity* of the Father and Son, and the *equality* of the two Persons." There was a blessed propriety in Paul's conjoining the Son with the Father in *this* petition, for it acknowledged Him as the One who holds the stars in His hand (Rev. 1:16) and opens and shuts all doors (Rev. 3:7).

The Grace of Love Now Especially Needed

"And the Lord make you to increase and abound in love one toward another, and toward all men, even as we do toward you" (v. 12). This is the second petition, but we shall not dwell upon it at the same length as the former: not because it is of less importance, but because it calls for less explanation. What is needed here is not so much exposition as the turning of these words into earnest supplication. If ever there was a time in the history of Christendom when God's people needed to entreat the throne of grace for an increase and an abounding in love, it is surely now. The exercise and manifestation of this cardinal grace is at an exceedingly low ebb. Sectarian bigotry, carnal strife, roots of bitterness, thrive on every hand. Yea, things are in such a deplorable state today that many of God's own people hold quite a wrong idea as to the nature and fruits of love. Most of them misconstrue natural affability and temperamental geniality for love. A hearty handshake, a warm welcome, may be had at the world's clubs and social centers where Christ is not even professed! The love for which the apostle here prayed was a holy, spiritual, and supernatural love.

Spiritual love proceeds from a spiritual nature and is attracted by the sight of the divine image in the saints. "Every one that loveth him that begat loveth him also that is begotten of him" (I John 5:1). No one can love holiness in another unless he has holiness in his own soul. Many love particular Christians because they find them to be sweet-tempered or generous-hearted, but that is merely *natural* and not spiritual love. If we would love the saints spiritually we must disregard what they are temperamentally by nature, and contemplate them as the objects and subjects of God's love, loving them for what we see of Him in them. Only thus shall we be able to rise above individual peculiarities and personal infirmities, and value them with a true spiritual affection. This does not mean that we shall ignore their offenses or condone their sins (Lev. 19:17). On the other hand, often what we regard as "slights" from them is due to our own pride. We are hurt because we do not receive the notice which we consider is our due. At times it is not good for the people of God to know too much of each other (Prov. 25:17). Familiarity may breed contempt.

Neither the reality nor the depth of Christian love is to be measured by honeyed words or endearing expressions. Actions speak louder than words. Gushy people are proverbially superficial and fickle. Those less demonstrative are more stable. Still waters run deep. Spiritual love always aims at the good of its object. It is exercised in edifying conversation, in seeking to strengthen and confirm faith, exalt God's Word, and promote piety. The more another magnifies Christ the more should he be endeared to us. We do not mean mere glib talk about Christ, but that overflowing of the heart toward Him which compels the mouth to speak of Him. We should love the saints for the truth's sake, for being unashamed to avow their faith in such a day as this. Those who reflect most of the image of Christ and carry about with them most of His fragrance should be the ones we love most.

Love for the brethren is ever proportioned to our love for the Lord Himself, which at once explains why the former is at such a low ebb. The sectarian bigotry and the bitterness growing all around us are not hard to explain. Love *to God* has waned! "Thou shalt love the Lord thy God with all thy heart, . . . soul and . . . strength" comes before "thou shalt love thy neighbour as thyself." But the love of material things and the cares of this world have chilled the souls of many toward God. Our affections must be set steadfastly upon the Head of the Church before they will wax warm to its members. When the Lord is given His rightful place in our hearts, His redeemed will also be given theirs. Then love will not be confined to that narrow ecclesiastical circle in which our lot is cast; it will embrace the entire household of faith. Then we shall have "love unto *all* the saints" (Eph. 1:15), and that will be evidenced by "supplication for all saints" (Eph. 6:18)—those in the four corners of the earth whom we have never seen. "Salute *every* saint" (Phil. 4:21)—poor as well as rich, weak as well as strong.

The Connection of This Petition with the Former One

At first glance there appears to be no connection, for what relation is there between one being guided in a journey and others loving one another? Yet the fact that this petition opens with "and" gives plain intimation that there *is* a coherence between them. A little meditation should discover what that is. What would have been the use of the apostle visiting the Thessalonian assembly if strife and division had prevailed in their midst? Under such circumstances the Lord would not have clothed Paul's words with power. Paul, instead of building up the Christians, would have had to reprove and rebuke them for their carnality, for most certainly he was not one of those who would ignore what was wrong and act as though things were all right. Nothing more quickly grieves and quenches the Spirit than dissension and a spirit of ill-will in an assembly.

"And the Lord make you to increase and abound in love one toward another." This petition was addressed more specifically to the Head of the Church, from whom the nourishment and increase of its members flow (Col. 2:19). From Him we receive His "fulness" (John 1:16); from Him we receive "the supply of the Spirit" (Phil. 1:19); yet we are required to seek for these. We are not to infer from the apostle asking for some particular thing that those for whom he supplicated were deficient therein, but rather the reverse. Because he perceived that a certain grace was in healthy exercise, he felt encouraged to ask God for *an increase* of the same. Such was unmistakably the case here. Paul had opened his epistle by referring to their "labour of love" (1:3). He later declared, "But as touching brotherly love ye need not that I write unto you: for ye yourselves are taught of God to love one another. And indeed ye do it toward all the brethren" (4:9-10). Why then this petition? "That ye [may] increase more and more" (4:10). The answer to this large petition is recorded in II Thessalonians 1:3.

The Object in View

"To the end he may stablish your hearts unblameable in holiness before God, even our Father, at the coming of our Lord Jesus Christ with all his saints" (v. 13). First, this verse expresses the design in Paul's petitions. Our hearts are sadly fickle and inconstant in their frames, and need divine establishing against the fear of man, the frowns of the world, and the temptations of Satan. Second, holiness before God was the grand *object* in view, and the abounding of love the *means* for promoting the same (Col 3:14). Third, the establishing our hearts (which God ever eyes) is our great need, yet how little concern we have about their state! Much head and hand religion, but the heart is neglected! So far as we recall, never once have we heard this petition used in public prayer! Fourth, at the return of Christ these desires will be fully realized.

Chapter 26

PRAYER FOR SANCTIFICATION OF THE YOUNG SAINTS

I THESSALONIANS 5:23-24

FIVE THINGS CLAIM OUR CONSIDERATION when pondering this prayer. First, its *connection:* the opening "and" of verse 23 links it to that which precedes, and that in turn supplies help to an understanding of the petition here. Second, its *addressee:* "the God of peace," the precise force of which address needs to be ascertained and then appropriated by faith. Third, its *request:* that these saints might be "sanctified wholly," concerning the meaning of which there has been much needless difference of opinion. Fourth, its *design:* that the saints should be so sanctified that they might "be preserved blameless unto the coming of our Lord Jesus Christ," an expression which calls for particularly careful and prayerful examination. Fifth, its *assurance:* "faithful is he that calleth you, who also will do it" (v. 24), which imports that the apostle had no doubt but that God would grant his request and accomplish his design—a proof that he had not asked for something which is unrealizable in this life by any of God's children. May the spirit of prayer be granted to our readers as they seek to mentally weigh what we have written.

Let us consider the *connection* of this prayer with what has preceeded. The order followed by the apostle is significant: exhortation to saints, then supplication to God. Paul called on the saints to perform their several duties, then he entreated God to further quicken them thereunto. Prayer was never designed to be a substitute for diligence in keeping God's precepts, but is a means whereby we obtain grace for obedient conduct. Diligent endeavor and fervent prayer are never to be separated.

As the apostle approached the end of this epistle he issued a series of short but weighty exhortations, the last of which was "Abstain from all appearance of evil" (v. 22). In the light of the verse immediately preceding, that signifies first to shun whatever savors of error. False doctrine is most dishonoring to God and highly injurious to the souls of His people, and therefore to be feared and avoided as a plague. God has warned concerning those men who teach anything contrary to His eternal truth, "Their word will eat as doth a canker" (II Tim. 2:17). Second, evil practice as well as evil doctrine is to be refrained from in the least degree, yea, in its very semblance. He who would avoid great sins must exercise conscience regarding little ones; and he who would avoid both great and little sins must consequently shun also the very appearance of sin.

Such things as extreme styles of apparel and overuse of jewelry, immoderate use of cosmetics, immodest attire, betray an absence of that spirit which hates even "the garment spotted by the flesh" (Jude 23).

The Moral Connection Between Verses 21 and 22

There is a real and close moral connection between "Abstain from all appearance of evil" and the exhortation immediately preceding: "Prove all things; hold fast that which is good" (v. 21). The word for "prove" signifies "examine, weigh, try." Whatever you hear and read, whatever counsel you receive even from Christians, whatever doubtful course of conduct others follow, bring all to the test of God's Word; and whatever survives that test "hold fast" and let not the sneers and frowns of men cause you to relinquish it. The more you make a practice of measuring all things by *that* standard, the keener will be your discernment to detect whatever falls short of it: "through thy precepts I get understanding: therefore I hate every false way" (Ps. 119:104). The latter cannot be said without the former. "I esteem all thy precepts concerning all things to be right; and I hate every false way" (Ps. 119:128). Only as we form the habit of "proving all things" and then "holding fast that which is good" are we morally enabled to "abstain from all appearance of evil."

On the other hand, our obedience to "prove all things, hold fast that which is good" does not render superfluous or needless our obedience to also "abstain from every appearance of evil," for no matter how well informed we may be from the Word, nor how strong may be our hatred of evil, there is still an enemy within ready to betray us. Therefore we need to spurn even the borders of evil and turn away our eyes from the very sight of it. If we do not, our souls will soon become receptive to the devil's lies. Matthew Henry declared, "Corrupt affections indulged in the heart and evil practices allowed in the life will greatly tend to promote fatal errors in the mind; whereas purity of heart and integrity of life will dispose men to receive the truth in the love of it. We should therefore abstain from all appearance of evil, from that which looks like sin or leads to it. He who is not shy of the appearances of sin, who shuns not the occasions of sin, who avoids not the approaches of sin, will not long abstain from the actual commission of sin." So much then for the connection or immediate context of this prayer.

"The God of Peace"

This particular title, "the God of peace," has at least a fivefold reference. First, it tells us what God is essentially, the Fountain of peace. Second, it announces what He is economically or dispensationally, the Ordainer or Covenantor of peace. Third, it reveals what He is judicially, a reconciled God, the Provider of peace. Fourth, it declares what He is paternally, the Giver of peace to His children. Fifth, it proclaims what He is governmentally, the Orderer of peace in the churches and in the world. Our present passage has most to do with the last three. First, it respects God in His judicial relationship with His people. When they sinned in Adam, a breach was made, so that God was legally alienated from them and they were morally alienated from Him. Though there was no change in His everlasting *love* for them, because of their apostasy from Him in the Adamic fall, and because of their own multiplied transgressions against Him, God as the moral Governor of the universe could not ignore that awful breach. As the Judge of all the earth His condemnation and curse rested upon them. The elect equally with the nonelect are "by nature the children of wrath" (Eph. 2:3), and as long as they remain in unbelief they are under the wrath of God (John 3:36), the objects of His penal hatred (Ps. 5:5), repulsive to the Holy One. But His wisdom devised a way whereby He could be reconciled to His alienated people.

God's Way of Deliverance

That way consists of what Christ did for them, what His Spirit works in them, and what they themselves are made willing to do. Christ obeyed the precept of the law on their behalf and suffered its penalty in their stead. Thereby the great Surety of the Church made complete satisfaction of God's justice, placated His wrath, and established an equitable and stable peace. When Christ endured the curse of the broken law, He "made peace [between God and His people] through the blood of his cross" (Col. 1:20), healing the fearful breach, reconciling the divine Judge to them, establishing a perfect and abiding amity and concord. In that way the divine interests were secured. But more: He secured for His people the Holy Spirit (Gal. 3:13-14) and thereby adequate provision was made to meet their dire needs. Desperate indeed is their case by nature and by practice: dead spiritually, rebels against God, their minds at enmity against Him, wedded to their idols, in love with sin. But by the quickening and illuminating power of the Holy Spirit they are convicted of their wickedness, made willing to throw down the weapons of their revolt, flee to Christ for refuge, and take His yoke upon them. Thereby they respond to the divine call "Be ye reconciled to God" (II Cor. 5:20) and thus they have "peace with God" (Rom. 5:1).

Thus we see the appropriateness of this divine title when the apostle was making request for the further sanctifying of the saints. The "God of peace" was the One who was pacified by the blood of Christ and reconciled to sinners when they turned from being lawless rebels and became loyal subjects of His government. The sanctifying Spirit was the surest evidence of their reconciliation to God. Proof of being brought into God's favor objectively is our enjoyment of His peace subjectively. The intolerable burden of guilt is removed from the conscience, and we "find rest unto . . . [our] souls." But if that rest is to be preserved in our souls we have to take the most diligent heed to our ways. If we are to enjoy communion with "the God of peace," then all details of our lives must be regulated by His Word. That calls for diligent watchfulness over our hearts, since sin, the archenemy of God, surrounds us. The apostle's injunction to the Roman saints is as relevant to us today: "Reckon . . . yourselves to be dead indeed unto sin, but alive unto God. . . . Let not sin therefore reign in your mortal body" (Rom. 6:11-12).

Our Enjoyment of God's Paternal Peace

Our enjoyment of the *paternal* peace of God is conditioned upon our obedience to Him: "O that thou hadst hearkened to my commandments! then had thy peace been as a river" (Isa. 48:18), full and unbroken. Our enjoyment of God's paternal peace is conditioned upon our making it a practice to cast all our care on Him: "Be careful [anxious] for nothing; but in every thing by prayer and supplication with thanksgiving let your requests be made known unto God. And the peace of God, which passeth all understanding, shall keep your hearts and minds through Christ Jesus" (Phil. 4:6-7). The enjoyment of God's *governmental* peace in the local church is a fruit of the unquenched Spirit operating in their midst by the exercise of love among the members and by the maintenance of scriptural discipline over them corporately. It is sin which produces strife and dissension among saints. "From whence come wars and fighting among you? Come they not hence, even of your lusts that war in your members?" (James 4:1). Then communion with the God of peace is at an end.

Third, let us consider the *request* of this prayer of the apostle. "And [Himself] the very God of peace sanctify you wholly." Why did the apostle make this request? Were not the Thessalonian saints already sanctified? Certainly they were, both as to their standing before God in Christ and as to their state in themselves as indwelt by the Holy Spirit. Then precisely what was it that Paul sought on their behalf? Sanctification is many-sided, and unless we distinguish between its many aspects, we shall not only have but a vague and blurred concept of the whole but we shall entertain erroneous ideas of the same and bring our hearts into bondage. As this is a most blessed, deeply important, yet little understood subject, we will now indicate its chief branches.

First, believers were sanctified by *God the Father* from all eternity. "To them that are sanctified by God the Father, and preserved in Jesus Christ, and called" (Jude 1). Note well the order: they were sanctified before their preservation (i.e., from death in their unregeneracy) and effectual call. The reference there is to the believers' eternal election, when in His decree the Father set apart His elect from the nonelect for His delight and glory, choosing them in Christ and blessing them with all spiritual blessings in Him before the foundation of the world. On that initial aspect of sanctification we will not dwell.

Second, all believers have been sanctified by *God the Son*. As that is little apprehended we will enter into more detail. Our sanctification by the Son, like that by the Father, is not subjective but objective, not something we experience within but something entirely outside ourselves. By the redemptive sacrifice of Christ the entire Church has been set apart, consecrated to and accepted by God in all the excellency of the infinitely meritorious work of His incarnate Son. "We are sanctified through the offering of the body of Jesus Christ once for all. . . . For by one offering he hath perfected for ever them that *are sanctified*" (Heb. 10:10, 14). Those blessed statements have no reference whatever to anything which the Spirit does *in* the Christian, but relate exclusively to what Christ has secured *for* him. They speak of that which results from our federal oneness with Christ. They tell us that by virtue of the sacrifice of Calvary every believer is not only accounted righteous in the courts of God's justice but is perfectly hallowed for the courts of His holiness. The blood of the Lamb not only delivers from hell but fits us for heaven. It is the believer's relation to Christ, and that alone, which entitles him to enter the Father's house. And it is his relation to Christ, and that alone, which now gives him the right to draw nigh to God within the veil (Heb. 10:19).

Every Believer Sanctified upon Believing

The grand fact is that the feeblest and least-instructed believer was as completely sanctified before God the first moment he trusted in Christ as he will be in heaven in his glorified state. Said the Saviour on the eve of His death, "For their sakes I sanctify myself, that they might be truly sanctified" (John 17:19, margin), that is, that they might be really and actually sanctified, in contrast with the merely typical and ceremonial sanctification which obtained under the Mosaic dispensation. Christ was on the point of dedicating Himself to the final execution of the work of making Himself the sacrifice for sin; as the surety of His people He was about to present Himself to the Father and place Himself on the altar as a vicarious propitiation for His church. As the consequence of Christ devoting Himself as a whole burnt offering to God, His people are perfectly sanctified. Their sins are forever put away. Their persons are cleansed from all defilement. The excellency of His work is imputed to them so that they are rendered perfectly acceptable to God, suited to His presence, fitted for His worship. Priestly nearness to God is their blessed portion as the consequence of Christ's priestly offering of Himself for them. They have the right of access to God as purged worshipers.

"But of him are ye in Christ Jesus, who of God is made unto us wisdom, and [even] righteousness, and sanctification, and redemption" (I Cor. 1:30). Observe well that this verse is not stating what we were made by Christ, but what God has made Christ to be to His believing people. The distinction is real and fundamental, and to ignore it is to deprive ourselves of the most precious half of the gospel. Christ is here said to be made four things to us or, as the Greek more nicely discriminates, one thing (wisdom), which is defined under three points, the whole speaking of the Church's completeness in her Head (Col. 2:10). God has made Christ to be all and in all to us objectively and imputatively. Christ is not only our righteousness but our sanctification, by the purity of His person and the excellency of His sacrifice being reckoned to our account. If Israel became a holy people (ceremonially) when sprinkled with the blood of bulls and goats, so that they were admitted and readmitted to Jehovah's worship, how much more shall the meritorious blood of Christ sanctify us actually, so that we may draw nigh to God with confidence as acceptable worshipers? My ignorance does not alter the fact, neither does the weakness of my faith to truly grasp the same impair it. My feelings and experience have nothing to do with it. God has done it, and nothing can alter it.

Aaron the High Priest

"And thou shalt make a plate of pure gold, and grave upon it, like the engravings of a signet, HOLINESS TO THE LORD. . . . And it shall be upon Aaron's forehead, that Aaron may bear the iniquity of the holy things, which the children of Israel shall hallow in all their holy gifts; and it shall be always upon *his* forehead, that *they* may be accepted before the LORD" (Exodus 28:36-39). That presents to us one of the most precious typical pictures to be found in all the Old Testament. Aaron, the high priest, was dedicated and devoted exclusively to the Lord. He served in that office on behalf of others as their mediator. He stood before God as the representative of the nation, bearing the names of the twelve tribes on his shoulders and on his heart (Exodus 28:12, 29). Israel, the people of God, were both represented by and *accepted in* Aaron. That was not a type of "the way of salvation," but it spoke of the approach to God of a failing and sinning people whose very prayers and praises were defiled but whose service and worship were rendered acceptable to the Holy One through their high priest. That inscription "HOLINESS TO THE LORD" on Aaron's forehead was a solemn appointment by which the people of Israel were impressively taught that holiness became the house of God, and that none who were unholy could possibly draw nigh to Him.

Now Aaron foreshadowed Christ, the great High Priest who is "over the house of God" (Heb. 10:21). Believers are both represented by and accepted in Him. The "HOLINESS TO THE LORD" which was *"always"* upon Aaron's forehead pointed to the mediatorial holiness of the One who *"ever"* liveth to make intercession" for us (Heb. 7:25). Because of our federal and vital union with Christ, *His* holiness is *ours*. The perfection of the great High Priest is the measure of our acceptance with God. Christ has also borne the iniquity of our holy things (Exodus 28:38); that is, He not only atoned for our sins but made satisfaction for the defects of our worship. Not only can nothing be laid to our charge but the sweet incense of His merits (Rev. 8:3) renders our worship "an odour of a sweet smell, a sacrifice acceptable, wellpleasing to God" (Phil. 4:18). Thus Christians are enabled to "offer up spiritual sacrifices, acceptable to God by Jesus Christ" (I Peter 2:5). Christ is the One who meets our every need both as sinners and as saints. In, through, and by Christ every believer has a flawless sanctification. The Holy One could not look upon us with the least favor, nor could we draw nigh to Him at all, unless He viewed us as perfectly holy; and this He *does* in the person of our Mediator.

A perfect holiness is as indispensable as a perfect righteousness in order for us to have access to and communion with the thrice holy God. In Christ we have the one as truly as we have the other. The glorious gospel reveals to us a perfect Saviour, One who has completely met every need of His people; yet it is absolutely necessary that we mix faith with that good news if we are to live in the power and comfort of the same. "Wherefore Jesus also, that he might sanctify the people with his own blood, suffered without the gate" (Heb. 13:12). The precious blood has not only made expiation for the sins of His people but has hallowed and consecrated them to God, so that He views them not only as guiltless and unreprovable but also as spotless and holy. The blood of Christ not only covers every stain of sin's defilement but in the very place of what it covers and cleanses, it leaves its own excellency and virtue. God sees us in the face of His Anointed as perfect as Christ Himself, and therefore as both justified and sanctified. His oblation has restored us to full favor and fellowship of God.

The word "sanctify" has a twofold meaning: primarily it signifies the bare setting apart of a thing. In Scripture it usually, though not always, has reference to setting apart to a sacred use, as the seventh day to be the Sabbath. Exceptions are found in such passages as Isaiah 66:17 where we read of men setting themselves apart to do evil, and Isaiah 13:3 where the Lord terms the Medes "my sanctified ones" when about to employ them in the destruction of Babylon. In the majority of cases in the Old Testament, "to sanctify" means "to separate some object from a common use to a sacred one," consecrating the same to God, yet without any change being effected in the object itself, as with all the materials and vessels used in the tabernacle. But in its secondary meaning (not secondary in importance, but as a derivative) "sanctify" is used in a moral sense, signifying "to make holy," rendering what was set apart fit for the end designed, first by a cleansing (Exodus 19:10), second by an anointing or equipping (Exodus 29:36). In the case of God's elect, sanctification signifies changing or purifying their dispositions. This brings us to the third main branch of our subject.

The Father's sanctification of His people in His eternal decree and the Church's sanctification in and by the Son federally and meritoriously are made good to and in them personally by *God the Spirit*: "being sanctified by the Holy Ghost" (Rom. 15:16). It is not until the Comforter takes up His abode in the heart that the Father's "will" (Heb. 10:10) begins to be actualized and the Son's "blood" (Heb. 13:12) evidences its efficacy toward us. It is not to be supposed for a moment that the perfect standing before God which the work of Christ secured for His people leaves their *state* unaffected; that their position should be so gloriously changed and their condition remain unaltered; that holiness should be imputed to them but not also imparted. The redemptive work of Christ was a means to an end, namely, to procure for His people the Holy Spirit who should make good in them what He had done for them. It is by the Spirit's quickening operation that we obtain vital union with Christ—by means of which the benefits of our federal and legal union with Him actually become ours. The "sanctification of the Spirit" (II Thess. 2:13) is an integral part of that salvation to which the Father chose us and which the incarnate Son purchased for us. Thus the Christian is sanctified by the triune Jehovah.

Union with Christ

Our *union with Christ* is the grand hinge on which everything turns. Without Him we have nothing. During our unregeneracy we were "without Christ" and therefore "strangers from the covenants of promise" (Eph. 2:12). But the moment the Spirit made us one livingly with Christ, all that He has became ours; we were made henceforth "joint heirs with him"—as a woman obtains the right to share all that a man has once she is wedded to him. By virtue of our union with the first Adam we not only had imputed to us the guilt of his disobedience but we also received from him a sinful nature which vitiated all the faculties of our souls; and by virtue of our federal union with the last Adam we not only have imputed to us the merits of His obedience but we receive from Him a holy nature which renews all the faculties of our souls. Once we become united to the Vine, the life and virtue which are in Him flow into us and bring forth spiritual fruit. Thus, as soon as the Spirit unites us to Him we are "sanctified *in* Christ Jesus" (I Cor. 1:2). "By one Spirit are we all baptized [spiritually] into one body [of which Christ is the vital and influential Head], . . . and have been all made to drink into one Spirit" (I Cor. 12:13).

"But of him [by no act of ours] are ye in Christ Jesus" (I Cor. 1:30). It is by the quickening operation of the Spirit that the elect are supernaturally and vitally incorporated with Christ, and it is then God makes Him to be to us "wisdom, even righteousness, and sanctification, and redemption." "For we are his workmanship, *created* in Christ Jesus" (Eph. 2:10). That new creation is effected by the Spirit and issues in our union with Christ's person. Just as both our standing and state were radically affected by our union with the first Adam, so they are completely changed by virtue of our union with the last Adam. As the believer has a perfect standing in holiness before God because of his federal union with Christ, so his state is perfect before God because he is now vitally one with Christ: he is in Christ and Christ is in him. "He that is joined unto the Lord is one spirit" (I Cor. 6:17). The moment they were born of the Spirit all Christians were sanctified in Christ with a sanctification to which no growth in grace, no attainments in holiness, can add one iota. The believer is "sanctified [made a saint] in Christ Jesus" (I Cor. 1:2), one of the "holy brethren" (Heb. 3:1), and just because he is such he is called upon to live a holy life.

Our relationship to God is changed when the Spirit sanctifies us by His quickening power, for we are then consecrated to God by the Spirit's indwelling us and making our body His temple. As He came upon the Head ("not . . . by measure," John 3:34), so in due time He is given to each of the members of the Head: "Ye have an unction [the Spirit] from the Holy One." "The anointing [the Spirit] which ye have received from him [Christ] abideth in you" (I John 2:20, 27). We derive our name from that very blessing, for "Christian" means "an anointed one," the term being taken from the type in Psalm 133:2. It is the indwelling of the Spirit which constitutes a believer a holy person. Our relationship to Christ is changed when the Spirit quickens us, for instead of being "without" Him in the world, we are now "joined" to Him. Our actual state is radically changed, for a principle of holiness is planted in the soul which powerfully affects all its faculties. God now occupies the throne of the heart, the affections are purged from their love of sin, the Word is delighted in so that the will chooses its precepts as its regulator. Nevertheless, the "flesh," or evil principle, remains unchanged.

Different Phases of the Believer's Sanctification

In one sense the believer's sanctification by the Spirit is complete at the new birth, so that he will never be made any holier than he is at that moment; in another sense his sanctification is incomplete and admits of progress. It is complete in that by virtue of the great change effected in him by the miracle of regeneration he is *then* "made meet to be [one of the] partakers of the inheritance of the saints in light" (Col. 1:12), virtually and personally united to Christ and, by the Spirit's taking up His abode in his heart, consecrated to God. It is incomplete in that the "flesh" principle is not then removed, in that the babe in Christ needs to grow in grace, and in that he is henceforth required to "put off the old man" and "put on the new man" in a practical way, cleansing himself "from all filthiness of the flesh and spirit, perfecting holiness in the fear of God" (II Cor. 7:1). To enable him in this, the Spirit renews him daily (II Cor. 4:16), stirs him up to the use of the means of the Word and prayer, quickens his graces, draws forth his spiritual life to spiritual acts in Christ's name; and thereby He continues and completes that "good work" (Phil. 1:6) which He wrought in the soul at regeneration.

Let us sum up. Sanctification is the first *blessing* to which the Father predestinated His people (Eph. 1:3-5). Second, it is a *gift*, an inalienable and eternal gift, which they have in and through Christ. Third, it is a *moral quality*, a holy principle or "nature" communicated by the Spirit. Fourth, it is a *duty* which God requires from us (I Peter 1:15-16). Or again we may say sanctification is a *relationship* into which we are brought with the thrice holy God. Second, it is a *status* we have by virtue of our union with Christ. Third, it is an *enduement* which we experience by the Spirit's operation within us. Fourth, it is a lifelong *work* to which we are called, but for which we are in constant need of more grace. "Perfecting holiness in the fear of God" (II Cor. 7:1) by no means intimates that the holiness which the Christian now possesses is defective and needs supplementing by his own efforts, but signifies that he is to carry out to its proper use and end that perfect holiness which *is his* in Christ. Compare I John 2:5, which means that by keeping God's commands the design of His love in us is reached. "By works was [Abraham's] faith made perfect" (i.e., achieved in design or intended result, James 2:22). The Christian is to be "in behaviour as becometh holiness" (Titus 2:3).

"Abstain from all appearance of evil. And the God of peace himself sanctify you wholly." Both the immediate context and the particular character in which God is here addressed serve to show which aspect of our sanctification is in view, namely, our practical holiness or purity of heart and conduct. Paul's prayer is for divine enablement to keep the foregoing commands—full sanctification for full obedience. To the preceeding exhortations the apostle added earnest supplication, knowing well that only the efficacious grace of God could supply either the will or the power to comply. The standard in verse 22 is an exceedingly high and exacting one: to abhor everything which carries even the appearance of uncleanness, to abstain from everything tending thereto. The more we eye that standard, the more conscious we are of its purity, the more we shall realize the need of much grace to measure up to it, and the more we shall perceive the suitability of this prayer to our case. We are still the targets of Satan, the archenemy of God. Yielding to Satan's temptations separates us from God's favor, produces disorder and confusion among all the faculties of our being, and causes dissension among the saints. To prevent such disaster, the apostle invokes the "God of *peace*."

The Christian's Work of Grace Not Perfected

The indulgence of our lusts and the allowance of sin derange all the faculties of our being so that the soul usurps the throne of the spirit (emotions and impulses directing us instead of our understanding or judgment), and the body seeks to dominate both spirit and soul—carnal affections opposing reason. But experimental and practical sanctification puts all into a right order again and causes peace and harmony. But only "the very God of peace" can *so* sanctify us. This is emphasized in our text: "the . . . God of peace [Himself]," which points up a contrast between the feeble efforts after holiness which we are capable of in our own spiritual strength and the almighty power which He can exert because of the peace and order which His sanctification brings to our whole being. The Christian is indeed sanctified, yet the work of grace begun in him at regeneration is not then completed. "First the blade, then the ear, after that the full corn in the ear" (Mark 4:28). The heart needs to be increasingly cleansed from the pollution of sin, the soul more fully conformed to the divine image, the daily walk more "worthy of the Lord" (Col. 1:10). Yet all the advances we make in the Christian life are but the effects, fruits, and evidences of the Spirit's sanctifying us at the new birth. Growth in grace is a *manifestation* of our holiness.

"And the . . . God of peace [Himself] sanctify you wholly" is to be taken in its widest latitude. First, as a request that all the members of the Thessalonian church, the entire assembly, might be thus sanctified. Second, that each individual member might be unreservedly devoted to God in the whole of his complex being. Third, that each and all of them might be energized and purified more perfectly, strengthened, and stirred up to press forward to complete holiness. Thus I Thessalonians 5:23 is almost parallel with Hebrews 13:20-21. The apostle prayed that all parts and faculties of the Christian might be kept under the influence of efficacious grace, in true and real conformity to God: that they might be so influenced by the truth as to be fitted and furnished for the performance of every good work. Though this be our bounden duty, yet it is the work of our reconciled God, by His Spirit in and through us; and this is to be the burden of our daily prayers. The exhortation of verse 22 makes known our duty: the prayer of verse 23 how to be enabled thereto. By nature our hearts were antagonistic to God's holy requirements, and only His power can produce an abiding change.

The Practical Aspect of Sanctification

This prayer is concerned with the practical aspect of sanctification: that the saint should be divinely enabled to manifest in his daily life that sanctification which he has in Christ and bring forth the fruits of the spirit's indwelling him, by the principle of holiness imparted at regeneration. He should be constantly "denying ungodliness and worldly lusts" and live "soberly, righteously, and godly, in this present world; looking for that blessed hope" (Titus 2:12-13). As to our standing and state before God, sanctification extends to the whole man— every part of our human nature being the subject of it. And so must be our devotedness to God. Our body as well as our spirit and soul is to be dedicated to Him (Rom. 12:1), and its members employed in the works of righteousness (Rom. 6:13). John Owen said, "In your whole nature or persons, in all that ye are and do, that ye may—not in this or that part, but—be every whit clean and holy throughout."

Fourth, we shall consider the *design* of the apostle's prayer. "Your whole spirit and soul and body be preserved blameless." It is difficult (and perhaps not necessary) for us to determine the precise relation of this clause to the previous one—whether it is an additional request, an explanatory amplification of the word *wholly*, or an expression of the apostle's aim in making that request. Personally, we consider it includes the last two. The American Standard Version gives it thus: "And the God of peace himself sanctify you wholly; and may your spirit and soul and body be preserved entire, without blame at the coming of our Lord Jesus Christ." Whatever rendition is preferred, it is clear the verse as a whole teaches that sanctification extends to our entire persons. Equally clear is it that man is a tripartite being, consisting of an intelligent spirit, a sensual or sensitive soul, and a material body. Man, with his customary perversity, reverses this order and speaks of "body, soul, and spirit," putting the body first because it occupies most of his care.

Man a Tripart Being

Since the tripart nature of man has been so widely denied we will make some brief observations. That man is a threefold (and not merely twofold) entity is definitely established by the fact that he was created in the image of the triune God (Gen. 1:26). It is intimated in the account of the Fall. "The woman saw that the tree was good for food"—it appealed to her bodily appetites. Second, she saw that it was "pleasant [margin, a desire] to the eyes"—it appealed to her sensitive soul. She thought it was "a tree to be desired to make one wise"—it appealed to her intelligent spirit (Gen. 3:6). It is a serious error to say that when man fell, his spirit ceased to be, and that only at regeneration is his spirit "communicated" to him.

Fallen man is possessed equally of "spirit and soul" (Heb. 4:12). God "formeth the spirit of man within him" (Zech. 12:1), and at death the "spirit shall return unto God who gave it" (Eccles. 12:7). We agree with the Reformer Zanchius that "the spirit includes the superior faculties of the mind, such as reason and understanding; the soul, the inferior faculties such as will, affections, and desires." By means of the "soul" we feel; by the "spirit" we know (Dan. 2:3 ff.). "Thou shalt love the LORD thy God with [1] all thine heart [spirit], and [2] with all thy soul, and [3] with all thy might" [physical energy] (Deut. 6:5). This corresponds with Paul's threefold distinction in our text. The constitution of man *as man* was once for all demonstrated when the Son of God became incarnate and assumed both human "spirit" (Luke 23:46) and "soul" (Matt. 26:38). Yet in saying that unregenerate man possesses a spirit, we do not affirm that he has a *spiritual nature,* for his spirit has been defiled by the Fall, though it was not annihilated and therefore is capable of being washed and renewed (Titus 3:5).

The whole nature of man is the subject of the Spirit's work in regeneration and sanctification. This fact is to be manifested by the Christian in a practical way, by every disposition and resource of his spirit, each faculty and affection of his soul, all the members of his body. His body has been made a member of Christ (I Cor. 6:15) and is the temple of the Holy Spirit (I Cor. 6:19). Since the Christian's body is an integral part of his person, and since its inclinations and appetites seek to usurp the functions of his spirit and soul and dominate his actions, he is required to bring his body under the control of the higher parts of his being, so that it is regulated by a scripturally enlightened reason and not by its carnal passions. "Every one . . . should know how to possess his vessel [his body] in sanctification and honour" (I Thess. 4:4). As in unregeneracy we yielded our members to sin, now we are to yield them as servants to righteousness unto holiness (Rom. 6:19). Someone has said, "Perfect holiness is to be the *aim* of saints on earth, as it will be the *reward* of the saints in heaven."

Saints Preserved Blameless

Christians *are* "sanctified wholly" in their desires and intentions, and that brings us to the meaning of *"preserved blameless."* It is not that blamelessness which the covenant of works required, but that of the covenant of grace wherein God accepts the will for the deed (Neh. 1:11; II Cor. 8:12). God accepts the deed by the will. He interprets as perfect the man who desires to be perfect, and He calls that man perfect who desires to have all his imperfections removed. It is sad that so few have been taught to distinguish between legal and evangelical blamelessness. When God's Word says that the parents of John the Baptist walked "in all the commandments and ordinances of the Lord blameless" (Luke 1:6) it does not mean that they lived sinlessly, as verse 20 shows, but that such was their sincere desire and earnest endeavor that they habitually walked in conscientious obedience to God and behaved in such a manner in the general tenor of their conduct that none could charge them with any open sin.

The word *blameless* in such passages as I Corinthians 1:8; Philippians 2:15 and I Thessalonians 3:13 should be compared with "Blessed are the *undefiled* in the way" (Ps. 119:1). The word *blameless* here is to be understood according to the tenor of the new covenant, which does not exclude (as the covenant of works did) God's exercise of mercy and the pardon of sin (see Ps. 130:3-4). The prayer which Christ has given us to use bids us ask not only for deliverance from temptation but for daily pardon. If God dealt with us according to the strict rigor of His law and required absolute "undefiledness," none would escape His condemnation. Evangelical undefiledness must be understood as the *sincerity* of our obedience and refrainment from that which would give others occasion to justly charge us with wrongdoing. While the Christian honestly and earnestly endeavors to show himself approved to God, while he is truly humble regarding his failures and penitently confesses them, while he diligently seeks to walk in the law of the Lord, he is *accounted* "blameless," or "undefiled," in the gospel sense of those words.

Fifth, let us briefly consider the *assurance* of the apostle's prayer. "Faithful is he that calleth you, who also will do it" (v. 24). Regeneration guarantees sanctification. Our effectual call by God is the earnest of our preservation. Divine grace will complete our experimental and practical holiness. "The LORD will perfect that which concerneth me: thy mercy, O LORD, endureth for ever" (Ps. 138:8). Whether we translate the end of verse 23 "be preserved blameless *unto* the coming of the Lord Jesus Christ" or "be preserved blameless 'at' . . ." as the "till" in Philippians 1:10, and the "in" of I Corinthians 1:8 show, both are equally the case. Thus the confidence of verse 24 is parallel with "he which hath begun a good work in you will perform it until the day of Jesus Christ" (Phil. 1:6).

Chapter 27

PRAYER FOR PERSEVERING GRACE:
OCCASION AND IMPORTUNITY

II Thessalonians 1:11-12

It is both interesting and instructive to compare and collate the different things Paul prayed for on behalf of the several assemblies. For the Roman saints he asked that they might be "like-minded one toward another" and be filled "with all joy and peace in believing" (Rom. 15:5, 13). Paul prayed that the Corinthians might "come behind in no gift" and be confirmed unto the end (I Cor. 1:7-8). Paul prayed that the Ephesians might have the eyes of their understanding opened so that they might apprehend the wonders of God's great salvation (Eph. 1:18-23), and be so strengthened by the Holy Spirit as to experimentally possess their possessions (3:16-21). The apostle prayed that the love of the Philippians might be regulated by knowledge (Phil. 1:9-11). He prayed that the Colossians might "walk worthy of the Lord unto all pleasing, being fruitful in every good work" (Col. 1:9-12). How rarely these blessings are made the burden of public prayers! There was no petition for justification!

The Spiritual State of the Thessalonian Saints

For the Thessalonian saints the apostle besought their entire sanctification. Their spiritual condition was much above the average as is evident from the whole of the opening chapter of the first Epistle, and for them he made an unusual request. They had progressed far in the school of Christ, and the apostle longed that they should attain the highest grade of all. Their case illustrates the principle that those Christians who give the least promise at the outset do not necessarily develop the least favorably, and those who make the best beginning do not always end well. In Acts 17:10-11 we read that those in Berea "were more noble than those in Thessalonica, in that they received the word with all readiness of mind, and searched the scriptures daily." Yet we are not told of a church being organized there; in fact, no further mention is made of them in the New Testament, whereas two epistles are addressed to the church of the Thessalonians! So also of the churches of Galatia: time was when they "did run well" but they ceased to do so (Gal. 5:7).

As to exactly what the apostle prayed for in this particular case there is considerable difference of opinion among the commentators; nor were our translators very sure, as appears from the words in italics. In the case of all regenerate souls God already *"hath wrought* . . . [them] for the selfsame thing" (II Cor. 5:5), i.e., for their "house not made with hands, eternal in the heavens" (v. 1). The meritorious and imputed righteousness of Christ has obtained for them an indisputable *title* to everlasting glory, and the regenerating work of the Spirit in their souls has experimentally *fitted* and qualified them for the same, as is clear from the case of the dying thief. Therefore, instead of striving to be worthy, or praying to God to make them so, it is their grand privilege and binding duty to be daily "giving thanks unto the Father, which *hath made us meet* to be partakers of the inheritance of the saints in light" (Col. 1:12), to praise Him for what His grace has effected for and in us. Second, we believers are to diligently and constantly seek enabling grace that we may *"walk* worthy of the vocation wherewith . . . [we] *are* called" (Eph. 4:1), that is, our conduct must accord with our high privilege, our daily lives should show that we have been thus marvelously favored.

"Wherefore also we pray always for you, that our God would count you worthy of *this* calling, and fulfill all the good pleasure of *his* goodness, and the work of faith with power" (v. 11). The two words in italics have been supplied by the translators, but as is so often the case they serve to obscure rather than elucidate. On this verse Bagster's Interlinear (which preserves in English the order of the words in the Greek and gives a literal translation) is to be preferred: "For which also we pray always for you, that you may count worthy of the calling of God, and may fulfill every good pleasure of goodness and work of faith with power." Not only is that far truer to the original but it is much sounder doctrine besides being more intelligible. It should also be pointed out that "may count worthy" is a single word in the Greek, and is not a forensic one, being quite different from the one rendered "counted" (i.e., legally accounted) in Romans 4:3-4 and "imputed" in Romans 4:8, 11. The Greek word in our text is *axioo* and is found again in Luke 7:7; I Timothy 5:17; Hebrews 3:3 and 10:29 where in each place it has the force of "deemed" or "esteemed."

Now whenever a verse presents any difficulty our initial concern should be to carefully ponder its context. That is particularly incumbent upon us here, for our verse opens with the word *wherefore.* Let us then consider the occasion of this prayer, for that will throw light upon its meaning. In verse 4, the key to all that follows to the end of the chapter, the apostle declares, "So that we ourselves glory in you in the churches of God for your patience and faith in all your persecutions and tribulations that ye endure" or "are bearing." They were being hotly assailed by the enemy and were passing through a great "fight of afflictions." So nobly had they conducted themselves that Paul held them up as a pattern to other assemblies. And now he seeks to comfort and strengthen them, first, by pointing out the present advantage of their severe trials. Their fortitude and faith supplied "a manifest token of the righteous judgment of God," that they might be counted worthy of the kingdom of God for which they had suffered (v. 5).

Judging Righteous Judgment

The Greek word for "manifest token" occurs again only in II Corinthians 8:24: "the *proof* of your love." The word for "righteous judgment" in verse 5 of our chapter is the same as in " Judge not according to appearance, but judge righteous judgment" (John 7:24) : that is, "Do not determine your estimate of others on superficial and surface grounds, but let your decision or evaluation be fair, impartial, adequate, and equitable." Thus, taking verse 4 and 5 together, the meaning of the latter should be obvious. By their becoming conduct in the furnace of affliction the Thessalonians had clearly attested themselves to be among the effectually called. Their "patience and faith" as surely evidenced their regeneration as did the bounty of the Corinthians give proof of their love. Consequently, their bringing forth that fruit in such an unfavorable season was proof of the just verdict of God in accounting them worthy of His kingdom for which they suffered. In other words, Wisdom was justified of her children: their deportment made it evident that they bore the image of God. "That ye *may* be the children of your Father which is in heaven" (Matt. 5:45) signifies that believers may *manifest* themselves as such by doing what is enjoined in verse 44.

Next, the apostle assured the Thessalonians that God in His righteousness would both deal with those who troubled them and exonerate His people at the revelation of the Lord Jesus from heaven (vv. 6-10). Their Redeemer Himself would take vengeance on those who knew not God and obeyed not the gospel of His Son; whereas He would be "glorified in his saints, and . . . admired in all them that believe." Here then was solid consolation for them. In due time their persecutors would be punished, while they would be richly rewarded and fully vindicated. Here we are shown one of the many practical advantages of the "blessed hope" of our Lord's return. That glorious event should not be made the subject of acrimonious controversy, but it should be a means of comfort (I Thess. 4:18) and an incentive to piety (I John 3:2-3). The second coming of the Lord and the glorification of His entire Church at that time should be constantly viewed by the redeemed with the eyes of faith, of hope, and of love. The more it is so viewed, the greater will be its holy influence upon their character and conduct; especially will it enable them amid tribulation to rest in the Lord and wait patiently for Him.

"Wherefore [for which] also we pray always for you." The correctness of our analysis of the context is here borne out by the word *also*. Paul is saying, "In addition to the grounds of consolation set forth by me as pertinent to your suffering [to which the opening 'for which' looks back], I would assure you that I make your case the subject of earnest prayer." (The "always" means "frequently.") And for what would we here expect the apostle to make request? That the Thessalonians might be delivered from their persecutions and tribulations? No indeed. That would be a natural or carnal desire, not a spiritual one. Paul had previously informed them that God's people "are appointed thereunto" (I Thess. 3:3), that they "must through much tribulation enter into the kingdom of God" (Acts 14:22). The members of Christ's mystical Body are first conformed to their Head before they are "glorified together" (Rom. 8:17). Their prayers must be regulated by the revealed will of God (I John 5:14) and not by the promptings of mere flesh and blood which are generally contrary thereto.

The Petitions of Paul's Prayer

Let us consider, second, the *petitions* of this prayer, using the more accurate rendering of the Interlinear: "that you may count worthy of the calling our God." Three things require elucidation: What is here signified by "the calling"? What is meant by "that you may count worthy of" the same? Why did Paul make such a request for them? In Ephesians 1:18 the apostle prayed that those saints might know "the hope of *his* calling." In II Peter 1:10 all Christians are exhorted, "Make *your* calling and election sure." It is one and the same "calling" of which God is the Author and we are the subjects. It is our call to Christianity. The same Greek word is rendered "walk worthy of your *vocation* or occupation" (Eph. 4:1). The artist's vocation is to paint pictures, the wife's vocation is to look after her home, the Christian's vocation is to serve, please, and glorify Christ. He is to make holiness his trade; his business is to *"shew* forth the virtues of him who hath called . . . [him] out of darkness into his marvellous light" (I Peter 2:9) and thereby "adorn the doctrine" which he professes.

The Christian's calling is described by a double attribute: "who hath saved us, and called us with an *holy* calling" (II Tim. 1:9); "wherefore, holy brethren, partakers of the *heavenly* calling" (Heb. 3:1). The former relates to the way, the other to the end. Therefore it is said that God has "called us to glory and virtue" (II Peter 1:3), meaning by "glory" our eternal inheritance, and by "virtue" grace and holiness. The latter is the way and means by which we arrive at the former. Both are to be viewed first as they are represented in the gospel offer: "God hath not called us unto uncleanness, but unto holiness" (I Thess. 4:7). Our daily work is to make holiness the business of our lives. God has also "called us unto his eternal glory by Christ Jesus" (I Peter 5:10). So far from suffering loss by accepting the gospel offer, we become incomparably the gainers. Second, our calling is to be considered as it is impressed upon us by the mighty operation of the Spirit. It is by His power that we truly respond to the gospel and are effectually called from death to life.

The Christian's Life a Vocation

This designating the Christian's life a calling or vocation denotes work for him to do, duties to be performed. It is not a life of daydreaming and emotional rapture, but rather the carrying out of tasks which are neither easy nor pleasant to the natural man, though pertaining to and delightful for the spiritual nature—such as the mortifying of his lusts and the cultivation of practical godliness. The Christian life is also represented as a race which has to be run, demanding putting forth all our energies. This life is likened to a long journey which is both arduous and dangerous for it lies through the enemy's territory (I John 5:19) and therefore is beset with many perils. Severe trials have to be endured, temptations resisted, powerful foes overcome, or we shall be overcome by them and perish in the conflict. The Christian career, then, is a persevering in grace, a holding on his way along the highway of holiness, which alone leads to heaven.

Much grace then is needed by the Christian that, "having put his hand to the plow," he does not look back and become unfit for the kingdom of God

(Luke 9:62); that, having enlisted under the banner of Christ, he does not yield to temptation and become a deserter because of the fierce opposition he meets from those who hate him and would bring about his utter ruin. This brings us to our second question—a harder one to answer. What is meant by "that you may count worthy of the calling our God"? All the prayers of the apostle may be summarized as requests for supplies of grace but, more specifically, for some particular grace suited to the case and circumstances of each company for whom he petitioned. Bearing in mind that these Thessalonians were enduring a great fight of afflictions, it is evident that the principal blessing Paul would seek on their behalf would be the grace of perseverance, that they might hold out steadfast under all their "persecutions and tribulations" and endure to the end of the conflict.

The Thessalonians Exhorted to Perseverance and Holiness

Paul had recently sent Timothy to establish and comfort them, "that no man should be moved by these afflictions" (I Thess. 3:3). In his former prayer he requested that they should be "preserved blameless" (I Thess. 5:23), and here he intimates *how* this was to be accomplished. These Thessalonian Christians had begun well, for which he thanked God (II Thess. 1:3), and now he makes supplication that they may end well, particularly in view of what they were suffering at the hands of their opponents. Calvin (in his *Institutes*) refers to this as a prayer for "the grace of perseverance." That it *was* their perseverance in faith and holiness which the apostle here had in view is definitely confirmed by each succeeding clause of this prayer, as we hope to make clear in our exposition of them.

"That you may count worthy of the calling our God." There is no idea whatever here of anything entitled to reward. It is not the worthiness of condignity but of congruity: that is, it is something which evidence meetness, and not that which is meritorious. As patience under suffering makes it manifest there has been wrought in us that which qualifies or fits us for the glory which is to be revealed. The Greek word for "may count worthy" is rendered "desire" in Acts 28:22: "We desire to hear of thee what thou thinkest": that is, "We deem it right or meet to give thee a fair hearing." The negative form of the word occurs in "But Paul *thought not* good to take him with them" (Acts 15:38). We have referred to these passages to enable the reader to form his own judgment of what is admittedly a difficult word. In I Thessalonians 2:11-12 the apostle had said, "Ye know how we . . . charged every one of you, as a father doth his children, that ye would walk worthy of God [suitably, becomingly], who hath called you unto his kingdom and glory." And here in our text Paul prays that they would be moved to do so by highly *esteeming* their calling and *acting* accordingly.

The apostle was making request for God's work of grace to be continued and completed in their souls, particularly that they might be stirred to discharge their responsibilities in connection with the same. The Greek word occurs again, in an intensified form (*kataziōthentes*) in "they which shall be accounted worthy [adjudged fit] to obtain that world, and the resurrection from the dead" (Luke 20:35), which denotes approbation. The same word is found in "Take heed to yourselves, lest at any time your hearts be overcharged with surfeiting, and drunkenness, and cares of this life, and so that day come upon you unawares. For as a snare shall it come on all them that dwell on the face of the whole earth. Watch ye therefore, and pray always, that ye may be *accounted worthy* to escape all those things that shall come to pass" (Luke 21:34-36). This passage clearly implies some difficulty in realizing this goal and some danger of coming short. As the seed sown, so the harvest: if we "sow to the spirit" then we shall "of the spirit reap life everlasting," but not otherwise.

In all of his prayers for the saints Paul sought further supplies of grace on their behalf in order that they might be more fully furnished and stirred up to the performing of their duty. God has called His people to a life of holiness, requiring them to be so "in all manner of conversation" (I Peter 1:15). At regeneration He imparts to them a holy nature, or principle, and then bids them, "Now yield your members servants to righteousness unto holiness" (Rom. 6:19). Yet that holy nature or principle is but an instrument, therefore far from being a self-sufficient entity. Like all other instruments it is dependent upon God for its life, development, and motions. But its possessor, like all other rational creatures, is endowed with the instinct of self-preservation and therefore is responsible to use all suitable means and measures for its well-being. Nevertheless that responsibility can only be effectually discharged by divine enablement. Therefore it is both our duty and privilege to seek from God all needed grace and trustfully count upon His goodness to supply the same. The particular grace needed will be determined by our varying cases and circumstances.

The Thessalonians Established and Comforted

The Thessalonians were being sorely oppressed by their enemies: so much so that Paul had sent Timothy to establish and comfort them concerning their faith and to urge, "No man should be moved by these afflictions: for yourselves know that we are appointed thereunto" (I Thess. 3:3). Note well that holy balance: though God had ordained those trials, their spiritual father did not conclude there was no reason for him to be concerned with the outcome; rather he dealt with them as moral and accountable agents. Though they had exercised much patience and faith in all their "persecutions and tribulations" (v. 4), the apostle was mindful of their frailty and the very real danger of their wavering and backsliding. Therefore he prayed much that persevering grace might be granted them; that they might walk worthy of their calling and hew steadfastly to the line of God's revealed will, thereby glorifying their Master. Such supplication on their behalf was intensified as Paul eyed the day of punishment and reward (vv. 6-9).

If any readers experience a difficulty in our statement that the apostle here prayed for persevering grace to be granted those sorely tried saints, seeing that the eternal security of all Christians is infallibly guaranteed by the divine promises, it is because of their onesided and defective views of the subject. That difficulty is a fancied rather than a real one. Before proceeding further let us point out that by "persevering grace" we mean divine quickening, strengthening, empowering, to enable the Christian to hold on his course and run the race which is set before him. Thus, in seeking from God food for the soul, deliverance from temptation, the help of His Spirit to mortify our lusts, we are really asking Him for grace to enable us to persevere in faith and holiness.

Lack of Scriptural Balance

There has been a deplorable lack of scriptural *balance* in the presentation of this subject. Calvinists have thrown their emphasis almost entirely upon God's preservation of His people, whereas Arminians have insisted only upon the necessity for their persevering. Since the great majority of our readers have been influenced far more by the former than the latter, let us point out first that God's Word teaches *both*. While it must be the power of God alone which preserves the saints from apostasy (total and final), and not in any degree their own grace, wisdom, strength, or faithfulness, yet we must not fail to press the fact that Christians are responsible to keep themselves: that is, to avoid and resist temptations, abstain from everything injurious, and make diligent use of all those means which God has appointed for their well-being. The Christian is exhorted to *"keep himself* unspotted from the world" (James 1:27). We are bidden, "Keep yourselves from idols" (I John 5:21), "Abstain from all appearance of evil" (I Thess. 5:22), and "Keep yourselves in the love of God" (Jude 21). It is criminal for preachers to ignore such passages as these.

Divine Grace and Human Responsibility

God's Word enjoins the saints to preserve themselves, and the Holy Spirit affirms that they actually *do so*. He moved David to aver, "By the word of thy lips I have kept me from the paths of the destroyer" (Ps. 17:4), "I kept myself from mine iniquity" (Ps. 18:23), "I have refrained my feet from every evil way" (Ps. 119:101). Those were not the boastings of self-righteousness, but rather testimonies to the sufficiency of God's enabling grace. The Apostle Paul, jealous as he ever was of the glory of God, after exhorting the saints, "So run that ye may obtain" (the "incorruptible crown"), and pointing out that the mastery over physical lusts calls for being "temperate in all things," affirmed, "I therefore run, not as uncertainly; so fight I, not as one that beateth the air: but *I keep* under my body, and bring it into subjection: lest that by any means, when I have preached to others, I myself should be a castaway" (I Cor. 9:26-27). Another wrote, "He that is begotten of God keepeth himself" (I John 5:18).

Someone may raise the objection, Does not God attribute too much to the creature, and divide the honors by ascribing the work of preservation partly to God and partly to ourselves? Our first answer is, God's Word is to be received with childlike simplicity, and not quibbled over: received as a whole and not merely those parts which appeal to us or accord with our own views. We have not set forth our *personal ideas* in the last two paragraphs, but have quoted the Scriptures—verses which, alas, have no place whatsoever in the preaching of most Calvinists today. If the reader is unable to fit those verses into his doctrinal system, it is evident there is something wrong with his system. But our second answer is an emphatic denial of such an imputation. For *our use* of the means God has appointed, our greatest diligence and efforts will all be unavailing unless *God blesses* the same. Yes, our utmost watchfulness and industry would avail us nothing whatever if God left us to ourselves.

Our own wisdom and strength, even as Christians, are altogether inadequate for the task assigned to us, and unless the Holy Spirit energized us and afforded success to our efforts our case would be like Gehazi's, who laid his staff upon the dead child (II Kings 4:31), but there was no quickening until his master came and acted! Though Christians do indeed keep themselves (and to deny that is to repudiate the passages quoted above), nevertheless, it is wholly from and by the power of God, so that they freely acknowledge, "By the grace of God I am what I am" (I Cor. 15:10). Yet, observe that the apostle added, "And his grace . . . was not in vain; but I laboured more abundantly than they all." Nevertheless he disavowed all credit for the same: "Yet not I, but the grace of God which was with me." He said again, "I also labour, striving according to his working, which worketh in me mightily" (Col. 1:29). Grace is given us to make use of, yet grace is required to use it.

We must therefore press upon another class of professing Christians that we are entirely dependent upon God. We can only work out our own salvation with fear and trembling as He works in us "both to will and to do of His good pleasure" (Phil. 2:12-13). The ax cannot cut unless it is wielded. Keeping ourselves from evil and destruction is not a distinct and separate work from God's preserving us, but a subordinate though a concurrent one. It is not as though He were one partial cause and we another—as when two persons unite in lifting one burden. Our keeping is from Him, by Him, and under Him, as the little child writes as the hand of his teacher guides his. Therefore there is no ground for boasting, no occasion for self-gratulation. All the praise belongs alone to our Enabler. Thus, while the responsibility of the Christian is duly enforced and his accountability preserved, yet the glory of our preservation belongs entirely to God.

The Power of God Necessary

As the miraculous power of God is absolutely necessary to the beginning of a work in any one's soul, so it is equally necessary for its continuance and progress. Unless God renewed the Christian daily he would perish eternally. Only its Giver "holdeth our soul in life" (Ps. 66:9). God preserves His people by breathing into them holy thoughts and quickening meditations which keep them in His fear and love; by stirring up His grace in us so that we are moved to holy action; by drawing us so that we run after Him; by inclining our hearts to love His law and walk in its statutes. God preserves us by giving us a spirit of prayer so that we are moved to seek fresh supplies of strength from Him; by restraining us from sin and delivering out of temptations; by working in us godly sorrow and causing us to penitently confess our sins; by His consolation when we are cast down, which puts new heart into us; by granting us foretastes of the glory awaiting us so that the joy of the Lord energizes us (Neh. 8:10).

If unfallen Adam was incapable of keeping himself, it is certain that we cannot do so independently of God. Indwelling sin is too potent, Satan too powerful to overcome in our own strength. Our falls demonstrate the need of God's preserving us. Nevertheless, Adam was responsible for keeping himself, and was fully condemned because he did not do so. Likewise, believers are responsible to avoid every path which leads to death, and to steadfastly tread to the very end that narrow way which alone leads to life. As a rational creature is morally responsible to shun known danger, to abstain from poisons, and to eat nourishing food for the sustaining of his body, so a spiritual creature is responsible to do likewise concerning his soul. If he is to guard against the spirit of self-confidence and self-sufficiency, he is also to beware of acting presumptuously. When the devil tempted Christ to cast Himself down from the pinnacle of the temple, assuring Him that the angels would preserve Him, He immediately denounced such recklessness with "Thou shalt not tempt the Lord thy God."

Means and Ends

We must never divorce the precept from the promise nor what God requires from us from what He has purposed for us. God has inseparably connected means and ends, and woe be unto us if we put them asunder. The same God who has predestinated that a certain end shall be accomplished, has also predestinated that it shall be accomplished via the employment of certain means. Thus His people are told, "God hath from the beginning chosen you to salvation through [1] sanctification of the Spirit and [2] belief of the truth" (II Thess. 2:13). Our "sanctification of the Spirit" is by His own operation, but "belief of the truth" is the act required of us, and we are not saved, nor will we ever be, till we perform it. Likewise we are told that the saints "are kept by the power of God," yet not to the setting aside of their concurrence, for immediately following are the words "through faith" (I Peter 1:5). The duty of keeping his faith healthy and vigorous devolves upon the Christian—seeking from God its strengthening, feeding upon suitable food. The duty of exercising that faith rests upon the Christian also: "Be sober, be vigilant; . . . resist [the 'roaring lion' who seeks to 'devour'] stedfast in the faith" (I Peter 5:8-9).

Christ stated, "If ye *continue* in my word, then are ye my disciples indeed" (John 8:31). "My sheep hear [heed, obey] my voice, . . . and they *follow* me: and I give unto them eternal life; and *they* [those who plainly evidence themselves to be of His 'sheep' by yielding to His authority and following the example which He has left them—and no others] shall never perish" (John 10:27-28). It is not honest to generalize the promise of verse 28: it must be restricted to the characters described in verse 27. The apostle guarded and qualified his statement in Colossians 1:22 with the succeeding verse: "If ye continue in the faith grounded and settled, and be not moved away from the hope of the gospel."

That prince of theologians among the Puritans, John Owen, preserved a holy balance of the truth. Said he, when exposing the sophistries of one who opposed the certainty of God's preservation of His people to eternal glory on the ground that it encouraged loose living: "Doth this doctrine promise, with height of assurance, that under what vile practices so ever men do live, they shall have exemption from eternal punishment? Doth it teach men that it is vain to use the means of mortification because they shall certainly attain the end whether they use the means or no? Doth it speak peace to the flesh, in assurance of blessed immortality, though it disport itself in all folly in the meantime? . . . The perseverance of the saints is not held out in the Scriptures on any such ridiculous terms, carry themselves well, or wickedly miscarry themselves, but is asserted upon the account of God's effectual grace preserving them in the use of the means and from all such miscarriages."

On Hebrews 3:14 Owen said, "Persistency in our subsistence in Christ unto the end is a matter of *great endeavour and diligence,* and that unto all believers. This is plainly included in the expression here used by the apostle: 'If we hold the beginning of our confidence stedfast unto the end.' The words denote our utmost endeavour to hold it fast and keep it firm. Shaken it will be, opposed it will be, kept it will not, it cannot be, without *our* utmost and diligent endeavour. It is true, persistency in Christ doth not, as to the issue and event, depend absolutely on our diligence. The unalterableness of our union unto Christ, on the account of the faithfulness of the covenant of grace, is that which doth, and shall eventually secure. But yet our own diligent endeavour is such an indispensable means for that end, *as without it,* it will not be brought about."

Pray for Persevering Grace

It may be thought that we have wandered far from the subject of our opening paragraphs. But have we? Our endeavor has been to demonstrate the very real need there is to *pray for persevering grace,* both for ourselves and for our brethren. Some ask, Why should we, since God has solemnly promised the eternal security of all His people? First, because our great High Priest has taught us (by His example) to do so: "Holy Father, *keep* through thine own name those whom thou hast given me. I pray not that thou shouldest take them out of the world, but that thou shouldest *keep* them from the evil" (John 17:11, 15). Second, as an acknowledgment of our dependency and a confession of our helplessness. Third, as our concurring with God's revealed will, seeking grace to use the appointed means. We place a very large question mark after the Christian profession of any man who is unconscious of his frailty and who deems such a prayer as "Leave me not, neither forsake me, O God of my salvation" (Ps. 27:9) as unsuited to *his* case. The present writer frequently cries, "Hold thou me up, and I shall be safe" (Ps. 119:117), knowing that the converse would be "Leave me to myself, and I shall assuredly perish."

Chapter 28

PRAYER FOR PERSEVERING GRACE:
PETITION, DESIGN, AND ACCOMPLISHMENT

II Thessalonians 1:11-12

THERE IS MORE DIFFERENCE OF OPINION among sermonizers and commentators on this prayer than on any other in the New Testament. It is not easy to make a translation of the Greek into simple and intelligible English, as appears from the additions made in our Authorized Version, for the insertion of the italicized words quite alters the scope and meaning of its clauses. Even where there is substantial concurrence as to the best English rendition, expositors are far from being agreed as to the precise meaning of its several petitions. We have therefore proceeded more slowly in our own attempt to open its contents, taking as our foundation the rendering of *Bagster's Interlinear,* which in our judgment is as close and literal an equivalent of the original as can be given: "For which also we pray always for you, that you may count worthy of the calling our God, and may fulfil every good pleasure of goodness and work of faith with power, so that may be glorified the name of our Lord Jesus Christ in you, and ye in Him, according to the grace of our God and of [the] Lord Jesus Christ."

First, we have carefully considered the *occasion* of this prayer or what prompted it, as its opening, "for which also [wherefore also, AV] we pray," requires us to do. We have pointed out that such an investigation takes us back to verse 4 where reference is made to the "persecutions and tribulations" which those saints were enduring. And we reminded the reader that the Thessalonians were being so sorely oppressed by their enemies that Paul had sent Timothy to "comfort and establish" them concerning their faith and to urge them "that no man should be moved by these afflictions" (I Thess. 3:3). In II Thessalonians 1:4-10 the apostle had sought to strengthen them by setting forth various considerations for their encouragement. He assured them that he specially remembered them before the throne of grace, earnestly supplicating God on their behalf. The "wherefore [for which cause] also we pray *always* for you" shows, second, the *importunity* of this prayer. He frequently interceded for them, which fact expressed both his deep affection and real concern for them.

Its Petitions

Third, coming to its *petitions,* we expressed the conviction that the principal blessing for which the apostle here made request was that further supplies of *persevering grace* should be granted these saints. We conclude this, first, from the very trying situation they were in. Second, they particularly needed that grace in order to conduct themselves suitably to their profession. Third, their allotted task was to "fulfil all the good pleasure of his goodness, and the work of faith with power," for which performance divine enablement was absolutely essential. Fourth, thereby they would glorify "the name of our Lord Jesus Christ." Fifth, on any other analysis of Paul's prayer its concluding words would be a redundancy. But if their perseverance was the apostle's concern, then the phrase "according to the grace of our God" would remove all ground of boasting and place the crown of honor where it rightly belonged. There is a holy balance between the truth of God's effectual preservation of His people and the imperative necessity of their continuing in faith and holiness.

By regarding this prayer (and each of his others) as an *implied exhortation,* we obtain a better understanding of the apostle's scope. For the chief reason why his prayers are recorded is that those for whom he prayed (and we who are informed of his petitions) might seek to realize the blessings he sought for God's children. In other words, those things for which the apostle made request are what God requires from His people, yet what they are unable to accomplish in their own strength. While there is nothing meritorious in them, yet the exercise of their graces is as necessary as the gospel and the glorifying of their Master. Consequently we see in this prayer, as everywhere in the Word of truth, a striking and blessed union of power and our perseverance and duty leading to attainment of blessedness. Here the exercise of divine sovereignty and the discharge of human responsibility concur. Never let us put asunder what God has joined together.

The Calling of God

"That you may count worthy of the calling of our God" is the first petition in the prayer we are now pondering. Since we have previously devoted several paragraphs to a consideration of its meaning, we must abbreviate our present remarks upon it. The "calling" has reference to that operation of divine grace by which these Christians had been brought out of darkness into God's marvelous light and made the willing subjects of the kingdom of His dear Son, which entailed that henceforth they must make personal holiness their trade or avocation. The petition was that they should be brought to highly esteem such a vocation—notwithstanding the bitter opposition it met with—and be stirred up to meekly discharge their responsibilities in connection with the same. Paul prayed not that they might be delivered from their "persecution and tribulation," but rather that they should be divinely enabled to hold out steadfast under the same and behave as the followers of Christ so that He should not be ashamed to own them as "His brethren." Paul's yearning was that by their becoming conduct they should clearly evince themselves to be among the effectually called of God.

God's Good Pleasure

"And fulfil all the good pleasure of his goodness" is the second petition. The reference is clearly to one of the divine excellencies, for God is expressly mentioned at the end of the preceding clause. The "good pleasure" of God signifies His free will, his entire independency, that He acts without any restraint, being a law to Himself. His "goodness" is His benignity and kindness. God has absolute power and sovereign right to dispose as He will of all creatures, as to not only their temporal but their eternal concerns (Matt. 20:15). That sovereign will is the sole reason why He passes by some and chooses others (Rom. 9:18). But that absolute will of God is sweetly tempered with goodness or rich favor to His own elect. He has gracious goodwill to them at all times. As the self-inclination which is in God to promote His people's welfare is free, it is called His "good pleasure," and as it moves Him to bestow benefits on them, it is termed His goodness, or benignity. All that the saints receive from Him proceeds from the goodwill which He bears them, and therefore all the praise for the same belongs alone to Him.

The Twofold Will of God

Note that these words, "fulfil all the good pleasure of his goodness," do not form part of a doctrinal statement affirming the certainty of the divine purpose; instead, they describe a duty incumbent upon Christians—a duty for which divine grace needs to be sought. It is therefore requisite that we call the reader's attention to a simple but necessary distinction. There is a twofold "will" of God referred to in Scripture, namely, His secret and revealed will—the former being the principal from which He works and which is invincible, the latter being the rule by which we are required to walk and which is never perfectly performed by any man (Dan. 4:35; Rom. 9:19; cf. John 7:17 and Luke 12:47). And there is a twofold "counsel" of God—the one referring to His eternal decree, and the other to His advice to us (Isa. 46:10; Acts 4:28; cf. Prov. 1:25; Luke 7:30). There is also the "good pleasure" by which God always acts (Eph. 1:9) and the "pleasure" of God by which we are called to act (Ps. 103:21). It is the latter of which our present verse speaks. The apostle prayed that these saints might be granted hearts framed to entire obedience to the divine statutes.

It is blessedly true that God does fulfill every good pleasure of His goodness in and through His people, yet it is equally true that they ought to aim at and rest content with nothing short of their fulfilling every divine precept which has been given them. The divine statutes are not only clothed with God's authority, which we disregard at our peril, but they are also expressions of His goodness, which we ignore to our loss. God manifests His "goodness" to us in many ways, not least in His commandments, which are designed for our welfare. "The sabbath was made for man"—because he needed it for his benefit. They who, like Jonah the prophet, follow their own inclinations rather than God's instructions "forsake their own mercy" (Jonah 2:8). A life of obedience is not only our duty but our comfort. The divine wisdom has so determined that whatever promotes His glory shall also advance the good of His people. Therefore as He has inseparably connected sin and misery, so He has holiness and happiness. "Great peace have they which love thy law" (Ps. 119:165). "He that keepeth the law, happy is he" (Prov. 29:18). "The way of transgressors is hard" (Prov. 13:15), but Wisdom's ways are "ways of pleasantness" (Prov. 3:17).

God Requires a Holy People

"And may fulfil all the good pleasure of his goodness." Again we observe what an exalted standard of conduct the apostle (by necessary implication) here sets before the saints. God requires His people to be "holy in all manner of conversation" (I Peter 1:15)—in thought, word, and deed. Nothing less than complete conformity to the rule God has given us must be our aim and earnest endeavor. No dispensation is granted us to pick and choose out of the Scriptures what we like best and pass by the rest. The divine promises must not be esteemed above the precepts. At this very point the emptiness of so many professors stands revealed. They are like backsliding Ephraim who "loveth to tread out the corn" but would not "break his clods" (Hosea 10:11). How many who call themselves "believers" approve the privileges of Christianity but disdain its duties, are all for saving grace, but nothing for the grace which teaches us to deny self. God requires that our obedience should be not only diligent but universal. Said the Psalmist, "Then shall I not be ashamed, when I have respect unto *all* thy commandments" (Ps. 119:6). Until we do so, we have cause to hide our faces in confusion.

Divine Wisdom Needed

But like everything else in the Christian's life, obedience to God is a *growth:* not in the spirit of it, not in sincere desire, not in determination to please God, for that is common to all the regenerate, but in actual performance. Light as well as love is necessary for this growth. Light comes to the Christian gradually as he is able to bear it—"more and more unto the perfect day" (Prov. 4:18). Increased wisdom is necessary in order to make right use of the light—to know when to speak and when to be silent, and so on. And that is largely a matter of experience. As babes in Christ are unable to feed upon the food of which the fully grown partake, so there are tasks performed by the latter of which the former are incapable as yet. Mark the discrimination in the apostle's language: "that you may fulfil all the good pleasure of his goodness." He did not employ the verb *teleioō* which means "to accomplish" but *pleroō* which signifies "to bring to completion." Paul had reference to a process which is performed gradually or by degrees. The same word occurs again in Acts 12:25; 14:21. The goal was that they "might walk worthy of the Lord unto all pleasing, being fruitful in every good work, and increasing in the knowledge of God" (Col. 1:10), thus performing all those duties Paul had assigned them.

Increased Grace Essential

The apostle here made supplication for increased *grace* as well as light and wisdom, essential for a fuller obedience. Once more we call attention to the *breadth* of his requests. He now besought God for a full supply of enabling grace for His people. Paul was no niggardly petitioner. Eyeing the good will which God bears His children, Paul did not hesitate to open his mouth when seeking favors for them—which far from being presumptuous was honoring to God as he availed himself of his rightful privilege. This feature is a very prominent one in all his prayers. It was as though he called to mind the example of the man after God's own heart, who asked, "Deal *bountifully* with thy servant, that I may live, and keep thy word" (Ps. 119:17). That was the very thing the apostle was doing here: beseeching God that He would impart to the Thessalonians a plentiful supply of grace that they might be spiritually alive and vigorous, in order that they should "keep his word," for in a renewed soul's estimation the best " bounty" is to have the heart furnished for full obedience to God's "good pleasure."

Let us not be stumbled then by the exalted standard of holiness which God has set before us, but let us rather be encouraged by the apostle's precedent to seek full supplies of grace from God to fit us for the performing of our duty. If we are believingly occupied with "the goodness" of our God we shall not be afraid to ask and look for bounteous blessings from Him. As one truly said, "We may be too bold in our manner of approach to God, but we cannot be too bold in our expectations from Him." God is able, God is willing, to do for us exceeding abundantly above all that we ask or think. The straitness is always in ourselves and never in Him: in the narrowness of our faith and not in the breadth of His promises. "For unto every one that hath shall be given, and he shall have *abundance*" (Matt. 25:29). Plead that word before Him. "God is able to make all grace abound toward you; that ye, always having all sufficiency in all things, may abound to every good work" (II Cor. 9:8). Ponder well that threefold "all"! What further inducements do we require to approach the throne of grace with large petitions? If your need and longing are great, see to it that your expectation is equally so.

It is neither honoring to God nor good for himself that the Christian should be contented with a little grace. These Thessalonians were not only regenerate persons but they had attained a considerable degree of eminence in faith and holiness. Nevertheless Paul prayed that such further supplies of grace would be vouchsafed to them that they would be enabled to "fulfil all the good pleasure of his goodness," i.e., that they would measure up to the whole revealed will of God. Do not be satisfied with the assurance that you have enough grace to take you to heaven, but seek that measure of it which will be not only for your comfort on earth but for the glorifying of your Saviour while you are left in this scene. "Covet earnestly the best gifts" (I Cor. 12:31). Pray for enlarged affections and expectations. Beg God to deal with you not according to your deserts but according to the largeness of His liberality, seeking from Him that "good measure" which is "pressed down and running over." Above all, plead the Redeemer's worthiness. God never denies those who make *that* their all-prevailing plea, for there is infinitely more merit in Christ's sacrifice than there is demerit in you and all your sins!

A Notional and Nominal Faith Worthless

"And work of faith with power" is the third petition, or thing which God required from the saints and which the apostle asked for them. A notional and nominal faith, which is without good works, is dead and worthless; but a spiritual faith which produces fruit to God's glory is living and authentic. The faith which God communicates to His elect is a vital and operative principle, therefore it has an office to discharge, a duty to fulfill. These words "the work of faith" are to be understood in precisely the same way as that little-understood expression "the work of the law" in Romans 2:15. The "work of the law" in that verse is to be regarded not as a principle of righteousness operating within the unregenerate Gentiles (a manifest absurdity) but as the design and function of the law. Its "work" is to prohibit and promise, to threaten or assure, reward. The "work of the law" refers not to the conduct it requires from us but to what the law itself *does*—accuses or acquits. So "the work of faith" refers to neither God's quickening of faith nor its fruits through us, but to the task allotted to it. It is not the invigorating of faith by God's Spirit which is here in view, but that function which God has assigned faith, that office which it is fitted to perform.

In his sermon on these verses, Mr. Philpot said on these words: "By 'the work of faith' we may understand two things: 1. the operation of God upon the heart, whereby from time to time faith is raised up and brought into living exercise upon the things of God; and 2. the work which faith has to do when thus raised up and strengthened in the soul." There are two sorts of work required of and ascribed to faith, namely, that which is internal and that which is external. The former consists of the mind's assent to the truth, the will's consent to what is there taught, and the heart's reliance on the promises of God, the whole soul resting on Christ, confiding its eternal interests to Him. The external work of faith consists of an open confession of Christ, boldly owning His ways before the world which despises them, and a ready obedience to the will of God in forsaking sin and walking in the path of His commandments, producing practical holiness. Therefore our obedience is designated "the obedience of faith" (Rom. 16:26).

The External Work of Faith

While not altogether excluding the internal work of faith, we think it is obvious, from both what precedes and what follows, that the external work of faith is chiefly in view—the honoring of Christ before men. The products of the work of faith make that faith evident to our fellows, for a holy walk brings more glory to Christ than a lot of frothy talk. Steadfast perseverance in duty in a time of persecution is more pleasing to Him than showy performance in a day of peace. Furthermore, in a time of acute suffering the saint will find it easier to determine his spiritual case by the objective rather than the subjective exercise of his grace. Thomas Manton stated, "The drift of his prayer is that God would enable them to ride out the storm of those troubles which came upon them for the Gospel's sake. And a Christian, in judging his condition, will discover it better in the external acts of faith than in the internal."

"The work of faith *with power,*" namely, the power of God in enabling faith to fulfill its functions. As the faith here spoken of is of God, so it is dependent upon God. Does faith support the soul under heavy trials? That is because it is sustained by the omnipotent One. Does it perform duties which are contrary to the dictates of carnal wisdom? That is because faith is energized by divine power. Does faith choose a path which is hateful to flesh and blood? It is because faith is strengthened by the might of its Giver. Does faith, in the midst of the most painful and bewildering situations, aver, "Though he slay me, yet will I trust in him"? This is so because the Almighty is its maintainer. Nevertheless, if our faith is small and feeble, the fault is entirely ours. God has expressly bidden us, "Be strong in the Lord, and in the power of his might" (Eph. 6:10); therefore it is both our privilege and duty to ask and expect Him to make good in us that which He requires from us. Surely that is evident from the Lord's rebuke to His disciples. He would not have reproved them for their fear and unbelief (Matt. 8:26) except that *they* were responsible to maintain it in healthy vigor.

Now we have, fourth, the *design* of this prayer; and fifth, its *accomplishment*. The mind of the apostle centered upon the honoring of Christ by the furthering of the salvation of His people, for in this world the Head of the church is now magnified through and by His members. The grand concern which occupied the heart, formed the thoughts, and motivated the activities of His ambassador was the exalting of his beloved Lord. The whole of Paul's strenuous and self-effacing Christian life is summed up in that memorable confession of his, "According to my earnest expectation and my hope, that in nothing I shall be ashamed, but that with all boldness, as always, so now also Christ shall be magnified in my body, whether it be by life, or by death. For to me to live is Christ, and to die is gain" (Phil. 1:20-21). Accordingly, we find that blessed aim actuated him equally in his prayers and in his preaching, during his ministerial labors or while suffering imprisonment.

Glorifying the Name of the Lord Jesus

In petitioning the throne of grace that these Thessalonians might be divinely enabled to highly esteem and walk worthy of their holy and heavenly calling, by performing every duty which the divine precepts outlined and by fulfilling the work of faith with power, the apostle aimed at the honoring of his Master. The design before him was that the name of the Lord Jesus Christ should be glorified in them and they in Him. In verse 10 he had comforted them with the declaration "He shall come to be glorified in his saints, and to be admired in all them that believe (because our testimony among you was believed) in that day." Therefore he had supplicated God fervently to that end, thereby teaching them (and us) *the effect* which that blessed prospect should have upon our walk. The advent of the Redeemer in glory with the glorification of the church at that time is set before us in Scripture as the grand consummation of the Christian vocation or calling. The hope of the church is a powerful dynamic in the promotion of her present holiness (I John 3:2-3). Only those who truly delight in and pant after holiness will spiritually long for Christ's return and cry, "Make haste, my beloved" (Song of Sol. 8:14).

It is often said that we are saved to serve. We prefer to say that we are saved to please and honor Christ. His redeemed are left for a season in this scene to represent Him, to show forth His praises (I Peter 2:9), to reflect (in their measure) His excellencies, to follow the example He left them—which may be summarized as living wholly to the glory of God and doing good to all men, especially those who are of the household of faith. The chief and highest end of the creature is to glorify its Creator; therefore the fundamental principle of godliness is this: "Whether therefore ye eat, or drink, or whatsoever ye do, do all to the glory of God" (I Cor. 10:31). Why did the apostle pray, "So that may be glorified the name of our Lord Jesus Christ" rather than "That *God* may be glorified"? Generally, because God has made Christ the partner of His glory: "that all should honour the Son, even as they honour the Father" (John 5:23); "that the Father may be glorified in the Son" (John 14:13). More specifically, because the "persecutions and tribulations" (v. 4) which the Thessalonians were enduring were for the gospel's sake, for the uncompromising profession of the Saviour's name.

Concern for the Divine Glory

The acts of the natural man are prompted by self-love and are done to advance his own interests, comforts, and glory: "Is not this great Babylon, that I have built . . . by the might of *my* power, and for the honour of *my* majesty?" (Dan. 4:30). The natural man does not act from any consideration of or concern for the honor of God. If he refrains from committing gross sins, it is for his own reputation and not from any regard for the divine law. Those who are liberal in contributing to the poor and needy distribute their charity out of pity for the suffering and not with their eyes on the divine precept. Even the unregenerate who claim to be Christians are regulated by what is agreeable to themselves and not by love to Christ and respect for His authority and glory. They are willing to please God just as far as it does not displease them. Others who wish to obtain a reputation for piety are like the Pharisees, who tithed and fasted and made long prayers to satisfy their own ambition—to be seen, heard, and praised by men. But where a miracle of grace is wrought in the soul, self-pleasing is displaced by self-denial, and gratitude and love now move the man to seek the glory of God.

Yet though a new nature is imparted at regeneration, the old nature is not removed or bettered. The principle of "the flesh" still indwells the soul and is continually clamoring for indulgence; thus there is a ceaseless conflict within the believer between carnality and holiness. The believer's responsibility and lifelong task is to mortify the one and nourish and exercise the other, to deny self and follow Christ. We should frequently test ourselves on this very point, as by this we may most surely ascertain whether we are growing in grace: to what extent we are dying to sin and living to God.

How far is my conduct determined by a concern for the divine glory? Have I formed the habit of challenging my inclinations and determinations with the question "Will this be for the glory of God"? Every plan we form, every act we perform, is either pleasing or displeasing to God, honoring or dishonoring to Him—there is no mean between those alternatives. Every project I entertain will either further the interests of self or serve to magnify Christ. I must pause and consider *which* of those alternatives my heart is really set upon; otherwise, what difference is there between me and the respectable worldling?

"Whatsoever ye do, do all to the glory of God" (I Cor. 10:31). Is a young man giving serious thought to choosing a wife? Then he should first solemnly ponder the question "Do I desire marriage for the glory of God?" If a man is contemplating a change of occupation or residence, or if his thoughts turn to planning a journey, before making the decision it is his Christian duty to ask himself, "Will such a course promote the honor of Christ? Am I making this move for His sake?" This principle must also actuate and regulate the minister of the gospel. It is a horrible profanation of the sacred office to seek the applause of men or covet the fame of being thought a great preacher. This principle must take precedence over seeking the good of souls. If the salvation of sinners and the edifying of saints are my supreme concerns, I am making an idol of the creature, and efforts after success rather than fidelity to my charge will determine my course. But if I labor with an eye single to the glory of God and aim at magnifying Christ, I shall be far more concerned about preaching the truth in its purity than in seeing results.

Motives for Seeking the Glory of God

There are many weighty reasons which should move the Christian to seek the glory of God in all that he does. That which is of the greatest value and consideration should be sought before all else in life. And surely God's glory has infinite excellence above all things, and therefore must be preferred before all material good. Then too, since God ever has our good in mind we ought ever to keep His glory in view. He never forgets us, nor should we forget Him. How concerned we ought to be to make restitution for our former dishonoring of God! In our unregenerate days we had no regard for Him: never a mercy but what we abused. How zealous then we ought now to be in ordering our conduct to His praise, manifesting the genuineness of our repentance over the past by living wholly for Him in the present! The example of Christ shows us our duty. He "pleased not himself" (Rom. 15:3) but ever cherished God's honor. Did He say, "Father, save *me* from this hour"? No, rather, "Father, glorify *Thy* name." (See John 12:27-28.) By His example Christ taught us to put the honor of God before our own interests and comforts.

Here are some of the ways by which God is glorified. By ascribing glory to Him, which is His due (Ps. 29:1-2). By proclaiming His worth to others (Ps. 34:3). By loving Him and making Him our supreme delight (Ps. 73:25). By implicit confidence in Him: Abraham "was strong in faith [thereby] giving glory to God" (Rom. 4:20). By dedicating our bodies to Him (I Cor. 6:20). By yielding obedience: "that they may see your good works, and glorify your Father which is in heaven" (Matt. 5:16). By our repentance (Rev. 16:9*b*). By confession of sin (Joshua 7:19). By cultivating the fruit of the Spirit in our lives: "Herein is my Father glorified, that ye bear much fruit" (John 15:8). By adoring God's excellency: "Whoso offereth praise glorifieth me" (Ps. 50:23). By readiness to suffer for Him and patiently bear afflictions (I Peter 4:14-16). By disowning any credit to ourselves, attributing to Him all good in and from us (Rom. 3:12*b*). "That God in *all* things may be glorified through Jesus Christ" (I Peter 4:11*b*) is the end we should ever aim at, avoiding whatever is contrary, making all subordinate and subservient.

Making the honor of Christ our supreme concern will preserve us from many snares and follies. All the disastrous bypaths into which we have wandered since we became Christians may be traced back to failure at this very point. Instead of being actuated and regulated by the determination to magnify Christ, we yielded to a spirit of self-love and self-pleasing. In seeking the glory of Christ we, at the same time, are furthering our own salvation, for we then act contrary to the promptings of the flesh and are being more conformed to the image of God's Son. Thus highly esteeming our calling and walking worthy of it, fulfilling every precept of God's goodness, and keeping our own faith healthy and in vigorous exercise, we both honor Christ and advance our own spiritual interests. Moreover, what an unspeakable privilege and dignity it is to serve such a Master as ours! Is it not glorious indeed to please—yea, to endure persecution for—such a glorious Saviour! "Rejoicing that they were counted worthy to suffer shame for His name" (Acts 5:41). But "if . . . we suffer with him" we shall also " be also glorified together" (Rom. 8:17).

Reference to the Life to Come

"And ye in him" has intimate reference to the next life: the consummation of our salvation, the reward for honoring Christ in this life. We quote from Thomas Manton: "God hath appointed this order, that we should glorify Him before He glorifies us, and there is much wisdom and righteousness in that appointment. It would greatly redound to God's dishonor if He should glorify those that do not glorify Him, and make no difference between the godly and the wicked, those that break His laws and those that keep them. If both should fare alike, it would eclipse the righteousness of God's government. . . . God hath not only appointed that we should glorify Him before He glorifies us, but that we should glorify Him upon the earth before He glorifies us in heaven. We have Christ for an example: 'I have glorified thee on the earth. . . . And now, O Father, glorify thou me' (John 17:4-5). . . . Christ takes special notice of those that glorify Him in the world and it is one of His pleas for His disciples: '[Father], I am glorified in them' (John 17:10). He is an Advocate in heaven for those that are factors for His kingdom upon earth. . . . This glory is promised: 'If any man serve me, him will my Father honour' (John 12:26*b*)."

"According to the grace of our God and [of] the Lord Jesus Christ" secures the fulfillment of this prayer. The wider reference is to all that precedes. Our acting suitably to God's holy calling, our fulfilling every good counsel of His goodness and the work of faith by His power, our glorifying His Son, is all from and by divine grace. Our salvation from the love, the guilt, the defilement, the power, and (ultimately) the presence of sin, is wholly by divine grace. Scripture is plain and emphatic on this point, and so also must be the tongue and pen of God's servants. His sovereign favor chose us in Christ before the foundation of the world. And each blessing which follows it is equally of His favor. Therefore we read of "the election of grace" (Rom. 11:5), that our calling is "according to his own purpose and grace" (II Tim. 1:9), that we have "believed through grace" (Acts 18:27), that we are "justified freely by his grace" (Rom. 3:24). It is the same wondrous grace which bears with our dullness and waywardness, which provides for our every need, which renews us day by day in the inner man, and which brings us safely to heaven.

"According to the grace of our God and the Lord Jesus Christ" refers more immediately to the preceding clause, "and ye in him," which principally refers to our glorification. For though our glorification be the issue and reward of our perseverance in faith and holiness, yet it is not a reward of debt but of grace, not something we have merited, but something bestowed by God's free bounty. Hence we read of "the grace that is to be brought unto . . . [us] at the revelation of Jesus Christ" (I Peter 1:13). Thus all ground for boasting is removed from us, and the praise and glory are His alone. Nothing but His wondrous grace could overcome our obstinacy and bring us into willing subjection to God. Nothing less is able to maintain and keep us in the paths of righteousness. We can only work out our own salvation with fear and trembling as God works in us "both to will and to do of his good pleasure" (Phil. 2:11-12). The world, the flesh, and the devil are far too powerful for us to overcome in our own might.

Saved by Grace Through Faith

But if the balance of truth is to be preserved, we must point out that the grace of God is the original cause of our salvation. Yet it does not preclude the worth and work of Christ as its meritorious cause, and neither does it exclude repentance, faith, and obedience as the means: "By grace are ye saved *through faith*." Though neither faith nor good works have any causal influence in our salvation, though they are not concauses with the grace of God and of Christ, yet God has appointed this method and way of salvation. Principal causes do not exclude necessary means, but comprise them; therefore we must not set grace against grace and say that the elect will be saved whether they believe or no, or that the regenerate will reach heaven no matter how they live. Grace is magnified by us only as we insist that it works "through righteousness" (Rom. 5:21) and as we bring forth its holy fruits. Basically and fundamentally our salvation flows from the sovereign pleasure of God (the goodwill which He bears us), and it is effectually wrought in us by His power. Yet instrumentally salvation issues from the discharge of our responsibility (for God ever treats us as moral agents), from the heeding of His warnings and in using the means He has appointed. *"We believe* to the saving of the soul" (Heb. 10:39) and are "kept by the power of God *through faith*" (I Peter 1:5).

It is all-important to insist that "salvation is of the Lord" (Jonah 2:9) so that all the glory is ascribed to Him, and so that we may be encouraged to seek grace from Him. For when we are aware of our undeservingness, only the realization of His abundant favor will keep our hearts from sinking. Yet it is nonetheless necessary to press the Christian's responsibility in the use of all proper means so that he may be preserved from lapsing into antinomianism and fatalistic inertia. There is a balance to be preserved here between a sense of our helplessness and our obligation to use the grace which we already have and to seek further and fuller supplies of grace (Heb. 4:16). Our entire dependency upon God and our full accountability to Him are not contradictory but are complementary parts of one whole. It is the grand privilege of faith to make free use of Christ, and it is our duty to live *unto* Him, yet that is only possible by constantly drawing from Him. Without Christ we can do nothing (John

15:5), but energized by Him we can do all things (Phil. 4:13). Then let us see to it that we are "strong in the grace that is in Christ Jesus" (II Tim. 2:1).

All Is Through the Grace of God

"According to the grace of our God" is to be regarded then as referring to *the whole* of His benignant design toward us. It is on that basis all our supplies must be asked for, it is from that fountain all the streams of blessing do flow, and it is to that divine attribute all must be ascribed. It is the grace which sets His power to work on our behalf. Were the operation of His power suspended for a moment, even the "new man" would instantly be paralyzed. He "holdeth our soul in life" (Ps. 66:9), and should He "let loose his hand" we would be at once "cut off" (Job 6:9). For the resisting of any sin or the performing of any duty we are in need of the gracious power of God moment by moment. Nevertheless, we are not mere automatons. "He which hath begun a good work in you will . . . [finish] it" (Phil. 1:6), yet not without our concurrence, as though we were blocks of wood. Finally, we must not so eye "the grace of our God" as to lose sight of "and of the Lord Jesus Christ." In the Greek there is only one article here, and it is in the singular number, which not only exhibits the unity of the divine nature but also reveals the two Persons engaged in a common work.

Chapter 29

PRAYER FOR COMFORT AND STABILITY

II THESSALONIANS 2:16-17

WE DESIRE TO EMPHASIZE the need and importance of preserving the balance of truth, for in so doing we are really calling attention to the method followed by the Holy Spirit in the Scriptures, and that cannot be ignored without our suffering serious loss. There is a most blessed mingling together in the Word of those different elements which are so essential to a well-rounded Christian life, as in the natural world God has provided various kinds of food suited to the several needs of our bodies. A striking example of this is found in the immediate context of that prayer which here engages our attention. In verses 13 and 14 one of the fundamental articles of our most holy faith is expressed, not in cold and formal manner, but rather as that which occasions deep and constant thanksgiving. Next, in verse 15, the corresponding duty is enforced, the obligations which such a disclosure of divine grace devolves upon the favored objects and recipients of it. Then follows our prayer which, as we shall see, really grows out of verses 13 to 15. Thus here we have doctrinal declaration, practical exhortation, and earnest supplication; that is what both preachers and hearers should ever blend together—in that order.

God's Sovereign Grace to His Elect

What has just been pointed out is too weighty for us to dismiss without a further word of amplification. After describing the fearful judgment which God sends upon those who receive not His truth in the love of it, the apostle turned to those who were the objects of the divine favor. This moved him to exclaim, "But we are bound to give thanks alway to God for you, brethren beloved of the Lord, because God hath from the beginning chosen you to salvation through sanctification of the Spirit and belief of the truth" (v. 13). That should ever be the effect on a child of God as he solemnly contemplates the doom of unbelievers. Hearty thanksgiving should issue from his soul at the realization that the Lord eternally set His heart upon an elect company which He appointed to deliverance from the wrath to come. But what we would here particularly note is that God's eternal election does not preclude effectual calling, nor does it render needless the exercise of our moral agency. Those "beloved of the Lord" (all of them, yet none other) are "chosen . . . to salvation *through* sanctification of the Spirit and belief of the truth." These three things must never be separated.

304

First, from the beginning the elect are "chosen . . . to salvation," God's sovereign and eternal decree being the originating cause of salvation. Second, that decree is fulfilled "through" or by means of the "sanctification of the Spirit," the reference being to His quickening operation, when by the miracle of regeneration He sets them apart from those who are dead in trespasses and sins. Third, God's eternal decree is only accomplished when the subjects of it personally appropriate the truth of the gospel to themselves. While in their unregenerate state they were incapable of any saving "belief of the truth," for their corrupt hearts were hostile to it, in love with error and sin. But when the miracle of grace is wrought within them their enmity to God is slain, and the gospel is welcomed as exactly suited to their dire need and is cordially embraced by them. Thus they spell out their election and evince their effectual call by the Holy Spirit through their "belief of the truth." Thereby the beloved of the Lord are brought to concur with God's will in their salvation in the way of His appointing. So, far from the elect being saved whether they believe or not, they do not enter into God's salvation except through their "belief of the truth."

Further, the regeneration of God's beloved (their belief of the truth, and their initial participation in God's great salvation) does not render them unfit subjects for exhortation: on the contrary, their accountability must be enforced and their moral agency brought into exercise. Those who have received spiritual life require instruction and encouragement to "stir up the gift which is in" them, and urging to perform their duties. Accordingly, we find the apostle bidding them, "Therefore, brethren, stand fast, and hold the traditions which ye have been taught, whether by word, or [by] our epistle" (v. 15). Paul did not consider such an exhortation legalistic or useless because he was assured that they would do the things which he commanded them (3:4). The operation of divine grace does not set aside the discharge of human responsibility, but it equips us for it. Our concurrence with God is required to the end of our earthly course. Yet such exhorting of the saints is far from implying any sufficiency in them to comply in their own strength. Paul knew full well that his order would prevail little with them without God's blessing and help, therefore he added supplication to his order.

The Apostle's Concern for the Thessalonian Saints

"Now our Lord Jesus Christ himself, and God, even our Father, which hath loved us, and hath given us everlasting consolation and good hope through grace, comfort your hearts, and stablish you in every good word and work" (vv. 16-17). As we have pointed out formerly, these Thessalonian saints were enduring a great fight of affliction from without, and therefore their ministerial father here sought to occupy them with the rich compensations and provisions which the divine lovers of their soul had made for their peace and cheer. They had been experiencing many "persecutions and tribulations" (1:4), and therefore he made earnest intercession for them that they might be further comforted by God and energized by His grace to the close of life. Having already considered the setting or connections of this prayer, let us ponder first, *its Addressees,* or the Objects to whom it is made; second, its *grounds of confidence* for an answer; third, its specific *requests,* and then seek to make application of the whole to ourselves today.

"Our Lord Jesus Christ himself, and God, even our Father" are the Addressees. In the original there is an emphasis which is not preserved in our more euphonious translation. The Greek reads, "Now himself Lord, our Jesus Christ, and God and Father our." First, let us carefully notice the fact that here is still another instance where prayer is made directly to the Redeemer. It is incumbent upon us to approach the Father and direct our petitions to Him in and through the mediation of our great High Priest, owning the fact that there is no other way or means of access to Him. Yet it is equally our privilege and duty to address ourselves immediately to the Son, that *He* may receive the honor and homage which are His due as being one with the Father. We should also acknowledge Him as the Purchaser and Bestower of all our spiritual blessings. The "which hath loved us, and given us everlasting consolation" that immediately follows takes in both the Son and the Father, and since we are indebted to the one as much as to the other, Each is to be equally loved, revered, and magnified by us. Faith should especially be placed in both the Father and the Son in a season of persecution and tribulation since we are assured both have our best interests at heart.

Christ Jesus Presented as the Lord

Second, let us carefully notice the manner in which the Son is here presented: "Now Himself Lord, our Jesus Christ." Order and emphasis are here which are sadly lacking in modern ministry. The apostle declared, "We preach . . . Christ Jesus *the Lord*" (II Cor. 4:5), "preaching peace by Jesus Christ: (he is Lord of all)" (Acts 10:36). Christ is "Lord" in two ways: first, by that right which pertains to Him as the Creator, which right belongs to Him equally with the Father and the Spirit. As the Creator of the world, He is the Sovereign of it as shown by the winds and waves obeying His word. Second, by right of dominion, which belongs to Him as Redeemer. This is partly by divine donation: "All power is *given* unto me in heaven and in earth" (Matt. 28:18). "Therefore let all the house of Israel know assuredly, that God *hath made* that same Jesus, whom ye have crucified, both Lord and Christ" (Acts 2:36); having "put all things under his feet" (Eph. 1:22). It is also His right by purchase and conquest: "For to this end Christ both died, and rose, and revived, that he might be Lord both of the dead and living" (Rom. 14:9). By His death He merited and by His resurrection He attained the exalted station of universal dominion, "upholding all things by the word of his power" (Heb. 1:3; cf. Rev. 1:18).

By *passive subjection* all creatures in heaven and in earth are under the power and dominion of the Son of God, our Redeemer, as will openly appear on the last great day when, in the name of Jesus, every knee shall bow "of things in heaven, and things in earth, and things under the earth; and . . . every tongue . . . [shall] confess that Jesus Christ is Lord, to the glory of God the Father" (Phil. 2:10-11). Therefore even kings and great men of the earth are now bidden to "serve the LORD with fear" (Ps. 2:10-11). Everyone who hears the gospel is also required to do so, for in the gospel Christ's dignities and rights are made known to men. Those who *"obey not* the gospel of our

Lord Jesus Christ . . . shall be punished with everlasting destruction from the presence of the Lord, and from the glory of his power" (II Thess. 1:8-9). Thus, the first duty of the evangelist is to press upon his hearers the claims of Christ, calling on them to throw down the weapons of their warfare against Him and to submit to His scepter, to cease serving sin and Satan and yield themselves to His sway. On His entrance into this world the divine announcement was made: "Unto you is born this day in the city of David a Saviour, which is Christ the Lord" (Luke 2:11). Only as the throne of the heart is freely offered to Christ does He become the "Saviour" of anyone, i.e., of those who cease being rebels against Him.

That which distinguishes Christians from non-Christians is their surrender to the authority of Christ. He is their Lord by voluntary submission. 'They . . . first gave their own selves to the Lord" (II Cor. 8:5). That is, they repudiated the world, the flesh, and the devil, took Christ's yoke upon them, and solemnly covenanted to henceforth love and serve Him alone (Isa. 26:13). The word to Christians is "As ye have therefore received Christ Jesus *the Lord,* so walk ye in him" (Col. 2:6). They have intelligently and freely accepted Him as their Lord, renouncing all other lords and idols, enthroning Him in their affections, desiring Him to rule their lives. That is exactly what true conversion consists of: turning from sin to Christ, ceasing from self-pleasing to be in subjection to His authority; and the sins of all such (and of none other) are pardoned as they trust in His blood. That is the order of our present verse: "Now himself Lord, our Jesus Christ." He is not *"our* Jesus Christ" until He has first been received as Lord! That is ever the order of the Scripture: "My soul doth magnify the Lord, and my spirit hath rejoiced in God my Saviour" (Luke 1:46-47). "The everlasting kingdom of our [1] Lord and [2] Saviour Jesus Christ" (II Peter 1:11). "Through the knowledge of the Lord and Saviour Jesus Christ" (II Peter 2:20). "Grow in grace, and in the knowledge of our Lord and Saviour Jesus Christ" (II Peter 3:18).

Accepting Christ as Personal Saviour

Man, with his invariable perversity, has reversed God's order. Modern evangelism urges giddy worldlings, with no sense of their lost condition, to "accept Christ as their personal Saviour"; and when such "converts" prove unsatisfactory to the churches, special meetings are arranged where they are pressed to "consecrate themselves to Christ as Lord." Christ must be received according to God's appointed terms. He is "the author of eternal salvation unto all them that *obey* him" (Heb. 5:9). But the heart language of all who despise and reject Him is "We will not have this one to reign over us" (Luke 19:14). In contrast, the attitude of the saints is "Himself Lord, *our* Jesus Christ." To which the apostle here added, "And God and Father our." He too stands in a double relation to us: our God by sovereign dominion, our Father by gracious regeneration. The two divine Persons were here jointly addressed to evince Their coequality and to teach us that we must not look to and rest in the Mediator to the exclusion or even the neglect of exercising a lively faith in the One who sent Him. Having referred first to the One whose work on the soul is the more immediate, the apostle guards against giving the impression that the Father is any less deeply interested in our welfare than is the Son.

"Which hath loved us, and hath given us everlasting consolation and good hope through grace." Those words reveal the various *grounds* for the apostle's confidence that an answer would be granted to the petitions which follow. They are regarded as "the grounds of audience and success," as they are well styled by Thomas Manton. This clause is immediately connected with the preceding one, as its opening "which" intimates, for that pronoun includes both the Persons here addressed. First, "Himself Lord, our Jesus Christ." In this divine adoration the apostle would exalt *Him* in the esteem of the saints as coequal with the Father. The emphatic "Himself" at the beginning of the sentence was designed to contrast *His* almighty power and infinite love with the comparatively feeble affection which Paul bore to the suffering Thessalonians and the ministerial assistance he sought to render them, as well as their inability to "stand fast" in their own strength. Second, "And God and Father our." He too had their welfare equally at heart and must be given equal place in their thoughts and affections as commended to them by the endearing "our" God and Father.

"Which hath loved us, and hath given us everlasting consolation and good hope through grace." Taking the three together, we may observe what a strong emphasis is here laid upon the fact that the saints' consolations and comforts proceed from pure and bounteous benignity. First, we are shown that divine love is their fountain or origin; then we are told the same are "given" us, and nothing is more free than a gift; and last, they are plainly declared to be "through grace." The apostle found encouragement in these truths and emboldenment to seek further blessings for these saints. And thus it needs to be with us when we are about to pray. Nothing is more assuring to the heart than the realization that we are approaching the bounteous One who "giveth to all men liberally, and upbraideth not" (James 1:5). Nothing is better suited to dispel all doubts and fears than the knowledge that we are invited to draw boldly nigh to "the throne of *grace*." Well suited is such a throne to beggars who have no merits of their own. Equally fitted for the ill-deserving and defiled who come to confess their sins. Let all such recall they are coming to "the God of all grace," whose mercy is free and infinite and "endureth for ever."

The Love of God the Spring of All Our Blessings

Considering separately or distinctly these grounds of assurance for a hearing at the mercy seat, we may view the divine love as the cause, and the everlasting consolation and good hope as the effects of the same. "Which hath loved us" refers to both the Son and the Father. In the economy of redemption the love of the Father is first, for though Christ communicated the love of the Father to His people, it was the Father's love which furnished Christ for them. "God so loved the world, that *he gave* his only begotten Son, that whosoever believeth in him should not perish, but have everlasting life." The love of God for His elect is the spring of all their blessings. It was His love which chose them in Christ before the foundation of the world: "in love having predestinated . . . [them] unto the adoption of children by Jesus Christ to himself" (Eph. 1:4-5). It was His love which provided a Saviour for them: "Herein is love, not that we loved God, but that he loved us, and sent his Son to be the propitiation for our sins" (I John 4:10). It was His love which gave the Holy Spirit to quicken us: "I have loved thee with an everlasting love: therefore with lovingkindness have I drawn thee" (Jer. 31:3). It is His love which chastens us when we sin (Heb. 12:6), and which suffers nothing to separate us from Him in Christ Jesus (Rom. 8:39).

The love of the Son is made equally manifest in His redemption of His people. It was His love for them which made Him willing to become their Surety, to take upon Himself the form of a servant, to be made in the likeness of sinful flesh. It was His love for them which moved Him to take upon Himself their debts and discharge their obligations, being made under the law that He might render perfect obedience to its precepts in their behalf and suffer its awful curse in their stead. "Christ also loved the church, and gave himself for it" (Eph. 5:25). "Greater love hath no man than this, that a man lay down his life for his friends" (John 15:13). How we need to pray with the apostle that we may *know* the love of Christ, which passeth knowledge" (Eph. 3:19); that is, that we may be constantly occupied with it, that we may have more spiritual conceptions of it, be nourished by and swallowed up in it. Says the Saviour of our souls, "As the Father hath loved me, so have I loved you" (John 15:9): we should particularly remember that as we draw nigh to Him in prayer. What liberty of approach and freedom of utterance are mine when I realize I am about to petition the One "who loved *me*, and gave himself for *me*" (Gal. 2:20) and that His love is ever the same toward me!

The Love of the Spirit

For the benefit of young preachers we will devote one paragraph to the love of the Spirit, for which we are as much indebted as the Father's and the Son's. "*God* is love" is to be understood equally of each of the three Persons. In Romans 15:30 distinct mention is made of "the love of the Spirit," yet how little is ever heard of the same! The entire ministry of the Spirit to the saints is one of fathomless and amazing love. In love He sought them out when they were dead in sin. In love He quickened them into newness of life, for nothing but love could have moved Him to take pity on such vile and leprous creatures. In incomprehensible love He takes up His abode in our hearts. What a marvel that the Holy Spirit should indwell such worms of the earth and make our bodies His temples! In love He bears with our infirmities and "maketh intercession within us." Infinitely patient is His long-suffering to us. In love He bears witness with our spirits that we are the sons of God. In love He teaches, guides, strengthens, fructifies, and preserves us to the end. Then let us be far more on our guard against *grieving* this Lover of our souls.

"Which hath loved us." That is what the apostle eyed first as he was about to make intercession for those tried saints, and that is what our faith must never lose sight of, for nothing else will keep our hearts warm and our affections fresh to God. All of God's dispensations to and all of His dealings with us should be considered in the light of His infinite and unchanging love for us. Yet that is only possible as *faith* is daily exercised regarding these facts. When God's providences are contemplated and interpreted by carnal reason, unbelief clouds our vision, and we give the devil an advantage to inject into our minds poisonous and blasphemous aspersions against God. It is one of the enemy's favorite devices to induce a Christian to entertain doubts of God's love toward him—especially so in a time of trial or tribulation—and nought but "the shield of faith" can stop his fiery darts. Faith resists his evil suggestions, looks away from the things seen, and lays hold upon the declarations and promises of Him who has covenanted with His people, "I will not turn away from them, to do them good" (Jer. 32:40). *There* is solid ground to rest upon amid the storms of life. This is an unfailing cordial for the fainting heart.

"God . . . hath loved us, and hath given us everlasting consolation and good hope through grace" (v. 16). Divine love is the fountain; everlasting consolation and good hope are the streams which flow from it. God's love for His people preceded their fall into sin, both historically and as foreseen by Him, for it was a love of goodwill and not of compassion or pity. As the first Adam was "the figure of him that was to come" (Rom. 5:14), so Eve was the original type of the Church as the Bride of Christ (Gen. 2:24; Eph. 5:31-32). Eve was created and given to Adam by God *before* he transgressed, and she was as pure and upright as he was, fully suited to be his wife and companion. A holy Adam and a holy Eve were united in wedlock prior to the entrance of evil into this world. That was a blessed foreshadowing of the fact that God appointed a sinless and holy Church to be the wife and companion of His Son, and accordingly she was given a marriage union with Him in the eternal purpose of God antecedent to His foreview of Adam's defection and the Church's fall in him, her federal head, for he was equally the head of all mankind. The fact that Eve did not keep her first estate in no wise affected the fact that she was Adam's sinless wife previously.

God's Immutable Love for His Elect

In Eden God typified in a most wonderful way His secret and everlasting counsels respecting His own elect. His love to them was like Himself: incomprehensible, infinite, immutable. Nothing could change or cloud it. Sin, far from quenching His love, only provided occasion for Him to manifest the strength and durability of that love, and to go forth in mercy and compassion. As Adam did not cast off his wife when she yielded to the serpent's wiles, neither did God revoke His benign purpose when the Church became dead in trespasses and sins through the fall. No, it seems clear from the Word that "Adam was *not* deceived" (I Tim. 2:14), that out of love to Eve he voluntarily and deliberately joined her in her fallen condition, thereby foreshadowing the abounding love of Christ for His Church in being willing not only to assume our nature and in all things "to be made like unto his brethren" (Heb. 2:17) but also to be "made . . . sin for us" (II Cor. 5:21) and to bear our iniquities, and in consequence be made a curse for us. Upon His foreview of our fall God entered into an everlasting covenant with Christ, wherein arrangements were made for Him to save His people from their sins and provide "everlasting consolation" for them.

"And hath given us everlasting consolation." There is some difference of opinion among the commentators whether that "consolation" is to be regarded as exclusively an objective one or whether it also includes our subjective experience. Personally, we consider it wholly objective, or outside of ourselves, though in proportion as faith acts upon it we shall enjoy the blessedness of it. We base that view first upon the tense of the verb *"hath* given," not "is now giving" us, as it would read if our present experience were being described. Second, because of the qualifying word *everlasting*, which signifies that the "consolation" here spoken of is a durable, immutable, eternal one; whereas nothing is more fluctuating and fleeting than the inward consolation which most of the saints enjoy in this life, for their moods and feelings appear to be almost as variable as the weather—now on the mountaintop, then in the valley, if not in the slough of despond. And third, unless we regard this "everlasting consolation" as an objective one, that is, as having reference to the matter or substance of our peace and joy, we confound it with the "comfort your hearts" in the next verse where the apostle makes request that they might have the experimental effect and personal sense of the same *within* them.

"And hath given us everlasting consolation." To what was the apostle referring? The answer to that question may be stated in two different forms. Manton terms it "in the new covenant," and that provides a satisfactory meaning, for under the "old covenant" with the nation of Israel the promises and blessings set forth were earthly and temporal. But the new covenant contains "a better hope" and "better promises" (Heb. 7:19; 8:6) as the whole of that Epistle is designed to set forth. But personally we prefer to say that God has given us "everlasting consolation" *in the gospel,* for though the gospel enunciates the new covenant, it is also primarily a transcript of the everlasting covenant which God made with Christ, viewed as the Head of His people; and the "everlasting covenant" is the foundation of all the believer's consolations and hopes. The Gospel reveals the contents of that everlasting covenant as Romans 16:25-26 affirms. Take away the gospel and the very foundation of our consolation and hope is removed. That is made clear in I Corinthians 15 where, after stating that the salient facts of the gospel are that Christ died for our sins according to the Scriptures, that He was buried, and that He rose again the third day according to the Scriptures, Paul pointed out to those who denied His resurrection, "If Christ be not risen, then is our preaching vain, and your faith is also vain" (v. 14).

Paul then went on to declare, "If in *this* life only we have hope in Christ, we are of all men most miserable" (v. 19), which was the reverse way of showing that in the gospel God has given us "everlasting consolation" ratified by Christ's resurrection. Those words of I Corinthians 15:19 make it clear that we have no ground for hope beyond this life except in the divine revelation made in the gospel. Nay, we may go further and affirm that even for this present life there is no hope for any sinner apart from the revelation of Christ in the gospel of God's grace. It cannot be too plainly and emphatically insisted upon today that if the gospel is jettisoned there is no well-grounded hope for any man, either in this life or the life to come. The Christless, whether they live moral or immoral lives, are described by the infallible pen of inspiration as "having no hope, and without God in the world" (Eph. 2:12). And such "hope" as they *do* cherish is but imaginary, blind, impudent, and presumptuous; in the moment of death it will be found to be empty deceit. "The hypocrite's hope shall perish" (Job 8:13). Make sure *your* hope is grounded upon the gospel.

Consolation Found Only in the Gospel

"Which hath loved us, and hath given us everlasting consolation." The word *consolation* means "the alleviation of misery, solace." In the gospel (and nowhere else) do we learn of the wondrous and gracious provision which God has made for His people considered as lost sinners. As intimated above, the "which hath loved us" goes back to the source of all, when the triune God set His heart upon the Church and blessed it "with all spiritual blessings in heavenly places in Christ" (Eph. 1:3). Then came the divine foreview of the Church's defection in the Adam fall, which opened the way for a further manifestation of God's superabounding grace. That was evidenced in the everlasting covenant in which arrangements were made for the Son to save His people from their sins, and for the Spirit to quicken them into newness of life. The gospel contains a transcript of that everlasting covenant, proclaiming the distinctive goodness and gracious acts of each of the Persons of the Godhead, which gospel is fully expounded in the Epistle to the Romans as its opening verse indicates (cf. 1:9, 16-17; 16:25-27). In the gospel God has given us everlasting consolation, revealing the remedy for sin, His provision for our holiness and happiness, the endless bliss He has "prepared for them that love him" (I Cor. 2:9).

The "everlasting consolation" is in marked contrast with the evanescent pleasure afforded by material comforts, which perishes with the using; it differs also from the temporal portion allotted Israel as a nation. That consolation which God has provided for His beloved Church is endless: it does not die with the body, but is as enduring as the soul, proceeding from God Himself, issuing from His free grace, grounded upon His sure Word. Of what does this "everlasting consolation" *consist?* In complete and effectual alleviation of the misery which our fall in Adam produced, and deliverance from all the dire consequences of the same. By Adam's disobedience the Church became judicially alienated from God and experimentally separated from Him. By the entrance of sin the favor, the life, the image of God in the soul, was lost and fellowship with Him totally severed. All of this was graphically represented by the driving out of man and God's placing "at the east of the garden of Eden Cherubims, and a flaming sword which turned every way, to keep the way of the tree of life" (Gen. 3:24). But the gospel makes known how the work of the last Adam reverses all that, resulting in the reconciliation of the Church to God, restoring her to His unclouded favor, renewing her after His image, and bringing her into communion with Him.

"And hath given us everlasting consolation and good hope through grace." Those gifts though quite distinct are really two parts of one whole, the former referring to the believer's present portion, the latter to his future. Both of them are the fruitage of that "everlasting righteousness" which Christ brought in for His people (Dan. 9:24), having wrought out the same for them as their Representative, by not only suffering in their stead the full penalty of the broken law but also by rendering perfect obedience to its precepts on their behalf. Thereby Christ not only makes complete atonement for all their transgressions, so that the guilt and pollution of the same are forever removed from the sight of the Judge of all, but thereby obtains for them a sure title to the *reward* of the law so that they are justified or pronounced righteous before Him with full acceptance. The reward of the law is "life" (Rom. 7:10) as its penalty is death. The gift of grace is eternal life, and accordingly we read of "eternal life, which God, that cannot lie, *promised* before the world began" (Titus 1:2), therefore before any part of the Scriptures was written. Consequently the reference must be to the promise made to our federal Head in the everlasting covenant. The believer enjoys now both an earnest and a foretaste of that "eternal life."

"And hath given us . . . good hope." This too refers not to any inward comfort but to that which is the sure *ground* of comfort. In this verse Paul contemplates not the grace of hope in the believer's soul but rather the object upon which that grace is to be exercised. The "good hope" equally with the "everlasting consolation" is here entirely objective, namely, that which is set before us in the gospel. "For the hope which is laid up for you in heaven, whereof ye heard before in the word of the truth of the gospel" (Col. 1:5). Here "hope" is the object, namely, the glorious and blessed estate which is reserved for us hereafter. In Scripture "hope" always contemplates something *future*, something of which we are not yet in actual possession: "Hope that is seen [experienced or possessed] is not *hope:* for what a man seeth, why doth he yet hope for? But if we hope for that we see not, then do we with patience wait for it" (Rom. 8:24-25. Here it is the *grace* of hope which is in mind. "That . . . we might have a strong consolation, who have fled for refuge to lay hold upon the hope *set before* us" (Heb. 6:18). Here again hope is the object, and as faith "lays hold" of the same, "strong consolation" is produced in the soul.

Good Hope Through Grace

In attempting to define the character and substance of our "good hope through grace" we cannot do better than pattern our outline after that of Thomas Manton. First, this hope is based on the personal return of our Redeemer: "Looking for that blessed hope, and the glorious appearing of our great God and Saviour Jesus Christ" (Titus 2:13). Hope is there described by its grand Object, when He shall be seen no more "through a glass darkly" but "face to face"; when all the holy longings and aspirations of His redeemed will be fully realized. Then Christ will see of the travail of His soul and be satisfied, possessing what He purchased, and conducting the Church into the eternal abode which He has prepared for her. In proportion as our faith is exercised on that promise, and as our love burns and yearns for the Lover of our souls, we shall be "looking for," eagerly awaiting, His appearing.

Second, the resurrection of the dead: "[I] have hope toward God . . . that there shall be a resurrection of the dead, both of the just and unjust" (Acts 24:15; cf. 26:6-8). At the return of Christ the living saints will be changed and the sleeping ones raised in power and glory, and "fashioned like to his glorious body" (Phil. 3:21; I Cor. 15; I Thess. 4:16-17).

Third, the vision of God in Christ, when we shall at length be admitted into

His presence, see Him as He is, and be made like Him both for holiness and happiness (I John 3:2).

Fourth, our heavenly inheritance: an inheritance which is "incorruptible, and undefiled, and that fadeth not away, reserved in heaven" for us (I Peter 1:4). That will consist of "fulness of joy" in God's presence, "pleasures for evermore" at His right hand (Ps. 16:11). You will agree, Christian reader, that all of that is "a good hope." It is wholly "through grace," and in no way earned by human merits. Have we not good cause, sure ground, to "rejoice in hope of the glory of God"? (Rom. 5:2). But only as we exercise faith on what God has revealed in the gospel do we *rejoice.* It was on this supreme good, namely, the eternal vision and fruition of God, that the eye of David was fixed when he said, "As for me, I will behold thy face in righteousness: I shall be satisfied, when I awake, with thy likeness" (Ps. 17:15). Then let us be more in prayer that the grace of hope within us may be more engaged with these glorious objects of hope without us.

This brings us to the special requests made by the apostle in this prayer: "comfort your hearts, and stablish you in every good word and work" (v. 17). In that first petition Paul was asking that the everlasting consolation and good hope given them in the gospel might be effectually applied to the souls of those persecuted saints. "Comfort your hearts," present tense, in contrast with the "hath given us" in the preceding verse. This is clear proof of the verse's entire objectivity, for if the "consolation" and "good hope" were in respect to their experience, there was no need to ask that their hearts be comforted. The supplication was that they might have inward enjoyment of the same, that the glorious contents of the gospel should be brought home in power to their hearts, that the substance of their consolation and the object of their hope would be made so real and solid as to fill them with peace and joy. Paul desired that they might have such a satisfying and blissful realization of the divine love and its manifestations to them that no tribulations and sufferings should be able to rob them or even becloud the same in their apprehensions.

The Coexistence of Faith and Hope

Here, as always, more was implied than was actually expressed. In order for such comfort to be experienced, their graces must be in exercise. The revelation which God has made to us in the gospel profits us nothing until it is personally appropriated by faith. The wonderful vista of the future which is there unveiled to the saints does not animate them unless the grace of hope is also employed. Though distinguishable, gospel faith and gospel hope, twin graces in the soul, are as fundamental to the believer as are light and heat to the sun. Faith does not exist without hope, and hope has no being apart from faith. As a Christian's faith is, so is his hope. They are alike founded on and rooted in God's Word. Faith receives Christ as He is there set forth; hope confidently expects all the blessings there promised. Christ is equally the Object of our faith and of our hope; yes, He *is* "our hope" (I Tim. 1:1): its substance and its cause. Both work by love (Gal. 5:6), which is the fulfilling of the law. Faith is more than intellectual, hope is more than emotional; both are spiritual and dynamic, conforming the soul to the character of their objective.

But while it is the believer's responsibility to keep his graces in constant exercise, it is not absolutely in his own power to do so, and therefore the apostle supplicated the Lord Jesus Christ and God the Father to "comfort the hearts" of the Thessalonians. It is a great mercy for the distressed to be truly comforted, yet it does not lie in the power of any creature to administer the same. That is the prerogative of the Almighty: "I, even I, am he that comforteth you" (Isa. 51:12). Therefore He is designated "the God of all comfort" (II Cor. 1:3), "God, that comforteth those that are cast down" (II Cor. 7:6). He may in His sovereign condescension use instruments in doing so, but the power and blessing are entirely His. In His gracious ministry to the Church, the Spirit is denominated "the Comforter" (John 16:7), for He is the immediate Author of all our experimental consolations as He is the Quickener, Maintainer, and Fructifier of our graces. Therefore we read that "we *through the Spirit* wait for the hope of righteousness" (Gal. 5:5). He alone can make us cheerful amid sufferings, patient during the period of waiting the fulfillment of the promise, persevering in duty when there is so much to discourage.

"Comfort your hearts, and stablish you in every good word and work." These two petitions are closely related. This appears more clearly when we understand the meaning of our English word *comfort: con fortis,* "with strength." The Greek word here rendered "comfort" is literally "to call alongside, to help." It is not a soporific or pain-deadener, as "comfort" implies in ordinary usage, but a renewing of moral energy, a spiritual vivification in view of trials yet to be faced. God alone is capable of imparting such "comfort." Thomas Manton defined comfort thus: "Comfort is a strengthening of the mind when it is in danger of being weakened by fears and sorrows, or the strength and stay of the heart in trouble: 'This is my comfort in my affliction: for thy word hath quickened me' (Ps. 119:50). 'Thou hast put gladness in my heart' (Ps. 4:7). God's comfort is like a soaking shower that goes to the root and refreshes the plants of the earth rather than a morning dew that wets only the surface. Other comforts tickle the senses and refresh the outward man, but this penetrates the heart."

These Petitions Imply Responsibilities on the Believer's Part

"And stablish you in every good word and work," which is only possible as God first comforts or strengthens with might in the inner man. As none but God can comfort or strengthen, so He alone can "stablish" us and enable us to persevere. There is a powerful tendency in us to stray (Ps. 119:176). It is good for us when we feel the need of crying,

> Prone to wander, Lord, I feel it,
> Prone to leave the God I love:
> Here's my heart, O take and seal it;
> Seal it for Thy courts above.

Nevertheless, we must bear in mind that these petitions imply *our* obligations. Though we cannot comfort ourselves, it is our responsibility to avoid the things which hinder: carnal fears, worldly delights, sins against conscience (which destroy our peace), grieving the Spirit. So too we must seek to be instruments in God's hand for comforting others: by speaking words to those who are weary, by lifting up the hands which hang down. Likewise it is our duty to use those means which promote our establishment in the faith, and to beware of everything that tends to make us waver and temporize. To falter in the path of duty chills our joy. We quote Thomas Manton again: "By 'every good work' is meant sound doctrine; by 'every good work" holiness of life. Establishment in faith and holiness is a needful blessing, and earnestly to be sought of God."

Paul's prayer is for increased grace and for the quickening of our graces, particularly that we may ever obey our Lord Jesus Christ and love our Father. The singular number of the verbs "comforted" and "stablish" (which is not reproduced in the English) intimates the unity of the two Persons which are the common Objects of the verbs (cf. I Thess. 3:11). The equality of the Persons is seen in these petitions being addressed jointly to both. The "hath loved" of verse 16 looks back to verse 13, the "good hope" to verse 14, and the petitions of verse 17 to the exhortation of verse 15.

Chapter 30

PRAYER FOR LOVE TOWARD GOD

II THESSALONIANS 3:5

THE ATTENTIVE READER will observe that more of Paul's prayers are recorded for the Thessalonians than for any other church or company of saints. There is yet another in verse 16 of our present chapter, though in view of our observations on Romans 15:33 and I Thessalonians 5:23 we do not propose to give it a separate consideration. Note that reference is made more frequently to the coming of Christ in the Thessalonian epistles than in any other of Paul's letters. We know of no writer who has attempted to give a reason for these conspicuous features. There is no doubt in our mind that they should be linked together, for a single explanation satisfactorily accounts for them both, namely, the extremely trying situation in which these particular saints were placed. As we have more than once pointed out, they were enduring a great fight of afflictions, meeting with strong opposition from unbelievers. Thus, we are here taught two important lessons regarding the Christian's special duty to his afflicted brethren: the one concerning the rank and file of God's people, the other pertaining more especially to ministers of the gospel.

Ministry to Suffering Saints

First, persecuted believers have a peculiar claim on the sympathies of the whole household of faith, and should therefore be given a special place in their supplications and intercessions. We are expressly told to "weep with them that weep" (Rom. 12:15). The cultivation and exercise of love one to another are incumbent upon us at all times, but especially in seasons when fellow saints are in distress. More reprehensible and unchristlike is the callous spirit which says, "I have troubles enough of my own without burdening myself with those of others." Different far was the attitude of Nehemiah, who, though in a palace, "wept, and mourned certain days, and fasted, and prayed before the God of heaven" when he heard of his fellow Jews being "in great affliction and reproach" (Neh. 1:1-4). We are required to "remember them that are in bonds, as bound with them" (Heb. 13:3), taking them to our hearts, having compassion toward them, seeking grace for them. Whenever we hear or read of an earthquake, famine, flood, we should at once approach the throne of grace and beg God to undertake for His own dear people in the stricken district (ponder Matt. 25:36, 40).

Second, the ministry best suited to and most appropriate for those who are suffering for Christ's sake is to direct their thoughts away from the present to the future, setting before them "that blessed hope, and the glorious appearing of our great God and Saviour Jesus Christ" (Titus 2:13). Not until His advent will a period be put to the oppressions of the Church. At that time all shall be richly rewarded who have been steadfast and faithful to Him. The intensely practical side of our "blessed hope" must not be lost sight of amid all the acrimonious and profitless speculations about the Millennium. This grand truth about our Lord's return is used by the Spirit as a most powerful motive for the discharge of Christian duties, as a quickener of our graces, as an incentive to piety, and as consolation to the grief-stricken. Our Lord Himself calmed the troubled hearts of the disciples with it (John 14:1-3), and His apostles bade bereaved saints to comfort each other with the same truth (I Thess. 4:13-18). A spiritual hope of our Lord's appearing produces ministerial fidelity (II Tim. 4:1-2; I Peter 5:3-4), Christian patience (James 5:7-11), sobriety (I Peter 1:13), purity (I John 3:2-3). They are greatly the losers who are not looking for His appearing.

"And the Lord direct your hearts into the love of God, and into the patient waiting for Christ." Three things in this prayer call for consideration. First, though briefly, its *connection* with foregoing verses. Second, and more specifically, its *Addressee*. Third, and at greater length, its important *petitions*. The opening word requires attention to its setting. It is blessed to note the link between the verses immediately preceding and the prayer which we last considered. In 2:15 the apostle had exhorted the saints, "Therefore, brethren, stand fast and hold the traditions which ye have been taught [i.e., the oral ministry of the apostles], whether by word, or our epistle." Then had followed the prayer in 2:16-17 that they might be comforted and established by an effectual application to them of the glorious contents of the gospel. Next he had solicited their prayers for himself and fellow ministers (3:1-2), after which he had declared, "But the Lord is faithful, who will stablish you, and keep you from evil. And we have confidence in the Lord touching you, that ye both do and will do the things which we command you" (vv. 3-4). Note, the apostle did not say, "We have confidence in you" but "We have confidence in the Lord touching you." Paul was assured that God, having begun a good work in them, would graciously complete it.

The Addressee of This Prayer

Let us now consider the Addressee of this prayer. Who is meant by "the Lord" here? We answer unhesitatingly, the third Person of the blessed Trinity, the One who is designated "Lord" in I Corinthians 12:5, and "the Spirit of the Lord" in II Corinthians 3:18. First, this is clear from the fact that in our present verse He is definitely distinguished from "God" and "Christ," so that reference is here made to the Eternal Three. Second, this fact is borne out by what is here asked of Him: "The Lord direct your hearts into the love of God and into patient waiting for Christ." Now it is the distinguishing work of the Spirit to develop our graces and to regulate their exercise. As "the love of God is shed abroad in our hearts by the Holy Ghost which is given unto us" (Rom.

5:5), so love is called forth into action by Him. Third, since the Spirit is co-essential and coeternal with the Father and the Son, He is worthy of our homage. Nowhere in Scripture is there the least hint that one Person in the Godhead must be excluded from the praises which we give to the Lord. On the contrary, the Spirit is to be publically owned and equally honored with the Father and the Son. This is clear from Matthew 28:19; to be baptized in His name is an act of worship. It is evident again from the place accorded Him in the Christian benediction (II Cor. 13:14).

We are expressly commanded to "worship and bow down . . . before the LORD our maker" (Ps. 95:6). That the third Person is included in that command is plain: "The Spirit of God hath made me, and the breath of the Almighty hath given me life" (Job 33:4; cf. Job 26:13 with Ps. 33:6). Instruction is given to pray to "the Lord of the harvest" (Matt. 9:38). During the days of His earthly ministry Christ sustained that office, as appears from His choosing the apostles and sending forth the seventy. But since His ascension, the Holy Spirit fulfills that ministry (see Acts 13:2, 4; 20:28). The Spirit now calls and equips the "laborers," assigns them their work, and blesses them in it.

The Holy Spirit a Divine Person

"The Lord direct your hearts." As the title "Lord" is expressive of the Spirit's dominion, so the action here mentioned indicates His Godhead, for it is one which none but a divine Person can perform. "The king's heart is in the hand of the LORD, as the rivers of waters: he turneth it whithersoever he will" (Prov. 21:1). All men's hearts are equally so.

"And the Lord direct your hearts into the love of God" may be taken either actively or passively: actively, as the love wherewith we love God; or passively, as the love wherewith we are loved by God. Personally, we are satisfied that the reference is to our love of God, rather than to His for us. Since the words may be understood either way, we will consider them in both ways. We regard the words in an active sense, first, because our apprehension and enjoyment of God's love to us were fully covered in the preceding prayer (2:16-17). Second, because the immediate context obviously requires us to do so. In verse 4 the apostle expressed his confidence in the Lord that they did and would do the things His servants *commanded* them, and he at once prayed that the Lord the Spirit would strengthen and direct them; so that practical love which issues in obedience is here in view—though perhaps it is not to be restricted absolutely to that. Third, because the second petition, "and into the patient waiting for Christ," is to be understood in an active sense, as pertaining to the discharge of their duty, namely, a steady endurance of persecution and a continuance in well-doing to the end of their earthly course.

"Direct your hearts into the love of God." This petition is of far too vital and vast importance for us to hurriedly and cursorily dismiss it. First, we are constantly to bear in mind that love to God and to our neighbor is the sum and substance of the moral law. "Thou shalt love the Lord thy God with all thy heart, and with all thy soul, and with all thy mind. This is the first and great commandment" (Matt. 22:37-38). It is not a new commandment; it is simply *renewed* in the gospel dispensation and pressed more strongly.

All Men Commanded to Love God

But though all men are required to so love the Lord their God, none in his natural condition is able to do so. Not that he lacks the necessary faculties, but because sin is in full possession of every part of his complex being, and therefore he is "alienated from God." As a result of the Fall every descendant of Adam is born into this world destitute of the slightest affection for God. To the religious Pharisees Christ said, "But I know you, that ye have not the love of God in you" (John 5:42). "If any man love the world, the love of the Father is not in him" (I John 2:15). Where is the man or woman who does not love the world until a miracle of grace is wrought within, and the bent and bias of the heart are changed? Not only is the heart of the natural man devoid of any love to God; it has a radical aversion to Him, for "the carnal mind is enmity against God" (Rom. 8:7). That was unmistakably demonstrated when the Son of God became incarnate, for far from being welcomed and adored, He was hated "without a cause" (John 15:25).

Where there is genuine love to God in anyone, that person has been made the subject of a miracle of grace. At regeneration the blessed Spirit slays our native enmity against God, and sheds abroad His love in our heart. A principle of life, of grace, of holiness, is communicated to the soul. There is "given us an understanding, that we may know him that is true" (I John 5:20). A personal revelation of God is made to the one born again, so that He "hath shined in our hearts, to give the light of the knowledge of the glory of God in the face of Jesus Christ" (II Cor. 4:6). The film of prejudice is removed, the mist of error is dispersed, and the soul perceives the majesty, the excellence, the loveliness of the divine character, and exclaims, "Who is like unto thee, O LORD, among the gods? who is like thee, glorious in holiness, fearful in praises, doing wonders?" (Exodus 15:11). Such a discovery and view of God draws out the heart to Him so that He is now its supreme delight. "The grace of our Lord was exceeding abundant with faith and love which is in Christ Jesus" (I Tim. 1:14). Those two graces of faith and love always go together, being implanted at one and the same time by one and the same hand.

The New Nature

It needs to be clearly recognized and constantly borne in mind that the principle of life and grace imparted to us at regeneration, that "new nature" as many term it, is entirely dependent for its continuance, development, and health upon its Author. Further, it must be remembered that the flesh, the world, and the devil are inveterately opposed to that "new creature," hence our urgent need for God to sustain, nourish, establish, guard it, as well as regulating all its activities. It was these considerations which prompted the apostle here, when he petitioned the Lord the Spirit to "direct their hearts into the love of God," for he well knew that they did not have the power to do so. Consciousness of his own weakness in the matter moved David to exclaim, "O that my ways were *directed* to keep thy statutes!" (Ps. 119:4-5). And after praying, "Make me to go in the path of thy commandments; for therein do I delight," David added, *"Incline* my heart unto thy testimonies" (Ps. 119:35-36).

But let us now consider more closely *of what* our "love to God" consists.

Its external and internal acts are desire after Him and delight in Him. Love to God implies an earnest seeking after Him, in order to attain the highest enjoyment that we are capable of in this life. The Psalmist cried, "My soul followeth hard after thee" (Ps. 63:8). The more constantly and earnestly we seek God, to enjoy more of His saving graces and benefits, the more we have of the love of God.

God is the supreme Object of our desire (Ps. 27:4) and also of our delight. Since love to God is the complacence of the soul in Him who is the sum of all perfection and our all-sufficient portion, it follows that we shall find our highest pleasure in Him. "If thou return to the Almighty, thou shalt . . . lift up thy face unto God" (Job 22:23, 26). Fullness of joy is reserved for heaven, yet even in this vale of tears "we also joy in God through our Lord Jesus Christ" (Rom. 5:11). It cannot be otherwise. As the soul perceives God's excellence and is admitted to communion with Him, it exults in Him: "I sat down under his shadow with great delight, and his fruit was sweet to my taste" (Song of Sol. 2:3). The saints look upon God reconciled as their best Friend: "My meditation of him shall be sweet: I will be glad in the LORD" (Ps. 104:34). "Because thy lovingkindness is better than life, my lips shall praise thee . . . My soul shall be satisfied" (Ps. 63:3, 5).

The external effects of love to God are summed up in these two things: doing and allowing His will. If we really love God, we shall be loath to offend Him and desirous of pleasing Him; consciousness of failure in either is the acutest grief experienced by the saint. "If a man love me," said Christ, "he will keep my words" (John 14:23). Love to God is the most powerful incentive, motive, and dynamic of all: "For this is the love of God, that we keep his commandments: and his commandments are not grievous" (I John 5:3) to His dear children, for they "delight in the law of God after the inward man" (Rom. 7:22). Faith is indeed a wonderful grace, yet only as it "worketh by *love*" (Gal. 5:6) does it produce that which is pleasing and glorifying to God. "Whoso keepeth his word, in him verily is the love of God perfected" (I John 2:5). None can be owned as a sincere lover of God except he that makes a point of obeying what He commands.

Love to God is also evidenced by a meek and cheerful submission to His will. The apostle prayed that God would direct the Thessalonians' hearts to love Him so that they would endure anything rather than deny the faith, and confess Christ whatever it cost them. Obedience, courage, and resolution are included in love. "Many waters cannot quench love, neither can the floods drown it: if a man would give all the substance of his house for love, it would be utterly contemned" (Song of Sol. 8:7). It is true of love in general, much more true of love to God. Love to God is an antidote against temptations. All the riches, pleasures, and honors of this world cannot bribe those that really love Christ. Nor can all the floods of persecution quench this holy desire. When once the heart is set toward God and heaven, it is set against anything that would turn it out of the way and divert it from its high aim and purpose.

A brief word on the properties of this love. "It is not speculative but practical, not consisting in lofty, airy streams of devotion, too high for the common rate of us poor mortals. No, it is put upon a surer and infallible test—our obedience to God. Again, it does not consist in a bold familiarity, but in a humble subjection and compliance with God's will: "He that hath my commandments, and keepeth them, he it is that loveth me" (John 14:21). God's love is a love of bounty, but ours is a love of duty; therefore we are properly said to love God when we are careful to please Him and fearful to offend Him: "Ye that love the Lord, hate evil" (Ps. 97:10). When we are fearful of committing or omitting anything which may be a violation of His law, a grief to His Spirit, or a dishonor to His name, then we are said to love God. However lofty our words of devotion may rise, they are empty without our active obedience, the proof of our love. Nothing but an honest endeavor to walk before the Lord unto all pleasing (Col. 1:10) must be made the touchstone of the genuineness of our love.

True Love to God

True lovers of God are not those who speak of Him as their "dear Father," nor those who talk about their intimate communion with Him, nor those who can discourse most accurately on His attributes. Rather they are those who are the most conscientious and diligent in performing for Him the duties which He has assigned them. Again, real love to God is a transcendent and preeminent one: He is loved above all others. "My son, give me thine heart, and let thine eyes observe my ways" (Prov. 23:26) is His peremptory demand. He requires the chief place in our affections and in our lives, so that glorifying Him is our supreme aim: otherwise we have no real love to Him. If His interests are subordinated to ours, then God is not loved as God. "He that loveth father or mother more than me is not worthy of me" (Matt. 10:37). By this too we must test our alleged love to God. "Whom have I in heaven but thee? and there is none upon earth that I desire besides thee" (Ps. 73:25). Unless that really is the language of our hearts, we are deceived if we imagine ourselves to be lovers of God.

But love to God, however sincere and transcendent, is not all there is in the Christian's heart: there are also powerful impulses which lust after ungodly things, and compete for his affections. Hence his urgent need of crying, "Unite my heart to fear thy name" (Ps. 86:11). Yet the very fact that the Christian is constrained to so cry, that he is acutely conscious of the feebleness of his love, is a sure evidence of his regeneration, for the natural man is a total stranger to any such pangs of soul. It is the same with the Christian's love as it is with his faith. Not until a divinely begotten faith is born within are we in the least conscious of the presence and workings of unbelief. Only as we become aware of the latter do we "with tears" say, "Lord, I believe; help thou mine unbelief" (Mark 9:24). So too the love of God has to be shed abroad in our hearts by the Holy Spirit before we can realize how disloyal to Him our affections really are. And as faith is dependent upon its Author for its continuance and growth, so love is dependent upon its Giver for its health and activities.

That brings us to consider more closely this petition: "The Lord direct your hearts into the love of God." The reference is not to the furnishing of counsels for our guidance but to the bending and setting straight of what is crooked and awry. Even after receiving God's grace, our hearts are apt to wander and return to their old bent and bias again.. Our love for God so quickly wanes. Many of God's dear children have reason to mourn the abating of their love toward God. Though the grace itself can never be lost, yet the freshness and fervor of it may. It is our sin and misery that we so often set our affections on wrong objects. Not only will an immediate pursuit of the things of this world chill our love: undue familiarity, fellowship with unbelievers and empty professors, will also do so. To many of His people Christ has reason to complain today, "I have somewhat against thee, because thou hast left ["not lost"] thy first love" (Rev. 2:4).

Many things seek to draw our hearts another way. Since the devil hates God, one of his chief employs is to draw off from Him the hearts of His people, both by attacking His character and by means of counterattractions. The devil gained the ear of Eve by causing her to doubt God's goodness. And when God's providences cross our wills and painful trials become our portion, the devil seeks to make us question God's loving-kindness. Or the devil endeavors to seduce the soul by material things, as in the case of Ananias and Sapphira. Therefore we are warned, "Be sober, be vigilant; because your adversary the devil, as a roaring lion, walketh about, seeking whom he may devour: whom resist steadfast in the faith" (I Peter 5:8-9). We must not tamely yield to him. Our own lusts tempt, seek to draw away from God, and entice us (James 1:14) and therefore the admonition is given, "Mortify therefore your members which are upon the earth" (Col. 3:5). The world offers many baits to the same end and purpose, and therefore we are commanded, "Love not the world, neither the things that are in the world" (I John 2:15). An undue attachment to any of the things of time and sense chill our affections for God. How many of the saints have proved this to their sorrow.

Our Need of Earnestly Praying

There is, then, a real and pressing need that we should earnestly supplicate the Lord the Spirit to "direct our hearts into the love of God." He can strengthen us with His might in the inner man, and thereby enable us to sternly resist every temptation to become attached to any earthly idol. We must ask Him to more and more enlighten our understanding to perceive the utter vanity of all earthly enjoyments and wean our fickle hearts from them. We must look to Him to graciously occupy us daily with the ineffable perfections of God and grant us such soul-ravishing views of Him as will deaden us to the empty baubles of this world. He can engage our minds more frequently and effectually with the wondrous love of God for us and thereby excite ours for Him. He can so enthrall us with His electing grace, His having singled us out to be the objects of His favor, the ones upon whom He set His heart from all eternity, that we shall be constrained to love Him with all our souls, minds, and strength. He can so melt us in adoration and appreciation of all Christ is to us that we shall be wholly devoted to Him, delight ourselves in Him, and seek to please and glorify Him in all things.

If we had a clearer concept of what the love of God consists of, we should be far more conscious of the defects of our love. This love is a powerful inclination and earnest bent of the heart toward God as our chief good and last end. It enables us to realize that God is infinitely worthy and desirable, so that all our efforts are directed to enjoying Him and pleasing Him. If that really is the dominant passion in our souls, then by it we shall decide what is to be avoided and what is to be employed as fit means to the realization thereof. We shall be conscious that not only are all sins contrary to the making of God's glory our supreme end or design but that all foolish and trifling actions are inconsistent with that end. Measuring our lives by such a standard, we realize how much we live for self, and how little for God! How many of our desires, schemes, words, and actions have no real respect to God at all! It is not sufficient that we surrender our hearts at conversion: we need to beg Him daily to reclaim them from their vain wanderings and bind them afresh to Himself, and to maintain and increase our love to Him.

Our Love Distracted from God

Not only are there innumerable objects in this scene to draw away our unstable hearts from God; the cares of this life and the slavish fears to which we so often give place, hinder our delight in Him. Such cares oppress, and such fears prevent comfortable communion with God in the means of grace. When we are worried over our present lot or harassed about supplies for the future, the heart is straitened and the spirit of praise is chilled. When we are occupied more with our sins than we are with Christ, more with our corruptions than with His blood, more with our failures than with God's covenant faithfulness, doubts will assail, assurance will be lost, and rejoicing in God becomes a thing of the past. In such a case the means of grace may still be used and duties performed, but there is no joy in the one or thankful gratitude behind the other. It is more the service of a slave than of a son. "There is no fear in love; but perfect love casteth out fear: because fear hath torment" (I John 4:18). But if our hearts are directed into the love of God, then our obedience to Him will be a delight, and we shall serve Him by inclination and not compulsion.

When the means of grace become irksome and tedious to us and the works of obedience distasteful and burdensome, it is a sure sign that our love to God has grievously declined. All goes spontaneously, easily, freely, when love motivates us. Seven years seemed as a few days to Jacob for the love he had for Rachel (Gen. 29:20). Thus it was with Christ Himself: love to His Father, love to His people, constrained all that He did. "The Lord is the portion of mine inheritance and of my cup." Therefore He added, "The lines are fallen unto me in pleasant places" . . . "I have set the Lord always before me. . . . Therefore my heart is glad" (Ps. 16:5-9). But when we yield to the promptings of self-love or to our carnal lusts, the light of God's countenance becomes eclipsed, our affections gradually cool off, and His ways are no longer our delight. The profits and pleasures of this world attract us, and we have a disinclination to the performance of spiritual duties. If we take our fill of carnal delights, the Spirit is grieved, and He ceases to take of the things of Christ and of the Father and show them to us.

Love is a tender, delicate plant. After it is planted in the soul, we must see that it gets rooted, that it grows, that it blooms and bears fruit. It is our sacred duty and Christian responsibility to care for our spiritual life as for our natural, es, far more so, as the latter exceeds in value and importance the former. We ɑust look after the health and well-being of our souls as well as that of our ɪodies. God has commanded us, "Keep thy heart with all diligence" (Prov. ɪ:23), and still more expressly, "Keep yourselves in the love of God" (Jude ɔ1), which means to preserve in a healthy state our love to God—that principle ɔf love which has been shed abroad in our hearts. Why is *that* termed "the love of God"? Because God is its Author, because He is its Object, because He is its Perfector. The great work committed to the Christian is to keep himself in the love of God, for if that is properly attended to, everything else will be well with him. It must be his daily care to see to it that that precious but tender plant is nourished, increased, and made manifest by its fruits.

The Believer's Responsibility

Once more we must remind ourselves of the clear implication in all the petitions of the apostle's prayers: namely, that it is *our* responsibility to produce the things asked for, yet that we can only do so properly by divine enablement. Asking God to direct our hearts into His love does not release us from our obligations. It is merely asking Him to quicken us in the discharge of them. As formerly pointed out, our first concern must be to see to it that our love to God is firmly established, "rooted and grounded in love" (Eph. 3:17). We must not be contented with occasional good moods and ecstatic feelings, nor with meltings under a sermon, but diligently seek after and pray for a solid, steady, durable affection for God. And how is that to be accomplished? By getting the heart fixed in *His* love to us. The firmer is our assurance of that, the more will our love to Him be inflamed, just as the more we walk in the genial rays of the sun, the warmer our bodies become. If we daily observe God's blessings both spiritual and temporal, a renewed realization of His goodness will renew our gratitude to Him.

At this point we take in or combine the *passive* sense of these words, "the love of God," for unless we bask often in the sunshine of God's love to us, ours to Him will be neither fervent nor fruitful. Certainly nothing is so invigorating to our love and more calculated to make us aware of how infinitely worthy God is of our love than the contemplation of His love to us. As Paul prayed for the Ephesians that they might be "rooted and grounded in love," their love firmly fixed and indeclinably settled upon God, so he requested for the Philippian saints that their love might "abound yet more and more in knowledge and in all judgment" (1:9), which could only be through a fuller, deeper apprehension of God's love for them. It is alike our privilege and duty to strive and pray that we may increasingly cleave to God as our absolute good and rest in Him as our supreme delight. Love will not remain static: if it does not grow and increase, it will inevitably weaken and diminish. Nothing is more conducive to the decline and decay of our love than to be content with and satisfied in the present measure or degree of it.

If our affections for God are to be preserved warm and fresh, we must avoid everything which has a tendency to chill them and draw the heart away from Him. The allowance of any known sin, conformity to the spirit and ways of the world, making too much of the creature, giving way to unbelief, slackness in using the appointed means of grace, are some of the evils which must be avoided if God is to have His proper place in our hearts. Every day that passes, the Christian should be more and more out of love with sin, with self, with the world, and more in love with God. We need to watch closely against any abatement in our love: that is obviously one part of the duty inculcated in "Keep thy heart with all diligence." If we fail to do so, if we become careless and indifferent to the measure and strength of our love, then it will rapidly deteriorate. Backsliding and openly dishonoring the Lord are only prevented by observing closely the first decline of our love. The longer that is unattended to, like the neglect of a bodily ailment, the more serious our case becomes. Love *has* certainly cooled when we are less diligent in seeking to please God and are less careful in striving against sin.

Love Must Be Actively Exercised

Not only do we need to get our love firmly rooted and steadily increased, but it also needs to be continually exercised. All religion is in effect love. Faith is thankful acceptance, and thankfulness is an expression of love. Repentance is love mourning. Yearning for holiness is love seeking. Obedience is love pleasing. Self-denial is the mortification of self-love. Sobriety is the curtailing of carnal love. If love is not activated and kept working, it will atrophy. The affections of man cannot be idle; if they do not go out to God, they leak out to worldly things. When our love for God decreases, the love of the world grows in our soul. Love's constraining influence keeps us from living to and for ourselves.

Work and love are often coupled in the Scriptures. Paul spoke of "your work of faith, and labour of love" (I Thess. 1:3). The writer of Hebrews said, "God is not unrighteous to forget your work and labour of love which ye have showed toward his name" (Heb. 6:10). Then how earnestly we should pray for the succoring, strengthening, and stimulating of our love! One of the Holy Spirit's ministries in us is to stir up our love to God.

Earnest prayer to God for the strengthening of love does not absolve us from a diligent use of means. Daily meditation on the nature and evidences of God's love to us is the most effectual way of feeding and increasing ours to Him. Ponder the freeness and sovereignty of His love. He did not set His heart on us because of any loveliness of ours, for His love antedated our existence, and therefore proceeded from His goodwill. God's love passed by multitudes and fixed itself on us: "Jacob have I loved, but Esau have I hated" (Rom. 9:13). Think of its immutability: it is as invariable as His nature. "Having loved his own which were in the world, he loved them unto the end" (John 13:1). That love proceeds from One "with whom is no variableness, neither shadow of turning" (James 1:17). God's love to us is everlasting, and therefore nothing can or shall ever separate us from it. Let us revel in its unparalleled degree: "God, who is rich in mercy, for his great love wherewith he loved us, even when we were dead in sins, hath quickened us together with Christ" (Eph. 2:4-5). Matchless, amazing love! "God is love" (I John 4:8) and therefore His love is infinite, incomprehensible, adorable. We may feed on it now, and it shall be our endless delight in heaven.

Chapter 31

PRAYER FOR PATIENCE

II THESSALONIANS 3:5

"THE LORD DIRECT YOUR HEARTS into the love of God and into the patient waiting for Christ." The Greek verb here rendered "direct" occurs twice elsewhere in the New Testament: in I Thessalonians 3:11, and in Luke 1:79 where it is translated "to guide our feet into the way of peace." Literally the word signifies "to make thoroughly straight what has gone awry, to turn back or straighten what has become crooked." The Christian's heart is apt to return to its old bias and become warped: this prayer is for the righting of that fault. We are prone to allow our affections to wander from God and make an idol of some creature; therefore we constantly need to beg Him to bind them to Himself, that our love may be unalterably fixed upon its true and only worthy Object. We are also prone to grow slack in the performance of duty, to become weary in doing good, especially when we meet with opposition and affliction; therefore we need to earnestly ask God for the grace of endurance, that our knees do not become feeble and that our hands do not hang down, but that we "hold fast the confidence and the rejoicing of the hope firm unto the end."

Consideration of the Meaning of "Patient Waiting"

Quite a lot is said about the grace and duty of "patient waiting" in the Scriptures, though there is comparatively little of it in the lives of most Christians, which fact is not only displeasing and dishonoring to God but detrimental to their own spiritual condition. Few of them have any clear scriptural conception of what "patient waiting" actually consists, for there has not been sufficient really definite and practical teaching on it; consequently the thoughts of few rise any higher than those of the natural man. When commenting upon Colossians 1:11, we threw out some general hints on this subject, and expressed the hope of later supplementing them. We shall therefore consider something of what God's Word teaches on this most necessary fruit of Divine grace.

The Saviour Himself exhorted us, "In your patience possess ye your souls" (Luke 21:19), and His apostle declared, "Ye have need of patience" (Heb. 10:36). Patience is a most necessary grace for the Christian. That requires little proof, for the experience of every believer confirms it. Some difficulty accompanies every duty and the putting forth of every grace, not only because the commandments of God run counter to our corruptions but also because they run counter to the spirit and course of this world. Therefore patience is required in order to perform our duties constantly, and to continue in the exercise of that grace. To swim against the tide of popular sentiment, willing to be deemed singular, plodding along the narrow way, which is an uphill course throughout, and not fainting near the end, calls for much fortitude and endurance.

This patient waiting for Christ may be defined as "the grace of hope fortifying our resolutions for God and His way, that we may be steadfast till our work is finished and our warfare is ended." There is a threefold patience spoken of in Scripture. First, a *laboring* patience, which consists in our doing the will of God in self-denying obedience, however irksome it proves to the flesh. The same Greek word rendered "patiently waiting" in our text is translated "patient continuance in well doing" in Romans 2:7, which is in contrast with those whose "goodness is as a morning cloud, and as the early dew it goeth away" (Hosea 6:4). Christ defined the stony-ground hearers as those "which for a while believe, and in time of temptation fall away." He described the thorny-ground hearers as they who "are choked with the cares and riches and pleasures of this life, and bring no fruit to perfection." But He declared that the good-ground hearers are they who "having heard the word, keep it, and bring forth fruit *with patience*" (Luke 8:13-15). "Many of his disciples went back, and walked no more with him" (John 6:66), but of the apostles He said, "Ye are they which have *continued* with me" (Luke 22:28).

Second, *suffering* patience, which meekly bears affliction and does not rebel against whatever God has appointed for us. Where that grace is thus exercised, the soul does not faint in the time of adversity nor turn back in the day of battle. When the dispensations of divine providence are most trying to flesh and blood, and we are tempted to resist them, we are enabled to say, "What? shall we receive good at the hand of God, and shall we not receive evil?" (Job 2:10). Piety does not exempt any from trouble and sorrow, but it does enable us to make manifest the sufficiency of divine grace in all conditions and circumstances. As God is honored by the exercise of our love and zeal in performing His precepts, so He is greatly glorified by our quietness and submission when He calls upon us to experience suffering. Our fidelity to Him must be tested by enduring evil as well as in doing good, and the exercise of patience is as much needed for an unrepining and unflagging bearing of the one as it is for the joyous and unremitting performance of the other.

Third, a *waiting* patience, which consists of quietly tarrying for God's pleasure after we have both done the preceptive will of God and fulfilled His providential will. Some find this more difficult to exercise than either of the former, yet it is required of us. "Be not slothful, but followers of them who through patience inherit the promises." "For ye have need of patience, that, after ye have done the will of God, ye might receive the promise" (Heb. 6:12; 10:36). God has anticipatory mercies which come without our tarrying for them; He also has rewarding mercies which must be waited for, for He is pleased to test our patience, and often there is no reward for doing His will unless we do wait. Though God is never behind *His* time, He seldom comes at *ours*. "It came to pass at the end of four hundred and thirty years, even *the selfsame day* it came to pass, that all of the hosts of the LORD went out from the land of Egypt. It is a night much to be observed unto the LORD for bringing them out" (Exodus 12:41-42). That great promise of deliverance was performed punctually, not only to the day but to the very hour. Those four hundred and thirty years expired during the hours of darkness, and God did not wait till the morning light.

We read of the "shortening" of evil times (Matt. 24:22) but not of their lengthening! God never keeps His people waiting for good any longer than He has purposed or promised. But though He keeps *His* time exactly, and works just at the moment He has ordained and made known, yet we are apt to antedate the divine promise and set a time before His. As one of the Puritans quaintly expressed it, "We are both short-sighted and short-breathed." That which is but a moment in the calendar of heaven seems an age to us, and therefore we have need of patience in referring all to God's pleasure. "The vision is yet for an appointed time, but at the end it shall speak, and not lie: though it tarry, wait for it; because it will surely come, it will not tarry" (Hab. 2:3). There appears to be a verbal contradiction there: "though it tarry" and "it will not tarry"; yet the meaning is simple. Though what is promised may tarry beyond our time, it shall not beyond the hour God has prefixed. There is no remedy or relief for us but in patiently waiting, calmly but confidently expecting the divine performance.

Waiting God's Time

This patient waiting for God's time to appear on our behalf is as much the saint's duty as is a steady persistence in rendering obedience to God's commandments and in meekly bearing His afflictions. It is the prerogative of God to *date* all events as well as to do all things for us. Our "times" as well as ourselves and all our affairs are in His hand (Ps. 31:15). The Lord is the Disposer of all things in regard to not only their means and instruments but also in regard to their seasons: "To every thing there is a season, and a time unto every purpose under the heaven" (Eccles. 3:1). And God requires us to acquiesce to His timetable and defer to His good pleasure, to bow to His sovereignty and confide in His wisdom, and not fret and fume because He is slower than we desire in undertaking for us. It is not sufficient that we make known our requests; we must also "rest in the LORD, and wait patiently for him" (Ps. 37:7). We must realize that our welfare is in safer hands than our own, and behave ourselves accordingly, composing our spirit, stifling the unrest of our hearts, and resisting all the workings of unbelief. "I waited patiently for the LORD, and he inclined unto me, and heard my cry" (Ps. 40:1).

It is extremely painful not to wait patiently, for it points out our unwillingness to accept God's timing, which is really a spirit of insubordination. Fretful impatience takes issue with God's authority and calls into question His goodness. Solemn indeed are the sins of this nature recorded in the Word. "When the people saw that Moses *delayed* to come down out of the mount, the people gathered themselves together unto Aaron, and said unto him, Up, make us gods, which shall go before us; for this Moses, the man that brought us up out of the land of Egypt, we wot not what is become of him" (Exodus 32:1). And Aaron yielded to their evil demand. When the servant of God bade Saul tarry seven days at Gilgal until he should come and offer sacrifices and show the king what he should do (I Sam. 10:8), because the prophet did not appear when Saul expected, he impatiently and impiously took matters into his own hand, and in consequence lost his kingdom (I Sam. 13:8-14). Fearful also was the wickedness of that king who asked, "Should I wait for the LORD any longer?" (II Kings 6:33). He grew weary of tarrying for the Lord and opposed his own will against Him.

Let the reader perceive what an evil thing it is not to quietly wait the Lord's time. Once we give way to a spirit of impatience, we open the door to many dangers. Those who do not tarry for God take things into their own hands, which is not only highly dishonoring to the Lord but attended with disastrous consequences for themselves. Thus Abraham found it. At the outset the Lord declared, "I will make of thee a great nation" and "Unto thy seed will I give this land" (Gen. 12:2, 7). Years later, when the patriarch told the Lord, "I go childless," he assured him, "He that shall come forth out of thine own bowels shall be thine heir" (Gen. 15:2, 4). Nevertheless, because Sarah remained barren, Abraham yielded to her suggestion of obtaining a son by Hagar. Though that carnal plan resulted in the birth of Ishmael, Abraham's impatience was a source of domestic trouble for years to come. Impatience leads to setting aside God's means and employing our own: "They said, There is no hope: but we will walk after our own devices" (Jer. 18:12). Alas, many organizations are, with their worldly methods, doing so today.

On the other hand, it is highly beneficial to us to exercise this grace: "Therefore will the LORD wait, that he may be gracious unto you. . . . *blessed* are all they that wait for him" (Isa. 30:18). "Blessed is the man that trusteth in the LORD, and whose hope the LORD is" (Jer. 17:7). "The LORD is good unto them that wait for him. . . . It is good that a man should both hope and quietly wait for the salvation [deliverance] of the LORD" (Lam. 3:25-26). Waiting is not only a duty but a benefit. This waiting patience is termed by Christ a "possessing" of our souls (Luke 21:19). Whatever *title* we have to our souls, we have no *possession* of them without patience. As faith puts us in possession of Christ, so patience gives us possession of our souls. The soul of an impatient person is dispossessed, for he no longer acts as a rational creature. The exercise of patience enables us to preserve a holy serenity of mind, keeping under the tumults of passion, so that neither terror nor grief prevents the dominion of reason. By resigning ourselves to God's will and confidently awaiting the fulfillment of His promises, we are kept calm and cheerful, and have a considerable enjoyment of His mercies amid trouble and tribulation.

Patience Exercised in Afflictions

It is impossible but that affections and passions will be stirred in a season of trial and affliction, but patience takes off their excess and fierceness, calming the storm within. It subdues the violence of emotion which rends the soul and distracts reason, enabling its possessor to rule his own spirit (Prov. 16:32), instead of roaring "as a wild bull in a net" (Isa. 51:20). Patience checks angry murmurings and brings us to acquiescing silence before God: "I opened not my mouth; because thou didst it" (Ps. 39:9). Since impatience proceeds from self-love and is a species of self-will, patience works the soul into a self-denying frame or attitude. When providences cross our designs or impede our expectations, we are provoked and restless; but when the trying of faith works patience, the heart is more weaned from the creature and brought to rest in God. Thus it produces a spirit of quietness and submission, causing us to realize that the trial is of our Father, and that when He deems best He will deliver us from this trouble or supply that which will be most for His glory and our highest welfare. We shall be able to say, "It is the LORD: let him do what seemeth him good" (I Sam. 3:18).

Such a thing is beyond our powers, out of reach of attainment, something contrary to flesh and blood. Yet it is not beyond the power of God to bestow or the sufficiency of His grace to effect. That is why we find the apostle here making supplication for these sorely tried saints that the Lord the Spirit would "direct their hearts into the patient waiting for Christ." Our feet have to be guided into the way of peace (Luke 1:79), for it is a track completely hidden from the natural man, even from the wisest of this world: "The way of peace have they not known" (Rom. 3:17). Equally so, none but God can rectify our evil proclivity to impatience. The plainest and most earnest sermons preached cannot, of themselves, effect it. What we have written will not do so unless God is pleased to apply and bless the same to the reader, by convincing him of his sinful failures, moving him to confess them and cry to Him for His quickening power, "that he may incline our hearts unto him" (I Kings 8:58) and that He will graciously stay our minds upon Himself (Isa. 26:3).

While our sense of weakness and inability should ever drive us to our knees for divine enablement, prayer is not to be substituted for diligence in other directions. It is our responsibility to avoid everything which hinders the exercise of patience, and to make due use of those means which promote it. It should also be remembered that in the answering of such prayers, God will not cease dealing with us as moral agents. God indeed "draws" us, but it is "with the cords of a man, with the bands of love" (Hosea 11:4), working upon us as rational beings. As the phrase "guide our feet into the way of peace" is preceded by "to give light to them that sit in darkness" (Luke 1:79), so Christ explained the expression "draw him" by adding "they shall all be taught of God" (John 6:44-45). We are not forced but directed. God's "drawing" is by teaching, without doing violence to the liberty of man. He convinces the judgment that it is fit and proper that we submit to and wait for Him; the will accepts the verdict of the understanding; then the affections are brought under the authority of the Word.

God Alone Can Direct Our Hearts

"The Lord direct your hearts into the love of God and into the patient waiting for Christ." There is both a general and a particular "directing." In His Word God has declared His mind to us through His statutes: "He hath shewed thee, O man, what is good; and what doth the LORD require of thee, but to do justly, and to love mercy, and to walk humbly with thy God?" (Micah 6:8). Yet, so intractable are we by nature that something more is necessary before any of us renders to God His due, namely, the inward operations of the Holy Spirit who teaches us how to apply the rule to the details of our lives and in the orderly exercises of our graces. God can direct our hearts, incline our minds, move our wills, without any violence done to our free agency. He *will* do so in answer to fervent prayer, yes, He has already begun to do so if our prayers are sincere. These prayers are really the breathings of holy desires which He has worked in us by the efficacy of His grace, by making attractive and desirable the duties to which He calls us.

There is a very close connection, in fact, an inseparable one, between the two things Paul here prayed for. Not only is patience an effect of love, but our patient waiting for God will be in proportion to our love for Him. Love to God produces patience; rather, faith working by love does so. "The trying of your faith worketh patience" (James 1:3), yet whenever spiritual faith operates, it "worketh *by love*" (Gal. 5:6). Love to God makes the soul cleave to Him and bear up under all the dispensations of His providence. "Blessed is the man that endureth [patiently bears] temptations [or trials]: for when he is tried, he shall receive the crown of life, which the Lord hath promised to them that *love* him" (James 1:12). That identifying mark is mentioned because it is love which enables one to meekly submit to the most painful trials. "What mean ye to weep and break mine heart? for I am ready not to be bound only, but also to die at Jerusalem for the name of the Lord Jesus" (Acts 21:13). It was love to Christ which fired Paul, as it was love to Him which caused Bunyan and a host of others to endure lengthy imprisonment not simply with unrepining patience but with triumphant joy. Love makes the will of God and the glorifying of Him in Christ dearer to us than all other aims.

How essential it is then that we should use our utmost endeavors for the quickening, strengthening, and increasing of our love to God; for if that cardinal task is neglected, it is certain that our patience will weaken and flag, whether in a steady continuance in performing God's preceptive will, meekly bowing to His providential will, or quietly waiting the fulfillment of His promises and His answers to our prayers.

Waiting for Christ

Not only does the love of God promote patience toward Him in a general way, but also specifically in connection with "waiting for Christ." Those that love God will point all their thoughts and desires to one aim: that God may be enjoyed and glorified. It is the yearning of the new nature to delight itself in God to the fullest measure and manner of its capacity, and therefore the language of the saint is, "As the hart panteth after the water brooks, so panteth my soul after thee, O God" (Ps. 42:1). Yet how little is that longing realized in this life! How distant and how broken is our communion with Him! So much in our daily duties prevents the direct occupation of the mind with His perfections! But it will not always be so. A full, immediate, uninterrupted, and eternal enjoyment of God in Christ is promised His people. But that will only be at Christ's coming. "We know that, when he shall appear, we shall be like him; for we shall see him as he is" (I John 3:2). We shall be like Him both in holiness and in happiness. Then He will say to each of His faithful servants, "Enter thou into the joy of thy lord" (Matt. 25:21), and then shall we be "for ever with the Lord."

Honor of the Lord's Name

They that truly love God not only long for an enjoyment of Him but sincerely desire that He may be glorified. The honor of God's name is valued high above that of their own. The publication of His gospel, the coming of His kingdom, the vindication of His truth, are what their hearts are most set upon. It is also the yearning of the new nature within which makes them strive to please Him. If the deepest aspiration of their hearts could be realized, never again would they do or say anything which might bring the slightest reproach upon God's cause; they would rather "shew forth his praise" continually. Alas, how often this aspiration is thwarted by the activities of indwelling sin. How often they find that the good they would do is not performed, and that the evil they hate breaks forth (Rom. 7:19). And how often they are made to mourn over the corruption of the gospel and the dishonor done to God's truth! But it will not always be thus. At the coming of Christ their longings will be realized. The divine promises and threatenings will be accomplished. "He shall come to be glorified in his saints" (I Thess. 1:10), and all His enemies will then be His footstool.

Where there is true love for God there will necessarily be the same for *Christ,* His incarnate Son, the anointed One. "Christ" ever refers to Him in His official character as Prophet, Priest, and Potentate. As God loves His people in Christ (Eph. 1:3-5) and for His sake (Rom. 8:39), so we love God in Christ. God can neither be known, approached, nor loved apart from the Mediator, the Son of His love. God is fully declared in and by Christ (John 1:18; II Cor. 4:6). They who imagine they love God, yet at the same time regard Christ as being merely a creature and do not rest their eternal hope on the sufficiency of His propitiatory sacrifice, are fatally deceived. Christ accounted for the hostility of the Jews toward Himself by saying, "Ye have not the love of God in you" (John 5:40, 42). And when they boasted that God was their Father, He told them, "If God were your Father, ye would love me" (John 8:41-42). Those who do not love the Lord Jesus Christ with all their hearts and do not render divine honors to Him are unregenerate and yet in their sins: "He that honoureth not the Son honoureth not the Father" (John 5:23).

Christ the Mediator is the grand Object of His people's affections. "Grace be with all them that love our Lord Jesus Christ in sincerity" (Eph. 6:24). He is by way of eminence, *He* whom they love. "Whom having not seen, ye love; in whom, though now ye see him not, yet believing, ye rejoice [that is, 'shall rejoice'] with joy unspeakable and full of glory" (I Peter 1:8). This is an essential element in the Christian character. When a soul is quickened by the Holy Spirit and brought to understand and believe the gospel, he perceives that in the Lord Jesus there is everything that is desirable, that in Him all excellencies center in their absolute perfection, and that the benefits that He has obtained for him are inestimable in value, countless in number, everlasting in duration. Contemplating His glory "(. . . the glory as of the only begotten of the Father,) full of grace and truth," the loving believer exclaims that he is "the chiefest among ten thousand" and "he is altogether lovely" (Song of Sol. 5:10, 16). Reflecting on what He has done and suffered, what He has given and promised, he declares, "I love Him because He first loved me."

Intimate Communion with Christ

It is the very essence of love to seek union with its object, to be present with and have intimate fellowship with it. So it is with the Christian in reference to the Object of his affections. Yet such longings can be but very imperfectly gratified in this life, for though faith in exercise makes Him real and precious to the soul, the believer sees Him through a glass darkly. The regenerated one looks forward to the time when he shall "see the King in his beauty," see Him "face to face." He knows that his joy will be immeasurably increased when he shall be bodily "present with the Lord," when he shall hear His voice with his outward ear: "Sweet is thy voice, and thy countenance is comely" (Song of Sol. 2:15). Not only are believers now absent from their Beloved but they are most imperfectly acquainted with Him. They know Him and are following on to know Him, counting all things but loss "for the excellency of the knowledge of Christ Jesus their Lord." Yet, despite their best efforts in the use of means, they know only "in part" in reference to Him whom they love. It will be otherwise by and by.

Final State of the Christian

The final state of the Christian will be very different from his present one. Here he encounters trials, numerous and painful; there he shall enjoy the glorious and blessed effects of them (II Cor. 4:17). Now, complete salvation—deliverance from the very presence of sin both internally and externally; full conformity to the image of God's Son—is but the subject of hope; then it will be wholly realized. At present Christ is apprehended through the Word by faith, imperfectly and fitfully; throughout the endless ages of eternity Christ will be bodily present with His redeemed, and their knowledge of Him will be direct and immediate. Then the desire of His heart shall be accomplished: "Father, I will that they also, whom thou hast given me, be with me where I am; that they may behold my glory, which thou hast given me" (John 17:24). This is a "season of heaviness"; that shall be one of unclouded bliss: "In thy presence is fulness of joy; at thy right hand there are pleasures for evermore" (Ps. 16:11). Here we follow after, that we may lay hold of that for which Christ Jesus has apprehended us; then each shall exclaim, "As for me, I will behold thy face in righteousness: I shall be satisfied, when I awake, with thy likeness" (Ps. 17:15).

Now this completion of the believer's salvation and the consummation of his longings will be at the coming of Christ, which will be a personal and visible appearing of Himself: "This same Jesus, which is taken up from you into heaven, shall so come in like manner as ye have seen him go into heaven" (Acts 1:11). "For the Lord himself shall descend from heaven with a shout, with the voice of the archangel, and with the trump of God: and the dead in Christ shall rise first: then we which are alive and remain shall be caught up together with them in the clouds, to meet the Lord in the air" (I Thess. 4:16-17). "The Son of man shall come in the glory of his Father with his angels, and then he shall reward every man according to his works" (Matt. 16:27). "When Christ, who is our life, shall appear, then shall ye also appear with him in glory" (Col. 3:4). In His glorified body Christ shall forever dwell in the midst of His people. His coming is also designated "the revelation of Jesus Christ" (I Peter 1:13) to His people, which implies a fuller manifestation of His excellencies to them, when a clearer discovery will be made of His personal glory and mediatorial honors, and when they shall know Him far better and more extensively than they do now.

God's Precious Promises

As faith lays hold of those precious promises and as love fires the heart, the believer yearns for the fulfillment of them. Both stimulate hope and give strength to patient waiting. Love craves Himself, and hope is fixed upon the realization. That expectation of hope and patient waiting is expressed in Scripture in three ways. Sometimes by *looking:* "Looking for that blessed hope, and the glorious appearing of the great God and our Saviour Jesus Christ" (Titus 2:13). "Unto them that look for him shall he appear the second time without sin unto salvation" (Heb. 9:28)—not as our Sinbearer, but as our Sinremover. Sometimes by *longing and loving:* "For in this [earthly house] we groan, earnestly *desiring* to be clothed upon with our house which is from heaven" (II Cor. 5:2); "Them also that *love* his appearing" (II Tim. 4:8). Sometimes by *waiting:* "Waiting for the coming of our Lord Jesus Christ" (I Cor. 1:7); "Ye turned to God from idols to serve the living and true God; and to wait for his Son from heaven" (I Thess. 1:9-10); "We through the Spirit wait for the hope of righteousness by faith" (Gal. 5:5). The waiting is in expectation of that which is confidently hoped for, and the longing is strengthened by the deferring of immediate realization: "For yet a little while, and he that shall come will come, and will not tarry" (Heb. 10:37) beyond the ordained hour.

Nineteen centuries have passed since the Redeemer left this scene and took His place on the right hand of the Majesty on high, and scoffers still say, "Where is the promise of His coming?" Daily there arises from the heart and lips of God's people the prayer "Thy kingdom come," and as yet it remains unanswered. Many have been wrongly taught to base their expectations of the nearness of Christ's return upon the conditions prevailing in this world, which are adduced as the fulfillment of prophecy, to the repeated disappointment of such an expectation. God's people are to walk by *faith* and not by sight. "Signs" are "not to them that believe, but to them that believe not" (I Cor. 14:22)! Our Lord plainly declared, "An evil and adulterous generation seeketh after a sign" (Matt. 12:39; 16:4). Faith looks upon Christ as if He had begun His journey and were now on the way, and makes the believer stand ready to meet and welcome Him. His coming is promised, and the time is certainly determined in God's decree. This is enough for faith.

"He That Shall Come Will Come"

Why has the Bridegroom "tarried" (Matt. 25:5)? Because the ordained hour of His return has not yet arrived. "The Lord is not slack concerning his promise, as some men count slackness; but is longsuffering to us-ward, not willing that any [of them] should perish, but that all [of His 'beloved,' v. 9] should come to repentance" (II Peter 3:9). The full number of His elect must be gathered in before Christ shall see of the travail of His soul and be satisfied.

Christ is now building the spiritual temple of the Lord (Zech. 6:13; Eph. 2:21-22), adding stone upon stone (I Peter 2:5), and not until it is complete will He come and "bring forth the headstone thereof with shoutings, crying, Grace, grace unto it" (Zech. 4:7). Meanwhile the word to His people is "Be patient therefore, brethren, unto the coming of the Lord. Behold, the husbandman *waiteth* for the precious fruit of the earth, and hath long patience for it, until he receive the early and latter rain. Be ye also patient; stablish your hearts: for the coming of the Lord draweth nigh" (James 5:7-8): *not* "has drawn nigh," as men say, but "draweth nigh." His coming is ever getting nearer.

The similitude of the husbandman patiently waiting for the fruits of his labors is a very apt and suggestive one. He sows his grain in faith, believing that in due course his toil will be rewarded. He waits in hope, expecting the harvest at the appointed season. The fruit does not immediately appear: he waits for weeks and sees nothing, and long months pass before his crop can be garnered. But he *will* have a harvest, for God has promised it (Gen. 8:22), and then his hope will be realized. So it is with the Christian: "Light is *sown* for the righteous, and gladness for the upright in heart" (Ps. 97:11). When Christ appears to reward His people, the joy of harvest will be theirs. How long did the Old Testament saints have to wait for the first advent of Christ? By faith Abraham saw it "and was glad" (John 8:56). Even if there should be twenty thousand years before Christ's second advent, what is that span of time in comparison with the endless ages of eternity? If our hearts are truly set upon His appearing, love will reduce the distance between our hope and its realization and enable us to "wait patiently" for Him.

The Greek may be rendered either "the patient waiting for Christ" or "the patience of Christ." Taking it as "the patience of Christ," the genitive case is virtually a discriptive adjective (as in "patience of hope": I Thess. 1:3), and thus signifies *Christlike patience*. In its full meaning, it is that patience which Christ requires and inculcated, which He personally exemplified and is still exercising, and of which He is the Author and Perfecter. During His earthly ministry Christ urged upon His disciples a *working* patience: "Son, go work to day in my vineyard" (Matt. 21:28). "No man, having put his hand to the plough, and looking back, is fit for the kingdom of God" (Luke 9:62). He exhorted them unto a suffering or *enduring* patience: "In your patience possess ye your souls" (Luke 21:19); "He that endureth to the end shall be saved" (Matt. 10:22). He called them to a *waiting* patience: "Let your loins be girded about, and your lights burning; and ye yourselves like unto men that wait for their lord" (Luke 12:35-36); "Watch therefore: for ye know not what hour your Lord doth come" (Matt. 24:42).

Patience Exemplified in Christ

Consider Christ's patience in *well doing*. At the age of twelve He said, "Wist ye not that I must be about my Father's business?" (Luke 2:49). Throughout His public ministry, though constantly opposed, He continually went about doing good. At nighttime He did not refuse to see Nicodemus (John 3); and though "wearied with his journey," nevertheless He ministered in grace to the Samaritan adulteress (John 4). "The multitude cometh together again, so that they could not so much as eat bread. And when his friends heard of it, they went out to lay hold on him: for they said, He is beside himself" (Mark 3:20-21). Said He, "I must work the works of him that sent me, while it is day: the night cometh, when no man can work" (John 9:4). With unflagging diligence and unwearied patience He continued, until at the close He could say, "I have finished the work which thou gavest me to do" (John 17:4).

Consider Christ's patience *under suffering:* in enduring such contradiction of sinners against Himself. "Who, when he was reviled, reviled not again; when he suffered, he threatened not" (I Peter 2:23). How patiently He bore with the dullness of His apostles! How many a master would have grown weary with such pupils, but in infinite love He continued still to teach them though they were so slow to learn. How tenderly and longsufferingly He dealt with their unbelief! When they petulantly asked, "Carest thou not that we perish?" He said, "Why are ye so fearful?" When they were skeptical of His feeding the multitude, He did not upbraid them. How meekly He submitted to the dispensations of God: "The cup which my Father hath given me, shall I not drink it?" (John 18:11). Though He was complete in all graces and perfect in all active obedience, the glory of His perfections is clearly displayed in His patience under suffering. The Captain of our salvation was "made perfect through suffering" (Heb. 2:10). That unmurmuring endurance of afflictions enhanced and exalted His obedience: "Though he were a Son, yet learned he obedience by the things which he suffered" (Heb. 5:8).

Consider Christ's *waiting* patience. When His brethren according to the flesh told Him to go into Judea that His disciples might there witness His miracles, saying, "For there is no man that doeth any thing in secret, and he himself seeketh to be known openly. If thou do these things, *shew thyself* to the world" (John 7:4), He replied, "My time is not yet come: but your time is alway ready." He would not then vindicate Himself by an open display of His glory. The appointed day when He would appear before the world in visible majesty and power was not then. It is written, "He that believeth shall not make haste" (Isa. 28:16), and Christ rendered perfect obedience to that precept, as to every other. He was never in a hurry. When the sisters of Lazarus sent word saying, "Lord, behold, he whom thou lovest is sick" (John 11:3), instead of rushing at once to Bethany, "he abode two days still in the same place where he was." It was not through any lack of compassion for those tried sisters, but because the right moment for Him to act and show Himself strong in their behalf had not arrived. He sought "the glory of God" (v. 4) and therefore waited God's time.

With perfect composure and confident expectation He looked for a happy issue from His sufferings: "My flesh also shall rest *in hope.* For thou wilt not leave my soul in hell, neither wilt thou suffer thine Holy One to see corruption. Thou *wilt* shew me the path of life" (Ps. 16:9-11). What is perhaps yet more remarkable, the Lord Jesus is even now exercising waiting patience. That little-understood expression "the kingdom and *patience* of [the ascended] Jesus Christ" (Rev. 1:9) is explained by "after he had offered one sacrifice for sins for ever, sat down on the right hand of God; from henceforth *expecting* till his enemies be made his footstool" (Heb. 10:12-13). The suffering Saviour has been invested with unlimited dominion, and nothing now remains but the accomplishment of those results which His sacrifice was designed to procure, namely, the saving of His elect and the subjugation of all revolters against God. Christ is now calmly waiting the fulfillment of His Father's promise, that day which God has "appointed" (Acts 17:31). Here too He sets us an example.

"The Lord direct your hearts into the love of God, and into the patient waiting for Christ," such patience as He Himself inculcated and exemplified and which He alone can bestow upon and perfect in us.

Chapter 32

PRAYER OF WORSHIP

I Timothy 1:17; 6:15-16

It may seem somewhat strange that in the Pastoral Epistles (which should receive special attention from all ministers of the gospel) there is no record of a single prayer which their author offered for any of the recipients, though they were his own "sons" in the faith. He did indeed inform Timothy that "without ceasing" he had "remembrance of him in his prayers night and day" (II Tim. 1:3), but no mention is made of any particular requests that he offered to God on his behalf. Probably several practical lessons may be learned from that silence. But may we not see in this omission a lovely delicacy of spirit? Had the apostle specified that he was begging God to strengthen this or that grace or to equip him for the discharge of certain duties, it probably would have conveyed the impression that Timothy was defective in the one or remiss in the other. Hence the absence of what might be regarded as casting reflection upon his spirituality. But while no petitionary prayers on his behalf are recorded, two most blessed doxologies are contained in the first epistle, thereby inculcating an essential ministerial duty, and setting before this young servant of Christ an admirable example which he did well to emulate.

"Now unto the King eternal, immortal, invisible, the only wise God, be honour and glory for ever and ever. Amen" (I Tim. 1:17). "Which in his times he shall shew, who is the blessed and only Potentate, the King of kings, and Lord of lords; who only hath immortality, dwelling in the light which no man can approach unto; whom no man hath seen, nor can see: to whom be honour and power everlasting. Amen" (I Tim. 6:15-16). We do not propose to treat these two prayers singly, but rather couple them together, for they both partake of the same character, are found in the same epistle, and obviously have much in common. In our contemplation of them we shall point out first their distinctive *nature;* second, the *Object* to which they are addressed; third, their *substance.* They are of a most elevated character; therefore one must be in a truly spiritual attitude in order to appreciate their sublime contents and make personal use of them.

General Classification of the Prayers of Scripture

Earlier we pointed out that for the purpose of general classification the prayers of Scripture may be described as those of humiliation, those of supplication, and those of adoration. The first are expressions of repentance, and

339

consist of confessions of sin. The second are expressions of faith, wherein we request God to supply the needs of ourselves and others. The third are expressions of veneration and love, wherein we are occupied with the perfections of God Himself, and pour out our hearts in worship before Him. The last are *doxologies,* which consist in magnifying the divine Being, celebrating His excellence. Both of the passages quoted above are of this nature. In them God is adored for what He is in Himself. We often request the Lord, "Teach us to pray," when we ought to entreat Him to cause us to make better use of what He has already taught us. He has graciously furnished us with all necessary instruction, both in His own recorded prayers and in those of His apostles. In them He has plainly revealed that our hearts should be engaged with God Himself, contemplating His wonderful attributes and seeking His glory; we should not be thinking solely of ourselves and the supply of our wants.

In that prayer which Christ has given His disciples He has supplied a perfect model. In it He has taught us not only that it is our privilege to ask for those things which are needful for ourselves and fellow believers, but also to ascribe to God those excellences which pertain to Himself. The due consideration that He is "our Father which art in heaven" and the expression of the fervent desire, "Hallowed be thy name" take precedence over presentation of our own personal requests. "Thine is the kingdom and the power and the glory" is to be heartily acknowledged, and a sense of the same should remain upon our souls at the conclusion of our petitions. To praise and adore God for what He is in Himself is an essential part of our duty. We are required to respond to the call "Stand up and bless the LORD your God for ever and ever: and blessed be thy glorious name, which is exalted above all blessing and praise" (Neh. 9:5). *That* is the chief end of worship: not to benefit ourselves but to honor God. Many of our petitions begin and end with self, and therefore in no way honor God. "Whoso offereth praise glorifieth me" (Ps. 50:23) is His own declaration. Praise is to be offered to God not because He needs it but because He is entitled to it, and because it is a testimony to our reverence, faith, and love for Him.

Occupied with the Glory of God

The hearts of the apostles being fully enthralled with the glory of God, their mouths and pens frequently gave expression to it. Often Paul broke forth in the midst of an argument or discussion to bless God. Thus in Romans 1, when charging the heathen for having changed the glory of the incorruptible God into that of the creature, he, with holy horror at such a dishonor done to the great God, interjected, "Who is blessed for ever. Amen" (v. 25). Also in Romans 9, on mentioning the name of Christ, the apostle added, "Who is over all, God blessed for ever. Amen" (v. 5). Concluding his discussion of election and reprobation in Romans 11, he was filled with awe and adoration at the depth of the riches both of the wisdom and knowledge of God and at the absolute independence and inscrutability of His sovereignty, and ended with "to whom be glory for ever. Amen" (v. 36). So too he concluded that epistle: "To God only wise, be glory through Jesus Christ for ever. Amen." At the beginning of the Galatian epistle, having mentioned the Father, he at once added, "To whom be glory for ever and ever" (1:5). The Ephesian epistle he began thus: "Blessed be the God and Father of our Lord Jesus Christ," and ended the third chapter with a fuller doxology. In the Philippian epistle he stated, "Now unto God and our Father be glory for ever and ever. Amen" (4:20).

In a narration of his conversion, Paul broke out in the first of the two doxologies which we are here considering; later, while mentioning "the appearing of our Lord Jesus Christ," he burst forth in the latter doxology. At the close of the letter to the Hebrews, after mentioning Christ the author added, "To whom be glory for ever and ever. Amen" (13:21). In like manner, Peter's heart was so full that he began his first epistle with "Blessed be the God and Father of our Lord Jesus Christ, which according to his abundant mercy hath begotten us again unto a lively hope." Later he uttered praise "that God in all things may be glorified through Jesus Christ, to whom be praise and dominion for ever and ever. Amen" (I Peter 4:11). Again in chapter 5 he adored the God of all grace thus: "To him be glory and dominion for ever and ever. Amen" (v. 11). The spirit of Jude was also elevated to such a height that he concluded, "To the only wise God our Saviour, be glory and majesty, dominion and power, both now and ever. Amen." John, at the beginning of the Revelation, followed the salutation from God the Father, the Spirit, and Jesus Christ with "Unto him that loved us, and washed us from our sins in his own blood, and hath made us kings and priests unto God and his Father; to him be glory and dominion for ever and ever. Amen" (1:5-6).

What fervor of heart, elevation of spirit, homage of soul, such utterances breathe! What an example they set before all the servants of God to exalt and magnify Him both in their own affections and before the saints! How they rebuke the formality of the modern pulpit and the coldness which now prevails in the pew! How they give point to that injunction "Give unto the LORD the glory due unto his name" (Ps. 29:2), that is, for what He is in Himself, and not simply for His benefits. It is a duty incumbent on us not only to return thanks to God for His mercies but to magnify Him for the excellence of His nature and the glory of His name. The ebullitions of praise quoted above are extracted from all blessings received, being spontaneous adorations of the divine perfections. They were attributes due to God Himself. How little venerating of the divine Majesty is now heard! It is sad indeed, a mark of the low level of spirituality now obtaining in the gatherings of the Lord's people, that they do not resound with His praises. The absence of praiseful worship indicates a grievous lack of the sense of God's excellence and the coldness of our affections, for out of the abundance of the heart the mouth speaks, as from its emptiness the lips are silent.

When the soul is in a healthy condition it cannot help but exclaim, "Bless the LORD, O my soul: and all that is within me, bless his holy name" (Ps. 103:1). Yet how rarely do we now hear such language as this: "Blessed be thou, LORD God of Israel our father, for ever and ever. Thine, O LORD, is the greatness, and the power, and the glory, and the victory, and the majesty: for all that is in the heaven and in the earth is thine; thine is the kingdom, O LORD, and thou art exalted as head above all" (I Chron. 29:10-11). The praises rendered to God by His saints are so acceptable and delightful to Him that they are termed a "habitation" for Him (Ps. 22:3). Note that that was what supported the Lord Jesus, though the nation treated Him as a "worm" (v. 6). Not only is praise due to God but it is fitting for us. Believers are "an holy priesthood" (I Peter 2:5), therefore they are to bring offerings to God. The offerings they present must accord with the nature of their priesthood; and since the one is spiritual, the other must be. Therefore the Church is urged, "By him therefore let us offer the sacrifice of praise to God continually, that is, the fruit of our lips, giving thanks to his name" (Heb. 13:15).

God to Be Worshiped Collectively and Individually

God should be worshiped by us not only collectively in the assembly but by the saint individually in private. "I will praise thee, O Lord my God, with all my heart: and I will glorify thy name for evermore" (Ps. 86:12). A gracious soul cannot really contemplate God without exalting Him and exclaiming, "Who is like unto thee, O LORD, among the gods? who is like thee, glorious in holiness, fearful in praises, doing wonders?" (Exodus 15:11). If our hearts were more engaged with the divine Being, and if our minds meditated more on His wonderful character, we would admire Him more and sound forth His worth.

The Psalmist exulted, "I will bless the LORD at all times; his praise shall continually be in my mouth" (Ps. 34:1). If such were the case with us, we should be lifted above the petty trials of this life and forget our minor aches and pains. Praising and adoring God is the noblest part of the saint's work on earth, as it will be his chief employ in heaven. The unregenerate are blind to the divine beauty and incapable of perceiving His glory, much more so of rejoicing in it. But those who behold Him with the eyes of faith as He is revealed in the Lord Jesus Christ cannot help but overflow in expressions of veneration and admiration of Him.

"Now unto the King eternal, immortal, invisible, the only wise God, be honour and glory for ever and ever. Amen"; "Which in his times he shall shew, who is the blessed and only Potentate, the King of kings, and Lord of lords; Who only hath immortality, dwelling in the light which no man can approach unto; whom no man hath seen, or can see: to whom be honour and power everlasting. Amen." Who is thus celebrated in these verses? Different answers have been given. Some, in view of John 1:18, say it is the Father; others, influenced by the context, regard it as the Son. While it is plain from John 5:23 that the incarnate Son is *entitled* to equal honor and homage as the Father, and while Revelation 5:12-13 compared with 4:11 makes it clear that in heaven He actually received the same, yet some of the expressions made use of in these doxologies scarcely appear applicable to the God-man Mediator. He is neither invisible nor unapproachable. Moreover, our Lord Jesus Christ Himself, in His times, shall show or demonstrate "who is the blessed and only Potentate." On the other hand, we would not personally restrict these ascriptions of worship to the Father; rather we regard them as having *the Godhead* in view.

It seems to the writer that these doxologies contemplate the triune Jehovah, the Godhead without distinction of Persons, yet not viewed abstractly but rather as revealed in and through the Mediator, the Lord Jesus. Admittedly that conducts us into deep waters where it behooves us to move with the utmost circumspection, and express ourselves in holy fear and trembling. The finite mind is utterly incapable of forming any concept of the essence of God in its absolute nature, infinity, and blessedness. The Father, the Son, and the Spirit exist, and coexist, in a manner quite incomprehensible to us. The unity of the divine essence and the trinity of Persons in the Godhead is inconceivable. We must go to the Scriptures for any proper conception of this. There we have the doctrine stated, but no explanation is furnished. The triune God is the great I AM: "Which is, and which was, and which is to come" (Rev. 1:4). Abstracted from all beings and things, He is of Himself and from Himself alone, self-existent, self-sufficient. But the *doctrine* of the Trinity is a revelation which God has given us concerning His nature, persons, and perfections in Christ. The eternal Three can only be known to us in Their covenant transactions and as They stand related to us in the Lord Jesus. We have nothing whatever to do with an absolute God, but with God as made known by that One in whom dwells "all the fulness of the Godhead bodily" (Col. 2:9).

Christ the Image of the Godhead

Christ is "the image of the invisible God" (Col. 1:15), not simply of the Father but of the Godhead. The Lord Jesus is "God [the triune God] manifest in flesh." In Him the blessed Trinity is declared, made known to Their uttermost discovery. He is the Partner of the Lord of hosts. He is "the brightness of his glory, and the express image of his person" (Heb. 1:3). Christ is the Medium and Mirror in which we behold Him, worshiping God in the acknowledgment of His Persons. Not that the three Persons are swallowed up in Christ, but that Their persons and perfections are revealed in and through Him. All thoughts of the Godhead apart from Christ and without the consideration of Him as God-man lead only to the contemplation of absolute Deity, and leave us without any view of the ineffable subject as it is declared in the gospel. Only as we view the eternal Three as they stand related to us in Christ can we form any right concepts of Them. The divine Persons have manifested Themselves in the distinctive acts of Their wills toward us, in Their purpose respecting us, in the salvation planned for us before time, and its accomplishment *in Christ*. The Father's everlasting love to us in Christ (Eph. 1:3-4), and the Spirit's office and work in us, are from Christ: making Him precious to us, conforming us to Him, maintaining our communion with Him. When Christ was openly declared at His baptism, the whole Trinity was manifest.

Turning now more directly to the substance or contents of these doxologies, we are taught how we are to conceive of the Glorious One, and why worship is due Him. A close comparison of the two prayers reveals that the same essential perfections of Deity are extolled in both of them, though various terms are employed, the one serving to amplify and cast light upon the other. Thus, we conceive that "the King eternal" of 1:17 signifies the same as the fuller expression "the blessed and only Potentate, the King of kings, and Lord of lords" of 6:15. The "invisible" of 1:17 is explained as "dwelling in the light which no man can approach unto; whom no man hath seen, nor can see." "The only wise God" in the former has no balancing clause in the latter. The one closes with "be honour and glory for ever and ever. Amen," the other with "be honour and power everlasting. Amen." Let us now try to contemplate these several perfections of the Godhead, begging Him for quickened minds and enlarged hearts.

"Now unto the King eternal"; "the blessed and only Potentate, the King of kings, and Lord of lords." The very expression "the King *eternal*" at once intimates that the essential perfections of Deity are here being exalted. In considering this expression our thoughts are lifted far above all dispensational relations or temporal considerations. Jesus Christ is indeed "the King of kings, and Lord of lords" (Rev. 19:16), but considered as God-man He has not been so eternally, for His humanity had no existence before time began; nor was He vested with such dominion during the days of His flesh. It was after His resurrection, as the reward of His unparalleled humiliation and suffering, and in testimony of His meritorious and finished work, that God so highly honored the Son of man, and that He Himself declared, "All power is given unto me in heaven and in earth" (Matt. 28:18). What has just been pointed out in no way conflicts with the fact that because Christ was the Son of God incarnate, worship was due Him from the moment of His birth, so that during the days of His public ministry He was entitled to obedience and subjection; yet it was subsequent to the completion of His earthly mission that God crowned Him with glory and honor. Hence it is Deity as such which is here owned and magnified as "the King eternal."

"The Blessed and Only Potentate"

"The blessed and only Potentate." The reference is to the Godhead itself, without distinction of Persons. God Himself, the triune God, is the source of all blessedness and joy. God is self-sufficient, infinitely blessed and happy in Himself, and nothing can impair or disturb His serenity and sublimity. "The blessed and only Potentate." God's blessedness and *dominion* are necessarily joined, for the glory of God especially appears in His unrivaled sovereignty and supremacy whereby He rules over all. It is His distinct honor that He has no equal, "for who in heaven can be compared unto the Lord?" (Ps. 89:6). He is "the *only* Potentate," for all subordinate, derivative authority is from Him: "By me kings reign, and princes decree justice" (Prov. 8:15); "There is no [magisterial] power but of God: the powers that be are ordained of God" (Rom. 13:1). When Pilate said to the Saviour, "Knowest thou not that I have power to crucify thee, and have power to release thee?" He answered, "Thou couldest have no power at all against me, except it were given thee from above" (John 19:10-11). "His kingdom ruleth over all" (Ps. 103:19); "None can stay his hand" (Dan. 4:35).

"The King eternal." He is "the high and lofty One that inhabiteth eternity" (Isa. 57:15). He is "high" in the excellence and transcendence of His being, "lofty" in His independence and dominion, inhabiting eternity when none of His creatures had a being, dwelling all alone in His self-sufficiency. It brings real and solid peace to a grace-touched soul to realize that God is on the throne of the universe, directing its affairs both small and great, and working all things after the counsel of His own will. As the believer views Him thus, he is constrained to say, "Who is like unto the LORD our God, who dwelleth on high, who humbleth himself to behold the things that are in heaven and in the earth!" (Ps. 113:5-6). If our hearts were more occupied with the King eternal we should be less perturbed by what is happening in the world. Indeed, if our renewed minds were truly engaged with the high and lofty One our response would be "I will extol thee, my God, O king; and I will bless thy name for ever and ever. I will speak of the glorious honour of thy majesty" (Ps. 145:1, 5).

"The blessed and only Potentate, the King of kings, and Lord of lords" (6:15). The apostle here gives glory to the triune God, first for that blessedness which is in Himself. To be "blessed" is to be richly endowed and joyous. Such is God to an infinite and inconceivable degree, for there is in Him such a meeting together and such a fullness of all His excellences as to render Him complete in Himself. God has no need to go outside Himself for perfect fulfillment. As the apostle declared to the Athenians, the great God who made and rules the world is not dependent on men for the worship of their hands "as though he needed any thing, seeing he giveth to all life, and breath, and all things" (Acts 17:25). God is obligated to none, being absolutely independent. Praise then is rendered to God as the "only Potentate," as sovereign over all. He has not only all-sufficiency and happiness within Himself but absolute power and dominion over all creatures and things. Put the two together— infinite fullness and infinite might—in Himself, and God is indeed "blessed," and is to be owned as such, yes, feared, admired, and adored as "the blessed One." "Blessed be the most high God" (Gen. 14:20). No less an honor is ascribed to Christ: "Who is over all, God blessed for ever" (Rom. 9:5).

The Immortality of God

"Who only hath immortality" (6:16). This is in apposition to, or is the complementary perfection of, "the King *eternal*." God is not only without beginning of days but without end of them also. "Who only hath deathlessness" would be a literal rendering of the Greek word. The reason why God is immortal is because He is impeccable, or not liable to sin. A different term used in 1:17 for "immortal" signifies "incorruptible." God cannot be tempted with evil (James 1:13). Why? Because He is its very opposite, the ineffably Holy One. Death is the wages of sin, and since God is impeccable and incorruptible, He is immortal, or deathless. Moreover, He is the living God: "With thee is the fountain of life" (Ps. 36:9). He has "life in himself" (John 5:26) by essence and not by participation. God is not only immortal but He "only hath immortality." The holy angels are immortal, as will also be the resurrected bodies of the redeemed, but that immortality is derived, bestowed by God. But God, and He alone, "*hath* immortality" essentially, underived, in full possession, in Himself and from Himself. He alone has immortality simply and absolutely, being the fountain of it. As such He is to be acknowledged and adored.

"Invisible" (1:17). Observe carefully this is also mentioned as another of the divine perfections. There is a fullness in the words of Scripture which is not present in man's words. Frequently there is more contained in and implied by the words of Scripture than is actually expressed. Such is the case here. God is not only invisible to sight but He is impalpable to the senses and incomprehensible to reason. He is, in Himself, inscrutable to all creature intelligence. Notwithstanding the revelation of Himself which God has been pleased to make by His Word and by His works, we still have to say, "Lo, these are parts of his ways: but how little a portion is heard of him? but the thunder of his power who can understand?" (Job 26:14). Matthew Henry said, "What we know of God is nothing in comparison with what is in God, and what God is. After all the discoveries which God hath made to us and all the inquiries we have made after God, still we are much in the dark concerning Him." We cannot conceive of His essential glory. Only as we entertain a due appreciation of the greatness of God and the immeasurable distance between Him and us shall we be filled with holy fear and awe for Him.

"Dwelling in the light which no man can approach unto." How is that to be harmonized with "Clouds and darkness are round about him" (Ps. 97:2)? First, the Psalmist had reference to the ways of God which are hidden from us. We are incapable of perceiving *how* He acts, much less of understanding *why*. His providences are a great deep; His counsels are inscrutable to the human mind. Second, that language was designed to reprove our curiosity and presumption. We are far too prone to pry into what is not revealed, instead of performing our known duty. Third, this was said to try our faith: God will be trusted and honored even when we cannot see His hand or perceive His undertaking for us. Fourth, after all, Psalm 97:2 approximates very closely I Timothy 6:16, for even the saint is utterly incapable of understanding the divine essence or nature. There is such an overwhelming light in God that it is inscrutable to us. As one said, "The most eagle-like eyes of a human understanding are not only dazzled but quite blinded by His brightness." We may indeed draw near by faith to Him who is light, but not by reason.

Deity Dwells in Unapproachable Glory

The symbolism of the old covenant taught the same truth, namely, the unapproachable glory in which Deity dwells. We see this in the setting of "bounds unto the people round about" the base of Sinai (Exodus 19:12) at the giving of the law; in the veiled darkness of the holy of holies in the tabernacle and the temple, where the Shekinah abode between the cherubim on the mercy seat, to which Solomon alluded at the dedication of the temple: "The LORD said that he would dwell in the thick darkness" (I Kings 8:12); and in the seraphim veiling their faces as they stood above the throne of Jehovah (Isa. 6:1-2). On the other hand, the figure is varied in "The light dwelleth with him" (Dan. 2:22) and "In thy light shall we see light" (Ps. 36:9). Putting the two together, "dwelling in light unapproachable" signifies that the divine glory is too ineffable for any creature to draw near to or apprehend. God only is able to apprehend Himself. Our most spiritual and exalted notions of Him are obscure and inadequate at best. There must forever remain an incalculable distance between the Infinite and the finite: the God-man Mediator is alone qualified to make known the One to the other, so far as it is for His glory and our good.

"Whom no man hath seen, nor can see." That fact is stated again and again in the Scriptures. Even the highly favored Moses, who was granted such intimate and prolonged communion with God, when he requested, "Shew me thy glory" received the answer "I will make all my goodness pass before thee, and I will proclaim the name of the LORD before thee. . . . Thou canst not see my face: for there shall no man see me, and live" (Exodus 33:18-20). And almost at the end of the New Testament we are told, "No man hath seen God at any time" (I John 4:12). God is invisible, though the whole universe is full of Him and exhibits Him. "The heavens declare the glory of God; and the firmament sheweth his handywork" (Ps. 19:1). Yet *that* is not to "see God" but only what He has wrought. It is evident *that* He is, for He clothes Himself with light as with a garment (Ps. 104:2). It is not evident *what* He is, for "he maketh darkness his secret place" (Ps. 18:11). The fullness of His glory can never be known by any creature: "His greatness is unsearchable" (Ps. 145:3). Even a beatific vision of heaven will not consist of a sight of God as God, but rather as He shines forth in a manifestative and communicative way in the person of Christ, as suited to finite capacities.

God Only Wise

"To the only wise God." As those words were previously discussed, they need not detain us now. They extol another of the perfections of Deity, namely, His omniscience. Yet when we utter such a term, how feebly we grasp its immeasurable purport. "His understanding is infinite" (Ps. 147:5). "There is no searching of his understanding" (Isa. 40:28). Someone has said, "The profoundest creature wisdom deserves not the name of it when compared with God's. The wisdom of the angels is but folly to Him." All creature wisdom is imparted by God: *His* wisdom is original, essential, incapable of addition or diminution. God "by wisdom made the heavens" (Ps. 136:5). "In wisdom hast thou made them all" (Ps. 104:24). But above all God is to be praised for that "hidden wisdom" which He ordained before the world for our glory. A contemplation of this fact moved the apostle to exclaim, "O the depth of the riches both of the wisdom and knowledge of God!" (Rom. 11:33). To the "only Potentate, . . . who only hath immortality, to whom be honour and power everlasting. Amen."

Chapter 33

PAUL'S PRAYER FOR PHILEMON

PHILEMON 4-6

THOUGH THE EPISTLE OF PHILEMON is one of the shortest books in the New Testament, it is one of the least read by God's people and is certainly one of the least preached from. We have therefore decided to devote a few paragraphs to it, though more in the way of general remarks than a detailed exposition of the prayer itself, for it is full of important instruction and valuable lessons. The epistle of Philemon is the only strictly private letter of Paul's which has survived the passage of time. Doubtless he wrote many more, but this one alone God saw fit to preserve in the canon of Scripture. All his others were either addressed to local churches or were pastoral letters of authoritative direction. This one, though written under the immediate guidance of the Holy Spirit, presents its writer to us from quite a different angle. Here we view the "prisoner of Jesus Christ" throwing off as far as possible his apostolic dignity and parental authority over his converts, speaking simply from the heart as one Christian to another, in an admirable strain of humility and courtesy. It is therefore of peculiar interest and value inasmuch as it falls outside of what may be termed Paul's official sphere of ministry, affording us an insight into his personal and private life.

In this epistle Paul throws off the restraint of authority and employs the language of familiar intercourse, addressing Philemon as "brother" (v. 7), which breathes the spirit of freedom and equality. We see how, under the apostolic mission, as well as under divine inspiration, there was room for the free play of personal character and intimate correspondence. We come to know Paul better as an apostle as we see him not as Paul the apostle, but as Paul the minister and the man. We learn the valuable lesson as to the place which true courtesy and delicacy occupy in Christian character. We see the worth of the greatest plainness of speech at the right time. We understand how true courtesy is distinct from artificial and technical culture of manners, and is the natural outcome of that "lowliness of mind" in which "each esteems other better than himself." We are moved by the sympathetic love which does not look only on its own things but even in greater degree on the things of others. A careful comparison of this letter with Paul's other letters will discover a marked difference of tone throughout it.

Regarding Philemon

Philemon appears to have been a Christian of some eminence, residing at Colossae (Col. 4:9), who had been saved under Paul's ministry (Philemon 19). Onesimus was one of his slaves who had robbed his master, forsaken his service, and fled five hundred miles to Rome. This was providentially overruled for his eternal good, for the hand of God directed him to hear Paul's preaching (Acts 28:30-31) which was blessed of the Spirit to his conversion (v. 10). Though Onesimus had greatly endeared himself to the one who was (instrumentally) his spiritual father, and had been useful to Paul in his imprisonment, Paul realized it was only right to send him back to his master. Accordingly he wrote this touching letter to Philemon, begging that his erstwhile refractory slave might be given a favorable reception. His design was to effect a reconciliation between Philemon and his fugitive servant, now a brother in Christ. The apostle had full confidence that his appeal would not be in vain. It is highly probable that Paul's request was granted, and that Onesimus was received into his master's favor and later given his freedom. Tradition says that he afterward became a minister of the gospel.

In the course of his letter Paul used the most touching arguments and affectionate inducements to move Philemon to grant his request. (1) An implied appeal to his love for the saints in general (v. 5). (2) From consideration of the one who made this request, who might have used his apostolic authority, but chose rather to entreat him in love, by an appeal to his own condition—aged, in prison (vv. 8-9). (3) From the particular relation of Onesimus to Paul—his own son in the faith (v. 10). (4) From the transformation which had been accomplished in him—he was "now profitable" (v. 11). (5) From the strong affection which Paul had for Onesimus (v. 12). (6) From his unwillingness to act without the approval of Philemon (vv. 13-14). (7) From the special relation Onesimus now sustained to Philemon—" a brother beloved" (vv. 15-16). (8) From the intimate bonds which existed between Paul and Philemon (v. 17). (9) From the assurance given by Paul that he would personally make good any loss which Philemon had incurred (v. 18). (10) From joy and refreshment which his granting of this plea would afford the apostle (v. 20). Was a more powerful appeal ever made, or such an earnest and winsome suing for the pardon and kindly reception of a disloyal slave!

Teaching of This Epistle

Many important truths are exemplified in this epistle. In it we have a striking demonstration of the sovereignty and abundant mercy of God on a dishonest slave. Though sin abounded, divine grace did much more abound. We are made to realize the Christian duty of peacemaking, seeking to bring together two brethren in Christ who are alienated. Paul's unhesitating acknowledgment of this runaway slave as "my very heart" (v. 12, ASV) intimates what ties of affection should be felt between the minister and his people, the parent and his child, the master and his servant, in all the circumstances of life. How delicately yet forcibly the apostle urged Philemon (and us), "Put on therefore, as the elect of God, holy and beloved, bowels of mercies" (Col. 3:12-13)! Admire and emulate the humility of Paul who did not consider it beneath him to be concerned in performing such an office as to reconcile a master to his servant. See here a blessed setting forth of the spiritual equality of all who are in Christ Jesus. The chief of the apostles freely owned this converted servant as " a brother beloved."

Yet observe the balance of truth here. Though there was such equality so far as their standing before God and their spiritual inheritance were concerned, yet those facts in no way set aside inequalities in other relations and respects. The rights which masters have over their servants are not canceled when the latter become Christians. That new relation into which we are taken by virtue of a living union with Christ must not be regarded as annulling the obligations of natural relations, nor of the arrangements and responsibilities of ordinary society so far as they are not sinful. Though in Christ there was now no difference between Philemon and Onesimus, that did not alter the fact that one was still a master and the other a servant; the saving grace which had been communicated to the soul of the latter would be most suitably exercised in showing forth the respect and submission which was due the former. There is a *natural* order established by God on earth between husband and wife, parent and child. There is also a *governmental* order which God has allowed men to institute by His authority, and He requires His people to conduct themselves suitably to the order He has ordained: "Submit yourselves to every ordinance of man for the Lord's sake" (I Peter 2:13-15).

Typical Teaching of the Gospel

Finally, note that we have in this epistle an exquisite typical picture of the grand truths set before us in the gospel. First, the sinner's deep need is portrayed in the case and condition of Onesimus. God is our Creator, Owner, and Ruler; therefore as creatures and subjects we are under bonds to serve and obey Him. But fallen man is "born like a wild ass's colt," thoroughly intractable, unwilling to bear the yoke. Not only is he a rebel against the divine government but he is, morally, a thief, misusing his time and talents, and thereby robbing God of His glory. In consequence, he is "alienated from God," a wanderer in the far country of self-pleasing and sin. See how all of this is illustrated in Onesimus, who became an unprofitable servant by revolting against his master, stealing from him, and becoming a fugitive. Note that the *"if* he hath wronged thee" (v. 18) is not an expression of doubt but of concession, meaning *"since* he hath" (compare John 14:3; Col. 3:1). Second, the experience of Onesimus shows that the condition of no sinner is hopeless (Luke 19:10; Heb. 7:25). Third, the ministry of one of God's servants was used in his conversion.

Fourth, in Paul's offering to be bondsman for Onesimus (v. 18) we have a figure of the grace of Christ in voluntarily becoming the Surety of His people, assuming the whole of their debt. "Put that on mine account" expresses the same readiness which the Redeemer had to be charged with the sins of His redeemed. Fifth, carefully note that more than a bare reconciliation was to be effected between Philemon and Onesimus: "Receive him *as myself"* (v. 17). Not only are the guilt and pollution of the believing sinner removed from before the sight of God, but he is "accepted in the beloved" (Eph. 1:6). Thus the basic truth of *imputation* was here illustrated. Onesimus was not only exempted from the punishment of his crimes but—through the benevolence of his benefactor—made partaker of benefits which he had not merited. Believers receive the reward of Christ's righteousness by a reciprocal transference (II Cor. 5:21). Sixth, in all of Paul's pleading on the behalf of Onesimus we have an image of the intercession of Christ for "his own." Seventh, the real change effected in the character and conduct of the one saved by Christ appears in the return of Onesimus to his master. A chief evidence of genuine repentance is a prompt performance of those duties which had previously been neglected.

Very few words must suffice upon Paul's prayer for Philemon. First, its *object:* "my God" (v. 4). The first lesson in prayer Christ taught us was that the special relationship which He sustains to His children should be owned by them: "Our Father which art in heaven" (Luke 11:2). "I will praise thee, O Lord my God" (Ps. 86:12). "God, even *our own* God, shall bless us" (Ps. 67:6). Second, its *heartiness:* "Making mention of thee *always* in my prayers." Paul was no casual supplicant. Third, its *occasion:* "I thank my God . . . hearing of thy love and faith." The fact that thanks were returned to God for those graces was an acknowledgment that He is the Author of them: they do not originate with man. They are the fruit of the Spirit, evidences of His regenerating work. Thanksgiving should be offered to God not for ourselves only but for our fellow Christians also. This was always Paul's custom (Rom. 1:8; Eph. 1:15-16; Col. 1:3-4).

"Hearing of thy love and faith, which thou hast toward the Lord Jesus, and toward all saints" (v. 5). Wherever one grace exists the other is found. In the mystical Body of Christ, believers have communion both with the Head and with all its members: with the One by faith, with the other by love. Hence we find the two things so often taught by the apostle, not only as equally essential but as equally necessary to prove our interest or participation in that Body. Without love for the saints we are no more members of Christ than without faith in Him. Fourth, its *petition:* "That the communication of thy faith may become effectual by the acknowledging of every good thing which is in you in Christ Jesus" (v. 6). Request was here made that Philemon might be divinely enabled to give still further proof of his faith and love, by bringing forth more abundant fruit, in acts of benevolence, in ministering to the needs of others. Thereby those graces would be "effectual" in promoting the glory of Christ and the welfare of fellow saints.

SCRIPTURE INDEX

353